Praise for the Original Edition

A Garden Book Club
Alternate Selection July 1988

"A fascinating compilation of letters, travel diaries, essays, and seed catalogues."—*American Horticulturist*

"Pure reading pleasure."—*The Avant Gardener*

"Marvelous excerpts."—*Booklist*

"Marranca's intelligent selections of examples of American garden writing draws on classics covering more than 300 years of gardening in America. . . . Those of us interested not only in American gardening but also in that subject's evolution and history now have a broad menu from which to begin our search for knowledge."—*Fine Gardening*

"It is difficult to imagine a more intelligently edited or consistently engaging collection of pieces for gardeners who love to read than this one."—*Garden Design*

"Bonnie Marranca has chosen writers who care for the earth—American earth—writers who, as she says in her preface, believe that 'to cultivate the land and the mind are activities of a responsible life.' Such a wide interpretation of the idea of "garden" provides an appropriately broad base for the developing field of American garden history. The rescue of long out-of-print, forgotten, or little-known authors, such as Alice Morse Earle and Frederick Pursh, makes this book a treasure. Thought-provoking and fun to read, it will send many a gardener right back to the armchair." —**Mac Griswold**, author of *Pleasures of the Garden: Images from the Metropolitan Museum of Art*

"A treasury of writing that reveals the extent and range of meaning the garden has had in American life. Extending far beyond the boundaries of horticulture, the ideas about gardens and cultivation published here stand as paradigms of American visions of political economy, moral and religious life, and a scientific way of ordering the world. Particularly helpful to those interested in literature, history, or the social sciences are Ms. Marranca's intelligent accompanying notes which point to larger social and cultural linkages." —**Wilma Hall**, American Studies Department, Skidmore College

"A fine and important anthology." —*Horticulture*

"Well-researched." —*House and Garden*

"A book of enchantment, a creative anthology of the best that has been written." —**Stanley Kunitz**, poet

"Highlights from writers who greatly enjoyed writing." —*Library Journal*

"A startlingly clear and new vision of American history as it is revealed in our own gardens and fields and front yards." —**Charles L. Mee Jr.**, historian and author of *The Genius of the People*

"No gardener, serious or occasional, will wish to miss this book's delightful and fascinating compilation of information on how gardens work and how to make them better, scientific plant lore, and the virtues of what most of us regard as botanical malefactors. . . . Delicious and stimulating." —*Newsday*

"An eclectic treasure trove of 50 garden writings form Colonial times to the present." —*Organic Gardening*

"Takes for granted the literary tradition in American garden writing." —*Pacific Horticulture*

"Historically important horticultural writing." —*San Francisco Chronicle*

to the anonymous gardener

decayed literature makes the best soil
THOREAU

BOOKS BY BONNIE MARRANCA

Ecologies of Theatre
Theatrewritings
American Playwrights: A Critical Survey (with Gautam Dasgupta)

AS EDITOR:

A Slice of Life: Contemporary Writers on Food
Conversations on Art and Performance
Plays for the End of the Century
Hudson Valley Lives
American Garden Writing
Interculturalism and Performance: Writings from PAJ
American Dreams: The Imagination of Sam Shepard
The Theatre of the Ridiculous
Animations: A Trilogy for Mabou Mines
The Theatre of Images

AMERICAN GARDEN WRITING

AN ANTHOLOGY

EDITED BY

BONNIE MARRANCA

TAYLOR TRADE PUBLISHING
Lanham • New York • Toronto • Oxford

First Taylor Trade Publishing edition 2003

This Taylor Trade Publishing paperback edition of *American Garden Writing* is an unabridged republication of the edition first published in New York in 1988, with the addition of eight new pieces and a new preface, the deletion of seven illustrations and the addition of two new illustrations, and one textual emendation. It is published by arrangement with the author.

Published by Taylor Trade Publishing
An imprint of The Rowman & Littlefield Publishing Group, Inc.
4501 Forbes Boulevard, Suite 200
Lanham, Maryland 20706

Publication of this book has been made possible in part by grants received from the National Endowment for the Arts, Washington, D.C., a federal agency, and the New York State Council on the Arts.

Every effort has been made to seek out and obtain permissions for the quoted passages and photos selected for inclusion in *American Garden Writing*. Page vii constitutes an extension of the copyright page.

Distributed by National Book Network
A previous edition of this book was catalogued as follows by the Library of Congress:

Library of Congress Cataloging-in-Publication Data
American Garden Writing
Library of Congress Catalog Card No.: 87-73280
ISBN: 1-58979-023-5

Printed in the United States of America

♾ ™ The paper used in this publication meets the minimum requirements of American National Standard for Information Sciences—Permanence of Paper for Printed Library Materials, ANSI/NISO Z39.48–1992. Manufactured in the United States of America.

EDITOR'S NOTE

In putting together an anthology of material that ranges from the seventeenth to the twentieth century, I was immediately confronted by the need to choose an editorial style that addressed the issues of whether or not to standardize typography, British spellings, capitalization, obsolete spellings, and so forth. The decision was further complicated by the variation in flower names over a period of hundreds of years. In the interest of preserving the spirit of writings before the twentieth century, I have settled on including them as they originally appeared, with minor changes in punctuation, spelling, and italicization, for purposes of clarity. In a few places I have indicated brackets to distinguish my corrections from those of previously edited selections. All entries from the twentieth century follow a standardized style which, I believe, violates neither the letter nor the spirit of each individual piece. The biographical note to each selection indicates the source used. Wherever necessary, I have relied on *Hortus Third* as a reference.

For the sake of clarity and liveliness, and in cases where they didn't already exist, I have titled the selections of the following authors:

Michel-Guillaume St. John de Crèvecoeur, Amos Pettingill, Helen Morgenthau Fox, Frank Hamilton Cushing, John Josselyn, Bernard M'Mahon, Shaker Seed Catalogue (D. C. Brainard), Celia Thaxter, Katharine S. White, William Bartram, Thomas Nuttall, Victoria Padilla, François André Michaux, Frederick Pursh, Thomas Jefferson, Garrett Eckbo, Louis Bromfield.

CONTENTS

EDITOR'S NOTE   ix

ACKNOWLEDGMENTS   xv

Bonnie Marranca: *Preface to the Expanded Edition*   xvii

Bonnie Marranca: *Preface to the Original Edition*   xxi

I. SEEDS OF INSPIRATION   3

Alice Morse Earle: *Front Dooryards*   5
Michel-Guillaume St. John de Crèvecoeur: *A Visit to*   13
    John Bartram's Garden
Amos Pettingill: *White Flower Farm*   20
Louise Beebe Wilder: *Pleasures of the Nose*   29
George Washington: *Letter to Arthur Young*   34
Helen Morgenthau Fox: *Gardening With Herbs*   39
Frank Hamilton Cushing: *Zuñi Fields*   44
Henry Ward Beecher: *Political Economy of the Apple*   50
Thomas Bridgeman: *The Matrimonial Garden*   55
J. I. Rodale: *Introduction to Organic Farming*   60
Louisa Yeomans King: *Garden Happiness*   65
Wendell Berry: *The Reactor and the Garden*   67
Henry Mitchell: *On the Defiance of Gardeners*   71
Elizabeth Lawrence: *The Mississippi Market Bulletin*   75

II. LIVES OF THE PLANTS   83

John Josselyn: *New England Natural History*   85
Bernard M'Mahon: *Advice for the Fall*   91
Shaker Seed Catalogue of 1873: *Selections*   96
John Lawson: *A Description of North Carolina*   107
Peter Henderson: *Planting of Lawns and Flower Beds*   113
Celia Thaxter: *The Altar and the Shrine*   118
Liberty Hyde Bailey: *Recent Progress in*   124
     American Horticulture
Roger B. Swain: *Hamburgers and Houseplants*   134
Frances T. Dana: *Wild Carrot • Bird's Nest*   138
     Queen Anne's Lace
Lester Rowntree: *On Top of the World*   140
Kent Whealy: *Our Vanishing Vegetable Heritage*   145
Katharine S. White: *The Changing Rose*   153

III. TRAVELERS AND THE TRAVELS OF PLANTS   159

John Bartram: *Selected Letters*   161
William Bartram: *The Bounteous Kingdom of Flora*   171
François André Michaux: *In a Charleston Garden*   181
Thomas Nuttall: *The Spontaneous Productions of Nature*   184
Victoria Padilla: *The Franciscan Missionaries*   190
     in Southern California
David Douglas: *First Impressions*   199
Ernest H. Wilson: *The Princess Kurume*   203
Frederick Pursh: *New Acquisitions to the American Flora*   210
David Fairchild: *The Flowering Cherry Trees*   218
     Are Planted in Washington

IV. THE PLAY OF ART AND NATURE   227

Ann Leighton: *Cemeteries Into Parks*   229
Thomas Jefferson: *Notes from a Garden Book*   237
Andrew Jackson Downing: *Essay on Landscape Gardening*   245
Frank Scott: *The Lawn*   254
Edith Wharton: *Italian Garden-Magic*   260

Frederick Law Olmsted: *Inspiration from Tropical Scenery*   265
   for Park Planting
Beatrix Farrand: *The Lovers' Lane Pool*   272
Garrett Eckbo: *Urban Landscapes*   276
Jane Baber White: *Restoration of a Poet's Garden*   279

V. REFLECTIONS IN A GARDEN WORLD   285

Henry David Thoreau: *The Bean-Field*   287
Allen Lacy: *Broom and Wisteria*   297
Richardson Wright: *And So To Bed*   302
Eleanor Perényi: *Woman's Place*   306
Louis Bromfield: *Summer 1945*   318
Joseph Wood Krutch: *The Moth and the Candle*   321

VI. EDUCATION OF THE GARDENER   329

Michael Pollan: *Compost and Its Moral Imperatives*   331
Diane Ackerman: *Deer*   341
Jamaica Kincaid: *My Garden (Book)*   347
William Woys Weaver: *Mr. Jack Tomato*   351
Gary Paul Nabhan: *The Parable of the Poppy and the Bee*   354
Joan Dye Gussow: *Eating My Yard*   361
Jim Nollman: *The Sentient Garden*   374
Sara B. Stein: *Purslane and Immortality*   381

INDEX   389

ACKNOWLEDGEMENTS

American Garden Writing could never have been organized without the vast human and institutional resources available for horticultural research in this country. I am indebted to several libraries which I consulted in the preparation of this book: The Garden Library, Dumbarton Oaks, Washington, D.C.; New York State Library, Albany; New York University, Elmer Holmes Bobst Library; The New York Botanical Garden Library; The Garden Club of America Library; The New York Public Library.

I am grateful for the accumulated knowledge booksellers in the horticultural and related fields were willing to provide. In particular, I would like to thank Warren F. Broderick for his time and interest in offering suggestions to expand the scope of the book; also, Elisabeth Woodburn of Booknoll Farm and Mike McCabe of Lion's Head Books for their discussions on bibliography; George Bibby and Jane Sutley for recommending information sources on the West Coast.

Librarians, archivists, and cataloguers were such a rich source of information and so helpful that I cannot thank them enough for their expertise in the areas of bibliographic and photo documentation. I am especially grateful to Laura Byers and Annie Thacher for the glorious week I spent practically living in The Garden Library at Dumbarton

Oaks; to Lothian Lynas, Elizabeth Hall and Bernadette Callery of The New York Botanical Garden Library who were always willing sources of information and assistance; to Anita Karg of the Hunt Institute for Botanical Documentation, Carnegie Mellon University, who offered generous help in photo research, as did Ellen McCallister Clark and Karen Van Epps Peters of The Mount Vernon Ladies' Association, and Barbara Milligan of Monticello; to Jan Christman, The Shaker Museum, Old Chatham, New York, for her willingness in searching out materials for my research there; to Barbara Pitschel and Jane Gates, Strybing—Helen Crocker Russell Library of Horticulture, San Francisco, for biographical and historical information. Several people around the country graciously made themselves available for phone consultations in my search for documents and other historical materials: Barbara Doyle of Middleton Place, South Carolina; Nancy Whight, Cherokee Garden Library, Atlanta; Thomas Scharf, San Diego Historical Society; Thomas Brown of San Francisco; Louise Smith of Alabama; and to these scholars whom I consulted in various research areas: anthropologist Diane Rothenberg of SUNY/Buffalo; Henry Louis Gates, Jr., Cornell University; Martia Goodson, Bernard Baruch College; Frances Foster, San Diego State University.

I am very proud to have had the support and recognition of a Guggenheim Fellowship during the period of work on this book.

On a more personal note, I wish to take this opportunity to acknowledge my gratitude to: Pamela Lord of The Garden Book Club for always believing in this book; Mary Ann and Bob Buckley for their hospitality in Washington, D.C.; Jordan Tamagni for help in checking over parts of the manuscript; Susan Bruner for her careful, steady work on the production of the book and its index. Finally, I was fortunate throughout my work to have the companionship of my husband Gautam Dasgupta who shared not only my interest in this project, but the numerous visits to libraries, booksellers, and gardens, and then supervised the actual preparation of the book for publication.

Preface to the Expanded Edition

In the years leading up to the work on the original edition of this book, published fifteen years ago, I was a beginning gardener. I remember being a bit awed by a neighbor who offered me some groundcover transplants while casually mentioning that it took twelve years to establish a garden. Oblivious to the long view of things, in the years that followed I went right along creating my own garden—more precisely, gardens—driven by the sheer force of will and enthusiasm for my new obsession. Forty feet of hostas and iris next to a forsythia hedge, a sprawling bank of lilies, specimen shrubs in a nearby meadow, shade gardens, cosmos gardens for cutting, a big vegetable garden, and a sixty-foot long perennial bed with stone edging, in addition to foundation plantings on all sides of the house and roses in the front yard along the fence. For years, whenever I was able to leave my home in New York City, I worked nearly the whole day in April, May, and June, even July, planting more spaces, ever envisioning new garden plans.

I learned to love working with plants, digging in soil, just being outdoors observing them, and, when indoors, looking out of the windows of my house into the yard and meadow beyond, dreaming through the old maple trees. My favorite time has always been the evening walk around the yard when I inspect all the plantings, trying to determine how each is doing, if any seem in exceptional form, or perhaps stressed out by the weather. It's the time just before the magisterial Hudson Valley twilight. I never tire of examining the plants, moving them from one place to another, even bandaging a broken stem from time to time (I got the idea from Chekhov).

Oh, like so many travelers, I have had my moments in European gardens picturing this or that plant or fence or wall or pond back home in Catskill. How I would love to see Italy's oleanders or umbrella pines or the linden trees from the allées of palaces on the continent in my own garden; if only our roadsides had the English plantings; if only the Hudson, more beautiful than the Rhine, had lovely vineyards trailing down its riverbanks. But, then, back home, little by little I become attached to my own garden because it is mine. Alas, no sooner had I gotten my garden in full swing—it did take at least twelve years—than I realized that I had made too many gardens to care for, especially since I was traveling abroad for much of the last decade during the summer months. I didn't like coming home to find that my deer neighbors, who were sometimes lounging under my picnic table in the morning, had eaten all the lily buds.

Now I am in my second life as a gardener, having grassed over the lily bed and the hosta and iris garden and the cosmos cutting patch and considerably shortened the perennial bed and the vegetable garden. I have taken out the conventional yews and planted many more beautiful or fragrant shrubs, today with greater attention to texture and patterns of growth and color, especially variegation and blue and silver hues. I learned to consolidate my plants rather than having too many different species all in one place. I became a ruthless pruner. I also learned to accept the independence of nature, by now having lost several old pines to aphids and two populars to the wind and numerous flowers to the winter frost and fruit trees to the passage of time. Plants, like texts, lead their own lives in the world, I have come to understand.

In thinking about the new edition of this book and reading over some of the original selections which mention the old flower favorites, it has become clear to me that in the years since I started gardening, so many of the old farmhouses in the Hudson Valley, particularly in Greene Country which I know best, no longer offer hospitality to the sweet pea and hollyhocks that used to adorn the front steps or barns. The houses

have been sold or destroyed and many of the old flowers are unfashion-
able today, like the flowery wallpaper that framed their parlors. The
old houses with prewar furnishings and plantings that I used to show
visiting friends searching for a country house are, two decades later,
mostly repopulated by New York City folk who have changed the
plantings to express the new species of desire.

In the years since this book was published there have been significant
changes in the region—to all intents and purposes, my garden world—
that serve as a microcosm of much larger national issues. Even as city
people seek out rural life, the loss of so much agricultural land has forever changed the countryside. Current environmental concerns have led
to local conflicts over business interests and historical restoration, zon-
ing laws, protection of farm land, and stricter legislation for waste sites
and cement plants. But, new social forces have also led to the rehabilita-
tion of formerly polluted land and to the designation of more nature
preserves and a renewed interest in the Hudson River. Environmental,
agricultural, economic, and political issues are all intertwined in the
ecology of the garden "plot" which is, after all, the story of a culture.

In Catskill and elsewhere in Greene County, many of the farms now
produce the organic fruits and vegetables that are sold in the farmer's
market in New York City's Union Square and are bought by the upscale
restaurants who tout their "local" offerings. The farms are worked by
a growing number of Mexican laborers, some of whom now populate
the upstate towns. These same farms also produce the food in co-op
organizations subscribed to by Manhattanites. Yet, many of the farmer's
market shoppers and restaurant customers don't know where their food
supply comes from and have never visited the Hudson Valley (perhaps
haven't even heard of it).

Paradoxically, this same produce is not available in the supermarkets
in Catskill whose fruits and vegetables are shipped across country before arriving here, often discolored and tasteless. When I asked one of
the workers at Price Chopper why the local apples were not available—in one of the major apple growing regions of the world—he didn't
seem to understand my question. This general lack of connection between gardening, place, and labor is fostered by the images in garden
books and magazines which tend to emphasize the garden alone, without human presence. The denial of its relation to culture is further ex-
emplified by the scant number of 20th-century American paintings

featuring gardens or gardeners, compared to, for example, French art. And yet, the other side of that absence is the impossible beauty of the glossy garden photograph, like the unreal bodies of models whose photos appear in fashion magazines. Most gardeners do their own work and what matters to them is observing over time the fruits of their labor.

The world of gardening has seen many transformations over the last decade, not the least of which is its growth as a major American pastime and industry, complete with designer tools and clothing and the continuing quest for bigger and brighter and hardier plants from more and more exotic places. Surely sight now takes precedence over smell in the garden experience. What has gradually taken place is the increased blurring of boundaries in garden writing, food writing and the writing of history. Likewise, attention to environmental and health issues and the controversies of biogenetic engineering, framed by new attitudes toward the natural world in both its urban and rural manifestations, has pushed the subject of gardening, like food, toward investigative journalism. The rise of the personal essay has also contributed to opening up many more aspects of human experience. The new edition of *American Garden Writing* acknowledges these changes, which is why I added the selections in the final section of the volume, titled "Education of the Gardener."

Poetic reveries of the garden have drifted naturally toward politics and culture, without denying the sheer pleasure of gardening as an activity with often deeply spiritual attachments. Garden writers have simply become more aware of the global implications of local life and increasingly activist in their concerns. But that just means that they are reconnecting to the ancient tradition which joins culture and horticulture in a more worldly historical perspective. Any way you approach life, it all began in the garden.

Bonnie Marranca
Catskill, New York
May 2003

PREFACE TO THE
ORIGINAL EDITION

WHEN THE EIGHTY-YEAR-OLD MARCUS TEREN-
tius Varro sat down in 37 B.C. to write *De re rustica* as a guide to
husbandry for his wife, he pointed out that fifty Greek sources on the
subject already existed, if she needed further assistance. That husband-
ly gesture seems hardly likely to occur again, so vast has the literature
in the field grown in the intervening two thousand years. Besides, too
few people, much less a statesman/landowner, have time to write the
six hundred or so books Varro produced in his lifetime.

But, more to the point, what the Greeks and Romans left as a foundation of thought demonstrates how expansive a range of topics such
treatises encompassed then: the care of fruits, crops, vines, animals;
religion, history, myth; ecology, philosophy, aesthetics. The concept of
cultivation described a way of being in the world, with the result that
the same word made civilization a synonym for husbandry. To cultivate both the land and the mind were regarded as activities of a responsible life, and so for centuries the idea has come down to us that the
measure of civilization is the attitude of a people to their land. Regrettably, in our time a misguided sense of progress has separated one kind
of knowledge from another: the mind from the body, humanities from
science, agriculture from ecology, philosophy from action, the in-

dividual from a common good.

Likewise, natural history is often isolated from our understanding of the history of the world. History books are filled with exclusions, among them the place of nature in human consciousness. They tell instead of wars, the lives of kings and queens and statesmen, of exploration and invention, the creation and destruction of cities and cultures. Few tales are told of any other species than the human one. How simple it would be to include with our other histories those of plants and animals in the world, their habits and habitats. How many know the names of the plants in their neighborhood, or the birds and butterflies that frequent them? If naming is the greater part of possession, we live as strangers in paradise.

Research on this book led me to the conclusion that there is a theme larger than the one I initially envisioned, in the way Americans thought and wrote about plants, and worked in their gardens. The evolution of gardens and gardeners is inseparable from patterns in American society. That the lives of plants follow the same developments as the lives of people is not surprising because they share the same cultural and economic circumstances. Horticulture, like art, commerce, or technology, is one more historical portrait of a nation, in any given time and place.

So close to recent times American gardeners have struggled to name, to plant, to study the species of a New World. Out of this effort has emerged a rich heritage of horticultural documentation that extends from the seventeenth century to the present. If the notion of a garden belongs to the history of ideas, then garden writing, like other literary genres, offers its own perspective of the American imagination.

We search for answers to the great questions in books and ancient wisdom, even in statistical data, the new oracle, when quite simply, there are times in history when knowledge grows on trees. Since the beginning of time philosophers and writers and craftsmen have made the symbol of the tree part of the poetic life of civilizations. My own favorite arboreal fantasy is depicted in Italo Calvino's joyful novel *The Baron in the Trees*, in which a young aristocrat in protest against society goes up into the tall trees of Northern Italy one day and never comes down again. From his leafy home the baron as an old man writes a "Project for the Constitution of an Ideal State in the Trees." Alas, we are not so fortunate in our time, having neither leaders who can imagine such a life, nor the network of trees to support us.

Those who like myself woke up early the morning of October 4 last fall to the white sound of cracking branches witnessed a stormier scene in the relations of people and trees. The unseasonal wind and snow blasts that sent trees toppling throughout the Hudson Valley, then moved on to stun English parks and gardens from the deep green sleep of time, showed that nature has no thought of us. We are the spectators, the setting. I wonder if the orioles, perennial boarders in an old silver maple, will come back to a Catskill tree whose unwitting new airiness has transformed its shape. As somebody once said, we don't live in the first chapter of Genesis. If I will never see Capability Brown's now damaged landscapes, I can console myself with poppies left in Etruscan tombs.

Now as I sit and write these words from the center of a city, snow is falling outside and I wait anxiously for spring to come again. Fantasies are easily packed in snowflakes. Yet, bare trees bring their own semaphoric calm to the glow of urban skies. I know that flowers need their privacy to go underground for a time of sexual frenzy unknown to us mortals who envy their abandon. When I look out the window the ground acts as a blank mask—a sheet of ice melting into a sheet of paper—on which I project my thoughts of how to write about ephemerality.

I judge a garden by the gardener who cares for it, the one who invests space with daydreams. What is a garden but a species of desire? How well I know the downward gaze into the face of the earth, the feeling of a luxurious body in good, dark soil that slips through the fingers in the rush to return to its dirty delirium. Each gardener creates an ideal world of miniature thoughts that drift languidly into each other like flowers on a dry afternoon. Here silence has the rhythm of wishes.

Gardens have that special resistance beautiful things offer to our understanding. Some days I think it is enough to watch a hummingbird wander into the sweet tunnel of a trumpet vine climbing up a summer sky. Maybe gardening is a form of worship.

Strangely enough, I feel at home in this ephemerality of time because I have spent many years experiencing it in the theatre as a theatre critic. I still feel the same sense of melancholy in a winter garden or an empty theatre. Even more of a coincidence, thirty years ago another theatre critic, Joseph Wood Krutch, edited a collection of garden writing, his *Gardener's World* featuring selections from around the world and through the ages. Really it is not so difficult to move from a theatre to a garden. Each creates a world in a space that celebrates pure presence, and the fabulous confusion of nature and artifice, which is to say, reality and illusion. At least one half of gardening is dreaming yourself into a new setting.

For me it started with a house in the country and a new landscape, then learning the names of plants, buying them, too many, dividing them for friends, getting their surplus, looking at catalogues and going to nurseries, buying more plants, now old garden books, eventually finding myself in a garden too big to care for unless I quit my job. This, I think, is the general pattern of a gardener's life in its beginning stages.

It is very rare for anyone except professionals in the field or retired people to have the luxury of doing nothing but gardening. This book is filled with contributions by gardeners who were also historians, explorers, statesmen, editors, architects, scientists, novelists, preachers, entrepreneurs. Little by little they discovered the world as a garden. At that point everything changes, and suddenly one's whole life becomes the life of a person who gardens.

The next step if one is a writer is to find a way to turn gardening into a book project, so you can explore gardening as writing, at last unable in any season to give up the pleasures of manual labor.

Catskill—New York City   Bonnie Marranca
January 1988

AMERICAN GARDEN WRITING

I

SEEDS OF INSPIRATION

FRONT DOORYARDS

ALICE MORSE EARLE

"There are few of us who cannot remember a front yard garden which seemed to us a very paradise in childhood. Whether the house was a fine one and the enclosure spacious, or whether it was a small house with only a narrow bit of ground in front, the yard was kept with care, and was different from the rest of the land altogether. . . . People do not know what they lose when they make way with the reserve, the separateness, the sanctity, of the front yard of their grandmothers. It is like writing down family secrets for any one to read; it is like having everybody call you by your first name, or sitting in any pew in church."

—*Country Byways,* Sarah Orne Jewett, 1881

OLD NEW ENGLAND VILLAGES AND SMALL towns and well-kept New England farms had universally a simple and pleasing form of garden called the front yard or front dooryard. A few still may be seen in conservative communities in the New England states and in New York or Pennsylvania. I saw flourishing ones this summer in Gloucester, Marblehead, and Ipswich. Even where the front yard was but a narrow strip of land before a tiny cottage, it was carefully fenced in, with a gate that was kept rigidly closed and latched. There seemed to be a law which shaped and bounded the front yard; the side fences extended from the corners of the house to the front fence on the edge of the road, and thus formed naturally the guarded parallelogram. Often the fence around the front yard was the only one on the farm; everywhere else were boundaries of great stone walls; or if there were rail fences, the front yard fence was the only painted one. I cannot doubt that the first gardens that our foremothers had, which were wholly of flowering plants, were front yards, little enclosures hard won from the forest.

The word yard, not generally applied now to any enclosure of elegant cultivation, comes from the same root as the word garden. Garth is another derivative, and the word exists much disguised in orchard. In the sixteenth century yard was used in formal literature instead of garden; and later Burns writes of ''Eden's bonnie yard, Where yeuthful lovers first were pair'd.''

This front yard was an English fashion derived from the forecourt so strongly advised by Gervayse Markham (an interesting old English writer on floriculture and husbandry), and found in front of many a yeoman's house, and many a more pretentious house as well in Markham's day. Forecourts were common in England until the middle of the eighteenth century, and may still be seen. The forecourt gave privacy to the house even when in the center of a town. Its readoption is advised with handsome dwellings in England, where ground space is limited—and why not in America, too?

The front yard was sacred to the best beloved, or at any rate the most honored, garden flowers of the house mistress, and was preserved by its fences from inroads of cattle, which then wandered at their will and were not housed, or even enclosed at night. The flowers were often of scant variety, but were those deemed the gentlefolk of the flower world. There was a clump of daffodils and of the poet's narcissus in early spring, and stately crown imperial; usually, too, a few scarlet and yellow single tulips, and grape hyacinths. Later came phlox in abundance—the only native American plant,—canterbury bells, and ample and glowing London pride. Of course there were great plants of white and blue daylilies, with their beautiful and decorative leaves, and purple and yellow flower-de-luce. A few old-fashioned shrubs always were seen. By inflexible law there must be a lilac, which might be the aristocratic Persian lilac. A syringa, a flowering currant, or strawberry bush made sweet the front yard in spring, and sent wafts of fragrance into the house windows. Spindling, rusty snowberry bushes were by the gate, and snowballs also, or our native viburnums. Old as they seem, the spireas and deutzias came to us in the nineteenth century from Japan; as did the flowering quinces and cherries. The pink flowering almond dates back to the oldest front yards, and Peter's wreath certainly seems an old settler and is found now in many front yards that remain.

The glory of the front yard was the old-fashioned early red "piny," cultivated since the days of Pliny. I hear people speaking of it with contempt as a vulgar flower—flaunting is the conventional derogatory adjective—but I glory in its flaunting. The modern varieties, of every tint from white through flesh color, coral, pink, ruby color, salmon, and even yellow, to deep red, are as beautiful as roses. Some are sweet-scented; and they have no thorns, and their foliage is ever perfect, so I am sure the rose is jealous.

I am as fond of the peony as are the Chinese, among whom it is flower queen. It is by them regarded as an aristocratic flower; and in old New England towns fine peony plants in an old garden are a pretty good indication of the residence of what Dr. Holmes called New England Brahmins. In Salem and Portsmouth are old "pinys" that have a hundred blossoms at a time—a glorious sight. A Japanese name is "flower-of-prosperity"; another name, "plant-of-twenty-days," because its glories last during that period of time.

Rhododendrons are to the modern garden what the peony was in the old-fashioned flower border; and I am glad the modern flower cannot drive the old one out. They are equally varied in coloring, but the peony is a much hardier plant, and I like it far better. It has no blights, no bugs, no diseases, no running out, no funguses; it doesn't have to be covered in winter, and it will bloom in the shade. No old-time or modern garden is to me fully furnished without peonies. I would grow them in some corner of the garden for their splendid healthy foliage if they hadn't a blossom. The *Paeonia tenuifolia* in particular has exquisite feathery foliage. The great tree peony, which came from China, grows eight feet or more in height, and is a triumph of the flower world; but it was not known to the oldest front yards. Some of the tree peonies have finely displayed leafage of a curious and very gratifying tint of green. Miss Jekyll, with her usual felicity, compares its blue cast with pinkish shading to the varicolored metal alloys of the Japanese bronze workers—a striking comparison. The single peonies of recent years are of great beauty, and will soon be esteemed here as in China.

Not the least of the peony's charms is its exceeding trimness and cleanliness. The plants always look like a well-dressed, well-shod, well-gloved girl of birth, breeding, and of equal good taste and good health; a girl who can swim, and skate, and ride, and play golf. Every inch has a well-set, neat, cared-for look which the shape and growth of the plant keeps from seeming artificial or finicky.

No flower can be set in our garden of more distinct antiquity than the peony; the Greeks believed it to be of divine origin. A green arbor of the fourteenth century in England is described as set around with gillyflower, tansy, gromwell, and ''Pyonys powdered ay betwene'' —just as I like to see peonies set to this day, ''powdered'' everywhere between all the other flowers of the border.

I am pleased to note of the common flowers of the New England front yard, that they are no new things; they are nearly all Elizabethan of date—many are older still. Lord Bacon in his essay on gardens names many of them: crocus, tulip, hyacinth, daffodil, flower-de-luce, double peony, lilac, lily-of-the-valley.

A favorite flower was the yellow garden lily, the lemon lily, *Hemerocallis*, when it could be kept from spreading. Often its unbounded luxuriance exiled it from the front yard to the kitchen dooryard. Its pretty old-fashioned name was Liricon Fancy, given, I am told, in England to the lily-of-the-valley. I know no more satisfying sight than a good bank of these lemon lilies in full flower. Below Flatbush there used to be a driveway leading to an old Dutch house, set at regular intervals with great clumps of lemon lilies, and their full bloom made them glorious.

The time of fullest inflorescence of the nineteenth century front yard was when phlox and tiger lilies bloomed; but the pinkish-orange colors of the latter (the oddest reds of any flower tints) blended most vilely and rampantly with the crimson-purple of the phlox; and when London pride joined with its glowing scarlet, the front yard fairly ached. Nevertheless, an adaptation of that front-yard bloom can be most effective in a garden border, when white phlox only is planted, and the tiger lily or cultivated stalks of our wild nodding lily rise above the white trusses of bloom. These wild lilies grow very luxuriantly in the garden, often towering above our heads and forming great candelabra bearing two score or more blooms. . . .

The tiger lily is usually thought upon as a truly old-fashioned flower, a veritable antique; it is a favorite of artists to place as an accessory in their colonial gardens, and of authors for their flower beds of Revolutionary days, but it was not known either in formal garden or front yard, until after ''the days when we lived under the King.'' The bulbs were first brought to England from Eastern Asia in 1804 by Captain Kirkpatrick of the East India Company's Service, and shared with the Japan lily the honor of being the first Eastern lilies introduced into European gardens. A few years ago an old gentleman, Mr. Isaac Pitman, who was then about eighty-five years of age, told me that he recalled distinctly when tiger lilies first appeared in our gardens, and where he first saw them growing in Boston. So instead of being an old-time flower, or even an old-comer from the Orient, it is one of the novelties of this century. How readily has it made itself at home, and even wandered wild down our roadsides!

The two simple colors of phlox of the old-time front yard, white and crimson-purple, are now augmented by tints of salmon, vermilion, and rose. I recall with special pleasure the profuse garden decoration at East Hampton, Long Island, of a pure cherry-colored phlox, generally a doubtful color for me, but there so associated with the white blooms of various other plants, and backed by a high hedge covered solidly with blossoming honeysuckle, that it was wonderfully successful.

To other members of the phlox family, all natives of our own continent, the old front yard owed much; the moss pink sometimes crowded out both grass and its companion the periwinkle; it is still found in our gardens, and bountifully also in our fields; either in white or pink, it is one of the satisfactions of spring, and its cheerful little blossom is of wonderful use in many waste places. An old-fashioned bloom, the low-growing *Phlox amoena*, with its queerly fuzzy leaves and bright crimson blossoms, was among the most distinctly old-fashioned flowers of the front yard. It was tolerated rather than cultivated, as was its companion, the arabis or rock cress—both crowding, monopolizing creatures. I remember well how they spread over the beds and up the grass banks in my mother's garden, how sternly they were uprooted, in spite of the pretty name of the arabis—''snow-in-summer.''

Sometimes the front yard path had edgings of sweet single or lightly double white or tinted pinks, which were not deemed as choice as box edgings. Frequently large box plants clipped into simple and natural shapes stood at the side of the doorstep, usually in the home of the well-to-do. A great shell might be on either side of the door-sill, if there chanced to be seafaring menfolk who lived or visited under the roof-tree. Annuals were few in number; sturdy old perennial plants of many years' growth were the most honored dwellers in the front yard, true representatives of old families. The roses were few and poor, for there was usually some great tree just without the gate, an elm or larch, whose shadow fell far too near and heavily for the health of roses. Sometimes there was a prickly semidouble yellow rose, called by us a Scotch rose, a sweetbrier, or a rusty-flowered white rose, similar, though inferior, to the Madame Plantier. A new fashion of trellises appeared in the front yard about sixty years ago, and crimson Boursault roses climbed up them as if by magic.

One marked characteristic of the front yard was its lack of weeds; few sprung up, none came to seed-time; the enclosure was small, and it was a mark of good breeding to care for it well. Sometimes, however, the earth was covered closely under shrubs and plants with the cheerful little ladies'-delights, and they blossomed in the chinks of the bricked path and under the box edges. Ambrosia, too, grew everywhere, but these were welcome—they were not weeds. . . .

Sarah Orne Jewett, in the plaint of *A Mournful Villager*, has drawn a beautiful and sympathetic picture of these front yards, and she deplores their passing. I mourn them as I do every fenced-in or hedged-in garden enclosure. The sanctity and reserve of these front yards of our grandmothers was somewhat emblematic of woman's life of that day: it was restricted, and narrowed to a small outlook and monotonous likeness to her neighbor's; but it was a life easily satisfied with small pleasures, and it was comely and sheltered and carefully kept, and pleasant to the home household; and these were no mean things.

The front yard was never a garden of pleasure; children could not play in these precious little enclosed plots, and never could pick the flowers—front yard and flowers were both too much respected. Only formal visitors entered therein, visitors who opened the gate and closed it carefully behind them, and knocked slowly with the brass knocker, and were ushered in through the ceremonious front door and the little ill-contrived entry, to the stiff foreroom or parlor. The parson and his wife entered that portal, and sometimes a solemn would-be sweetheart, or the guests at a tea party. It can be seen that every one who had enough social dignity to have a front door and a parlor, and visitors thereto, also desired a front yard with flowers as the external token of that honored standing. It was like owning a pew in church; you could be a Christian without having a pew, but not a respected one. Sometimes when there was a "vandue" in the house, reckless folk opened the front gate, and even tied it back. I attended one where the auctioneer boldly set the articles out through the windows under the lilac bushes and even on the precious front yard plants. A vendue and a funeral were the only gatherings in country communities when the entire neighborhood came freely to an old homestead, when all were at liberty to enter the front dooryard. At the sad time when a funeral took place in the house, the front gate was fastened widely open, and solemn men-neighbors, in Sunday garments, stood rather uncomfortably and awkwardly around the front yard as the women passed into the house of mourning and were seated within. When the sad services began, the men too entered and stood stiffly by the door. Then through the front door, down the mossy path of the front yard, and through the open front gate was borne the master, the mistress, and then their children, and children's children. All are gone from our sight, many from our memory, and often too from our ken, while the lilacs and peonies and flowers-de-luce still blossom and flourish with perennial youth, and still claim us as friends.

At the side of the house or by the kitchen door would be seen many thrifty blooms: poles of scarlet runners, beds of portulacas and petunias, rows of pinks, bunches of marigolds, level expanses of sweet Williams, banks of cheerful nasturtiums, tangles of morning glories and long rows of stately hollyhocks, which were much admired, but were seldom seen in the front yard, which was too shaded for them. Weeds grew here at the kitchen door in a rank profusion which was hard to conquer; but here the winter's fuchsias or geraniums stood in flower pots in the sunlight, and the tubs of oleanders and agapanthus lilies.

The flowers of the front yard seemed to bear a more formal, a "company" aspect; conventionality rigidly bound them. Bachelor's buttons might grow there by accident, but marigolds never were tolerated —they were pot herbs. Sunflowers were not even permitted in the flower beds at the side of the house unless these streched down to the vegetable beds. Outside the front yard would be a rioting and cheerful growth of pink bouncing Bet, or of purple honesty, and tall straggling plants of a certain small flowered, ragged campanula, and a white mallow with flannelly leaves which, doubtless, aspired to inhabit the sacred bounds of the front yard (and probably dwelt there originally), and often were gladly permitted to grow in side gardens or kitchen dooryards, but which were regarded as interloping weeds by the guardians of the front yard, and sternly exiled. Sometimes a bed of these orange-tawny daylilies which had once been warmly welcomed from the Orient, and now were not wanted anywhere by anyone, kept company with the bouncing Bet, and stretched cheerfully down the roadside.

When the fences disappeared with the night rambles of the cows, the front yards gradually changed character; the tender blooms vanished, but the tall shrubs and the peonies and flower-de-luce sturdily grew and blossomed, save where that dreary destroyer of a garden crept in—the desire for a lawn. The result was then a meager expanse of poorly kept grass, with no variety, color, or change—neither lawn nor front yard. It is ever a pleasure to me when driving in a village street or a country road to find one of these front yards still enclosed, or even to note in front of many houses the traces of a past front yard still plainly visible in the flourishing old-fashioned plants of many years' growth.

*

From *Old Time Gardens*, Alice Morse Earle (1853-1911). New York: The Macmillan Company, 1901. *Old Time Gardens* is a classic in American garden literature by an author with a sturdy historical sense and real love of gardens as sites of the imagination. Earle's books emphasize the often overlooked truth that the best garden writing is both social and horticultural document. *Sun Dials and Roses of Yesterday* claims equal attention as a thoroughly enjoyable work, but there are many more that tell of lost, different worlds, namely, *Colonial Days in Old New York, Stage Coach and Tavern Days,* and *Two Centuries of Costume in America.* Here is a writer to return to again and again, for that special kind of history that uncovers the little pleasures of everyday life.

A Visit to John Bartram's Garden

Michel-Guillaume St. John de Crèvecoeur

EXAMINE THIS FLOURISHING PROVINCE, IN whatever light you will, the eyes as well as the mind of an European traveller are equally delighted; because a diffusive happiness appears in every part: happiness which is established on the broadest basis. The wisdom of Lycurgus and Solon never conferred on man one half of the blessings and uninterrupted prosperity which the Pennsylvanians now possess: the name of *Penn*, that simple but illustrious citizen, does more honour to the English nation than those of many of their kings.

In order to convince you that I have not bestowed undeserved praises in my former letters on this celebrated government; and that either nature or the climate seems to be more favourable here to the arts and sciences, than to any other American province; let us together agreeable to your desire, pay a visit to Mr. John Bertram [*sic.*—ed.], the first botanist, in this new hemisphere: become such by a native impulse of disposition. It is to this simple man that America is indebted for several useful discoveries, and the knowledge of many new plants. I had been greatly prepossessed in his favour by the extensive correspondence which I knew he held with the most eminent Scotch and French botanists; I knew also that he had been honoured with that of Queen Ulrica of Sweden.

His house is small, but decent; there was something peculiar in its first appearance, which seemed to distinguish it from those of his neighbours: a small tower in the middle of it, not only helped to strengthen it but afforded convenient room for a staircase. Every disposition of the fields, fences, and trees, seemed to bear the marks of perfect order and regularity, which in rural affairs, always indicate a prosperous industry.

I was received at the door by a woman dressed extremely neat and simple, who without courtesying, or any other ceremonial, asked me, with an air of benignity, who I wanted? I answered, I should be glad to see Mr. Bertram. If thee wilt step in and take a chair, I will send for him. No, I said, I had rather have the pleasure of walking through his farm, I shall easily find him out, with your directions. After a little time I perceived the Schuylkill, winding through delightful meadows, and soon cast my eyes on a new-made bank, which seemed greatly to confine its stream. After having walked on its top a considerable way I at last reached the place where ten men were at work. I asked, if any of them could tell me where Mr. Bertram was? An elderly looking man, with wide trousers and a large leather apron on, looking at me said, "My name is Bertram, dost thee want me?" Sir, I am come on purpose to converse with you, if you can be spared from your labour. "Very easily," he answered, "I direct and advise more than I work." We walked toward the house, where he made me take a chair while he went to put on clean clothes, after which he returned and sat down by me. The fame of your knowledge, said I, in American botany, and your well-known hospitality, have induced me to pay you a visit, which I hope you will not think troublesome: I shall be glad to spend a few hours in your garden. "The greatest advantage," replied he, "which I receive from what thee callest my botanical fame, is the pleasure which it often procureth me in receiving the visits of friends and foreigners: but our jaunt into the garden must be postponed for the present, as the bell is ringing for dinner." We entered into a large hall, where there was a long table full of victuals; at the lowest part sat his negroes, his hired men were next, then the family and myself; and at the head, the venerable father and his wife presided. Each reclined his head and said his prayers, divested of the tedious cant of some, and of the ostentatious style of others. "After the luxuries of our cities," observed he, "this plain fare must appear to thee a severe fast." By no means, Mr.

Bertram, this honest country dinner convinces me, that you receive me as a friend and an old acquaintance. "I am glad of it, for thee art heartily welcome. I never knew how to use ceremonies; they are insufficient proofs of sincerity; our society, besides, are utterly strangers to what the world calleth polite expressions. We treat others as we treat ourselves. I received yesterday a letter from Philadelphia, by which I understand thee art a Russian; what motives can possibly have induced thee to quit thy native country and to come so far in quest of knowledge or pleasure? Verily it is a great compliment thee payest to this our young province, to think that anything it exhibiteth may be worthy thy attention."

After dinner we quaffed an honest bottle of Madeira wine, without the irksome labour of toasts, healths, or sentiments; and then retired into his study.

I was no sooner entered, than I observed a coat of arms in a gilt frame with the name of *John Bertram*. The novelty of such a decoration, in such a place, struck me; I could not avoid asking, Does the society of Friends take any pride in these armorial bearings, which sometimes serve as marks of distinction between families, and much oftener as food for pride and ostentation? "Thee must know," said he, "that my father was a Frenchman, he brought this piece of painting over with him; I keep it as a piece of family furniture, and as a memorial of his removal hither." From his study we went into the garden, which contained a great variety of curious plants and shrubs; some grew in the greenhouse, over the door of which were written these lines:

> Slave to no sect, who takes no private road,
> But looks through nature, up to nature's God!

He informed me that he had often followed General Bouquet to Pittsburgh, with the view of herbalising; that he had made useful collections in Virginia, and that he had been employed by the king of England to visit the two Floridas.

Our walks and botanical observations engrossed so much of our time, that the sun was almost down ere I thought of returning to Philadelphia; I regretted that the day had been so short, as I had not spent so rational a one for a long time before. I wanted to stay, yet was doubtful whether it would not appear improper, being an utter stranger. Knowing, however, that I was visiting the least ceremonious people in the world, I bluntly informed him of the pleasure I had enjoyed, and with the desire I had of staying a few days with him. ''Thee art as welcome as if I were thy father; thee art no stranger; thy desire of knowledge, thy being a foreigner besides, entitleth thee to consider my house as thine own, as long as thee pleaseth: use thy time with the most perfect freedom; I too shall do so myself.'' I thankfully accepted the kind invitation.

We went to view his favourite bank; he showed me the principles and method on which it was erected; and we walked over the grounds which had been already drained. The whole store of nature's kind luxuriance seemed to have been exhausted on these beautiful meadows; he made me count the amazing number of cattle and horses now feeding on solid bottoms, which but a few years before had been covered with water. Thence we rambled through his fields, where the right-angular fences, the heaps of pitched stones, the flourishing clover, announced the best husbandry, as well as the most assiduous attention. His cows were then returning home, deep bellied, short legged, having udders ready to burst; seeking with seeming toil to be delivered from the great exuberance they contained: he next showed me his orchard, formerly planted on a barren sandy soil, but long since converted into one of the richest spots in that vicinage.

''This,'' said he, ''is altogether the fruit of my own contrivance; I purchased some years ago the privilege of a small spring, about a mile and a half from hence, which at a considerable expense I have brought to this reservoir; therein I throw old lime, ashes, horse-dung, etc., and twice a week I let it run, thus impregnated; I regularly spread on this ground in the fall, old hay, straw, and whatever damaged fodder I have about my barn. By these simple means I mow, one year with another, fifty-three hundreds of excellent hay per acre, from a soil, which scarcely produced *five fingers* [a small plant resembling strawberries] some years before.'' This is, Sir, a miracle in husbandry; happy the country which is cultivated by a society of men, whose application and taste lead them to prosecute and accomplish useful works. ''I am not the only person who does these things,'' he said, ''wherever water can be had it is always turned to that important use; wherever a farmer can water his meadows, the greatest crops of the best hay and excellent after-grass, are the sure rewards of his labours. With the banks of my meadow ditches, I have greatly enriched my upland fields, those which I intend to rest for a few years, I constantly sow with red clover, which is the greatest meliorator of our lands. For three years after, they yield abundant pasture; when I want to break up my clover fields, I give them a good coat of mud, which hath been exposed to the severities of three or four of our winters. This is the reason that I commonly reap from twenty-eight to thirty-six bushels of wheat an acre; my flax, oats, and Indian corn, I raise in the same proportion. Wouldst thee inform me whether the inhabitants of thy country follow the same methods of husbandry?'' No, Sir; in the neighbourhood of our towns, there are indeed some intelligent farmers, who prosecute their rural schemes with attention; but we should be too numerous, too happy, too powerful a people, if it were possible for the whole Russian Empire to be cultivated like the province of Pennsylvania. Our lands are so unequally divided, and so few of our farmers are possessors of the soil they till, that they cannot execute plans of husbandry with the same vigour as you do, who hold yours, as it were from the Master of nature, unencumbered and free. Oh, America! exclaimed I, thou knowest not as yet the whole extent of thy happiness: the foundation of thy civil polity must lead thee in a few years to a degree of population and power which Europe little thinks of! ''Long before this happens,'' answered the good man, ''we shall rest beneath the turf; it is vain for mortals to be presumptuous in their conjectures: our country is, no doubt, the cradle of an extensive future population; the old world is growing weary of its inhabitants, they must come here to flee from the tyranny of the great. But doth not thee imagine, that the great will, in the course of years, come over here also; for it is the misfortune of all societies everywhere to hear of great men, great rulers, and of great tyrants.'' My dear Sir, I replied, tyranny never can take a strong hold in this country, the land is too widely distributed: it is poverty in Europe that makes slaves. ''Friend Iwan, as I make no doubt that thee understandest the Latin tongue, read this kind epistle which the good Queen of Sweden, *Ulrica*, sent me a few years ago. Good woman! that she should think in her palace at Stockholm of poor John Bertram, on the banks of the Schuylkill, appeareth to me very strange.'' Not in the least, dear Sir; you are the first man whose name as a botanist hath done honour to America; it is very natural at the same time to imagine, that so extensive a continent must contain many curious plants and trees: is it then surprising to see a princess, fond of useful knowledge, descend sometimes from the throne, to walk in the gardens of Linnaeus? " 'Tis to the directions of that learned man," said Mr. Bertram, "that I am indebted for the method which has led me to the knowledge I now possess; the science of botany is so diffusive, that a proper thread is absolutely wanted to conduct the beginner." Pray, Mr. Bertram, when did you imbibe the first wish to cultivate the science of botany; were you regularly bred to it in Philadelphia? "I have never received any other education than barely reading and writing; this small farm was all the patrimony my father left me, certain debts and the want of meadows kept me rather low in the beginning of my life; my wife brought me nothing in money, all her riches consisted in her good temper and great knowledge of housewifery. I scarcely knew how to trace my steps in the botanical career; they appear to me now like unto a dream: but thee mayest rely on what I shall relate, though I know that some of our friends have laughed at it." I am not one of those people, Mr. Bertram, who aim at finding out the ridiculous in what is sincerely and honestly averred. "Well, then, I'll tell thee: One day I was very busy in holding my plough (for thee seest I am but a ploughman) and being weary I ran under the shade of a tree to repose myself. I cast my eyes on a *daisy*, I plucked it mechanically and viewed it with more curiosity than common country farmers are wont to do; and observed therein very many distinct parts, some perpendicular, some horizontal. *What a shame, said my mind, or something that inspired my mind, that thee shouldst have employed so many years in tilling the earth and destroying so many flowers and plants, without being acquainted with their structures and their uses!* This seeming inspiration suddenly awakened my curiosity, for these were not thoughts to which I had been accustomed. I returned to my team, but this new desire did not quit my mind; I mentioned it to my wife, who greatly discouraged me from prosecuting my new scheme, as she called it; I was not opulent enough, she said, to dedicate much of my time to studies and labours which might rob me of that portion of it which is the only wealth of the American farmer. However her prudent caution did not discourage me; I thought about it continually, at supper, in bed, and wherever I went. At last I could not resist the impulse; for on the fourth day of the following week, I hired a man to plough for me, and went to Philadelphia. Though I knew not what book to call for, I ingeniously told the bookseller my errand, who provided me with such as he thought best, and a Latin grammar beside. Next I applied to a neighbouring schoolmaster, who in three months taught me Latin enough to understand Linnaeus, which I purchased afterward. Then I began to botanise all over my farm; in a little time I became acquainted with every vegetable that grew in my neighbourhood; and next ventured into Maryland, living among the Friends: in proportion as I thought myself more learned I proceeded farther, and by a steady application of several years I have acquired a pretty general knowledge of every plant and tree to be found in our continent. In process of time I was applied to from the old countries, whither I every year send many collections. Being now made easy in my circumstances, I have ceased to labour, and am never so happy as when I see and converse with my friends. If among the many plants or shrubs I am acquainted with, there are any thee wantest to send to thy native country, I will cheerfully procure them, and give thee moreover whatever directions thee mayest want.''

*

From *Letters from an American Farmer*, Michel-Guillaume St. Jean de Crèvecoeur (1735-1813). London: Thomas Davies, 1782. Crèvecoeur was a Frenchman who served as mapmaker and engineer under Montcalm in the French and Indian War. He settled for many years in this country in the turbulent days before the creation of the republic, and lived with his wife and children on a farm in the Hudson Valley's Dutchess County. In 1783 Crèvecoeur became French consul in New York, helping to set up early trade agreements between France and his adopted country. Crèvecoeur's not altogether factual though much acclaimed *Letters* remains one of the best available accounts of eighteenth-century rural American life. In it he used the literary conceit of a series of letters, pretending to be a ''Russian gentleman'' for his recollection of a 1765 visit to the by then world-renowned botanist John Bartram. The book was praised in Great Britain by the likes of William Hazlitt and Charles Lamb; it gained Crèvecoeur entrance into Parisian literary salons, under the guidance of Rousseau's good friend Mme. d'Houdetot. George Washington modestly thought it ''embellished with rather too flattering circumstances,'' and D. H. Lawrence, a century later, would criticize the author as ''an *intellectual* savage.'' *St. John de Crèvecoeur: The Life of an American Farmer,* a new biography by Allen and Asselineau, reconstructs his life amidst revolutions on two continents.

WHITE FLOWER FARM

AMOS PETTINGILL

IN THE LATE 1930s JANE GRANT AND I MADE A house out of a small barn in Litchfield, Connecticut. The idea was to have ''a little place in the country'' to which we could bring our work, and where we could vacation. We were writers, and it seemed reasonable that writing could be done as well in the country as in New York City. Other people did it. We did it. But for me, trying to write in Litchfield was torture, for nature beckoned so seductively that I spent far more time with her than with my work. This book, a record of my first-hand experiences as a gardener, starts properly from the day when I stopped pushing furniture from one place to another inside and went outside and found, with some amazement, that we needed a lawn.

To get the other principal character in this cast into the reader's mind at this point, I shall explain that Jane Grant and I are married. She is a professional woman who has always kept her maiden name on the grounds that it's the only thing she has so really her own it can't be taken away, and that as men don't lose their names on a marriage day she sees no logic in a woman losing hers in this unequal tradition. . . .

When we moved into our house in the Litchfield hills (the contractors-builders were no different from those today), Grant and a friend took over the inside of the house; my work, except for shoving heavy stuff around for them, was on the outside. The builder's litter came up quickly, and the useless bits made a fine fire. Heavier pieces were saved; I still have a few of them stored away for that day when they may become useful. Our lot consisted of one and one-third acres. It was knee high in hay, except where it had been battered down by the workmen. When I discovered that we needed a lawn, I decided that to get one we would have to plow up a bit of the meadow and seed it. But this idea met with no enthusiasm—Grant said that dust would blow into our nice new quarters during the rest of the summer. I certainly did not want to do the inside cleaning, including windows, that would be necessary, although I had been offered the job, not very politely, if. . . .

A neighbor, the woman who had sold us the barn and the land, and who was a gracious lender of tools offered me a scythe and a hayfork. I had used a scythe years before; it was a tool for which I had never developed any affection. But I got hers, and though I found it just as demanding as the one I had used years before, I hacked down the hay, carted it to a pile, and burned it. Today, of course, the grass would go straight to a compost heap, but at that time I had never heard of such a thing. . . .

Grant came out one day and said, ''What are you playing?'' I said that I was playing digging dandelions out of the lawn, a weed that had plagued me in Colorado, and plantain, another broadleaf weed whose name Jim Bristol had told me. She said she would play, too, and from that moment on she became one of the world's most competent weeders. I guess a good gardener always starts as a good weeder. Weeding is always hard at first if the things have been allowed to grow big enough to be noticed. Later she learned to attack them when they could just be seen; their destruction then is so easy that weeding might even be called a pleasure. Anyway, killing them when they are that small is not much work.

In September, George Luca and I seeded the lawn. We scraped the surface lightly with iron rakes, sowed the seed, and then, with a makeshift drag made of a gunny sack, worked the seed lightly into the surface. Afterward, we pushed the mower over it, making believe it was a light roller. The fall rains came, the nights cooled and the new grass shot up, some of it almost immediately. It turned out that the seed which germinated so quickly was annual rye, which I later learned was called ''real estate'' grass, because speculative builders, who want their houses to look like homes quickly, use it for its rapid growth and deep green color. The only trouble is that it doesn't last over the winter. The cheap mixture I had bought contained 30 percent of the stuff, but there was enough Kentucky Bluegrass in it so that we at least had the start of what was to become, after a while, a fairly respectable lawn.

Meanwhile, Grant had the inside of the house in such good order that she started to give parties for friends. This required flowers. She discovered that dandelions with stems cut short and massed and floated in a bowl made sprightly, short-lasting bouquets. She also saw many different kinds of wild flowers in bloom in the surrounding hay meadows. She picked these largely from the edge of the meadow bordering my so-called lawn.

"There is a big patch of blue ones out there," I said, pointing to a slight rise about 200 feet from the house.

"Come on and help me get them," she said. At the moment I was busy trying to get 15 coats of paint off an old pine table we had picked up at an antique shop.

"I play weeding dandelions with you—you should play picking pretty flowers with me. It's only fair," she added.

That seemed logical. In a few moments the flowers were harvested and I went back to taking paint off with sandpaper, decidedly the hardest way to remove anything.

In about an hour I heard her in the living room talking sternly to the wild flowers. That's the nice way to describe her remarks. Never have flowers been cussed out so expertly. There are no swear words Grant doesn't know. Her education in them, which is *magna cum laude*, came from sitting in the society department when she first joined *The Times* and hearing, through the thin partition that separated the two departments, the sports writers and the various fighters who visited them discuss ordinary matters in extraordinary language, known in these gentler days as filthy—words that anyone can see now chalked on walls or on display advertising signs in the city subways. "You're a bunch of — — ingrates," she said at the end of a blacker sentence, "and to think I risked my life to pick you."

"Such language, Grant," I said.

"Look at them," she said. "Dead in 15 minutes!" . . .

To console her on the afternoon of the great wild flower collapse, I

said, ''Next summer I'll grow some flowers for you that will be better
and prettier in a bowl than any wild flower.'' This was sheer imagination, for I had never grown any flower, except sweet peas. Mother had
had rose gardens, but she only picked the blooms; the bushes were
planted and cared for by a Russian woman who worked for us for years.
The sweet pea period of my life came after World War I, when I attempted to run the family's ranch east of Boulder, Colorado. Mother
insisted that I grow sweet peas for her. Dutifully, every year on St.
Patrick's Day, I planted sweet peas, because that was the traditional
day to plant peas of any kind. It was simple. I ran a furrow about 100
feet long, distributed seed, covered them with about a half inch of soil,
cut some branches from the willows at the creek, and stuck them into
the furrow for the peas to climb on. The furrow, only partially filled
with soil, served as a ditch into which irrigation water could be turned.
When the flowers started to bloom, Mother and a friend would appear
daily in her aged Hupp-Yeats electric brougham, which she had learned to drive forward but had never learned to back, and they would pick
the blooms. One can readily see that a slight knowledge about growing
alfalfa, sugar beets, and sweet peas from seed, the first two planted and
harvested with machinery, was poor preparation for making good my
promise.

Late that fall I turned over a small bed close to a stone wall near the
house. It was about 30 feet long and 3 feet wide. Until then I'd never
seen so many rocks outside a gravel pit. It was a very large garden for a
beginner, particularly for a fellow with a completely inadequate water
supply. My garden book told me to make a pH test, without being
specific about how to do it, in order to determine how much lime the
soil needed. It didn't take long to dig the details of pH out of an encyclopedia, so I discussed the problem with our Litchfield druggist,
who offered to make the test. He did this with litmus paper and distilled
water, and charged $1.50 for it. (I later bought a small roll of graded lit-
mus for 25 cents, got a pint of distilled water from the local filling station and did it myself.) The druggist's test showed the soil to be slightly
acid, which the garden book said it should be. However, I had already
bought a bag of hydrated lime, so I put on a little, anyway, and raked it
in.

''Putting on a little, anyway,'' of anything handy, particularly fertilizer, I found to be a habit that was hard to break, for like most people

starting to garden it seemed to me that if a little was good, more of the
same would be better. It isn't. That fall I planted a fine little flowering
peach tree on the lawn and added far more fertilizer than was called for.
Its buds all bloomed the next spring, but it shriveled up and died soon
after. . . .

Right after Christmas that first year it obviously became time to do
some studying about annuals, so I bought a little book devoted exclusively to them, and discovered it said no more than my slightly
larger general garden book. The fact is that in comparing them I found
that even the language seemed similar. Both told me a lot that I really
didn't want to know and neither book got down to the real nuts and
bolts—the simple ''how-to's'' that I needed. It seemed to make the
growing of annuals a complicated business. So I visited a store on
Madison Avenue that I had always marveled at. It was Max Schling,
Seedsman, owned by the Max Schling who was also the famous Fifth
Avenue florist. There I was greeted by a huge man, a Mr. Platt, who
managed the store. It was a no-nonsense garden store, large, its walls
covered with small drawers in which countless varieties of seeds were
stored in small, neatly arranged envelopes. Various garden tools, all
hand-held kinds, were displayed on tables. There were few bulbs. I told
Mr. Platt my problem and the amount of space I had. Mr. Platt said it
would be easy. Even though I might get better results by starting some
of the annual seeds indoors or in a greenhouse, he said that under the
circumstances I should plant the seeds directly in the ground—I'd get a
somewhat shorter blooming period, but excellent results nonetheless.
He told me to plant the seeds as soon as the soil dried and was easily
worked into a bed with a smooth surface. The very fine seeds should be
planted a bit later, and instead of covering them with soil they should
be pressed into it by using a piece of two-by-four about five inches long.
He drew a small plan and suggested kinds to plant in each space. The
bill came to $5.55. He escorted me to the door and said, ''Good luck.
Let me know how you come out.'' . . .

I got Mr. Platt's seeds in the ground, successfully in most instances,
and they grew well. He had warned me to plant not more than half of
the seeds in each packet, in order to have a reserve if anything happened to the first planting. After seeing how few seeds there were in each
tiny packet, I cheated a bit, as do all new gardeners, and as a result had

much thinning to do. Mr. Platt had thoughtfully written thinning distances on each packet, and had told me that if the bed was rich more thinning would be needed as the plants developed. There was no doubt about the bed being rich—I had seen to that. At first I didn't have the heart to pull out enough seedlings so that good ones would be left to develop on 4- to 6-inch centers—they all looked like good plants. It's remarkable how much top one silly little seedling can throw in a short time, particularly if the shoots are pinched out to make it thick and sturdy.

"What a pretty bed of flowers," a visitor remarked that year in late July.

"Yes, it is nice, and I planted it myself from seed," I remember saying, fatuously. . . .

After three summers with annuals I tired of them and asked Mr. Platt what else he had that might be used in a garden. He wondered if I had heard of perennials. Of course I had heard of perennials. Every Sunday the news in the papers waited until I had finished the garden sections; I subscribed to four garden magazines; I now owned six garden books—how could I have kept from hearing about perennials? But that I knew nothing about growing perennials was obvious to Mr. Platt. He tried to sell me plants. They seemed expensive. The seeds, which he picked out, were perennials of different heights and colors and bloomed at different seasons, facts that he noted on each packet. They added up to about $40, and it turned out to be a surprising amount of seed. Seeds of perennials, he said, should not be sown where they were to grow. They had to be started in flats, then transplanted to 2¼-inch thumb pots, and only when they had developed into sturdy little plants were they ready for the border. We had built a small garden house on the northwest corner of the property, and had run a pipe to it from our precious water supply to take care of spot watering, by hand from a can, of a small garden plowed up in front of it. Because a friend had given us a few plants of Cymbidium orchids, we had built a miniature lathhouse at the end of the little garden house to house them during the summer. This left barely enough room to protect about 35 small flats of seedlings, which I made by cutting down tomato crates. Looking back, I feel sure that no other gardening project I have since attempted was grander than this first go at growing perennials from seed. Also, it was at this point that my gardening books became indispensable.

As soon as the weather warmed up, in mid-May, George Luca, Grant and I spent from Friday until Monday planting the seeds in flats—some 30 different varieties of about 20 genera. We covered them with glass to keep them from drying out, shaded them from light, and protected them from wind and rain as well as we could. George was charged with inspecting them daily. I had a fair idea of when they would sprout, for I had looked up their germination periods. By the second weekend there still was no germination, for the weather had been in the 40s. Then they started to pop. I told Platt we would soon need those clay thumb pots. I ordered 1000 at 3 cents each. When they arrived no one was around to instruct the driver, so he dumped them in the driveway, about 50 yards from the garden house and up a rather steep grade. One thousand 2¼-inch clay pots turned out to be far too heavy for George and me to handle. We had a wheelbarrow, bought at a country auction and painted a fine shade of green, but it had an idiosyncracy—whenever it was loaded, even lightly, the wheel dropped off. So I broke open the crate and carried the pots to the garden house as they were needed.

"Why don't you use a coolie pole?" Grant asked. She was the smarty who had been to China.

By this time many of the seedlings had produced pairs of true leaves. When this happened, the books said, they should be "pricked" off. Seedlings at this stage are small and frail compared to fingers, and during the first two dozen attempts my fingers turned out to be all thumbs—the gossamer roots broke and the little leaves pulled off. However, the knack of handling them came quickly, and when the first flat (of delphinium) had been transplanted the 40-odd little plants looked great. I could imagine them in flower, although I must admit that at the time I had only the vaguest idea of their shapes or colors. I went ahead, doggedly, with the second variety. Now a few over 100 plants were finished, but it was apparent I would not come out even—there would not be enough pots. There also were not enough flats to grow all of them and certainly not enough garden to plant them in if they grew. So I began transplanting only 18 seedlings per variety. By the time I was finished I had had my fill of them—and so had my managing editor. I had explained to him that I needed a week off as sick leave because my presence was needed to perform the duties of a mid-wife to a lot of plants I was bearing.

Platt had said that as I didn't have a greenhouse it would be wise to transplant more seedlings than I could use. He was right. Casualties were high. Storms took some off, and once George let the watering go too long "because it was going to rain" that night. By the time they were planted in our new perennial border, there were about 180 plants, representing a few of all the varieties that had germinated. We planted all of them. Then the things just sat, growing tops, but never showing a flower. I complained to Platt. He said, "Oh, none of them will bloom until next year." It was a point the books had neglected to mention. Grant said she would rather have had annuals—at least they bloomed and were not so much work. The next spring this simple perennial garden of ours threw bloom the likes of which have never been seen, and when 19 surviving delphinium plants reached to a regal 6 or 7 feet in July—well, I was hooked, as the saying goes, as a gardener. The winds were kind and did not blow and I did not have to stake the stately things.

One evening as the shadows lengthened in the dusk, Grant came over to where I stood looking at the lovely sight. "I thought I'd come out with you and watch them grow," she said.

When World War II came along we switched to vegetables. The small plot of ground at the garden house was enlarged. It didn't seem large then, but a piece of land 45 feet by 100 feet is a sizable piece, and produces a surprising amount of food—even when a third of its rows are planted with annual and perennial plants. Grant and I took care of it with minimum help from George, who by then spent most of his time caring for our now sizable lawn. At this time we were in Litchfield only on weekends and holidays. . . .

The nice lady who had sold us the barn died the following year, and in her will let us have first refusal on the 18 acres that surrounded our small property. We bought it for protection. Shortly after, Dr. Turkington trudged up the hill from the Turnpike, and instead of turning into his place, he entered ours. He looked distressed. "Turk," the nickname we did not use to his face, had not much liked the idea of our moving in close to him, but when he discovered that we ran a neat place he became friendly. He told us he had just had his two horses shot and buried on the hill across the Turnpike, that he was not well enough to ride anymore, and that he was going to sell his farm. He offered us first refusal. He is not the kind of man one attempts to trade with. We shook hands on the deal on the spot.

"Gees!" Grant said that night as we had cocktails, "there's nothing like owning a house and one acre and protecting it with 90 acres, two houses, a 3-car garage, a hay barn, a horse barn, and a dog kennel. What are we going to do with them?"

We had better than a year to think about it, because Dr. Turkington did not want to give immediate possession. Our Litchfield friends, many with larger farms than ours, were becoming gentlemen farmers. Some established fancy herds of purebred dairy cattle, others started to raise purebred sheep. I wanted no part of 4-legged animals—I'd had enough of them in Colorado. Also, a gentleman farmer quickly turns into a roustabout when his herdsman quits or becomes ill. One evening, obviously after one more drink than necessary, we said, "Let's start a nursery." . . .

*

From *The White-Flower-Farm Garden Book*, Amos Pettingill (1900-1981). New York: Alfred Knopf, 1971. Amos Pettingill was the pen name of William Harris who, with his wife, founded the famous nursery in Litchfield, Connecticut in 1947. Katharine S. White, in her *Onward and Upward in the Garden*, was the first to suspect "Pettingill" was a pseudonym, referring to its creator as "the sage of White Flower Farm." Indeed, the company's catalogues are characterized by a crusty, know-it-all flavor and hard-won industry, its founder still very much a part of the nursery in spirit, if not letter.

Pleasures of the Nose

Louise Beebe Wilder

A GARDEN FULL OF SWEET ODORS IS A GARDEN full of charm, a most precious kind of charm not to be implanted by mere skill in horticulture or power of purse, and which is beyond explaining. It is born of sensitive and very personal preferences yet its appeal is almost universal. Fragrance speaks to many to whom color and form say little, and it ''can bring as irresistibly as music emotions of all sorts to the mind.'' Besides the plants visible to the eye there will be in such a garden other comely growths, plain to that ''other sense,'' such as ''faith, romance, the lore of old unhurried times.'' These are infinitely well worth cultivating among the rest. They are an added joy in happy times and gently remedial when life seems warped and tired.

Nor is the fragrant garden ever wholly our own. It is, whether we will or no, common property. Over hedge or wall, and often far down the highway, it sends a greeting, not alone to us who have toiled for it, but to the passing stranger, the blind beggar, the child skipping to school, the tired woman on her way to work, the rich man, the careless youth. And who shall say that the gentle sweet airs for a moment enveloping them do not send each on his way touched in some manner, cheered, softened, filled with hope or renewed in vigor, arrested, perhaps, in some devious course?

In medieval times there was a widespread belief in the efficacy of flower and leaf scents as cures or alleviations for all sorts of ills of the flesh, but more especially of the spirit, and as a protection against infection. This belief is testified to again and again in early horticultural and medical works. ''If odours may worke satisfaction,'' wrote Gerard, ''they are so sovereign in plants and so comfortable that no confection of apothecaries can equall their excellent virtue.'' In the *Grete Herball* it is written, ''Against weyknesse of the brayne smel to Musk.'' The scent of basil was thought stimulating to the heart and ''it taketh away melancholy and maketh a man merry and glad.'' The fragrance of sweet marjoram was deemed remedial for those ''given to over much sighing.'' The smell of violets was thought an aid to digestion, and of rosemary it was written, ''Smell of it and it shall keep thee youngly.'' ''As for the garden of mint,'' wrote Pliny, ''the very smell of it alone recovers and refreshes our spirits, as the taste stirs up our appetite for meat.'' To smell of wild thyme was believed to raise the spirits (and does it not?) and the vital energies, while the odor of garlic preserved those who partook of it or carried it about with them from infection.

Nor need we peer back into the dim past for corroboration. We all know persons who are affected for better or for worse by certain odors. A woman once told me that the smell of white lilac revived her no matter how low she might feel in mind or body. My father was made actively ill by the scent of blossoming ailanthus trees and he carried on a small but animated feud with a neighbor who had two in her garden and refused to part with them—quite unreasonably, thought my father. To me the smell of clove pinks is instantly invigorating, while that of roses (the true old rose scent such as is possessed by the lovely dark red rose Etoile de Hollande) is invariably charming. Over and over again I have experienced the quieting influence of rose scent upon a disturbed state of mind, feeling the troubled condition smoothing out before I realized that roses were in the room, or near at hand. The soothing effects of lavender preparations are well known, and certain flower odors have an opposite effect, causing headache or nausea, even to the point of catastrophe, especially in a close room.

Miss Rohde (*Old English Gardening Books*) quotes from the writings of a Dutchman who traveled in England in 1560. He wrote of the English people that ''their chambers and parlours strawed over with sweet herbes refreshed mee; their nosegays finely intermingled with sundry sorts of fragraunte floures, in their bed-chambers and privy rooms, with comfortable smell cheered me up, and entirely delyghted all my senses.'' Perhaps we do not realize that so fragile and subtle an influence as a pleasant fragrance in our living rooms and gardens has the power to cheer us up and delight all our senses. But it is true. ''For smell often operates powerfully not only in surreptitiously enriching and invigorating the mental impression of an event but also in directing the flow of ideas into some particular channel independent of the will.'' (''Aromatics and the Soul,'' McKenzie)

But the subject is full of indistinctness, for a perfume that is a delight to one individual may be a horror to another. Memory, imagination, sentiment, a weak or strong stomach, are inextricably involved in our reactions. But do not many of us know from experience that a chance whiff from a hayfield, a pine grove, the wayside bramble, the sea, often changes the mood of a whole day? A very old man once told me that whenever he smelled freshly sawed wood he felt instantly young and vigorous for a time. His youth had been passed in a New England village where there was a large saw mill and the acrid odor of fresh-cut wood was so strongly associated in his mind with youth and its abounding energy that it affected him physically.

Of course some persons are far more sensitive to such influences than others. Some there are, sadly enough, who are partially, or totally, anosmic, or nose blind, and to these a whole world of sensation and experience is closed. But there is undoubtedly a close and intimate connection between the sense of smell and the nerve centers and it is probably not fully understood how far reaching and profound is the influence of odor upon our mental state and physical makeup. Montaigne wrote:

> Physicians might in mine opinion draw more use and good from odors than they doe. For myself have often perceived that according unto their strength and qualitie, they change and alter and move my spirits and worke strange effects in me which make approve the common saying that the invention of insense and perfumes in churches, so ancient and so far dispersed throughout all nations and religions, had a special regard to rejoyce, to comfort, to quicken, to rouse, and to purify the senses, so that we might be the apter and readier unto contemplation.

In early times living rooms, banqueting halls, churches and police courts were strewn with sweet scented herbs and flowers to disguise the odors arising from filthy and unsanitary conditions, and dandies and great ladies hung about their necks gold and silver filigree baubles filled with fragrant gums to preserve their delicate nostrils from the vile effluvia arising from the piles of garbage and filth rotting in the streets. Today we are proud of our sanitary conditions but are not our noses assaulted by almost as vile effluvia, the reek of gasoline and oil that pollutes the air of our cities and even rises triumphant above the delicate scents of the countryside? Perhaps it may again become fashionable to carry about with us little perforated balls of gold or silver filled with precious sweet smelling gums and resins to offset the unpleasant olfactory contacts that assail us. . . .

The gardens of my youth were fragrant gardens and it is their sweetness rather than their patterns or their furnishings that I now most clearly recall. My mother's rose garden in Maryland was famous in that countryside and in the nearby city, for many shared its bounty. In it grew the most fragrant roses, not only great bushes of Provence, damask and Gallica roses, but a collection of the finest teas and Noisettes of the day. Maréchal Niel, Lamarque and Gloire de Dijon climbed high on trellises against the stone of the old house and looked in at the second-story windows. I remember that some sort of much coveted distinction was conferred upon the child finding the first long golden bud of Maréchal Niel. Once a week, on Friday, a great hamper of freshly cut roses was loaded into the back of the ''yellow wagon'' —its physical aspect in no way bore out its sprightly name—and with ''old Tom'' in the driver's seat we fared into the city and distributed to the sick, the sad and the disgruntled, great bunches of dewy fragrant roses. . . .

Why do garden makers of today so seldom deliberately plan for fragrance? Undoubtedly gardens of early times were sweeter than ours. The green enclosures of Elizabethan days evidently overflowed with fragrant flowers and the little beds in which they were confined were neatly edged with some sweet-leaved plant—thyme, germander, lavender, rosemary, cut to a formal line. The yellowed pages of ancient works on gardening seem to give off the scents of the beloved old favorites—gilliflower, stock, sweet rocket, wallflower, white violet. Fragrance, by the wise old gardeners of those days, was valued as much as if not more than other attributes. Bacon said immortal things about sweet scented flowers in his essay, ''Of Gardens,'' as well as in his less known curious old ''Naturall Historie.'' Theophrastus devoted a portion of his *Inquiry Into Plants* to odors, chiefly floral and leaf odors. Our books of today make sadly little of the subject.

Our great grandmothers prized more highly than any others what they called their posy flowers, moss rose, southernwood, bergamot, marigold, and the like. Indeed it would seem that save in that strangely tasteless period of the nineteenth century, when all grace departed from gardens and hard hued flowers were laid down upon the patient earth in lines and circles of crude color like Berlin wool-work, geranium, calceolaria, lobelia, and again geranium, calceolaria, lobelia, no period has been so unmindful of fragrance in the garden as this in which we are now living. We have juggled the sweet pea into the last word in hues and furbelows, and all but lost its sweetness; we have been careless of the rose's scent, and have made of the wistful Mignonette a stolid and inodorous wedge of vulgarity. We plan meticulously for color harmony and a sequence of bloom, but who goes deliberately about planning for a succession of sweet scents during every week of the growing year?

*

From *The Fragrant Path*, Louise Beebe Wilder (1878-1938). New York: The Macmillan Company, 1932. Among the author's many books are *Colour in My Garden*, *Problems and Pleasures of a Rock Garden*, and *Adventures in a Suburban Garden*. *The Fragrant Path* is a celebration of the many sweet smells of the garden, and an early warning about increased lost pleasures through ''modernization'' in horticulture. Wilder is another of the early writers who brought a well-rehearsed and amicable knowledge to her work, leaving behind a thoughtful account of flower fashions in different ages. A leading exponent of rock gardens before they became popular, in her own Bronxville garden she grew thousands of plants believed to be unsuited to the East Coast climate.

LETTER TO ARTHUR YOUNG

GEORGE WASHINGTON

Mount Vernon, Dec. 4, 1788.

 SIR,

I have been favoured with the receipt of your letter dated the first day of July; and have to express my thanks for the three additional volumes of the Annals, which have also come safely to hand.

The more I am acquainted with agricultural affairs, the better I am pleased with them; insomuch, that I can no where find so great satisfaction as in those innocent and useful pursuits. In indulging these feelings, I am led to reflect how much more delightful to an undebauched mind, is the task of making improvements on the earth, than all the vain glory which can be acquired from ravaging it, by the most uninterrupted career of conquests. The design of this observation, is only to shew how much, as a member of human society, I feel myself obliged, by your labours to render respectable and advantageous, an employment which is more congenial to the natural dispositions of mankind than any other.

I am also much indebted to you, for the inquiries you were so kind as to make respecting the threshing machines. Notwithstanding I am pretty well convinced from your account, that the new-invented Scotch machine is of superior merit to Winlaw's; yet I think to wait a little longer before I procure one. In the intermediate time, I am not insensible to your obliging offers of executing this, or any other commission for me; and shall take the liberty to avail myself of them as occasions may require. . . .

I would willingly have sent you a lock of the wool of my sheep, agreeably to your desire, but it is all wrought into cloth, and I must therefore defer it until after the next shearing. You may expect it by some future conveyance. A manufacturer from Leeds, who was lately here, judges it to be of about the same quality with the English wool in general—though there is always a great difference in the fineness of different parts of the same fleece. I cannot help thinking that increasing and improving our breed of sheep, would be one of the most profitable speculations we could undertake; especially in this part of the Continent, where we have so little winter, that they require either no dry fodder, or next to none; and where we are sufficiently distant from the frontiers, not to be troubled with wolves or other wild vermin, which prevent the inhabitants there from keeping flocks. Though we do not feed our sheep upon leaves, as you mention they do in some parts of France, yet we cannot want for pastures enough suitable for them. I am at a loss, therefore, to account for the disproportion between their value and that of black cattle; as well as for our not augmenting the number. So persuaded am I of the practicability and advantage of it, that I have raised near 200 lambs upon my farm this year. I am glad to find that you are likely to succeed in propagating the Spanish breed of sheep in England, and that the wool does not degenerate: for the multiplication of useful animals is a common blessing to mankind. I have a prospect of introducing into this country a very excellent race of animals also, by means of the liberality of the King of Spain. One of the jacks which he was pleased to present to me (the other perished at sea) is about 15 hands high, his body and limbs very large in proportion to his height; and the mules which I have had from him, appear to be extremely well formed for service. I have likewise a jack and two jennetts from Malta, of a very good size, which the Marquis de la Fayette sent to me. The Spanish jack seems calculated to breed for heavy slow draught; and the others for the saddle, or lighter carriages. From these, altogether, I hope to secure a race of extraordinary goodness, which will stock the country. . . .

Since I wrote to you formerly, respecting the objection made by my labourers to the weight of the ploughs, I have had sufficient experience to overcome the ill-founded prejudice, and find them answer the purpose exceedingly well. I have been laying out my farm into fields of nearly the same dimensions, and assigning crops to each until the year 1795. The building of a brick barn has occupied much of my attention this summer. It is constructed according to the plan you had the goodness to send me; but with some additions. It is now, I believe, the largest and most convenient one in this country. Our seasons in this country (or at least in this part of it) have been so much in the two opposite extremes of dry and wet, for the two summers past, that many of my experiments have failed to give a satisfactory result, or I would have done myself the pleasure of transmitting it to you. In the first part of the last summer, the rains prevailed beyond what has been known in the memory of man; yet the crops in most parts of the United States are good. They were much injured, however, in those places on my farm, where the soil is mixed with clay, and so stiff as to be liable to retain the moisture. I planted a large quantity of potatoes, of which only those that were put in as late as the end of June, have produced tolerably well. I am, notwithstanding, more and more convinced of the prodigious usefulness of this root, and that it is very little, if any thing, of an exhauster. I have a high opinion also of carrots. The same unfavorableness of the season, has rendered it unimportant to give a detail of my experiments this year in flax, though I had sowed 25 bushels of the seed. In some spots it has yielded well; in others very indifferently, much injured by weeds and lodgits.

As to what you suggest at the close of your letter, respecting the publication of extracts from my correspondence, in your Annals, I hardly know what to say. I certainly highly approve the judicious execution of your well-conceived project of throwing light on a subject, which may be more conducive than almost any other to the happiness of mankind. On the one hand, it seems scarcely generous or proper, that any farmer, who receives benefit from the facts contained in such publications, should withhold his mite of information from the general stock. On the other hand, I am afraid it might be imputed to me as a piece of ostentation, if my name should appear in the work. And surely it would not be discreet for me to run the hazard of incurring this imputation, unless some good might probably result to society, as some kind of compensation for it. Of this I am not a judge—I can only say for myself, that I have endeavored, in a state of tranquil retirement, to keep myself as much from the eye of the world as I possibly could. I have studiously avoided, as much as was in my power, to give any cause for ill-natured or impertinent comments on my conduct: and I should be very unhappy to have any thing done on my behalf (however distant in itself from impropriety), which should give occasion for one officious tongue to use my name with indelicacy. For I wish most devoutly to glide silently and unnoticed through the remainder of my life. This is my heart-felt wish; and these are my undisguised feelings. After having submitted them confidentially to you, I have such a reliance upon your prudence, as to leave it you to do what you think, upon a full consideration of the matter, shall be wisest and best. I am, with very great regard and esteem, Sir,

Your most obedient and obliged humble servant,

G. Washington.

Arthur Young, Esq.

*

From *Letters from His Excellency General Washington to Arthur Young*, George Washington (1732-1799). London: B. McMillan, 1801. Washington settled with his wife at Mt. Vernon in 1759, residing there forty-five years until his death on the eve of the next century. After resigning his commission as commander of the continental forces, he returned to his beloved estate in 1783, only to be called into service as his nation's first president in 1789. Washington was among the most progressive farmers of his day. Close to 3000 of his nearly 8000-acre English-style estate, which was divided into 5 farms, was under cultivation. He experimented with new farming methods, crop rotation, intensive plowing, and fertilizers. His diaries and letters are filled with notations concerning the productivity of crops, soil conditions, animal husbandry, landscape design, and architectural plans.

Washington carried on a lengthy correspondence with Arthur Young, then one of Britain's most distinguished writers on agriculture. He also helped the Marquis de Lafayette and Crèvecoeur transport seeds and trees to the Jardin du Roi in Paris. Those interested in advanced techniques in land management willingly traded information, experiments, and plants. Seeds and seedlings were among the earliest American materials for foreign trade.

In this period of history, before culture was separated from agriculture, and the life of a man from the life of his country, responsible citizens were breaking new ground for democracy and for science.

Gardening With Herbs

Helen Morgenthau Fox

As I WEED AND CULTIVATE THE BASILS, SAVOR-
ies, and thymes in my garden, touch their furry or glossy leaves, and
breathe in their spicy scent, they seem like such old friends it is difficult
to realize that only three years ago these aromatic herbs, except for the
parsley, sage, and mint, were quite unknown to me.

Before writing a book about the herbs I decided to grow every plant
to be described so that I could watch the seed unfurl into a leafy plant,
the buds thicken and swell into flowers, and these drop their petals and
in turn ripen their seeds. Since exceptionally wet, cold, dry, or hot
spells affect the development of the plants, I grew them for three summers before I was sure I really knew them well enough to describe
them.

During the first year, five of my friends sent me copies of Mrs.
Bardswell's book, *The Herb Garden*; some, no doubt, in the hope that
if I saw how excellent a book already existed on the subject I would
desist from further efforts and behave as a normal, social being once
more, instead of spending my days in the herb garden and my evenings
in talking about it. Mrs. Bardswell, however, lives and grows her plants
in England, the paradise of gardeners, and since the only literature on
growing herbs in America consisted of a slender volume and some

government pamphlets, I persisted in the attempt to write a book about
how this group of aromatics smelt, tasted, and behaved in our quite different climate.

The first spade into the soil of herb lore was to consult two favorite
catalogues, an English one which offered twenty-two herbs and a
French one which under the heading of *Graines des Plantes Officinales*
listed ninety-one herbs, many of them medicinal plants. I ordered all
the herbs in both these catalogues, although there were some
duplicates, for I thought these would cover the mortalities, inevitable in
all horticultural undertakings. After I had learned where to look for
them I found that seeds of thirty different herbs are obtainable from
commercial sources in America, and that plants of rosemary, lavender,
wormwood, and sage as well as a few of the mints and thymes can be
bought here. At present the seeds of all unusual varieties of basil,
savory, or lavender have to be secured from Europe.

When the seeds arrived during the month of May, they were planted
in a well-drained, sunny space which had been prepared for them. It
was a warm season with almost no rain, and as many of the herbs are
native to southern lands the little plants felt at home and grew lustily.

The first task was to find out which herbs to include and which to
leave out of the book, and when the first crop matured I saw that a few
of them like chicory, celandine poppy, and viper's bugloss were weeds,
and others like melilot and tussilago were forage plants. After working
over the problem for a long time I decided, with some exceptions, to
choose the herbs some portion of which could be used as a condiment
in cooking, or in the preparation of homemade sachets and perfumes,
and which were easy for the amateur to grow in his garden.

To find out about the cultural requirements of the herbs, their
background of history and legend, and which portion of each was the
part used, when it was the seed, the leaves, stems, roots, or flowers
which were to be dropped into the soup or minced into the chicken
dressing, I first searched through all the old and modern books in my
own library on the subject. Books were sent for from England, France,
and Germany, and the collection of cook books in the Vassar College
Library, and other sources, in the libraries of the Massachusetts Horticultural Society and the New York Public Library were consulted. In
fact, for one year when not out in the garden I spent every spare hour
in taking notes. The study finally culminated in two weeks at

Washington in the Congressional Library and the Library of the Department of Agriculture.

Any available printed word which described the herbs was searched through, including the cook books which down through the ages have mentioned the herbs used in flavoring foods and brewing drinks. The diaries of travelers, such as Kalm and Bartram, the journals of the Folk Lore Society, articles on ethnobotany, government pamphlets, and as with all research on gardening subjects, the horticultural journals in English, French, and German and even some pamphlets in Spanish and Italian were read, although in these last only the high spots were understood.

The books found most useful and which have spent the last two years on my study table were Piesse, *The Art of Perfumery*; Poucher, *Perfumes, Cosmetics and Soaps*; F. A. Hampton, *The Scent of Flowers and Leaves*; *The Toilet of Flora*; Pliny's *Natural History*; Eleanor Rohde, *A Garden of Herbs*; Sturtevant's *Notes on Edible Plants*; Fernie's *Herbal Simples*; Robinson's translation of Vilmorin's *The Vegetable Garden*; John Parkinson's *Herbal* and *Paradisi in Sole*; Gerard's *Herball*; and Culpeper's *De Candolle, Origin of Cultivated Plants*; Correvon, *Le Jardin de l'Herboriste*; Merck's *Index*; Rehder's *Manual of Cultivated Trees and Shrubs*, and Bailey's *Manual of Cultivated Plants*.

Making out a list was simple enough, but locating the seeds and plants was quite another matter. Although most of them had been grown for thousands of years and had been described from Theophrastus' time in the fourth century B.C. down to Mrs. Grieve's in the twentieth, they were not listed in any seed catalogue and their whereabouts were unknown to horticulturists. In answer to my queries I was told repeatedly, ''Seeds of this plant can be secured only from some country woman in a remote village,'' and for a time it seemed as if to obtain them I should have to embark upon an expedition of exploration through the cottage gardens of Europe.

One afternoon I told my troubles to the members of the Poughkeepsie Garden Club who had come to see my lilies, and to my great joy one of the members said her grandmother had grown costmary and that they still had plants of it, while another had ambrosia. With the generosity typical of all true gardeners they sent me a few of each. Friends sent me slips of fragrant geraniums, and the gardener of a famous herb garden in Connecticut drove seventy miles to bring me an unusual santolina I had seen and admired when visiting him.

There were, however, still others to be garnered into the confines of my garden and having been unsuccessful in my appeals to the commercial people, except for Sutton's who have always been most helpful and this time got me a huge packet of *Nigella sativa* seeds. I turned to the authorities in cap and gown. Professor Hamblin sent me a few of the rare herbs and told me of the custom obtaining among botanical gardens of the world of exchanging seed lists with one another in January of each year. Mr. Benjamin Yoe Morrison of the Department of Agriculture was helpful in every way. Not only has he gone over my proofs, but he assisted me in securing "a preferred amateur's permit" to enable me to import all the plants not to be grown from seeds. He sent me the precious lists from the botanic gardens and told me to mark the "herbs" I wanted with my initials, and as I wrote "H.M.F." in the margins opposite the thymes, or sages so rare that they had not even been described in any of the books I had come across, I felt as if I had been permitted to enter the innermost sanctum of the botanical élite under government auspices. Copies of my tentative list of herbs were sent to Dr. E. D. Merrill of the New York Botanic Gardens, and Dr. C. Stuart Gager of the Brooklyn Botanic Gardens who helped me secure many treasures. Regius Director Smith of the Royal Botanic Gardens in Edinburgh, besides giving me addresses of people to write to, sent me plants of mints, nepetas, and satureias. Other plants were obtained from English nurseries and some from faraway India. I collected many varieties of mints, thymes, tansies, and sages other than the ones used for flavor and fragrance, for I felt I could understand the individual better by knowing the whole family. I corresponded with horticulturists and botanists in China, India, and Europe as well as distant portions of America, all of whom were amazingly kind in answering letters and giving advice and information.

Either the seeds or plants of every herb on my list, and many more besides, were finally gathered together. In February, as the second spring was coming, seed packets arrived from Algiers, Portugal, Spain, India, France, England, and Scotland. By the end of March seedlings filled my little greenhouse to capacity.

The detective work, furthered by kind friends, had been perfect, but as the season advanced our brilliant beginning was somewhat dimmed by several horticultural disappointments and our pride, as usual, took a tumble. The sweet cicely sickened and died and our only angelica plant to grow up turned yellow and did not have the vigor to flower as it should have in its second season in the garden; a friend, however, sent me a flat full of little plants. Because of its place in the religious practices of the Hindus, I had particularly wanted to grow the holy basil, *Ocimum sanctum*, and compare it with the other basils used for flavoring. After much difficulty I had finally obtained three packets, but no matter how we treated the seeds, although we put some of them in the sun, others in the shade, and kept some of them indoors and a few outside, they would germinate and raise our hopes and then disappoint us by suddenly expiring. One packetful finally grew and flowered and smelt quite vilely and we thought, ''this is it and perhaps the Hindus who like it and we differ about pleasantness in smells,'' but Dr. Merrill said these plants were a variety of *Ocimum basilicum* and not *Ocimum sanctum*.

In spite of the mishaps we managed to raise some three hundred different varieties of herbs. Planted at the top of the sloping cut-flower garden in three long terrace-like rows with little paths running between them and with a pink and white hedge of flowering cosmos behind them, they made an imposing array.

Every day with paper, pencil, and measuring tape I would sit on the ground beside the herbs, and measure, describe, taste, and smell them.

*

From *Gardening with Herbs for Flavor and Fragrance*, Helen Morgenthau Fox (1884-1974). New York: The Macmillan Company, 1933. This highly-respected author worked in the garden half a century, writing her last of seven books approaching eighty. A gardener of great style and graciousness, she viewed plants from the dual perspectives of humanist and scientist. After first raising a family, she went to Columbia University to study botany, then worked under A. B. Stout at The New York Botanical Garden. In addition to works which include *Garden Cinderellas, Gardening for Good Eating, Adventure in My Garden,* and a biography of André Le Nôtre, Fox also translated important writings from the French, such as *Abbé David's Diary*. This sophisticated lady once wrote, ''Herb gardening has been compared to chamber music. Both are appreciated in small places. . . .''

Zuñi Fields

Frank Hamilton Cushing

No BRANCH OF THE INDUSTRIAL ARTS OF THE
Zuñi Indians is shown so clearly as in their farming customs and
methods, first the influences of climatic environment on a people's
religion and culture, then the effects of this belief and philosophy on
their daily life. . . .

When a young Zuñi wishes to add to his landed possessions, he goes
out over the country, to all appearance caring nothing at all for
distance. He selects the mouth of some *arroyo* (deep dry gully or
stream-course) which winds up from the plain into the hills or mountains, and seeking, where it merges into the plain, some flat stretch of
ground, his first care is to "lift the sand." This is done by striking the
hoe into the earth at intervals of five or six yards, and hauling out the
little heaps of soil until a line of tiny boundary mounds has been formed
all around the proposed field. Next in this space he cuts away the
sagebrushes with his heavy hoe, and clods of grass, weeds, etc., all of
which he heaps in the middle of the field and burns. He then throws up
long banks of sand on the line first indicated by the heaps of soil. Each
embankment is called a *so'-pit-thlan* ("sand-string"). At every corner
he sets a rock, if possible columnar, sometimes rudely sculptured with
his tokens. It is rare he does anything more to the piece in a single year.

Not infrequently even years before the land is actually required for cultivation, the "sand is lifted" and a stone of peculiar shape is placed at one corner as a mark of ownership. Ever after, the place is, unless relinquished, the exclusive property of the one who lifted the sand, or, in case of his death, of the clan he belonged to.

In riding over the ancient country of the Zuñis, I have sometimes found these rows of little soil heaps as many as forty miles away from the central valley. Even after the lapse of years, overgrown with grasses, each the bases of a diminutive sand-drift, these marks of savage preëmption are distinct. Thus too, for ages they will remain to serve the archeologist, when the Zuñi and his theme shall have passed away, as material for speculation. Distance could not have been the sole cause for the abandonment of these pieces, as some fields, still under the hoe, are equally as far away; yet give evidence of having been cultivated, probably in consequence of great fertility, for several generations.

With the Zuñis one half the months in the year are "nameless," the others are "named." The year is called "a passage of time," the seasons "the steps" (of the year), and the months "crescents"— probably because each begins with a new moon. New Year is called the "Mid-journey of the sun"; that is, the middle of the solar trip between one summer solstice and another, and, occurring invariably about the nineteenth of December, usually initiates a short season of great religious activity. The first month after this is now called *I'-koh-pu-yä-tchun*, "Growing white crescent," as with it begins the Southwestern winter—the origin of the name is evident. The ancient name of the month seems to have been different in meaning, although strikingly similar in sound, *I-shoh-k'o' a-pu-yä-tchun* or "Crescent of the conception," doubtless a reference to the kindling of the sacred fire by drilling with an arrowshaft into a piece of soft, dry wood-root, a ceremony still strictly observed. Interesting evidence of this meaning may be found on the old notched calendar-sticks of the tribe, the first month of the new year being indicated by a little fire-socket at one end.

The second month is *Ta'-yäm-tchu-yä-tchun*, so named from the fact that it is the time when boughs are broken by the weight of descending snow.

Then follows *O-nan-ul'-ak-k'ia-kwum-yä-tchun*, or the month during which "Snow lies not in the pathways," with which ends winter, or the "Sway of cold."

Spring, called the "Starting time," opens with *Thli'-te-kwa-na-k'ia-tsa-na-yä-tchun*, or the month of the "Lesser sand-storms," followed by *Thli'-te-kwa-na-k'ia-thla'-na-yä-tchun*, or the month of the "Greater sand-storms," and this, the ugliest season of the Zuñi year, is closed by *Yä-tchun-kwa-shi'-am-o-na*, the "Crescent of no name." Summer and autumn, the period of the "months nameless," are together called *O'-lo-i-k'ia*, the season "Bringing flour-like clouds." In priestly or ritualistic language these six months, although called nameless, are designated successively the "yellow, blue, red, white, variegated or iridescent, and black," after the colors of the plumed prayer-sticks sacrificed in rotation at the full of each moon to the gods of the north, west, south, east, the skies, and the lower regions respectively.

In common parlance, these months and the minute divisions of the seasons they embrace, are referred to by the terms descriptive of the growth of corn-plants and the development and naturescence of their grain. The Zuñis make corn the standard of measurement and comparison not only for time, but for many other things, by the reproduction of a singular song of one of the sacred orders.

Early in the month of the "Lesser sand-storms" the same Zuñi, we will say, who preëmpted, a year since, a distant *arroyo*-field, goes forth, hoe and axe in hand, to resume the work of clearing, etc. Within the sand embankment he now selects that portion which the *arroyo* enters from above, and cutting many forked cedar branches, drives them firmly into the dry stream-bed, in a line crossing its course, and extending a considerable distance beyond either bank. Against this row of stakes he places boughs, clods, rocks, sticks, and earth, so as to form a strong barrier or dry-dam; open, however, at either end. Some rods below this on either side of the stream-course, he constructs, less carefully, other and longer barriers. Still farther down, he seeks in the "tracks" of some former torrent, a ball of clay, which, having been detached from its native bank, far above, has been rolled and washed, down and down, ever growing rounder and smaller and tougher, until in these lower plains it lies embedded in and baked by the burning sands. This he carefully takes up, breathing reverently from it, and places it on one side of the stream-bed, where it is desirable to have the rain-freshets overflow. He buries it, with a brief supplication, in the soil, and then proceeds to heap over it a solid bank of earth which he extends obliquely across, and to some distance beyond the *arroyo*. Returning, he continues the embankment past the clay ball either in line of, or at whatever angle with the completed portion seems to his practiced eye most suited to the topography. . . .

My hope has been in so minutely describing these beginnings of a Zuñi farm to give a most precious hint to anyone interested in agriculture, or who may possess a field some portions of which are barren because too dry. We may smile at the superstitious observances of the Indian agriculturist, but when we come to learn what he accomplishes, we shall admire and I hope find occasion to imitate his hereditary ingenuity. The country of the Zuñis is so desert and dry, that times out of number within even the fickle memory of tradition, the possession of water for drinking and cooking purposes alone has been counted a blessing. Yet, by his system of earth banking, the Zuñi Indian, and a few of his western brothers and pupils, the Moquis, have heretofore been the only human beings who could, without irrigation from living streams, raise to maturity a crop of corn within its parched limits.

The use of the principal barriers and embankments may be inferred from the terms of the invocation with which the field is consecrated after the completion of all the earthworks. The owner then applies to whatever corn-priest is keeper of the sacred ''medicine'' of his clan or order. The priest cuts and decorates a little stick of red willow with plumes from the legs and hips of the eagle, turkey, and duck, and with the tail-feathers from the Maximilian's jay, night-hawk, yellow-finch, and ground-sparrow, fastening them on, one over the other, with cords of fine cotton. From the store of paint which native tradition claims was brought from the original birthplace of the nation (a kind of plumbago), he takes a tiny particle, leavening with it a quantity of black mineral powder. To a sufficient measure of rainwater he adds a drop of ocean water with which he moistens the pigment, and with a brush made by chewing the end of a yucca-leaf, applies the paint to the stick. With the same paint he also decorates a section of cane filled with wild tobacco supposed to have been planted by rain, hence sacred. These two objects, sanctified by his breath, he gives to the applicant. Taking them carefully in his left hand, the latter goes forth to his new field. Seeking a point in the middle of the *arroyo* below all his earth-works, he kneels, or sits down on his blanket, facing east. He then lights his cane

cigarette and blows smoke toward the north, west, south, east, the
upper and lower regions. Then holding the smoking stump and the
plumed stick near his breast, he says a prayer. From the substance of
his prayer which, remarkably curious though it may be, is too long for
literal reproduction here, we learn the important facts relative to his in-
tentions and his faith. We find he believes that: He has infused the consciousness of prayer into the plumed stick; that with his sacred
cigarette he has prepared a way 'like the trails of the winds and rains'
[clouds] for the wafting of that prayer to the gods of all regions. That,
having taken the cloud-inspiring down of the turkey, the strength-
giving plume of the eagle, the water-loving feather of the duck, the
path-finding tails of the birds who counsel and guide summer; having
moreover severed and brought hither the flesh of the water-attracting
tree, which he has dipped in the god-denizened ocean, beautified with
the very cinders of creation, bound with strands from the dress of the
sky-born goddess of cotton—he beseeches the god-priests of earth, sky,
and cavern, the beloved gods whose dwelling places are in the great em-
bracing waters of the world, not to withhold their mist-laden breaths,
but to canopy the earth with cloud banners, and let fly their shafts little
and mighty of rain, to send forth the fiery spirits of lightning, lift up the
voice of thunder whose echoes shall step from mountain to mountain,
bidding the mesas shake down streamlets. The streamlets shall yield
torrents; the torrents, foam-capped, soil-laden, shall boil toward the
shrine he is making, drop hither and thither the soil they are bearing,
leap over his barricades unburdened and stronger, and in place of their
lading, bear out toward the ocean as payment and faith-gift the smoke-
cane and the prayer-plume. Thus thinking, thus believing, thus yearn-
ing, thus beseeching (in order that the seeds of the earth shall not want
food for their growing, that from their growth he may not lack food for
his living, means for his fortune), he this day plants, standing in the
trail of the waters, the smoke-cane and the prayer-plume.

The effect of the network of barriers is what the Indian prayed for (attributes, furthermore, as much to his prayer as to his labors), namely,
that with every shower, although the stream go dry three hours afterward, water has been carried to every portion of the field, has deposited
a fine loam over it, and moistened from one end to the other, the
substratum. Not only this, but also, all rainfall on the actual space is retained and absorbed within the system of minor embankments.

At the stage of operations above last described, the field is again left for a year, that it may become thoroughly enriched. Meanwhile, during the same month (the first of spring) each planter repairs the banks in his old fields, and proceeds to adopt quite a different method for renewing or enriching the soil.

Along the western sides of his field, as well as of such spots throughout it as are worn out or barren, he thickly plants rows of sagebrush, leaving them standing from six inches to a foot above the surface. As the prevailing winds of the Zuñi plains hail from the southwest, and, as during the succeeding month (the ''Crescent of the greater sand-storms''), these winds are laden many tens of feet high in the air with fine dust and sand, behind each row of the sagebrush a long, level, deep deposit of soil is drifted. With the coming of the first (and as a rule the only) rainstorm of spring-time, the water, carried about by the embankments and retained lower down by the ''earth bins,'' redistributes this ''soil sown by the winds'' and fixes it with moisture to the soil it has usurped.

Thus, with the aid of nature's hand, without plow or harrow, the Zuñi fits and fertilizes his lands, for the planting of Maytime, or the Nameless month.

*

From *Zuñi Breadstuff*, Frank Hamilton Cushing (1857-1900). New York: Indian Notes and Monographs, Vol. VIII, Museum of the American Indian/Heye Foundation, 1920; originally published in 1884 in *The Millstone*, an Indianapolis monthly devoted to milling and mechanical interests. In 1879 Cushing arrived among the Zuñi of western New Mexico as part of a Smithsonian expedition, the first field research project for the recently created Bureau of Ethnology, under John Wesley Powell. Cushing didn't simply observe the Zuñi from a scientific distance, but participated in their culture, formally becoming a member of the tribe. He learned their language and skills, and wore their clothes. He was called by them ''medicine-flower.'' Praised for his writings on Zuñi customs, myths, social and religious structures by the likes of Edmund Wilson and Claude Lévi-Strauss, Cushing made a pioneering contribution to the field of ethnology.

POLITICAL ECONOMY OF THE APPLE

HENRY WARD BEECHER

THE APPLE IS, BEYOND ALL QUESTION, *THE* American fruit. It stands absolutely alone and unapproachable, grapes notwithstanding. Originating in another hemisphere, neither in its own country, nor in any other to which it has been introduced, has it flourished as in America. It is conceded in Europe that, for size, soundness, flavor, and brilliancy of coloring, the American apple stands first,—a long way first.

But it is American in another sense. This is a land in which diffusion is the great law. This arises from our institutions, and from the character which they have imprinted upon our people. In Europe, certain classes, having by their intelligence and wealth and influence the power to attract all things to themselves, set the current from the center toward the surface. In America, the simple doctrines that the common people are the true source of political power, that the government is directly responsible to them, and therefore that moral culture, intelligence, and training in politics are indispensable to the common people, on whom every state is to rest safely, have wrought out such results that in all departments of justice and truth, as much as in politics, there is a tendency toward the popularizing of everything, and learning, or art, or any department of culture, is made to feel the need of popularity; a word which is very much despised by classicists, but which may be used in a sense so large as to make it respectable again. Things that reach after the universal, that include in them all men in their better and nobler nature, are in a proper sense *popular*; and in this country, amusement and refinement and wealth itself, first or last, are obliged to do homage to the common people, and so to be *popular*. Nor is it otherwise in respect to horticulture. Of fruits, I think this, above all others, may be called the true democratic fruit. There is some democracy that I think must have sprung from the first apple. Of all fruits, no other can pretend to vie with the apple as the fruit of the common people. This arises from the nature of the tree and from the nature of the fruit.

First, as to the tree. It is so easy of propagation, that any man who is capable of learning how to raise a crop of corn can learn how to plant, graft or bud, transplant, and prune an apple tree,—and then eat the apples. It is a thoroughly healthy and hardy tree; and that under more conditions and under greater varieties of stress than perhaps any other tree. It is neither dainty nor dyspeptic. It can bear high feeding and put up with low feeding. It is not subject to gout and scrofula, as plums are; to eruptions and ruptures, as the cherry is; or to apoplexy, as the pear is. The apple tree may be pampered, and may be rendered effeminate in a degree; but this is by artificial perversion. It is naturally tough as an Indian, patient as an ox, and fruitful as the Jewish Rachel. The apple tree is among trees what the cow is among domestic animals in northern zones, or what the camel of the Bedouin is. . . .

The apple tree is homely; but it is also hardy, and not only in respect to climate. It is almost indifferent to soil and exposure. We should as soon think of coddling an oak tree or a chestnut; we should as soon think of shielding from the winter white pine or hemlock, as an apple tree. If there is a lot too steep for the plow or too rocky for tools, the farmer dedicates it to an apple orchard. Nor do the trees betray his trust. Yet, the apple loves the meadows. It will thrive in sandy loams, and adapt itself to the toughest clay. It will bear as much dryness as a mullein stalk, and as much wet, almost, as a willow. In short, it is a genuine democrat. It can be poor, while it loves to be rich; it can be plain, although it prefers to be ornate; it can be neglected, notwithstanding it welcomes attention. But, whether neglected, abused, or abandoned, it is able to take care of itself, and to be fruitful of excellences. That is what I call being democratic.

The apple tree is the common people's tree, moreover, because it is the child of every latitude and every longitude on this continent. It will grow in Canada and Maine. It does well on the Atlantic slope; and on the Pacific the apple is portentous. Newton sat in an orchard, and an apple, plumping down on his head, started a train of thought which opened the heavens to us. Had it been in California, the size of the apples there would have saved him the trouble of much thinking thereafter, perhaps, opening the heavens to him, and not to us. Wherever Indian corn will grow, the apple will thrive; and wherever timothy grass will ripen its seed, the apple will exist fruitfully. . . .

The apple comes nearer to universal uses than any other fruit of the world. Is there another that has such a range of season? It begins in July, and a good cellar brings the apple round into July again, yet unshrunk, and in good flavor. It belts the year. What other fruit, except in the tropics, where there is no winter, and where there are successive growths, can do that?

It is a luxury, too. Kinds may be had so tender, so delicate, and, as Dr. Grant—the General Grant of the vineyards—would say, *so refreshing*, that not the pear, even, would dare to vie with it, or hope to surpass it. The Vanderveer of the Hudson River, the American Golden Russett, need not, in good seasons, well ripened, fear a regiment of pears in pomological convention, even in the city of Boston. It may not rival the melting qualities of the peach, eating which one knows not whether he is eating or drinking. But the peach is the fruit of a day,—ephemeral; and it is doubtful whether one would carry through the year any such relish as is experienced for a few weeks. It is the peculiarity of the apple that it never wearies the taste. It is to fruit what wheaten bread is to grains. It is a life-long relish. You may be satisfied with apples, but never cloyed. Do you remember your boyhood feats? I was brought up in a great old-fashioned house, with a cellar under every inch of it, through which an ox-cart might have been wheeled after all the bins were full. In this cellar, besides potatoes, beets, and turnips, were stored every year some hundred bushels of apples,—the Rhode Island Greening, the Roxbury Russet, the *Russet round the Stem*, as it was called, and the Spitzenberg; not daintily picked, but shaken down; not in aristocratic barrels set up in rows, but ox-carts full; not handled softly, but poured from baskets into great bins, as we poured potatoes into their resting-place. If they bruised and rotted, let them. We had enough and to spare. . . .

Now I enter upon the realm of uses, culinary and domestic, where, were I an ancient poet, I should stop and invoke all the gods to my aid. But the gods are all gone; and next to them is that blessing of the world, the housewife. Her I invoke, and chiefly one who taught me, by her kitchen magic, to believe that the germ of civilization is in the art and science of the kitchen. Is there, among fruits, one other that has so wide a range, or a range so important, so exquisite, so wonderful, as the range of the apple in the kitchen? . . .

It only remains that I should say a single word on the subject of the apple as an article of commerce. Whether fresh or dried, it is still, in that relation, a matter of no small importance. The home market is enlarging every year; and as soon as the apple shall become so cheap that all men may have it no matter how poor they may be, the market must of necessity have become very much augmented. Many men suppose that as orchards increase and fruit multiplies the profits diminish. Such is not the fact. As the commoner kinds multiply, and the common people learn to use them as daily food, the finer kinds will bear proportionally higher prices; and cheapness is one of the 'steps to profit in all things that are consumed in the community. And I should be glad to see the day when, for a few pence, every drayman, every common laborer in every city, should be able to bring as much fruit to his house every day as his family could consume in that day. I should be glad to see in our cities, what is to be seen to some extent in the cities of Europe, the time when a penny or two will enable a man to bring home enough flowers to decorate his table of food twice a day.

We have not merely in view the profits of raising fruit when we exhort you to bestow your attention on the apple more and more as an article of commerce; we have also in view the social influence which it may be made to exert. I hold that when in any respect you lift the common people up, whether by giving them a better dwelling, by placing within their reach better furniture, or by enabling them to furnish their table better, you are raising them toward self-respect; you are raising them toward the higher positions in society. For, although all men should start with the democracy, all men have a right to stop with the aristocracy. Let all put their feet on the same level; and then let them shoot as high as they please. Blessed is the man who knows how to overtop his neighbors by a fair development of skill and strength. And every single step of advance in general cultivation, even though it is brought about by so humble an instrumentality as the multiplication of fruit, or anything else that augments the range of healthful enjoyment among the common people, not only stimulates their moral growth, but, through that growth, gives the classes above them a better chance to grow. One of the most efficient ways of elevating the whole community is to multiply the means of livelihood among the poorest and commonest.

*

From *Pleasant Talk about Fruits, Flowers and Farming*, Henry Ward Beecher (1813-1887). New York: J.B. Ford and Company, 1874; expanded and revised new edition of 1859 publication. A clergyman with a national reputation for his emotional sermons, Beecher was an outspoken anti-slavery voice. In 1839 he was pastor of the Presbyterian Church in Indianapolis and also wrote articles on horticulture for *Indiana Farmer and Gardener* (later called *Western Farmer and Gardener*), a popular farm magazine in the Midwest. One of the founders in 1840 of the Indiana Horticultural Society, he also wrote *Seven Lectures to Young Men* and a *Life of Jesus Christ*. Beecher's 1864 speech printed here, with its mixture of politics and morality, transforms the forbidden fruit into the core of democratic thought. The Rhode Island Greening which he mentions is said by fruit authority U. P. Hedrick to be perhaps the earliest named apple to originate in this country.

THE MATRIMONIAL GARDEN

THOMAS BRIDGEMAN

MAN IS FORMED FOR SOCIAL ENJOYMENT, AND if it be allowed that ''it is not good for man to be alone,'' it may be justly inferred that it is not good that woman should be alone; hence a union of interests indicates a union of persons for their mutual benefit. By this union, a sort of seclusion from the rest of our species takes place; and as a garden is a retired apartment, appropriated to culture and improvement, the married state may not be inaptly compared with it in many respects.

It is good and honorable for the human species, prudently and cautiously to approach this delightful enclosure. Its entrance in general is extremely gay and glittering, being strewed with flowers of every hue and every fragrance, calculated to charm the eye and please the taste; but they are not all so; and as there are many persons who may wish to enter this garden at some time or other, who are yet strangers to its various productions, their attention should be directed to the cultivation of those plants which are beneficial, and to the avoiding or rooting up of those which are injurious.

And first, let me caution adventurers in this garden not to dream of *permanent* happiness; if you should so dream, experience will soon make you wiser, as such happiness never existed but in visionary heads. If you are desirous that this garden should yield you all the bliss of which it is capable, you must take with you that excellent flower called GOOD HUMOUR, which, of all the flowers of nature, is the most delicious and delicate; do not drop it or lose it, as many do soon after they enter the garden—it is a treasure that nothing can supply the loss of. When you get to the end of the first walk, which contains about thirty steps, commonly called "the Honey Moon Path," you will find the garden open into a vast variety of views, and it is necessary to caution you to avoid many productions in them which are noxious, nauseous, and even fatal in their nature and tendency, especially to the ignorant and unwary. There is a low, small plant, which may be seen in almost every path, called INDIFFERENCE.—This, though not perceived in the entrance, you will always know where it grows, by a certain coldness in the air which surrounds it. Contrary to the nature of plants in general, this grows by cold and dies by warmth; whenever you perceive this change in the air, avoid the place as soon as you can. In the same path is often found that baneful flower called JEALOUSY, which I advise you never to look at, for it has the strange quality of smiting the eye that beholds it with a pain that is seldom or never got rid of. Jealousy is a deadly flower; it is the aconite of the garden, and has marred the happiness of thousands.

As you proceed, you will meet with many little crooked paths. I advise you as a friend, never to go into them; for although at the entrance of each, it is written in large letters, I AM RIGHT, if you do enter, and get to the end of them, you will find the true name to be PERVERSENESS. These crooked paths occasion endless disputes, and as it is difficult to make the crooked straight, it is better to avoid them altogether, lest, as it sometimes happens, a total separation be the consequence, and you take different paths the rest of your lives. Near this spot, you will meet with a rough, sturdy plant, called OBSTINACY, which bears a hard knotty fruit that never digests, and of course must injure the constitution; it even becomes fatal, when taken in large quantities. Turn from it, avoid it as you would the cholera.

Just opposite to this, grows that lovely and lively shrub, called COMPLIANCE, which, though not always pleasant to the palate, is very salutary, and leaves a sweetness in the mouth; it is a most excellent shrub, and produces the most delicious fruit.—Never be without a very large sprig in your hand; it will often be wanted as you go along, for you cannot be happy without it in any part of the garden.

In one of the principal compartments, stands a very important plant, called ECONOMY; it is of a thriving quality; cultivate this fine plant with all your care; for it adorns and enriches at the same time. Many overlook it, some despise it, and others think that they will never want it; it is generally overlooked in the gaiety and levity with which people enter the place, but the want of it is generally deplored with bitter repentance. There are two other plants of the same species, which are very closely connected, called INDUSTRY and FRUGALITY, and I must take leave to tell you, that unless both the male and the female partake largely of their branches, very little success can be expected; in this they must both unite. Take care that you provide yourself and partner with a supply of each as soon as possible after you enter the garden.

There are two or three paths which run much into one another, and deserve the closest attention of the softer sex; I mean REGULARITY, EXACTNESS, and SIMPLICITY. Do not think, as some do, that when you once have got into the garden, you may be neglectful of these paths. Remember that your companion will see your neglect, which will affect his eye, and may alienate his heart. Enter on these departments, then, as soon as you enter the garden, and when you are once fairly in, you are in for life; the danger is that if you do not get into them at an early period, you will not find them afterwards. Near these walks is to be found that modest plant, called HUMILITY:

It is the Violet, ''born to blush unseen,
And waste its sweetness on the desert air.''

It appears of little worth in itself, but when joined with other virtues, it adds a charm to life, and spreads a fragrance around its wearer. Cultivate, then, with all your care, this sweet little plant, and you will find it prevent the growth of all poisonous and noxious weeds.

Allow me also to drop a hint on the subject of CULTIVATION, as connected with PROPAGATION, as that most probably will be your employment in this garden, sooner or later. Should you have the rearing of a young plant, remember that it is frail in its nature, and liable to be destroyed by every blast, and will demand all your care and attention. Should you witness a blast on its dawning beauties, Oh! how your fond heart will bleed with tenderness, affection, and sympathy! The young shoot will naturally twine around all the fibres of your frame. Should it live and thrive, spare no pains to ''train it up in the way it should go.'' Weed it, water it, prune it; it will need all the cultivator's skill. Without this, many weeds and baneful plants will grow up with it, and blast your fondest hopes. Be ever mindful that this is a TRUST for which both parties are accountable.

Without careful cultivation, what can you expect but the most luxuriant growth of unruly appetites, which, in time, will break forth in all manner of disgraceful irregularities? What, but that ANGER, like a prickly thorn, will arm the temper with an untractable moroseness? That PEEVISHNESS, like a stinging nettle, will render the conversation irksome and forbidding? That AVARICE, like some choking weed, will teach the fingers to gripe, and the hands to oppress? That REVENGE, like some poisonous plant, replete with baneful juices, will rankle in the breast, and meditate mischief to its neighbor. While unbridled LUSTS, like swarms of noisome insects, taint each rising thought, and render ''every imagination of the heart only evil continually?'' Such are the usual products of unrestrained nature! Such the furniture of the uncultivated mind!

By all means, then, pay due attention to culture. By suitable discipline, clear the soil; by careful instruction, implant the seeds of virtue. By skill and vigilance, prune the unprofitable and over-luxuriant branches:—''direct the young idea how to shoot,''—the wayward passions how to move. The mature man will then become the chief ornament of the garden. Around him CHARITY will breathe her sweets, and in his branches HOPE expand her blossoms. In him the personal virtues will display their graces, and the social ones their fruit—the sentiments become generous, the carriage endearing, the life useful, and the end happy and peaceful.

*

From *The Florist's Guide*, Thomas Bridgeman (?-1850). New York: self-published, 1840; third edition of volume first published in 1835. A florist and seedsman who came to the U.S. from England in 1824, Bridgeman had a successful nursery business in New York City in the first half of the nineteenth century. He wrote several popular books of advice for planting flowers, vegetables, shrubs, fruit trees, and indoor plants, including *The Young Gardener's Assistant* and *The Kitchen Gardener's Instructor*. Bridgeman's "Matrimonial Garden" is a bit of allegorical kitsch that reflects the morality and sentimentality of domestic culture in this era, offered as an "appendage" to his practical, and hence easier to follow, directions and monthly calendar.

Introduction to Organic Farming

J. I. Rodale

The subject of organic farming is new to the majority of farmers. In this country it has been taken up on a limited scale, only in the last few years. In Europe,—England, Denmark, Switzerland and Germany especially—it has been in use on a more extensive scale for many years and its advantages have been tested widely. There are two methods that have been used, the Bio-Dynamic system and the Indore method, the latter receiving its name from the city of Indore in India where it was first tried by Sir Albert Howard. They both have one thing in common, which is that they frown on the use of so-called chemical fertilizers.

What is claimed roughly for these organic methods of farming is that they increase the fertility of the soil, produce much better tasting crops, crops that are healthier for man and beast, reduce weeds, do away with the necessity of using poisonous sprays, improve the mechanical structure of the soil, enable it to retain moisture, and reduce soil erosion, etc.

Sir Albert Howard, advocate of the Indore method of farming, has said that ''artificial manures (chemicals) lead inevitably to artificial nutrition, artificial animals, and finally to artificial men and women.''

A few years ago in an English health magazine published in London there appeared a brief account of an experiment in the feeding of children which had a tremendous significance in connection with bodily resistance to disease. There were two groups of children. One group was fed on vegetables raised by ordinary methods with the liberal use of chemical fertilizers. The second ate vegetables grown by the use of compost fertilizer only, containing no chemicals. The latter children enjoyed a singular immunity to colds whereas the former suffered from the regular, normal condition as to colds, coughs, etc.

Compost fertilizer is a purely organic material as distinguished from mineral fertilizers (chemicals). It is made by mixing manure with such plant materials as weeds, leaves, grass clippings, etc. By a natural process, decay takes place and the resultant material, which has a rich woodsy brown color, goes back into the land to enrich it in a manner that the roots of the plants can appreciate and absorb, as against unnatural chemicals which the roots cannot as efficiently work with.

This was the first time that I had ever heard a question raised as to the methods used in raising crops insofar as it affected our health. Having read, extensively over a long period of time in medical journals, health magazines and books and never having seen this point discussed, it reacted as something of overwhelming importance.

I have obtained and read several times over Sir Albert Howard's book entitled *An Agricultural Testament* which treats the entire subject in adequate detail. The Bio-Dynamic method is described in a book called *Bio-Dynamic, Farming and Gardening* by Dr. Ehrenfried Pfeiffer.

Since July, 1941, we have been making compost heaps, using manure obtained from a herd of 20 steers. There is no question that the making of these heaps means extra labor, but it will be shown in the columns of this magazine that this extra work will be more than repaid by getting better crops and selling them at higher prices. The use of organic materials exclusively means greater profits for the farmer.

Plant growth depends on a bacteriological process in the soil and in this process there is a certain relationship or cooperation between bacteria and certain fungi called *mycorrhiza*. These two work as a team in feeding the organic matter of the soil to the roots. In the presence of artificial chemical fertilizers the efficiency of the bacteria and *mycorrhiza* is greatly reduced and the resultant food products do not have the fine taste of those raised with natural organic fertilizer materials, also called humus. In other words not only would we be much healthier if we ate food grown under the above-mentioned correct methods, but our farm animals, if fed on them, would be healthier and the income we get through them would be higher.

Where much chemical fertilizers are used with insufficient application of organic substances the soil is gradually becoming hard-packed and the earthworms which nature put there for a well-defined purpose are being killed off. By boring in the earth these tiny creatures produce openings which help in getting oxygen into the soil. But their most important duty is actually to swallow earth, mix it with matter from their digestive process and excrete one of the finest natural fertilizer materials ever made. Many soils today are almost barren of worms because of the constant dumping into the soil of artificial fertilizers. By the use of humus, or the natural organic fertilizers, the amount of earthworms in the soil is greatly increased because they can live and multiply in this element which is natural for them.

It is rather paradoxical that the medical profession and its thousands of scientific workers are spending so much time measuring the amount of vitamins in various food products and formulating interesting principles regarding their application to health problems, yet disregarding the basis or foundation of the food products. Plants are not like money for example. A one dollar bill always means 100 cents. But two different pea-pods each representing the same weight do not have the same amount of vitamins.

One of these fine days the public is going to wake up and will pay for eggs, meats, vegetables, etc., according to how they were produced. A substantial premium will be paid for high quality products such as those raised by organic methods. It is possible that if you feed chickens on home raised feeds produced without the use of chemical fertilizers, instead of getting 30 or 40¢ a dozen your eggs will command 50 or 60¢ a dozen. The better-earning class of the public will pay a high price if they can be shown its value, and that they will save on doctor bills.

Dr. Alexis Carrel, in his world-famous book *Man the Unknown*, wrote: ''Chemical fertilizers, by increasing the abundance of crops without replacing the exhausted elements of the soils, have contributed indirectly to change the nutritive value of our cereal grains and our vegetables.''

It has been proven that not only may food crops be grown without the aid of chemical fertilizers, but that when natural organic fertilizers are used, the food thus grown not only produces greater body resistance to disease when eaten by either man or animal, but the taste of food is by far more delicious and natural.

In New Zealand practically all the farms are treated with chemical fertilizers. A few years ago, *Lancet*, the famous London medical magazine, said, ''In 1936 Dr. G. B. Chapman, of the Physical and Mental Welfare Society of New Zealand, persuaded the authorities of a boys' school hostel to grow their fruit and vegetables on soils treated with humus. This has since been done, and a striking improvement is reported in general health and physique, particularly as regards freedom from infections, alimentary upsets and dental caries.''

In India, the Hunzas of the north have been found to have the best health and physique of the entire country. They are a ''hardy, agile, and vigorous people,'' says Sir Albert Howard. ''They have marvelous agility and endurance, good temper and cheerfulness. These men think nothing of covering the 60 miles to Gilgit in one stretch, doing their business and then returning . . . health and physique enjoyed by the Hunza hillmen appears to be due to the efficiency of their ancient system of farming.'' It was found that they return to the soil all human, animal, and vegetable wastes after being made into compost heaps as described earlier in this article. Chemicals do not enter into their farming formula.

In overpopulated China, where the soil is literally ''worked to death,'' and land is so precious, this method of using compost heaps has been in use for over 5000 years. The full advantage in China, however, cannot be secured on account of overpopulation in the first place and secondly because of frequent crop failures due to insufficient rainfall. Had chemical fertilizers been extensively used there over a period of not thousands, but only hundreds of years, China today would be a barren wasteland.

The dust storms in midwestern United States are partly due to the lack of organic humus in the soil. The humus that the farmer can make in the form of compost heaps, after being worked into the soil will improve the moisture retaining capacity of the earth. That is one of the very important aspects of this method of fertilization. The earth will retain moisture during long periods of drought. Ground which is overchemicalized, as in the dust-bowl regions, becomes hard packed and powdery, and is bound to become worthless eventually.

Unless more organic material is returned to the soil, the future of this country looks somewhat disheartening, because industry and prosperity are closely bound to and dependent upon agriculture. It is said that the decline of Rome was due to a deterioration of its crop lands. There are many other examples in History where carelessness in the handling of the soil resulted in the practical extinction of races, or reduction to a low status.

*

From *Organic Farming and Gardening* magazine, Vol. I, No. 1, J. I. Rodale (1898-1971). Emmaus, Pennsylvania: Rodale Press, 1942. The excerpt published here is Rodale's editorial in the first issue of the magazine now known as *Rodale's Organic Gardening.* Interestingly, the Dr. Pfeiffer mentioned in his editorial was influenced by the ''bio-dynamic'' method of German philosopher and anthroposophist Rudolf Steiner, a linkage which situates Rodale's own ideas, and his interests in playwriting, in a fascinating cultural-historical continuum. Years before it was a popular position, he was a tireless advocate of a healthy, non-chemical way of life—in the garden, in the home—and an experimenter with natural fertilizers when such practices were unknown to most Americans. For decades the Rodale enterprise has alerted readers to safe and productive planting and composting methods in the homey, advice-filled *Organic Gardening,* America's most popular garden magazine. Other publications were devoted to agricultural interests, continued today in *The New Farm,* and to health, centered in *Prevention.*

In addition to prolific contributions to his magazines, Rodale published books and reference sources, including *Pay Dirt, The Encyclopedia of Organic Gardening,* and *The Complete Book of Composting.* The Rodale Research Center, established in 1972, conducts gardening and farming experiments based on the concept of ''regeneration.'' In issues relating to the soil and to the body, the Rodale credo emphasizes environmentally-sound, healthy measures and minimum reliance on synthetic means. In the single-minded pursuit of his salutary vision Rodale founded a total world of good living, and eventually Americans found him.

GARDEN HAPPINESS

LOUISA YEOMANS KING

THIS VERY EVENING, IN THE DUSK, I WAS WALKing in my garden alone. The air was full of sweetness from great walls or cascades of the mock orange, from heavy peonies in full bloom, whose white or rose-colored petals weighed the plants almost to the ground, from valerian or garden heliotrope, white with flowers. Outside the wall of green made by tall spruces, I heard voices. One said: "Do look at those peonies—aren't they wonderful!" I called to the strangers, asking them to enter, to wander where they would. In they came, and we spent a few moments together enjoying the soft sight of many blooming flowers, the sweet scents in the dew, the rich greens of foliage and turf in the fading light; then I left them still exclaiming over the beauty of what they saw. But we had had together, these three unknown women and I, that satisfaction of the common beauty of the common things of the common life; and such moments leave one happier. They make for friendships through a common and rarely fine interest, an interest in the things that grow, an interest than which there is no better for body, mind, or spirit. Each one has his own most real thing. Mine is the garden. And the best wish I can wish for any one is that he may have a garden of his own, a little garden in which, through work and sweet imaginings he may find a creative happiness unknown to those without this dear possession.

*

From *Chronicles of the Garden,* Louisa Yeomans King (1863-1948). New York: Charles Scribner's Sons, 1925. Mrs. Francis King, as she was known in her books, was one of the founders in 1913 of the Garden Club of America, and a year later she was elected the first president of the Women's National Farm and Garden Association. The author of ten books, she was an enthusiastic supporter of garden clubs, grassroots organizations, and careers for women. *The Well-Considered Garden* and *The Flower Garden Day by Day* reflect the emphasis on color and on practicality in her approach.

THE REACTOR AND THE GARDEN

WENDELL BERRY

THE BEST KIND OF GARDENING IS A FORM OF home production capable of a considerable independence of outside sources. It will, then, be ''organic'' gardening. One of the most pleasing aspects of this way of gardening is its independence. For fertility, plant protection, etc., it relies as far as possible on resources in the locality and in the gardener's mind. Independence can be further enlarged by saving seed and starting your own seedlings. To work at ways of cutting down the use of petroleum products and gasoline engines in the garden is at once to increase independence and to work directly at a real (that is, a permanent) solution to the energy problem.

A garden gives interest a place, and it proves one's place interesting and worthy of interest. It works directly against the feeling—the source of a lot of our ''environmental'' troubles—that in order to be diverted or entertained, or to ''make life interesting,'' it is necessary to draw upon some distant resource—turn on the TV or take a trip.

One of the most important local resources that a garden makes available for use is the gardener's own body. At a time when the national economy is largely based on buying and selling substitutes for common bodily energies and functions, a garden restores the body to its usefulness—a victory for our species. It may take a bit of effort to realize that perhaps the most characteristic modern "achievement" is the obsolescence of the human body. Jogging and other forms of artificial exercise do not restore the usefulness of the body, but are simply ways of assenting to its uselessness; the body is a diverting pet, like one's Chihuahua, and must be taken out for air and exercise. A garden gives the body the dignity of working in its own support. It is a way of rejoining the human race.

One of the common assumptions, leading to the obsolescence of the body, is that physical work is degrading. That is true if the body is used as a slave or a machine—if, in other words, it is misused. But working in one's own garden does not misuse the body, nor does it dull or "brutalize" the mind. The work of gardening is not "drudgery," but is the finest sort of challenge to intelligence. Gardening is not a discipline that can be learned once for all, but keeps presenting problems that must be directly dealt with. It is, in addition, an agricultural and ecological education, and that sort of education corrects the cheap-energy mind.

A garden is the most direct way to recapture the issue of health, and to make it a private instead of a governmental responsibility. In this, as in several other ways I have mentioned, gardening has a power that is political and even democratic. And it is a political power that can be applied constantly, whereas one can only vote or demonstrate occasionally.

Finally, because it makes backyards (or front yards or vacant lots) productive, gardening speaks powerfully of the abundance of the world. It does so by increasing and enhancing abundance, and by demonstrating that abundance, given moderation and responsible use, is limitless. We learn from our gardens to deal with the most urgent question of the time: How much is enough? We don't soup our gardens up with chemicals because our goal is *enough*, and we know that *enough* requires a modest, moderate, conserving technology.

Atomic reactors and other big-technological solutions, on the other hand, convey an overwhelming suggestion of the poverty of the world and the scarcity of goods. That is because their actuating principle is excessive consumption. They obscure and destroy the vital distinction between abundance and extravagance. The ideal of "limitless economic growth" is based on the obsessive and fearful conviction that more is always needed. The growth is maintained by the consumers' panic-stricken suspicion, since they always want more, that they will never have enough.

Enough is everlasting. Too much, despite all the ballyhoo about "limitless growth," is temporary. And big-technological solutions are temporary: the lifetime of a nuclear power plant is thirty years! A garden, given the right methods and the right care, will last as long as the world.

If you grow a garden you are going to shed some sweat, and you are going to spend some time bent over; you will experience some aches and pains. But it is in the willingness to accept this discomfort that we strike the most telling blow against the power plants and what they represent. We have gained a great deal of comfort and convenience by our dependence on various public utilities and government agencies. But it is obviously not possible to become dependent without losing independence—and freedom too. Or to put it another way, we cannot be free from discomfort without becoming subject to the whims and abuses of centralized power, and to any number of serious threats to our health. We cannot hope to recover our freedom from such perils without discomfort.

Someone is sure to ask how I can suppose that a garden, "whose action is no stronger than a flower," can compete with a nuclear reactor. Well, I am not supposing that exactly. As I said, I think the protests and demonstrations are necessary. I think that jail may be the freest place when you *have no choice* but to breathe poison or die of cancer. But it is futile to attempt to correct a public wrong without correcting the sources of that wrong in yourself.

At the same time, I think it may be too easy to underestimate the power of a garden. A nuclear reactor is a proposed "solution" to "the energy problem." But like all big-technological "solutions," this one "solves" a single problem by causing many. The problems of what to do with radioactive wastes and with decommissioned nuclear plants, for example, have not yet been solved; and we can confidently predict that the "solutions," when they come, will cause yet other serious problems that will come as "surprises" to the officials and the experts. In that way, big technology works perpetually against itself. That is the limit of "unlimited economic growth."

A garden, on the other hand, is a solution that leads to other solutions. It is a part of the limitless pattern of good health and good sense.

*

From *The Gift of Good Land: Further Essays Cultural and Agricultural,* Wendell Berry (1934-). San Francisco: North Point Press, 1981. A poet, novelist, and essayist, Berry is an activist writer committed to the knowledge that the measure of a civilization is its treatment of the land. His writing addresses environmental and energy issues, agribusiness, technology, land maintenance and just plain living in a very personal, political vision of rural economy and human values. The organic life he advocates, and practices on his own farm in Kentucky, is pursued in his many books, among them, *Standing by Words, Home Economics,* and *Sabbaths.*

On the Defiance of Gardeners

Henry Mitchell

As I write this, on June 29, it's about time for another summer storm to smash the garden to pieces, though it may hold off until the phlox, tomatoes, daylilies, and zinnias are in full sway.

I detect an unwholesome strain in gardeners here, who keep forgetting how very favorable our climate is, and who seem almost on the verge of ingratitude. Disaster, they must learn, is the normal state of any garden, but every time there is wholesale ruin we start sounding off—gardeners here—as if it were terribly unjust. Go to any of those paradise-type gardens elsewhere, however, and see what they put up with in the way of weather, and you will stop whimpering. What is needed around here is more grit in gardeners.

Now I guess there is no garden in the world more dreamworthy than the one at Tresco Abbey in the Scilly Isles. It rarely approaches freezing there, off the mild coast of England, and wonders abound. Palms grow luxuriantly against soft old stonework, medieval in origin, and there is hardly an exotic rarity of New Zealand or South Africa or Madeira that does not flourish. And yet they can have their daffodils, too, for it never gets hot in those islands, either; and if you view such a garden in the long slanting light of a summer's late afternoon, you will think you have got to heaven in spite of yourself. Indeed, almost any garden, if you see it at just the right moment, can be confused with paradise. But even the greatest gardens, if you live with them day after decade, will throw you into despair. At Tresco, that sheltered wonderland, they wake up some mornings to discover 500 trees are down— the very shelter belts much damaged. The cost of cleanup is too grim to dwell on, but even worse is the loss not of mere lousy Norway maples, but of rare cherished specimens that were a wonder to see in flower.

Or there may be—take the great gardens of Gloucestershire—a drought, and the law forbids you to run the hose. Not just a little dry spell, either, but one going on month after month. There you sit in your garden, watching even the native oaks dry up, and as for the rarities imported at such cost, and with such dreams, from the moist Himalayas, the less said of their silent screams the better.

Or take another sort of garden, in which the land to begin with is a collection of rusting bedsprings and immortal boots. Old shoes simply do not rot, in my opinion, but just stay there forever. The chief growth the gardener finds (I am speaking now of the great garden of Sissinghurst in Kent) is brambles and bracken and dock, maybe broken up by patches of stinging nettles. Amenities include the remains of an old pig sty. You convert it, let's say, into one of the sweetest gardens of the world, with roundels of clipped yew and a little alley of lindens, rising over a wide walk, almost a terrace, of concrete cast in big blocks (not one in a thousand knew it was concrete) with spaces for a riot of primroses and spring bulbs, bursting out everywhere in lemon and scarlet and gentian and ivory. The lindens all die. The pavement has to be replaced. The primroses start dying out—they develop a sickness, they wear out the soil, and no mulches of manure, no coddling of any sort will preserve them. So you grub out the dying and start anew with something else.

Wherever humans garden magnificently, there are magnificent heartbreaks. It may be 40 heifers break through the hedge after a spring shower and (undiscovered for many hours) trample the labor of many years into uniform mire. It may be the gardener has nursed along his camellias for 25 years, and in one night of February they are dead. How can that be? Well, it can be. You have one of the greatest gardens of the Riviera, and one night the dam of the reservoir breaks. The floor of the house is covered with a foot of mud once the water subsides. The reservoir was built at endless labor and cost, since the garden would die without water from it. And now it is gone, and in the flood everything has gone with it. Be sure that is not the day to visit that great garden.

I never see a great garden (even in my mind's eye, which is the best place to see great gardens around here) but I think of the calamities that have visited it, unsuspected by the delighted visitor who supposes it must be nice to garden here.

It is not nice to garden anywhere. Everywhere there are violent winds, startling once-per-five centuries floods, unprecedented droughts, record-setting freezes, abusive and blasting heats never known before. There is no place, no garden, where these terrible things do not drive gardeners mad.

I smile when I hear the ignorant speak of lawns that take 300 years to get the velvet look (for so the ignorant think). It is far otherwise. A garden is very old (though not yet mature) at 40 years, and already, by that time, many things have had to be replaced, many treasures have died, many great schemes abandoned, many temporary triumphs have come to nothing and worse than nothing. If I see a garden that is very beautiful, I know it is a new garden. It may have an occasional sur- viving wonder—a triumphant old cedar—from the past, but I know the intensive care is of the present.

So there is no point dreading the next summer storm that, as I predict, will flatten everything. Nor is there any point dreading the winter, so soon to come, in which the temperature will drop to ten below zero and the ground freezes forty inches deep and we all say there never was such a winter since the beginning of the world. There have been such winters; there will be more.

Now the gardener is the one who has seen everything ruined so many times that (even as his pain increases with each loss) he com- prehends—truly knows—that where there was a garden once, it can be again, or where there never was, there yet can be a garden so that all who see it say, ''Well, you have favorable conditions here. Everything grows for you.'' Everything grows for everybody. Everything dies for everybody, too.

There are no green thumbs or black thumbs. There are only gardeners and non-gardeners. Gardeners are the ones who ruin after ruin get on with the high defiance of nature herself, creating, in the very face of her chaos and tornado, the bower of roses and the pride of irises. It sounds very well to garden a "natural way." You may see the natural way in any desert, any swamp, any leech-filled laurel hell. Defiance, on the other hand, is what makes gardeners.

*

From *The Essential Earthman,* Henry Mitchell (1923-   ). Bloomington: Indiana University Press, 1981. Garden correspondent for *The Washington Post,* where his "Earthman" column appears, Mitchell offers sound, unhurried advice to the gardener in his writing. He takes a hands-on, roll-up-your-sleeves approach, and cuts through all silliness and sentimentality with his punchy humor. Unwittingly, Mitchell's resigned calm serves as a fitting coda to thoughts of the October 1987 devastation that first swept through the Hudson Valley, and later England. Once again gardeners were reminded that Nature has its own design, beyond art, beyond history.

The Mississippi Market Bulletin

Elizabeth Lawrence

THE FARM WOMEN ARE GREAT LETTER WRITers, and usually answer (delightfully and often at length) if a stamped and addressed envelope is enclosed. One advertiser says, "If information is wanted, enclose ten cents," which seems fair enough, but usually questions are answered freely, willingly, and with love. I think my only unanswered letter is one that was returned from a crossroads post office. I expect the lady had died, for I had gotten her name out of an old issue. I can never bear to throw away old market bulletins, and I am always going back to them.

I thought Mrs. Ottice Breland's sweet horsemen must be horsemint, so I wrote to ask if I had guessed right and to beg for some more local names for a book I meant to write. She replied:

> Concerning your Flower Book I am a true flower lover and grower, and I am glad to help you in any way I can, but I might send you a bunch of names, and you would already have them. Let me know about your book, when you finish, how many names are in it. The flower you sent me is sweet horsemint. There are other kinds of mints, but this is the only one I have. I will send you bride bouquet, the calico border plant, and weeping Mary. Weeping Mary is advertised by some as purple butterfly (buddleia).

Bride bouquet proved to be bouncing Bet (*Saponaria officinalis*), a wayside flower with many old names—goodbye-summer, wild sweet William, and lady-at-the-gate. In Georgia it is called Sally-at-the-gate, but I never heard bride bouquet before. Mrs. Breland grows the handsome double form that was cultivated in English gardens in the seventeenth century. On summer evenings the fragrance of the flowers is so intense that they were described by one old writer as "fulsomely sweet."

The calico border plant is the common yarrow, *Achillea millefolium*. The genus was named for Achilles, who used the leaves to treat his soldiers' wounds. Yarrow has been put to many other uses, including brewing beer and making a tea to cure colds and rheumatism. People have chewed the leaves to relieve toothaches and to drive away sad thoughts. Another old name for it is nosebleed, for plant lore has it that the leaves, if held to the nose, will make it bleed and thus relieve migraine. I wonder if the pink form of this yarrow is what some country women list as pink Queen Anne's lace.

When I asked Mrs. Breland about the Virginia rose, which she describes as making a small tree with large, double pink blooms in fall, she offered to send me a plant.

> I am still in the mud with sick folks, so I am late again answering your letter. I am going to send you sometime next week, I hope, a moon lily and a Virginia rose. I would say put the Virginia rose in a large pot or bucket, and keep it in shade until it begins to grow. When it starts to grow it likes sun. Keep it in the house this winter, and put it out next spring. It will bloom next fall, and will come up from the roots each spring if protected from freezes. I paid a dollar for one plant that is supposed to bloom this fall, but I don't think it will. A neighbor sent me some moon lily seeds real late, so the plant I am sending you is small. Cover the moon lily good with green bushes until it starts to grow. It will come up from the roots each spring. In winter, cover the roots with leaf mold, straw, old sacks, or anything. It may bloom late. Guess you are tired of my advice on growing plants, but if I can help you don't fail to let me know. I will be at your service.

She signed herself "a true flower lover," and added a postscript: "I am going to see my sister tomorrow. Maybe I can gather your plants and get them off Wednesday or Thursday."

Mrs. Breland must have gotten them off on Wednesday, for they arrived on Saturday, carefully labeled and damp-packed. The moon lily, as I guessed, was *Datura inoxia* subsp. *inoxia,* still generally sold under its old name *D. meteloides,* a perennial native to the Southwest from Texas to California. It is easily grown from seed, and with me will bloom the first season. In the North, it can be grown as an annual if the seeds are sown indoors, but in cool northern summers the plants may not bloom. The moon lily is low and spreading, with wide, gray leaves and lavender-tinted stems, and blossoms like great white trumpets faintly washed in lavender. The flowers open at dusk and pour their fragrance all over the garden. But the moon lily should never be grown in a garden where there are children, for it is as poisonous as it is beautiful.

The Virginia rose proved to be the Confederate rose, *Hibiscus mutabilis*—called *mutabilis* because the flowers open white, turn pink, and then red by evening. I shall take Mrs. Breland's advice about keeping it indoors the first winter, for it comes from the tropics, but after that I mean to leave it to its fate. In ordering plants from the market bulletin, incidentally, it must be remembered that there are three zones of plant hardiness in Mississippi: Zone 9 along the Gulf Coast, Zone 8 in the center of the state, and Zone 7 in the northern part. Mrs. Breland lives in Neely, which is Zone 8. Charlotte is in the same zone, but she is in the southern half, we in the northern, and this difference sometimes is crucial for borderline plants such as *Hibiscus mutabilis.*

Mrs. Breland is the kind of gardener who grows some of everything, but especially daylilies and camellias, which she collects. Once she advertised ''Chinese pink morning glory seeds, large green leaves eight inches across, vine soft thorny kind, very pretty and makes a quick shade.'' I sent for some, and when they came there was a letter in the envelope: ''Soak the seed overnight before planting, and put a cloth over the hill to keep the dirt soft and deep. Put water on the cloth every day until they begin coming up. The first leaves are so large they don't come up through dry hard dirt very good. If you haven't seen this vine you are in for a surprise.''

Mrs. Breland also sent a plant she called Turk's-cap, which I already knew from Miss Nancy Holder, who had advertised it as ''bright red ladies' eardrops.'' When I asked Miss Holder to send me a flower, she wrote: ''Kind Flower Lover, I am sending you a twig of Ladies' eardrops with a tiny flower on it. The flowers are about an inch and a half in summer days, but this one is late on the bush, and small. Thanks for writing me." I ordered plants, and when they came wrote to tell Miss Holder how fresh they were. "I am glad your order was in good shape," she replied. "I pack in deep moss, and it requires more postage but the plants go through much better. . . . Thanks for writing me, and I trust you get a good grow."

Later, I sent a specimen of this plant to Dr. Sigmond Solymosy at the University of Southwestern Louisiana. He identified it as *Malvaviscus arboreus drummondii,* a shrub native to Texas and Mexico. It is called Mexican apple because the edible fruits look like tiny red apples. Another species, *M. arboreus mexicanus,* is showier but less hardy. (*Hortus Third* says Turk's-cap is *M. pendulifloras.*) In *Flower and Vegetable Garden,* James Vick describes *M. arboreus drummondii* as a bedding plant and "a good house plant that blooms continuously. The flower is bright scarlet, and remains in perfect condition for a long time. In pot culture it usually grows about two feet high, but when placed in the garden it grows quite strong."

Lady's-eardrop is of course also an old name for another plant, the fuchsia. In *Flowers and Flower Lore,* a book where I find many of the old names that turn up in the market bulletins (sometimes attached to the same plants, sometimes to different ones), Hilderic Friend reminisces about the fuchsias that went under this name in his childhood:

> Who has not heard the old folk speak of the Fuchsia as the Lady's Eardrop? I distinctly remember when I was a lad going from time to time with my mother on a visit to my grandmother, an elderly lady, and one who was very proud of her flower-garden. She almost always took us to see her Lady's Eardrop, as she preferred to call her Fuchsia, when it was in bloom. The older people in Devonshire still speak of the plant under the same name, and I was told on the borders of Dartmore quite recently that it is not many years since Lady's Eardrop was the only name there known. In American works on botany, too, the Fuchsia is often thus spoken of, the people who emigrated from England years ago probably carrying the familiar name with them.

Friend is right, for Alphonso Wood in 1876 called the fuchsia lady's-eardrop in his *Flora Atlantica.* And I can easily see how this old name was transferred from the fuchsia to the drooping red flowers of *Malvaviscus arboreus drummondii.*

Another plant I got from Mrs. Breland, many years ago when I was living in Raleigh, was the Jerusalem thorn (*Parkinsonia aculeata*), a little, prickly tree with fine, twice-pinnate leaves and long drooping racemes of fragrant golden flowers. It did not survive its first winter, but it is much planted in the Low Country and has even escaped into the wild from gardens in Beaufort County, South Carolina. Why the genus should have been named for a sixteenth-century herbalist who died more than a hundred years before it was brought to England from tropical America, I cannot imagine, and Jerusalem thorn seems equally inappropriate.

After some time went by when I didn't see any of Mrs. Breland's advertisements in the market bulletin, I wrote to ask if she could send me a tuber of her potato vine, described in an old issue as having "green heart-shaped leaves up to eight inches long; seed balls grow on vine."

Her son answered my letter. He said his mother had had a stroke and now lived with him. He sent me two round, silvery tubers, the size of a very small new Irish potato. "I hope this is what you want," he wrote. "She says the price is about fifty cents."

The vine was the air potato, *Dioscorea bulbifera,* native to tropical Africa. I had tried it once, years ago, but it is not hardy in these parts. In Florida it makes a quick screen and a dense shade. . . .

Not everyone who advertises plants in the market bulletins is a farm woman; there is also Mr. Kimery. My correspondence with him began with the wisteria vine. He wrote:

> Thank you for your order. The wisteria vine may not come up until spring. If it don't come up, let me know, and I will send you another free. It blooms in June, or mine does, long white blooms, about four inches. I'll write you a letter in a few days and tell you about what I have got, and a little about myself. Thanks again, and I hope you luck with all your flowers.

When he sent the list he promised, he enclosed a sheaf of colored pictures cut out of plant catalogues to identify some of his offerings.

> I have plenty of all, but I am out of the tuberose. You will know all about them. If you want anything I have almost all kinds of bulbs, plants and shrubs. I'll be glad to help you. I have about one acre of flowers. It keeps me busy at time to keep them clean, but I have loved flowers all my life. Oh yes, my mother said when I was large enough to crawl, she would have to go out and get me out of the hot sun. Ha. I have been in the flower business about thirty years; have mailed orders to every state in the U.S.

Along with the colored pictures, he enclosed two paper cutouts. On one was printed "Kim's hand at six months," on the other "Kim's foot at six months."

Mr. Kimery's post office is in Saulsbury, Tennessee, but his acre, Hilltop Nursery, is over the line in Mississippi. In 1970 his wife died. "I am staying at home," he wrote, "and I am making it just fine, but it will never be the same." He has brothers and sisters and two sons living nearby, and a daughter in Oregon. He flew there on a jet for a visit. One of his sisters is the alto in a quartet of gospel singers. Mr. Kimery is the tenor. "We are on the go a lot of the time," he wrote, "and we enjoy it. We have some beautiful songs on a record. We went to Memphis to make it." I asked if it was for sale. It was, and at a discount to flower friends. When I found "The Church in the Wildwood" among the hymns, I thought of *Losing Battles*:

> Oh come—come—come—come the bass voice of Uncle Noah Webster started, and they came in with "Come to the church in the wild wood, oh come to the church in the dell."

I sent another record to Eudora. "I love the way they all 'come,' " she wrote, "especially his sister. I only wish they had had enough room to give all the verses. You get the very air in the room, and the smell of the country flowers—I expect zinnias and gladiolus and salvia in a tub —and the warm day. It's all so expressive and Sunday-like. How did you and Mr. Kimery intersect on Gospel by way of flowers?" I told her that it happened because she had put my name on the mailing list of the bulletin some thirty years ago.

I asked Mr. Kimery about some of the names on his plant list: Chinese hollyhock (striped flowers), cat-bells, spider legs, sensitive vine, and the yellow rose of Texas. When I wrote, a little striped mallow that I had been trying to name for some time was in bloom, so I sent a flower and asked whether it was the Chinese hollyhock. It was. It is a biennial, but it reseeds itself indefinitely. I am always coming on it in old gardens, but no commercial seed companies seem to list it, despite its attractive pink blossoms with lavender stripes and its resistance to heat and drought. Later, Dr. Solymosy identified it as *Malva sylvestris,* a native of Europe that has become naturalized in this country. Park Seed sells this as *Malva alcea* "zebrina." Its medicinal uses are no longer taken seriously, but in earlier times all parts were used for various ills, the root, Culpeper said in his *Complete Herbal and English Physician,* having the most virtue.

The cat-bell, Mr. Kimery said, ''was called that name years ago by old people; they said the Indians called them cat-bells. They have small seeds in black pods, and when you shake them they sound like little bells. The kids around here play with them. This is all I know to tell you.'' He added a postscript: ''I sure have mailed a lot of cat-bells.'' In Caroline Dorman's *Flowers Native to the Deep South* I found that this small, insignificant wild flower is *Crotalaria sagittalis.* This specific name, though not listed in *Hortus Third,* came from the conspicuous stipules, shaped like arrowheads and pointing down the stem.

Spider legs was Mr. Kimery's name for cleome, and a very good one to describe its dangling seed pods. The usual name, spider flower, is not at all appropriate for the delicate orchid-like blossoms. Four color forms of *Cleome hasslerana* are listed in Park's catalogue, as well as the yellow-flowered *Cleome lutea,* which as I had it in my former garden in Raleigh was not worth growing. Pink Queen, which is pink and white, is the one grown most often. There is a Purple Queen and a Rose Giant. The most beautiful of all is Helen Campbell with its very large, airy heads of pure white. Although they droop in the midday sun, these cool flowers are a blessing to midsummer borders in the morning and the evening.

The sensitive vine is the sensitive brier, a thorny vining legume that trails on the ground. Mr. Kimery says it is called shame vine because it will close up when touched. The flowers are like those of its relative, the mimosa, little pink balls of fluff, and they have the fragrance of hyacinths. About this plant, which can be one of two closely related native American species, either *Schrankia microphylla* or *S. nuttallii,* Mrs. Lounsberry says that the mountaineer who steps on it with bare feet in a sandy meadow is unlikely to appreciate its beauty, ''but to the well shod it is one of the sweetest and most unique personalities of all native plants.''

''The rose of Texas,'' Mr. Kimery wrote, ''is double yellow. I sent you all I have. They will live. Hope so.'' I hope so too, for one I got earlier died before I had a chance to tell anything about it except that its thorns were sharp and numerous, which made me think it was the old brier, Harison's Yellow (1830), common in gardens and of American origin. The yellow rose of Texas appears often in the market bulletins, but sometimes it is not a rose at all but double kerria (*Kerria japonica*).

Mr. Kimery lives so peacefully on his hilltop, with his flowers and trips to Memphis with the quartet, that I forgot that there is violence in the world. One of his letters startled me out of this illusion.

> Just to let you know what happened here. Wednesday night someone put some kind of bomb in my mailbox and some more. So last night a man watched his, and he caught them. So the law is holding them, and the FBI will come from Memphis tomorrow and get them. They have been doing that for two years, but they are going where they can't do it anymore. If you ever want any flowers let me know. I have so many of such a lot of things. I can let you have them cheap.
>
>   Ain't this world getting in a sinful mess? Everything from that Watergate to raping and killing. Memphis is so mean. We don't know when we go to bed at night if someone will come in and kill us for a dime. They never think about hereafter, or don't care.

I think about Mr. Kimery, about all who sell their seeds and plants through the market bulletin. And I care.

*

From *Gardening for Love: The Market Bulletins,* Elizabeth Lawrence (1904-1985), edited with an introduction by Allen Lacy. Durham: Duke University Press, 1987. It was Katharine S. White who admitted in her own book, "I, a Northern amateur, come lately to any real knowledge of what gardening is about, have learned more about horticulture, plants, and garden history and literature from Elizabeth Lawrence than from any other person." *A Southern Garden* and *The Little Bulbs* are other much admired works by one of the finest American garden writers in literature. Lawrence wrote with the most refined sense of pleasure and decency about plants and people, her words respecting the separate but intertwined lives of each. She credits novelist Eudora Welty for introducing her to the market bulletins where rural gardeners traded seeds and plants and personal feelings. In her *Charlotte Observer* obituary a good friend called her "the Jane Austen of the gardening literary world."

II

*L*IVES OF THE *P*LANTS

New England Natural History

John Josselyn

And now I come to the plants of the Countrie. The plants in New-England for the variety, number, beauty, and vertues, may stand in Competition with the plants of any Countrey in Europe. Johnson hath added to Gerard's *Herbal* 300 and Parkinson mentioneth many more; had they been in New-England they might have found 1000 at least never heard of nor seen by any Englishman before: 'Tis true, the Countrie hath no Bonerets, or Tartarlambs, no glittering coloured Tuleps; but here you have the American Mary-Gold, the Earth-nut bearing a princely Flower, the beautiful leaved Pirola, the honied Colibry, &c. They are generally of (somewhat) a more masculine vertue, than any of the same species in England, but not in so terrible a degree, as to be mischievous or ineffectual to our English bodies. . . .

Now I shall present to your view the Shrubs; and first of the Sumach Shrub, which as I have told you in *New-Englands* rarities, differeth from all the kinds set down in our English Herbals; the root dyeth wool or cloth reddish, the decoction of the leaves in wine drunk, is good for all Fluxes of the belly in man or woman, the whites, &c. For galled places stamp the leaves with honey, and apply it, nothing so soon healeth a wound in the head as Sumach stampt and applyed once in three dayes, the powder strewed in stayeth the bleeding of wounds: The seed of Sumach pounded and mixt with honey, healeth the Hemorrhoids, the gum put into a hollow tooth asswageth the pain, the bark or berries in the fall of the leaf, is as good as galls to make Ink of.

Elder in New-England is shrubbie, & dies once in two years: there is a sort of dwarf-Elder that growes by the Sea-side that hath a red pith, the berries of both are smaller than English-Elder, not round but corner'd, neither of them smell so strong as ours.

Juniper growes for the most part by the Sea-side, it bears abundance of skie-coloured berries fed upon by Partridges, and hath a woodie root, which induceth me to believe that the plant mention'd in Job 30.4, *"Qui decerpebant herbas é salsilagine cum stirpibus: etiam radices Juniperorum cibo erant illis,"* was our Indian plant Cassava. They write that Juniper-coals preserve fire longest of any, keeping fire a whole year without supply, yet the Indian never burns of it.

Sweet fern, see the rarities of *New-England*, the tops and nucaments of sweet fern boiled in water or milk and drunk helpeth all manner of Fluxes, being boiled in water it makes an excellent liquor for Ink.

Current-bushes are of two kinds red and black, the black currents which are larger than the red smell like cats piss, yet are reasonable pleasant in eating.

The Gooseberry-bush, the berry of which is called Grosers or thorn Grapes, grow all over the Countrie, the berry is but small, of a red or purple colour when ripe.

There is a small shrub which is very common, growing sometimes to the height of Elder, bearing a berry like in shape to the fruit of the white thorn, of a pale yellow colour at first, then red, when it is ripe of a deep purple, of a delicate Aromatical tast, somewhat stiptick: to conclude, always observe this rule in taking or refusing unknown fruit: if you find them eaten of the fowl or beast, you may boldly venture to eat of them, otherwise do not touch them.

Maze, otherwise called Turkie-wheat, or rather Indian-wheat, because it came first from thence; the leaves boiled and drunk helpeth pain in the back; of the stalks when they are green you may make Beverage, as they do with Calamels, or Sugar-canes. The raw Corn chewed ripens felons or Cats hairs, or you may lay Samp to it: The Indians before it be thorow ripe eat of it parched. Certainly the parched corn that Abigail brought to David was of this kind of grain, I Sam.

25.18: ''The Jewes manner was (as it is delivered to us by a learned Divine) first to parch their corn, then they fried it, and lastly they boiled it to a paste, and then tempered it with water, Cheese-Curds, Honey and Eggs, this they carried drye with them to the Camp, and so wet the Cakes in Wine or milk; such was the pulse too of Africa.''

French-beans, or rather American-beans, the Herbalists call them kidney-beans from their shape and effects, for they strengthen the kidneys; they are variegated much, some being bigger a great deal than others; some white, black, red, yellow, blew, spotted; besides your Bonivis and Calavances and the kidney-bean, that is proper to Ronoake, but these are brought into the Countrie, the other are natural to the climate. So the Mexico pompion which is flat and deeply camphered, the flesh laid to, asswageth pain of the eyes. The water-mellon is proper to the Countrie, the flesh of it is of a flesh colour, a rare cooler of Feavers, and excellent against the stone. *Pomum spinosum* and *palma-Christi* too growes not here, unless planted, brought from Peru; the later is thought to be the plant, that shaded Jonah the Prophet, Jonas 4.6: ''*Paraverat enim Jehova Deus ricinum qui ascenderet supra Jonam, ut esset umbra super caput ejus ereptura eum à malo ipsius; laetabaturque Jonas de ricino illo laetitia magna.*'' *Ricinum*, that is *palma-Christi*, called also *cucurbita*, and therefore translated a Gourd.

Tobacco, or Tabacca so called from Tabaco or Tabago, one of the Caribbe-Islands about 50 English miles from Trinidad. The right name, according to Monardus, is *picielte*, as others will *petum, nico-tian* from Nicot, a Portingal, to whom it was presented for a raritie in *Anno Dom.* 1559 by one that brought it from Florida. Great contest there is about the time when it was first brought into England, some will have Sir John Hawkins the first, others Sir Francis Drake's Mariners; others again say that one Mr. Lane imployed by Sir Walter Rawleigh brought it first into England; all conclude that Sir Walter Rawleigh brought it first in use. It is observed that no one kind of forraign Commodity yieldeth greater advantage to the publick than Tobacco, it is generally made the complement of our entertainment, and hath made more slaves than Mahomet. There is three sorts of it Marchantable, the first horse Tobacco, having a broad long leaf piked at the end; the second round pointed Tobacco; third sweet scented Tobacco. These are made up into Cane, leaf or ball; there is little of it planted in New-England, neither have they learned the right way of curing of it. It is sowen in April upon a bed of rich mould sifted, they make a bed about three yards long, or more according to the ground they intend to plant, and a yard and a half over; this they tread down hard, then they sow their feed upon it as thick as may be, and sift fine earth upon it, then tread it down again as hard as possible they can, when it hath gotten four or six leaves, they remove it into the planting ground; when it begins to bud towards flowring, they crop off the top, for the Flower drawes away the strength of the leaf. For the rest I refer you to the Planter, being not willing to discover their mysteries. The Indians in New-England use a small round leafed Tobacco, called by them, or the Fishermen Poke. It is odious to the English. The vertues of Tobacco are these, it helps digestion, the Gout, the Tooth-ach, prevents infection by scents, it heats the cold, and cools them that sweat, feedeth the hungry, spent spirits restoreth, purgeth the stomach, killeth nits and lice; the juice of the green leaf healeth green wounds, although poysoned; the Syrup for many diseases, the smoak for the Phthisick, cough of the lungs, distillations of Rheume, and all diseases of a cold and moist caufe, good for all bodies cold and moist taken upon an emptie stomach, taken upon a full stomach it pre-cipitates digestion, immoderately taken it dryeth the body, enflameth the bloud, hurteth the brain, weakens the eyes and the sinews.

White Hellebore is used for the Scurvie by the English. A friend of mine gave them first a purge, then conserve of Bear-berries, then fumed their leggs with vinegar, sprinkled upon a piece of mill-stone made hot, and applied to the fores white Hellebore leaves; drink made of Orpine and sorrel were given likewise with it, and Sea-scurvie-grass. To kill lice, boil the roots of Hellebore in milk, and anoint the hair of the head therewith or other places.

Mandrake, is a very rare plant, the Indians know it not, it is found in the woods about Pascataway, they do in plain terms stink, therefore Reubens Flowers that he brought home were not Mandrakes, Gen. 30.14, 15, 16. They are rendered in the Latine *Amabiles flores*, the same word say our Divines is used in Canticles, 7.4. "*Amabiles istos flores edentes odorem, & fecundum ostia nostra omnes pretiosos fructus, recentes simulac veteres, dilecte mi, repono tibi.*" So that the right translation is, Reuben brought home amiable and sweet smelling Flowers; this in the Canticles (say they) expounding the other.

Calamus Aromaticus, or the sweet smelling reed, it Flowers in July;

see *New-Englands* rarities.

Sarsaparilla or roughbind-weed (as some describe it) the leaves and whole bind set with thorns, of this there is store growing upon the banks of Ponds. See the rarities of *New-England*. The leaves of the Sarsaparilla there described pounded with Hogs grease and boiled to an unguent, is excellent in the curing of wounds.

Live for ever, it is a kind of Cud-weed, flourisheth all summer long till cold weather comes in, it growes now plentifully in our English Gardens, it is good for cough of the lungs, and to cleanse the breast taken as you do Tobacco; and for pain in the head the decoction, or the juice strained and drunk in Bear, Wine, or Aqua vitae, killeth worms. The Fishermen when they want Tobacco take this herb being cut and dryed.

Lysimachus or Loose-strife: there are several kinds, but the most noted is the yellow *Lysimachus* of Virginia, the root is longish and white, as thick as ones thumb, the stalkes of an overworn colour, and a little hairie, the middle vein of the leaf whitish, the Flower yellow and like Primroses, and therefore called Tree-primrose, growes upon seedie vessels, &c. The first year it growes not up to a stalke, but sends up many large leaves handsomely lying upon one another, Rose fashion, Flowers in June, the seed is ripe in August, this as I have said is taken by the English for Scabious.

St. John's wort, it preserveth Cheese made up in it, at Sea.

Spurge or Wolfes milch there are several sorts.

Avens, or herb-bennet; you have an account of it in *New-Englands* rarities, but one thing more I shall add, that you may plainly perceive a more masculine quality in the plants growing in New-England. A neighbour of mine in Hay-time, having overheat himself, and melted his grease, with striving to outmowe another man, fell dangerously sick, not being able to turn himself in his bed, his stomach gon, and his heart fainting ever and anon; to whom I administered the decoction of Avens-Roots and leaves in water and wine, sweetening it with Syrup of Clove-Gilliflowers, in one weeks time it recovered him, so that he was able to perform his daily work, being a poor planter or husbandman as we call them.

*

From *An Account of Two Voyages to New-England*, John Josselyn
(1630-1675). London, 1674. Boston: William Veazie, 1865. An Englishman
who visited his brother in the New World in 1638-39, and again 1663-1671,
Josselyn wrote two of the most important books of their kind, *New-Englands
Rarities Discovered* and *An Account of Two Voyages to New-England*.
Together they contribute the fullest contemporary account of natural history
in New England in the seventeenth century. These charming, hoary volumes
are filled with descriptions of plants, beasts, fishes, birds, insects, and stones, of
Indian custom and colonists' distemper. Josselyn offers a fascinating account of
the manner in which the early settlers integrated plants into their religious,
cultural, and medical systems of thought. Reading him on home remedies and
the art of simpling is great fun, always full of surprise and provocation—especially when viewed against the distance our own overly scientific,
synthetic age has created between people and nature.

Anyone who has ever taken a field guide into the wilds knows how difficult a
task it is to identify plants, even with the aid of photographs. Josselyn's
attempt to describe, name, and sometimes draw (he reportedly made the first
image of a pitcher plant) the flowers and trees of a foreign land was indeed an
extraordinary endeavor.

ADVICE FOR THE FALL

BERNARD M'MAHON

THE VINEYARD

GRAPES MAY BE KEPT FRESH A LONG TIME BY the following method: before the autumn frosts have killed the leaves, let the bunch with the shoot be carefully cut off the vine; then let the lower end of the shoot be put into a bottle filled with water; which hang up with the shoot and branch in a warm room, or in a Green-house.

The bottle should be filled with fresh clear water every ten or twelve days, and at the same time a thin paring should be cut off the bottom of the shoot, whereby the pores will be made to imbibe the water with greater facility.

By this method grapes may be kept fresh and good till the middle of February.

Or let the grapes hang on the vines as long as they will continue on with safety; the late ripening kinds will be best for this purpose, provided they are of good flavour and have obtained full maturity. When the frosts begin to set in sharp then gather them. Where there are several bunches on one branch cut it off, leaving about six inches in length, or more, of the wood, according to the distance between the bunches, and a little on the outside of the fruit at each end; seal both ends of the branch with some common sealing wax, or with such as wine merchants use for sealing their bottles with; then hang them across a line in a dry room, which is to be kept perfectly free from frost, taking care to clip out, with a pair of scissors, any of the berries that begin to decay or become mouldy, which if left would taint the others. In this way grapes may be kept fresh a long time: if they are cut before the bunches are very ripe, they will keep longer, but their flavour will not be so fine.

Having plenty of fresh grapes in winter makes a great addition to the table and if properly kept they will be of a much superior flavour to the imported grapes.

Grapes may also be kept in jars; every bunch when well aired and perfectly dry, should be wrapped up loosely in soft white paper, laid in layers, and each layer covered with bran, which should be perfectly well dried before it is used: first lay a little of the dry bran in the bottom of the jar, then a layer of the wrapped up grapes, and so on, a layer of bran and a layer of grapes alternately, till you have filled the jar; then shake it gently and fill it to the top with bran: cover the top with paper, and over this a piece of bladder doubled, which tie firmly round to exclude the air: then put on the top or cover of the jar, observing that it fits as close as possible. These jars should be kept in a room where they will not be exposed to damps, frosts, or too much heat.

In order to preserve a few of your finest bunches for this purpose, from the depredations of birds and insects, let some small bags made of thin gauze or crape be drawn over them, or rather let the bunches be put into the bags; the sun and air will have free access through the crape, and when wet it will dry very soon.

THE ORCHARD

Winter pears and apples should, generally, be gathered this month; [October—ed.] some will be fit for pulling in the early part, others not before the middle or latter end thereof.

To know when the fruits have had their full growth, you should try several of them in different parts of the trees, by turning them gently one way or the other; if they quit the tree easily, it is a sign of maturity and time to gather them.

But none of the more delicate eating pears, should be suffered to remain on the trees till overtaken by frost, for if they are once touched with it, it will occasion many of them to rot in a very short time. Indeed it would be needless, even wrong, to suffer either apples or pairs to remain on the trees, after the least appearance of ice upon the water; as they would be subject to much injury, and receive no possible kind of benefit afterwards.

Observe in gathering the principal keeping fruits, both pears and apples, to do it when the trees and fruit are perfectly dry, otherwise they will not keep so well; and that the sorts designed for *long keeping*, be all carefully hand pulled, one by one, and laid gently into a basket, so as not to bruise one another.

According as the fruits are gathered, carry them into the fruitery, or into some convenient dry, clean, apartment, and lay them carefully in heaps, each sort separate, for about ten days, or two weeks, in order that the watery juices may transpire; which will make them keep longer, and render them much better for eating, than if put up finally as soon as pulled.

When they have lain in heaps that time, wipe each fruit, one after another, with a clean, dry cloth, and if you have a very warm dry cellar, where frost is by no means likely to enter, nor the place subject to much dampness; lay them singly, upon shelves, coated with dry straw, and cover them with a layer of the same.

Or, you may wrap some of the choice sorts, separately, in white paper, and pack them in barrels, or in baskets, lined with the like material. Or, after being wiped dry, lay layer about of fruit and *perfectly dry* sand, in barrels, and head them up as tight as possible. In default of sand, you may use barley chaff, bran, or *dry* saw dust.

Another method, and a very good one, is to be provided with a number of large earthen jars, and a quantity of moss, in a perfectly dry state; and when the fruits are wiped dry as before directed, your jars being also dry, lay therein layer about of fruit and moss, till the jars are near full, then cover with a layer of moss.

Suffer them to remain in this state for eight or ten days, then examine a stratum or two at the top to see if the moss and fruits are perfectly dry; and if you find them in a good condition, stop the jars up with some melted rosin to keep out air. The pears and apples to be used this way should be of the latest and best keeping kinds, and such as are not, generally, fit for use till February, March, or April.

After the jars are sealed as above, place them in a warm dry cellar or room on a bed of *perfectly dry* sand, at least one foot thick; and about the middle of November, or sooner if there is any danger to be apprehended from frost, fill up between the jars with very dry sand, until it is a foot thick round and over them. Thus you may preserve pears in the greatest perfection, for eight, or nine months, and apples twelve.

Be particularly careful to examine every fruit as you wipe it, lest it is bruised, which would cause it soon to rot and communicate the infection, so that in a little time much injury might be sustained, in consequence of a trifling neglect in the first instance: but above all things, place your fruit whatever way they are put up, completely out of the reach of frost.

The common kinds for more immediate use, after being sweated and wiped as before directed, may be packed in hampers or barrels layer about of fruit and straw, and placed where they will neither be exposed to damps or frost.

*

From *The American Gardener's Calendar*, Bernard M'Mahon (1775-1816). Philadelphia: B. Graves, 1806. M'Mahon's work resulted in the most influential gardening book of the first half of the nineteenth century. Appearing in eleven editions, it was the first horticultural volume created specifically for American growing conditions. Organized by month, it featured a glorious treasury of sound advice to follow—in the kitchen garden and flower garden, the orchard, the vineyard, the greenhouse, and pleasure-grounds—for every month of the year. Now, more than 180 years later, it is still a marvel to read his practical directions for when and how to plant, to prune, to preserve, to design all manner of plants around the home. In his important *History of Horticulture in America to 1860*, U. P. Hedrick claims that M'Mahon's nursery catalogue, included at the back of his extensive calendar, is a reliable account of what was then available in America—more than 3500 species of plants.

M'Mahon came to Philadelphia from Ireland in 1796. Within a decade he became a major distributor of seeds to Europe as part of his nursery business. His office was a meeting place for the botanists and horticulturists passing through or living in Philadelphia, men who would eventually found the Pennsylvania Horticultural Society in 1827. Both George Washington and Thomas Jefferson ordered plants and seeds from M'Mahon who was also entrusted with some of the specimens brought back from the Lewis and Clark expedition begun in 1804. Later the botanist Thomas Nuttall would name one of these plants—the Oregon grape holly (Mahonia)—after him. M'Mahon, like many of his time who found themselves in a land so desperately trying to define itself, generously saw his work in an expansive social and historical context. In 1806 he sent *The American Gardener's Calendar* to President Jefferson with a note: "I have much pleasure in requesting your acceptance of one of my publications on Horticulture which I forward to you by this mail. Should my humble efforts, meet with your approbation, and render any service to my adopted and beloved country, I shall feel the happy consolation of having contributed my mite to the welfare of my fellow man." It was the start of a horticultural friendship.

Shaker Seed Catalogue of 1873

Selections

It is with real pleasure that we again greet our friends and patrons, and trust we are fully prepared to respond to your esteemed orders satisfactorily. During the last season we have used the utmost exertions to secure an ample stock of such seeds as cannot fail to please. The largely increasing demands for our seeds, assure us that our efforts are appreciated. Persons have but to make a trial to become convinced that we can always supply just such seeds as they need, and such as are always reliable. We almost invariably hear it remarked by those who have tried our seeds for the first time, that they never before raised plants so large and fine, and feared they should never get seeds of so good quality again. But we assure those who patronize us, that we shall in no case suffer the quality of our seeds to deteriorate; and it will be for their interest to get a fresh supply each season rather than to save seeds of their own raising, or to procure them from uncertain sources. We spare no pains or expense in procuring and testing every new variety brought to notice, and such as possess any real merits we recommend, but shall be slow to notice anything, the name of which constitutes its only value. . . .

BEANS, BUSH OR SNAP

Plant in spring, after the ground becomes warm, in dry, warm soil, lightly manured; cover one inch deep; hoe often, but not when wet.

Early Round Yellow, Six Weeks.—One of the earliest, hardy and prolific. Seed orange yellow. A quart will plant about two hundred and twenty hills.

Early Long Yellow, Six Weeks.—Hardy and a good bearer. Seed a pale yellow. A quart will plant one hundred and fifty hills, or two hundred feet of drill.

Early Red Speckled Valentine.—Early, pod round, tender, and succulent. A quart will plant one hundred and seventy-five hills, or two hundred feet of drill.

Brown Speckled Valentine, or Refuge.—Early, pod round and succulent. Excellent for string or for pickling. A prolific bearer. A quart will plant two hundred hills, or two hundred and fifty feet of drill.

Early China.—A good bearer and an excellent variety. Seeds white, having the eye spotted with red. A quart will plant two hundred hills, or two hundred and fifty feet of drill.

Early Mohawk.—Hardy and very prolific. Seeds variegated with purple, drab, and brown. A quart will plant one hundred and fifty hills, or two hundred feet of drill.

Black Wax Bush.—A new variety unsurpassed for string or for shell while green. Pods transparent, of a waxy yellow, thick and very tender. A quart will plant two hundred hills, or two hundred and fifty feet of drill.

White Kidney, or Royal Dwarf.—One of the best varieties for shell, green or ripe. Seeds kidney-shaped, large and white. A quart will plant one hundred and fifty hills, or one hundred and seventy-five feet of drill.

White Marrow.—A prolific bearer. Excellent for shell while green; also fine for cooking when ripe. A quart will plant one hundred and fifty hills, or one hundred and seventy-five feet of drill.

BEANS, POLE OR RUNNING

Horticultural Cranberry, or Wrens Egg.—A good bearer. Seeds light red and cream colored, speckled. Good either in the pod or shelled. A quart will plant one hundred and thirty hills.

German Wax.—This is really one of the best varieties in cultivation, either for snaps or for shelling while green. Pods a waxy color, very succulent, fine and tender. When ripe, the seeds become black. A quart will plant one hundred and fifty hills.

White Dutch Case Knife,—Early and very prolific. Pods long and flat with white seeds, which are good green or dry. A quart will plant one hundred and seventy-five hills.

French Yard Long.—Pods grow in large clusters and of great length, and fine for string. Seeds dun color. A quart will plant one hundred and seventy-five hills.

Large Lima.—This is the best shell bean known, but it requires a long season for it to mature. A quart will plant one hundred hills.

Scarlet Runner.—Flowers a brilliant scarlet. Seeds variegated with black or deep purplish brown. Form broad, kidney-shaped. A quart contains five hundred seeds, and will plant eighty hills.

BROCCOLI

This vegetable is allied to the Cauliflower—more hardy, but not so fine.

Culture.—For early use, sow in February, and transplant in spring. For fall use, sow in spring in drills, and transplant in July, in deep, rich soil, two feet apart each way; cultivate same as Cabbage. An ounce will produce five thousand plants.

Early Purple Cape.—This is the variety most generally cultivated, producing large, close heads, of a brownish purple, and is of an excellent flavor.

White Cape.—A later sort; heads large, white and compact.

CABBAGE

Culture.—In the South, Cabbage for early use may be sown in the fall, and protected through the winter by a cold frame or a covering of straw, but in the Northern latitudes, it is better to sow in hot-beds, and transplant in the spring, after the ground becomes warm. The largest kinds should be set three feet apart each way. To have fine Cabbage the ground must be dug deep, heavily manured, and well tilled. An ounce of seed will produce six thousand plants.

Early York.—This is one of the earliest, and a popular variety; heads heart-shaped, firm, tender, and fine flavored.

Large Early York.—Larger and later than the Early York, and endures the heat well.

Early Sugar Loaf.—One of the earliest varieties, and popular at the North.

Early Paris.—This is one of the earliest sorts, but tender if sown early in the spring.

Early Erfurt.—Heads very large; white, and of fine quality.

Early London.—Stem tall, leaves of medium size, head white, compact and fine.

CORN

Early Sweet or Sugar.—One of the earliest varieties, and very sweet. Ears good size, generally twelve rowed. One quart will plant two hundred hills.

Evergreen Sweet.—Very sweet and prolific, a single stock bearing from three to five ears, some of which remain green till frost.

Mammoth Sweet.—Large and late. Ears twelve to sixteen rowed; and well filled. Very prolific. Quality excellent.

Asylum Sweet.—Ears medium size. Corn sweet and good flavored.

Early Canada.—Very early. Stock four or five feet high. Ears eight-rowed and small size.

Tuscarora.—Large eight-rowed variety. Kernels white and a little indented.

Eight-Rowed White Flint.—Ears very long and handsome. One of the best kinds for field culture.

White Pop Corn.—The best variety for parching.

Adam's Early or Burlington.—An early market variety. Ears good size but short. Kernel white and a little indented.

CUCUMBER

Culture.—Prepare the hills for planting, by using a shovelful of well-rotted manure in each hill. Cover this two inches deep with fine earth, on which plant the seed. When beyond the reach of insects thin to four plants in a hill, which should be six feet apart each way. Hoe often. An ounce of seed will plant one hundred hills.

Early Russian.—Earliest in cultivation, being ten days earlier than the Early Cluster, which it resembles. Fruit sets in pairs, and when fully grown is three or four inches in length. Fine flavored.

Early Cluster.—A short, prickly variety. Usually grows in clusters. Is a prolific bearer, and, excepting the Early Russian, is the earliest sort. Flavor excellent.

Early Frame.—The standard variety and a most prolific bearer. Fruit medium size, and excellent for using in green state or for pickling.

Early White Spine.—Fruit large size and smooth, and retains its color several days after being plucked. An excellent variety.

Long Green.—The largest variety. Long, straight, smooth and solid, sometimes growing eighteen inches in length. Excellent for pickling.

West India Gherkin.—A very small variety, used wholly for pickling.

ENDIVE

Grown principally for winter salads.

Culture.—Sow from early spring to middle of summer, in drills. When up, thin to eight inches. An ounce of seed will sow a seed-bed eighty feet square.

Green Curled.—The hardiest sort, with beautifully curled, dark green leaves, tender and crisp. Generally cultivated in this country for salads.

Broad Leaved.—Leaves broad and nearly plain. Used principally for flavoring soups and stews.

LETTUCE

Culture.—The richer the soil and the higher the state of cultivation the larger and finer will be the heads produced, and the more rapidly the plants are grown the more tender and brittle will be their quality. Lettuce succeeds best in rich and rather moist soil. For early use sow in a hot-bed, and as soon as the ground is warm enough transplant in rows; or sow in seed-bed in September, and protect through winter with a cold frame or a covering of straw or litter, and transplant in spring. When a few inches high, thin to ten or twelve inches in the row. Head lettuces need plenty of room or they will not be strong. One ounce of seed will sow a bed one hundred feet square.

Early Curled Silesia.—A excellent early variety of strong growth. Leaves large. Color light yellow and wrinkled. Heads large, loose and fine flavored.

Royal Cabbage.—Leaves light yellow. Head good size, close and well formed. Stands the heat well.

Ice Drumhead.—Heads readily, is crisp, tender and well-flavored.

Large India Head.—Heads very large, white, crisp, and tender. This variety stands the heat well.

Ice Coss.—Head cone-shaped. An excellent variety for early spring or for fall use, but does not stand the heat well.

Brown Dutch.—A very hardy lettuce not easily affected by the frost. Well adapted for fall sowing.

MELON

Culture.—Melons thrive best in a warm, rich, sandy loam, and in a sheltered exposure. If the soil is heavy, dig large holes two feet in diameter and eighteen inches deep; fill with stable manure; cover this with soil three inches deep; on this plant the seeds. When out of the reach of insects, thin to two or three plants in a hill. Melons should not be planted near pumpkins or squashes, as they will mix.

Musk Varieties

Fine Netted Nutmeg.—A popular variety. Fruit roundish. Flesh thick, and excellent flavor.

Pine Apple.—A dark green oval melon. Medium size. Rough netted, flesh thick, juicy and sweet.

Green Citron.—A large roundish fruit, flattened at the ends, and rough netted. Melting and fine flavored.

Jenny Lind.—Size small, but very delicious.

Water Varieties

Mountain Sweet.—The most popular variety, and very productive;

large in size; long, oval-shaped; flesh scarlet; excellent flavored, and solid quite to the centre.

Ice Cream.—A variety similar to the last-mentioned; it is prolific, early and well adapted for cultivation in cold localities.

Mountain Sprout.—A large, long, striped variety; flesh, bright scarlet color, and excellent flavored; seeds drab color.

Black Spanish.—A round variety; color dark green; flesh scarlet; seeds black.

Citron for Preserves.—Grows round and smooth; striped, and marbled with light green.

NASTURTIUM, OR INDIAN CRESS

Leaves and flowers used as a Salad. The pods when plump and tender make good pickles.

Culture.—Sow in spring in drills one inch deep; the tall variety by a fence or trellis.

Tall.

Dwarf.

PARSLEY

A well-known savory herb for flavoring.

Culture.—Parsley succeeds best in mellow, rich soil. As the seed vegetates slowly—sometimes remaining in the ground four or five weeks before the plants appear—the sowing should be done as early in the spring as the ground will admit. Soak the seed in warm water a few hours before sowing. The best Curled Parsley is obtained by repeatedly transplanting. Rows should be eighteen inches apart, and the plants a foot apart in the rows. One ounce contains seven thousand seeds, and will sow one hundred and fifty feet of drill.

Plain Parsley.—This is the hardiest and most productive sort; leaves dark green; plain, and better for flavoring than the curled.

Double Curled.—Leaves beautiful, and fine for garnishing.

PEAS

Culture.—Peas should be sowed in drills and not broadcast. For earliest crop, select a warm, light, rich spot of ground which should be manured the season previous. Sow in drills and cover three inches deep. Later sowings should be covered five inches deep. If the ground is poor, it will require to be more heavily manured. For the dwarf varieties the ground can hardly be too rich. If the soil is wet and recently manured, it will cause the vines to grow much taller. A quart of small seeded sorts will sow a row one hundred and twenty feet in length. A quart of the large sorts will sow a row one hundred and seventy-five feet in length.

Extra Early

Extra Early.—This is the earliest Pea cultivated; productive, hardy, and good flavored; height 2½ feet.

Carter's First Crop.—Similar to the above, but more delicate.

Caractacus.—A new variety, and one of the earliest; a vigorous grower, and good flavored.

Daniel O'Rourke.—A popular early sort; hardy, and a good bearer, but not so early as the Extra Early, or Caractacus; height 3 feet.

Alpha.—A new wrinkled variety, one of the earliest; flavor excellent; height 2½ feet.

McLean's Advancer.—A green wrinkled marrow of fine flavor; early, and a good bearer; height 2½ feet.

McLean's Little Gem.—An early wrinkled dwarf, and one of the best in cultivation; berry large size, and possessing an excellent sugary flavor; very prolific; height 2½ feet.

Second Early

Eugenie.—A white wrinkled marrow; an abundant bearer; pods long and well filled; good flavored; height 3 feet.

Bishop's Long-Podded Dwarf.—An early dwarf, and a good bearer; height 1 foot.

General Crop

Champion of England.—One of the best Peas in cultivation; a great bearer and of a delicious flavor; height 3 to 4 feet.

Dwarf Blue Imperial.—A good bearer; flavor fine; height 3 feet.

Tall Sugar.—Edible pods; height 5 feet.

Dwarf Sugar.—Edible pods; height 2 feet.

Large White Marrowfat.—An old variety, and a favorite market sort; height 6 feet.

Dwarf Marrowfat.—Similar to the Large White Marrowfat, but dwarfish habits.

Black Eyed Marrowfat.—An excellent market variety, and a good bearer; height 4 feet.

SQUASH

Culture.—Same as the cucumber. Hills for bush varieties should be four feet apart. The running varieties should be eight or nine feet apart.

Early Yellow Scollop Bush.—An early flat scollop bush variety. Rind deep yellow color, and smooth. Used, when tender, for boiling.

Early White Scollop Bush.—Larger and later than the yellow. Used mostly at the South.

Early Summer Crook-Neck Bush.—Very early and productive. Flesh very fine and rich.

Winter Crook-Neck.—Raised extensively in the Eastern States for winter use. Color sometimes green, but when fully ripe, is often cream yellow. Flesh salmon yellow, and fine flavored. Grown to a considerable extent for feeding stock.

Hubbard.—A fall variety, and, for table use, the best squash known. Shape oval, eight or ten inches long and seven or eight inches in diameter. Shell or rind hard and about an eighth of an inch thick. Color dull olive green. Flesh rich salmon yellow, very thick, fine grained, sweet, dry, and of a most excellent flavor.

Boston Marrow.—Fruit ovate, pointed at the extremity. Rind remarkably thin, cream yellow at the time of ripening. Flesh rich salmon yellow, fine grained, dry and sweet.

TOMATO

Culture.—Sow in hot-beds, and transplant after the weather becomes warm. Transplanting several times makes the vine more strong and vigorous. A warm, light soil is best. Tomatoes will produce much better if supported by trellises or bushes. An ounce contains twenty thousand seeds.

Early Smooth Red.—One of the earliest. Medium size, very smooth, round, and a good bearer.

Large Smooth Red.—Large size and smooth. Color bright red. A good market variety.

Tilden.—Color bright scarlet. Oval shaped, good size, smooth and solid. Flavor fine.

Feejee.—A pink colored, handsome smooth sort. Large size and good flavored.

Trophy.—New. One of the earliest varieties. The heaviest, smoothest and best tomato known.

Yellow pear shaped.—An excellent sort for pickling and for preserves.

Red Cherry.—A small, red tomato of the size and shape of a cherry.

Yellow Plum.—Oval and perfectly smooth. Color lemon yellow. Used for preserves.

*

From *Descriptive Catalogue of Vegetable Seeds*, Raised at New Lebanon, New York, 1873. A handful of Shakers, seeking religious freedom and a devoutly communal way of life, left England to settle in an area near Albany, New York, in 1774. In the decades that followed Shaker communities, soon supported by their self-sufficient agrarian and cottage industries, spread throughout rural New York, several New England states, Ohio, Kentucky, and Indiana. By the last two decades of the eighteenth century Shakers in various communities had started selling seeds, which were first peddled by wagon, later by mail, and even sent to Europe. Shakers were among the first in the country to offer seeds in paper packets, and to develop a systematic classification of medicinal herbs. They grew poppies and for a time most of the opium used in America came from the Shakers. Their herbal extracts and fruit products were in great demand. They also produced new vegetable varieties, putting on the market in the 1880s Shakers' Early Sweet corn, which was subsequently introduced by the reputable Thorburn seed house.

DeWitt Clinton Brainard (1828-1897), who headed the operations at Mt.

Lebanon (originally called New Lebanon), N.Y. which issued the catalogue excerpted here, was a noted Shaker seedsman of his day. His name appears on many of the now rare, colorful Shaker seed labels.

The Shakers, and their celibate, utopian ideals, are virtually extinct now. But the spirit of their quality workmanship is still to be savored in the tools, boxes, architecture, and, most triumphantly, in the furniture that reflects the simple, functional beauty of things unadorned.

A Description of North Carolina

John Lawson

THE WHEAT OF THIS PLACE IS VERY GOOD, SEL-dom yielding less than thirty fold, provided the Land is good where it is sown; Not but that there has been Sixty-six Increase for one measure sown in Piny-Land, which we account the meanest Sort. And I have been inform'd, by People of Credit, that Wheat which was planted in a very rich Piece of Land, brought a hundred and odd Pecks, for one. If our Planters, when they found such great Increase, would be so curious as to make nice Observations of the Soil, and other remarkable Accidents, they would soon be acquainted with the Nature of the Earth and Climate, and be better qualified to manage their Agriculture to more Certainty, and greater Advantage; whereby they might arrive to the Crops and Harvests of Babylon, and those other fruitful Countries so much talk'd of. For I must confess, I never saw one Acre of Land manag'd as it ought to be in Carolina, since I knew it; and were they as negligent in their Husbandry in Europe, as they are in Carolina, their Land would produce nothing but Weeds and Straw.

They have try'd Rye, and it thrives very well; but having such Plenty of Maiz, they do not regard it, because it makes black Bread, unless very curiously handled.

Barley has been sowed in small quantities, and does better than can be expected; because that Grain requires the Ground to be very well work'd with repeated Ploughings, which our general Way of breaking the Earth with Hoes, can, by no means, perform, tho' in several Places we have a light, rich, deep, black Mould, which is the particular Soil in which Barley best thrives.

The naked Oats thrive extraordinary well; and the other would prove a very bold Grain; but the Plenty of other Grains makes them not much coveted.

The Indian Corn, or Maiz, proves the most useful Grain in the World; and had it not been for the Fruitfulness of this Species, it would have proved very difficult to have settled some of the Plantations in America. It is very nourishing, whether in Bread, sodden, or otherwise; And those poor Christian Servants in Virginia, Maryland, and the other northerly Plantations, that have been forced to live wholly upon it, do manifestly prove, that it is the most nourishing Grain, for a Man to subsist on, without any other Victuals. And this Assertion is made good by the Negro-Slaves, who, in many Places, eat nothing but this Indian Corn and Salt. Pigs and Poultry fed with this Grain, eat the sweetest of all others. It refuses no Grounds, unless the barren Sands, and when planted in good Ground, will repay the Planter seven or eight hundred fold; besides the Stalks bruis'd and boil'd, make very pleasant Beer, being sweet like the Sugar-Cane.

There are several sorts of Rice, some bearded, others not, besides the red and white; But the white Rice is the best. Yet there is a sort of perfum'd Rice in the East-Indies, which gives a curious Flavour, in the Dressing. And with this sort America is not yet acquainted; neither can I learn, that any of it has been brought over to Europe; the Rice of Carolina being esteem'd the best that comes to that Quarter of the World. It is of great Increase, yielding from eight hundred to a thousand-fold, and thrives best in wild Land, that has never been broken up before.

Buck-Wheat is of great Increase in Carolina; but we make no other use of it, than instead of Maiz, to feed Hogs and Poultry: and Guinea Corn, which thrives well here, serves for the same use.

Of the Pulse-kind, we have many sorts. The first is the Bushel-Bean, which is a spontaneous Product. They are so called, because they bring a Bushel of Beans for one that is planted. They are set in the Spring, round Arbours, or at the Feet of Poles, up which they will climb, and cover the Wattling, making a very pretty Shade to sit under. They continue flowering, budding, and ripening all the Summer long, till the Frost approaches, when they forbear their Fruit, and die. The Stalks they grow on, come to the Thickness of a Man's Thumb; and the Bean is white and mottled, with a purple Figure on each side of it, like an Ear. They are very flat, and are eaten as a Windsor-Bean is, being an extraordinary well-relish'd Pulse, either by themselves, or with Meat.

We have the Indian Rouncival, or Miraculous Pease, so call'd from their long Pods, and great Increase. These are latter Pease, and require a pretty long Summer to ripen in. They are very good; and so are the Bonavis, Calavancies, Nanticokes, and abundance of other Pulse, too tedious here to name, which we found the Indians possess'd of, when first we settled in America; some of which sorts afford us two Crops in one Year; as the Bonavis and Calavancies, besides several others of that kind.

Now I am launch'd into a Discourse of the Pulse, I must acquaint you, that the European Bean planted here, will, in time, degenerate into a dwarfish sort, if not prevented by a yearly Supply of foreign Seed, and an extravagant rich Soil; yet these Pigmy-Beans are the sweetest of that kind I ever met withal.

As for all the sorts of English Pease that we have yet made tryal of, they thrive very well in Carolina. Particularly, the white and gray Rouncival, the common Field-Pease, and Sickle-Pease yield very well, and are of a good Relish. As for the other sorts, I have not seen any made tryal of as yet, but question not their coming to great Perfection with us.

The Kidney-Beans were here before the English came, being very plentiful in the Indian Corn-Fields.

The Garden-Roots that thrive well in Carolina, are Carrots, Leeks, Parsnips, Turneps, Potatoes, of several delicate sorts, Ground Artichokes, Radishes, Horse-Radish, Beet, both sorts, Onions, Shallot, Garlick, Cives, and the Wild-Onions.

The Sallads are the Lettuce, Curl'd, Red, Cabbage, and Savoy. The Spinage round and prickly, Fennel, sweet and the common Sort, Samphire in the Marshes excellent, so is the Dock or Wild-Rhubarb, Rocket, Sorrel, French and English, Cresses of several Sorts, Purslain wild, and that of a larger Size which grows in the Gardens; for this Plant is never met withal in the Indian Plantations, and is, therefore, suppos'd to proceed from Cow-Dung, which Beast they keep not. Parsley two Sorts: Asparagus thrives to a Miracle, without hot Beds or dunging the Land, White-Cabbage from European or New-England Seed, for the People are negligent and unskilful, and don't take care to provide Seed of their own. The Colly-Flower we have not yet had an Opportunity to make Tryal of, nor has the Artichoke ever appeared amongst us, that I can learn. Colewarts plain and curl'd, Savoys; besides the Water-Melons of several Sorts, very good, which should have gone amongst the Fruits. Of Musk-Melons we have very large and good, and several Sorts, as the Golden, Green, Guinea, and Orange. Cucumbers long, short, and prickly, all these from the Natural Ground, and great Increase, without any Helps of Dung or Reflection. Pompions yellow and very large, Burmillions, Cashaws, an excellent fruit boil'd; Squashes, Simnals, Horns, and Gourds, besides many other Species, of less Value, too tedious to name.

Our Pot-herbs and others of use, which we already possess, are Angelica wild and tame, Balm, Bugloss, Borage, Burnet, Clary, Marigold, Pot-Marjoram, and other Marjorams, Summer and Winter Savory, Columbines, Tansey, Wormwood, Nep, Mallows several Sorts, Drage red and white, Lambs Quarters, Thyme, Hyssop of a very large Growth, sweet Bazil, Rosemary, Lavender: The more Physical, are *Carduus Benedictus*, the Scurvy-grass of America, I never here met any of the European sort; Tobacco of many sorts, Dill, Carawa, Cummin, Anise, Coriander, all sorts of Plantain of England, and two sorts spontaneous, good Vulneraries; Elecampane, Comfrey, Nettle, the Seed from England, none Native; Monks Rhubarb, Burdock, Asarum wild in the Woods, reckon'd one of the Snake-Roots; Poppies in the Garden, none wild yet discover'd; Wormfeed, Feverfew, Rue, Ground-Ivy spontaneous, but very small and scarce, *Aurea virga*, four sorts of Snake-Roots, besides the common Species, which are great Antidotes against that Serpent's Bite, and are easily rais'd in the Garden; Mint; James-Town-Weed, so called from Virginia, the Seed it bears is very like that of an Onion; it is excellent for curing Burns, and asswaging Inflammations, but taken inwardly brings on a sort of drunken Madness. One of our Marsh-Weeds, like a Dock, has the same Effect, and possesses the Party with Fear and Watchings. The Red-Root whose Leaf is like Spear-Mint, is good for Thrushes and sore Mouths; Camomil, but it must be kept in the Shade, otherwise it will not thrive;

Housleek first from England; Vervin; Night-Shade, several kinds; Harts-Tongue; Yarrow abundance, Mullein the same, both of the Country; Sarsaparilla, and abundance more I could name, yet not the hundredth part of what remains, a Catalogue of which is a Work of many Years, and without any other Subject, would swell to a large Volume, and requires the Abilities of a skilful Botanist: Had not the ingenious Mr. Banister (the greatest Virtuoso we ever had on the Continent) been unfortunately taken out of this World, he would have given the best Account of the Plants of America, of any that ever yet made such an Attempt in these Parts. Not but we are satisfy'd, the Species of Vegetables in Carolina, are so numerous, that it requires more than one Man's Age to bring the chiefest Part of them into regular Classes; the Country being so different in its Situation and Soil, that what one place plentifully affords, another is absolutely a stranger to; yet we generally observe, that the greatest Variety is found in the Low Grounds, and Savanna's.

The Flower-Garden in Carolina is as yet arriv'd but to a very poor and jejune Perfection. We have only two sorts of Roses; the Clove-July-Flowers, Violets, Princes Feather, and *Tres Colores*. There has been nothing more cultivated in the Flower-Garden, which, at present, occurs to my Memory; but as for the wild spontaneous Flowers of this Country, Nature has been so liberal, that I cannot name one tenth part of the valuable ones.

*

From *A New Voyage to Carolina*, John Lawson (?-1712). London: W. Taylor, 1709; 1714 edition. Apparently, Lawson ended up in the Carolinas in 1700, after hearing exciting reports about the new country in England. He stayed on for eight years, becoming surveyor general. All the while Lawson familiarized himself with the seacoast, inland and mountain areas, and the animals, plants, minerals, the settlers and Indians living there; in general, the habits and habitats of human and other lives. He collected and shipped to England numerous plant and animal specimens. Lawson then wrote one of the pioneering natural histories of the country, his witty, observant *A New Voyage to Carolina* which was a promotional volume of sorts to excite other would-be travelers to the colonies. Historian Ann Leighton writes enthusiastically in *American Gardens in the Eighteenth Century* that ''not for another generation, until the travels of John and William Bartram, was Carolina so to stir the imagination of the Old World.'' Mark Catesby's stunning, illustrated natural history, which followed in the third and fourth decades of the eighteenth century, further whetted scientific and literary appetites abroad.

After returning to England for a year, Lawson made a second trip to the colonies, bringing with him several hundred Swiss and German immigrants who would found New Bern, South Carolina. Like many adventurers in the wild new land (the Mr. Banister referred to in the selection never completed his natural history of Virginia because he was accidentally shot while out botanizing), Lawson came to an unfortunate end. He was captured and killed by the Tuscarora Indians in 1712.

Planting of Lawns and Flower Beds

Peter Henderson

THE OLD-FASHIONED MIXED BORDERS OF FOUR or six feet wide along the walks of the fruit or vegetable garden, were usually planted with hardy herbaceous plants, the tall growing at the back, with the lower growing sorts in front. These, when there was a good collection, gave a bloom of varied color throughout the entire growing season. But the more modern style of flower borders has quite displaced such collections, and they are now but little seen, unless in very old gardens, or in botanical collections. Then again, we have the mixed borders of bedding plants, a heterogeneous grouping of all kinds of tropical plants, still holding to the plan of either placing the highest at the back of the border if it has only one walk, or if a bed has a walk on each side, the highest in the middle, and the plants sloping down to the walk on each side. The mixed system still has its advocates, who deprecate the modern plan of massing in color as being too formal, and too unnatural a way to dispose of flowers. But be that as it may, we will not stop to argue the matter further than to state, that in a visit to England in 1872, it was most evident that the ''carpet styles'' of massing plants as done at Battersea Park, London, were interesting to the people in a way that no mixed border could ever be. Any one who has not yet seen the wonderful effects produced by the massing of plants in this way, has a treat before him. Nearly all the public parks in and about London are so planted, and thousands of cottage gardens vie with each other in imitation of the parks. But to plant in patterns or in ribbon lines requires for immediate effect a large number of plants, for the reason that they must be so set out that they will meet to form continuous masses shortly after planting.

Of course it will be understood that a bed of any shape can be planted in this manner as well as circular beds, only keeping in view the width of the bed. For example, a bed having a diameter of ten feet may require eight or ten different kinds of plants to form the necessary contrast, while that of five feet will not require more than half that number. The following named plants are well suited for planting in masses or ribbon lines; they are named as nearly as possible in the order of their height, number one in each case being the tallest. Many of them will require to be ''pinched back'' to keep at the proper height, so that the outline will form a regular slope from the center or highest point, down to the front or lowest point—thus in list No.1, Canna Indica zebrina will grow six feet high, while Lobelia Paxtoni, the lowest, is less than six inches.

LIST NO. 1   *Average height in feet*

1. Canna Indica zebrina, leaves green and brown striped..6
2. Salvia splendens, flowers scarlet...5
3. Golden coleus, leaves orange and brown...4
4. Achyranthes Lindeni, leaves rich crimson 3
5. Phalaris arundinacea var., leaves white and green...2½
6. Achyranthes Gilsoni, leaves carmine...2
7. Bronze geranium, leaves golden bronze...1½
8. Centaurea candida, leaves white...1
9. Alternanthera latifolia, leaves crimson and yellow ....¾
10. Lobelia Paxtoni, flowers blue...½

LIST NO. 2   *Average height in feet*

1. Caladium esculentum, leaves large green 5
2. Japanese maize, leaves striped white and yellow...5
3. Coleus Verschaffeltii, leaves chocolate crimson 4
4. Delphinium bicolor, flowers blue and white 3
5. Cyperus alternifolius var., leaves white and green...2½
6. Achyranthes Verschaffeltii, leaves crimson...2
7. Mountain of snow geranium, leaves white and green 1½

8. Tropaeolum, Ball of Fire, flowers flame color..1

9. Echeveria metallica, leaves gray, metallic lustre..¾

10. Alternanthera amoena, yellow and carmine...½

It will be understood that these lists of plants can be transposed in any way necessary to suit beds of all widths, keeping in view that where small beds are placed near walks the lower growing kinds are most suitable, while for beds at greater distances from walks, or other points of view, the taller growing kinds must be used. Very fine effects are produced by planting on a lawn a single specimen of stately habit, such as some varieties of the ricinus, or castor-oil bean, which grow ten and twelve feet in height in one season, and are particularly striking plants. Or instead of this, a mass of six, eight, or twelve plants of scarlet sage will form a group six feet high by as many in diameter, and its dazzling scarlet color, contrasting against the green of the lawn, is superb. Many of the amaranths are also well suited for planting in single groups. *Amarantus tricolor gigantea* (Joseph's coat), grows to the height of six feet, and its leaves in the late summer and fall months exceed in brilliancy of color anything we know of in foliage; scarlet, crimson, and golden yellow predominating. Another, the *Amarantus bicolor ruber*, grows to the height of five feet, and is plumed with scarlet crimson. In contrast to these, plants of a more somber tint may be used, in individual specimens or in a group of such as pampas grass (*Gynerium argenteum*), or the ravenna grass (*Erianthus Ravennae*), each of these attain a height from six to ten feet, and have a graceful appearance. The tanyah, *Caladium esculentum*, a tropical looking plant growing three or four feet in height, and producing leaves sometimes eighteen inches across.

THE CARPET STYLE OF FLOWER BEDS

Planting, as practiced at Battersea and other parks in London, is as yet but little seen with us; our public parks here have shown a lamentable want of taste in this matter, especially those of New York and Brooklyn; Philadelphia and Boston have done better, but all of these are weak attempts when compared with the grounds of some of our private gentlemen, notable among whom are H. W. Sargent, of Peekskill, N.Y., and H. H. Hunnewell, of Boston. The grounds of

Mr. H. are thrown open to the public, who have the opportunity of seeing effects in this style of planting, nearly equal to anything in Europe,
entirely at the expense of the munificent owner. The carpet style, so
called, consists in using plants that can be kept down to a few inches
above the level of the lawn. A great variety of succulent plants are
used, such as echeverias, sedums, mesembryanthemums, etc., together
with numerous low-growing alpine plants, such as ajugas, cerastiums,
lysimachias, lobelias, ivies, alternantheras, etc., etc. This style of
bedding requires an immense number of plants. One bed in the carpet
style at Battersea Park, containing less than 1000 square feet, required
4000 plants to produce the desired effect in the design, and not a leaf of
these was more than six inches above the lawn. Planting in this style
admits of unlimited variety in the form of the beds, and contrasts of
colors; so great is the care exercised abroad in arranging the designs
that colored papers, giving the exact tints of the leading flowers and
colored foliage, are supplied by the dealers, in order that colored
designs may be made and studied before putting them into execution; a
single misplaced color may spoil the effect of the whole. In works of this
kind the parts of the design should be separated by well defined portions of turf, as the color of each member of it is brought out more
clearly and distinctly, and the whole has a much better effect if a liberal
amount of green is introduced.

*

From *Gardening for Pleasure*, Peter Henderson (1822-1890). New York:
Orange Judd Company, 1875. Henderson came to the U.S. from Scotland in
1843. His early years here he worked for nurserymen George Thorburn and
Robert Buist, and shortly afterwards started a market gardening business with
his brother in Jersey City, New Jersey. In the years 1871-1890 he ran the
famous seed and garden supply house, Peter Henderson and Company, in New
York City. An authority on floriculture, he wrote several successful books,
including *Gardening for Profit*, *Handbook of Plants*, and *Henderson's Practical Floriculture*, in the last quarter of the nineteenth century.

In the excerpt published here, Henderson champions the geometric carpet
bedding and ribbon styles of planting, the antithesis of natural design. A few

years after *Gardening for Pleasure* was written, William Robinson published his highly influential book, *The English Flower Garden*, which criticized the Victorian custom of bedding-out. Nonetheless, now more than a hundred years later, carpet-like beds of flowers can be seen about such diverse sites as palace gardens, parks, highways, schools, museums, railroad stations, state buildings, and gas stations—in the U.S., Europe, and Great Britain.

The Altar and the Shrine

Celia Thaxter

OPENING OUT ON THE LONG PIAZZA OVER THE flower beds, and extending almost its whole length, runs the large, light, airy room where a group of happy people gather to pass the swiftly flying summers here at the Isles of Shoals. This room is made first for music; on the polished floor is no carpet to muffle sound, only a few rugs here and there, like patches of warm green moss on the pine-needle color given by the polish to the natural hue of the wood. There are no heavy draperies to muffle the windows, nothing to absorb the sound. The piano stands midway at one side; there are couches, sofas with pillows of many shades of dull, rich color, but mostly of warm shades of green. There are low bookcases round the walls, the books screened by short curtains of pleasant olive-green; the high walls to the ceiling are covered with pictures, and flowers are everywhere. The shelves of the tall mantel are splendid with massed nasturtiums like a blazing torch, beginning with the palest yellow, almost white, and piled through every deepening shade of gold, orange, scarlet, crimson, to the blackest red; all along the tops of the low bookcases burn the fires of marigolds, coreopsis, large flowers of the velvet single dahlias in yellow, flame, and scarlet of many shades, masses of pure gold summer chrysanthemums, and many more—all here and there interspersed with blossoming grasses for a touch of ethereal green. On one low bookcase are Shirley poppies in a roseate cloud. And here let me say that the secret of keeping poppies in the house two whole days without fading is this: they must be gathered early, before the dew has dried, in the morning. I go forth between five and six o'clock to cut them while yet their gray-green leaves are hoary with dew, taking a tall slender pitcher or bottle of water with me into the garden, and as I cut each stem dropping the flower at once into it, so that the stem is covered nearly its whole length with water; and so on till the pitcher is full. Gathered in this way, they have no opportunity to lose their freshness, indeed, the exquisite creatures hardly know they have been gathered at all. When I have all I need, I begin on the left end of this bookcase, which most felicitously fronts the light, and into the glasses put the radiant blossoms with an infinite enjoyment of the work. The glasses (thirty-two in all) themselves are beautiful: nearly all are white, clear and pure, with a few pale green and paler rose and delicate blue, one or two of richer pink, all brilliantly clear and filled with absolutely colorless water, through which the stems show their slender green lengths. Into the glasses at this end on the left I put first the dazzling white single poppy, the Bride, to lead the sweet procession—a marvelous blossom, whose pure white is half transparent, with its central altar of ineffable green and gold. A few of these first, then a dozen or more of delicate tissue paper-like blossoms of snow in still another variety (with petals so thin that a bright color behind them shows through their filmy texture); then the double kind called Snowdrift, which being double makes a deeper body of whiteness flecked with softest shadow. Then I begin with the palest rose tints, placing them next, and slightly mingling a few with the last white ones—a rose tint delicate as the palm of a baby's hand; then the next, with a faint suffusion of a blush, and go on to the next shade, still very delicate, not deeper than the soft hue on the lips of the great whelk shells in southern seas; then the damask rose color and all tints of tender pink, then the deeper tones to clear, rich cherry, and on to glowing crimson, through a mass of this to burning maroon.

The flowers are of all heights (the stems of different lengths), and, though massed, are in broken and irregular ranks, the tallest standing a little over two feet high. But there is no crushing or crowding. Each individual has room to display its full perfection. The color gathers, softly flushing from the snow white at one end, through all rose, pink, cherry, and crimson shades, to the note of darkest red; the long stems of tender green showing through the clear glass, the radiant tempered gold of each flower illuminating the whole. Here and there a few leaves, stalks, and buds (if I can bring my mind to the cutting of these last) are sparingly interspersed at the back. The effect of this arrangement is perfectly beautiful. It is simply indescribable, and I have seen people stand before it mute with delight. It is like the rose of dawn.

To the left of this altar of flowers is a little table, upon which a picture stands and leans against the wall at the back. In the picture two tea roses long since faded live yet in their exquisite hues, never indeed to die. Before this I keep always a few of the fairest flowers, and call this table the shrine. Sometimes it is a spray of Madonna lilies in a long white vase of ground glass, or beneath the picture in a jar of yellow glass floats a saffron-tinted water lily, the chromatella, or a tall sapphire glass holds deep blue larkspurs of the same shade, or in a red Bohemian glass vase are a few carmine sweet peas, another harmony of color, or a charming dull red Japanese jar holds a few nasturtiums that exactly repeat its hues. The lovely combinations and contrasts of flowers and vases are simply endless.

On another small table below the ''altar'' are pink water lilies in pink glasses and white ones in white glasses; a low basket of amber glass is filled with the pale turquoise of forget-me-nots, the glass is iridescent and gleams with changing reflections, taking tints from every color near it. Sweet peas are everywhere about and fill the air with fragrance; orange and yellow Iceland poppies are in tall vases of English glass of light green. There is a large, low bowl, celadon-tinted, and decorated with the boughs and fruit of the olive on the gray-green background. This is filled with magnificent Jacqueminot roses, so large, so deep in color as to fully merit the word. Sometimes they are mixed with pink Gabrielle de Luizets and old-fashioned damask roses, and the bowl is set where the light falls just as it should to give the splendor of the flowers its full effect. In the center of a round table under one of the chandeliers is a flaring Venice glass as pure as a drop of dew and of a quaintly lovely shape; on the crystal water therein lies a single white water lily, fragrant snow and gold. By itself is a low vase shaped like a magnolia flower, with petals of light yellow deepening in color at the bottom, where its calyx of olive-green leaves clasps the flower. This has looking over its edge a few pale yellow nasturtiums of the Asa Gray variety, the lightest of all. With these, one or two of a richer yellow (Dunnett's Orange), the flowers repeating the tones of the vase, and with them harmoniously blending. A large pearly shell of the whelk tribe was given me years ago. I did not know what to do with it. I do not like flowers in shells as a rule, and I think the shells are best on the beach where they belong, but I was fond of the giver, so I sought some way of utilizing the gift. In itself it was beautiful, a mass of glimmering rainbows. I bored three holes in its edge and suspended it from one of the severely simple chandeliers with almost invisible wires. I keep it filled with water and in it arrange sometimes clusters of monthly honeysuckle sparingly; the hues of the flowers and the shell mingle and blend divinely. I get the same effect with hydrangea flowers, tints and tones all melt together; so also with the most delicate sweet peas, white, rose, and lilac; with these I take some lengths of the blossoming wild cucumber vine with its light clusters of white flowers, or the white clematis, the kind called "Traveler's Joy," and weave it lightly about the shell, letting it creep over one side and, running up the wires, entirely conceal them; then it is like a heavenly apparition afloat in mid air. Sometimes the tender mauve and soft rose and delicate blues of the exquisite little Rose Campion, or Rose of Heaven, with its grassy foliage, swing in this rainbow shell, making another harmony of hues.

Sometimes it is draped with wild morning glory vines which are gathered with their buds at evening; their long wiry stems I coil in the water, and arrange the graceful lengths of leaves and buds carefully, letting a few droop over the edge and twine together beneath the shell, and some run up to the chandelier and conceal the wires. The long smooth buds, yellow-white like ivory, deepen to a touch of bright rose at the tips close folded. In the morning all the buds open into fair trumpets of sea-shell pink, turning to every point of the compass, an exquisite sight to see. By changing the water daily these vines last a week, fresh buds maturing and blossoming every morning.

Near my own seat in a sofa corner at one of the south windows stands yet another small table, covered with a snow-white linen cloth embroidered in silk as white and lustrous as silver. On this are gathered every day all the rarest and loveliest flowers as they blossom, that I may touch them, dwell on them, breathe their delightful fragrance and adore them. Here are kept the daintiest and most delicate of the vases which may best set off the flowers' loveliness—the smallest of the collection, for the table is only large enough to hold a few. There is one slender small tumbler of colorless glass, from the upper edge of which a crimson stain is diffused half way down its crystal length. In this I keep one glowing crimson Burgundy rose, or an opening Jacqueminot bud; the effect is as if the color of the rose ran down and dyed the glass crimson. It is so beautiful an effect one never wearies of it. There is a little jar of Venice glass, the kind which Browning describes in ''The Flight of the Duchess''—

> With long white threads distinct inside,
> Like the lake-flower's fibrous roots that dangle
> Loose such a length and never tangle.

This is charming with a few rich pinks of different shades. Another Venice glass is irregularly bottle-shaped, bluish white with cool sea-green reflections at the bottom, very delicate, like an aqua-marine. It is lightly sprinkled with gold dust throughout its whole length; toward the top the slender neck takes on a soft touch of pink which meets and mingles with the Bon Silene or La France rose I always keep in it. Another Venice glass still is a wonder of iridescent blues, lavenders, gray, and gold, all through, with a faint hint of elusive green. A spray of heaven-blue larkspur dashed with rose is delicious in this slender shape, with its marvelous tints melting into the blue and pink of the fairy flowers.

A little glass of crystal girdled with gold holds pale blue forget-me-nots; sometimes it is rich with orange and yellow erysimum flowers. In a tall Venetian vase of amber a *Lilium auratum* is superb. A low jar of opaque rose-pink, lost at the bottom in milky whiteness, is refreshing with an old-fashioned damask rose matching its color exactly. This is also exquisite with one pink water lily. The pink variety of the Rose Campion is enchanting in this low jar. A tall shaft of ruby glass is radiant with poppies of every shade of rose and lightest scarlet, with the silvery green of a few oats among them. A slender purple glass is fine with different shades of purple and lilac sweet peas, or one or two purple poppies, or an aster or two of just its color, but there is one long gold-speckled Bohemian glass of rich green which is simply perfect for any flower that blows, and perfect under any circumstances. A half dozen Iceland poppies, white, yellow, orange, in a little Japanese porcelain bottle, always stand on this beautiful table, the few flecks of color on the bottle repeating their tints. I never could tell half the lovely combinations that glow on this table all summer long.

*

From *An Island Garden*, Celia Thaxter (1835-1894). Boston: Houghton Mifflin, 1894. Childe Hassam illustrated the original edition of this book, with several beautiful Impressionist paintings of Thaxter's garden and surroundings on the Isles of Shoals, off the Maine coast. Her family ran a large resort hotel on Appledore Island, whose guests included Richard Henry Dana, Thoreau, Emerson, Hawthorne, James Russell Lowell, and Sarah Orne Jewett. A poet whose work appeared in *Scribner's, Harper's* and *Atlantic Monthly,* and an expert gardener, Thaxter was positively rhapsodic about everyday life among her flowers. Over the last ten years the Shoals Marine Laboratory has begun the work of reconstructing her famous garden from the detailed accounts of it she left in her writing.

Recent Progress in American Horticulture

Liberty Hyde Bailey

There is a large class of our horticultural public which disparages these modern times as in no way so good as those of several or many years ago. These men are mostly gardeners who were apprenticed in their youth. There is another class which decries the introduction of new varieties of plants, thinking these novelties to be unreliable and deceitful. There are others who are content with the older things, and who have never had occasion to ask if there has been any progress in recent years. Others have looked for progress, but have not found it. A professor of horticulture told me a few days ago that nothing new or interesting seems to be transpiring in the horticultural world. Some people even deny outright that any progress is making [sic—ed.] at the present time. On the other hand, there are some, perhaps the minority, who contend that they see great advancement. . . .

I may say here that I care little for any facts or illustrations of progress merely as facts. There must be some law, some tendency, some profound movement underlying it all, and this we must discover. I shall not attempt, therefore, to indicate how great the progress has been in any definite time, but endeavor to ascertain if there is progression which gains impetus with the years.

1. *There is a progressive variation in plants.* Horticulture is concerned with the cultivation of plants. The plant is the beginning and the end. For the plant we till the soil, build greenhouses, and transact the business of the garden. All progress, therefore, rests upon the possibility of securing better varieties—those possessing greater intrinsic merit in themselves, or better adaptations to certain purposes or regions. In other words, all progress rests upon the fact that evolution is still operative, that garden plants, like wild animals and plants, are more or less constantly undergoing modification.

American horticulture may be said to have begun with the opening of the century. It was in 1806 that Bernard M'Mahon wrote his *American Gardener's Calendar.* This work contains a catalogue of 3700 "species and varieties of the most valuable and curious plants hitherto discovered." Among the cultivated varieties of fruits and vegetables, the present reader will see few familiar names. He will observe among the fruits, however, some American types, showing that even at that date American pomology had begun to diverge from the English and French which gave it birth. This is especially true of the apples, for of the 59 kinds in the catalogue, about 66 percent are of American origin. Several nurseries were established in the next 30 years, and fresh importations of European varieties were made, so that when Andrew Jackson Downing, in 1845, described the 190 apples known to be growing in this country, American varieties had fallen to 52 percent. In 1872, however, when almost 2000 varieties were described in Downing's second revision, the American kinds had risen to 65 or more percent, or to about the proportion which they occupied at the opening of the century. At the present time the percentage of varieties of American origin is much higher, and if we omit from our calculations the obsolete varieties, we find that over 80 percent of the apples actually cultivated in the older apple regions at the present time are of American origin. The percentage of native varieties, in other words, has risen from nothing to 80 percent since the apple settlement of the country, and at least once during this time the native productions have recovered from an overwhelming onslaught of foreigners. Except in the cold north and northwest, where the apple industry is now experiencing an immigration not unlike that which befell the older states early in the century, few people would think of importing varieties of apples with the expectation that they shall prove to be a commercial success in America. Other plants have shown most astounding development. In 1889 39 varieties of chrysanthemums were introduced in North America, in 1890 57 varieties, and in 1891 121 varieties. The chrysanthemum is now the princess of flowers, yet in 1806 M'Mahon barely mentioned it, and there were no named varieties.

All this is evidence of the greatest and most substantial progress, and much of it is recent; and there is every reason to believe that this rapid adaptation of plants to new conditions is still in progress in all cultivated species. In fact, the initial and conspicuous stage of such adaptation is just now taking place in the Russian apples in America, in which the American seedlings are even now gaining a greater prominence than some of their parents. Both the parent stock and the seedling brood are radical and progressive departures of recent date. The same modification to suit American environments is seen in every plant which has been cultivated here for a score or more of years. The mulberries are striking examples, for our fruit-bearing varieties are not only different from those of Europe, whence they came, but many of them belong to a species which in Europe is not esteemed for fruit. The European varieties of almonds are now being superseded in California by native seedlings, which are said to be much better adapted to our Pacific climate than their recent progenitors are.

There is another feature of this contemporaneous variation which must be considered at this point—the great increase in numbers of varieties. This increase is in part simply an accumulation of the varieties of many years, so that our manuals are apt to contain descriptions of more varieties than are actually cultivated at the time. But much of this increase is an actual multiplication of varieties. That is, there are more varieties of nearly all plants in cultivation now than at any previous time. M'Mahon mentions 6 beets as grown at his time; in 1889 there were 42 kinds. Then there were 14 cabbages, now there are over 100. Then there were 16 lettuces, against about 120 now. He mentions 59 apples; now there are about 2500 described in our books. He mentions 40 pears, against 1000 now. There were something over 450 species of garden plants native to the United States mentioned by M'Mahon; now there are over 2000 in cultivation. These figures are average examples of the marvelous increase in varieties during the century. I may be met here with the technical objection that M'Mahon did not make a complete catalogue of the plants of his time. This may be true, but it was meant to be practically complete, and it is much the fullest of any early list. Gardening occupied such a limited area a century ago that it could not have been a burdensome task to collect very nearly all the varieties in existence; and any omissions are undoubtedly much overbalanced by the shortcomings of the contemporaneous figures which I have given you. It is certainly true that during the nineteenth century, varieties of all the leading species of cultivated plants have multiplied in this country from 100 percent to 1000 percent. This variation still continues, and the sum of novelties of any year probably exceeds that of the preceding year. Every generation sees, for the most part, a new type of plants.

But I suppose that these statements as to the increase of varieties will be accepted without further proof. The question is whether all this increase represents progress. Many poor varieties have been introduced, beyond a doubt, but I am convinced that the general tendency is decidedly progressive. You may cite me the fact that we have not improved upon the Rhode Island Greening and Fall Pippin apples, the Montmorenci cherry, the Green Gage plum, and other varieties which were in cultivation at the opening of the century, as proof of a contrary conviction; but I shall answer that we now have a score of apples as good as the Greening, although we may have none better. This habit of saying that we have not improved upon certain old plants is really a fallacy, for the reference is always made to quality of fruit alone; and, furthermore, the test of progress is not the supplanting of a good variety, but the origination of varieties which shall meet new demands. The more numerous and diverse the varieties of any plant, the more successful will be its cultivation over a wide area, because the greatest number of different conditions—as soils, climates and uses—will be satisfactorily met. If we had at present only the apples which were grown in M'Mahon's time, apple culture in the prairie states, in our bleak northwest, and even in some of the apple sections of Ontario, would be impossible. We are constantly extending our borders of the cultivation of all fruits by means of these new varieties. The horticultural settlement of our great west and of the cold north is one of the wonders of the time. . . .

2. *There is a constant augmentation in new specific types of plants, both from our native flora and by importation from without.* I suppose

that there is no parallel to the marvelous evolution of native fruits in America. Within a century we have procured the grapes, cranberries, the most popular gooseberries, some of the mulberries, the raspberries and blackberries, the pecans and some of the chestnuts, from our wild species. Perhaps some of the strawberries can be traced to the same source. There are many men still living who remember when there was no commercial cultivation of these fruits. Here is progress enough for one century; yet an overwhelming host of new types is coming upon us. I sometimes think that the improved native plants are coming forward so rapidly that we do not properly appreciate them. Witness the perplexing horde of native plums, the varieties even now reaching nearly 200, which are destined to occupy a much larger area of North America than the European plum now occupies. New species of grapes are now coming into cultivation. The dewberries, juneberry, Crandall currant type, buffalo berry, wild apples, and more than a score of lesser worthies, are now spreading into our gardens. Many of these things will be among the staples a hundred years to come. One hundred and eighty-five species of native plants, some for fruit but mostly for ornament, were introduced into commerce last year; and the number of plants native to North America north of Mexico which have come into cultivation is 2416. Under the stimulus of new conditions, some of these species will vary into hundreds, perhaps thousands, of new forms, and our horticulture will become the richest in the world. It is a privilege to live when great movements are conceived and new agencies first lend themselves to the dominion of man.

Many species have come to us from various parts of the world throughout the century, but the immigration still continues, and perhaps is greater now than at any previous time. It is well nigh impossible to chronicle the new types of ornamental plants which have come to America during the last two decades. Consider the overwhelming introduction of species of orchids alone. Even the wholly new types of fruits are many. Over 25 species of edible plants have come to America comparatively recently from Japan alone, and some of these species are already very important. Two of them, the Japanese persimmons and the Japanese plums, are most signal additions, probably exceeding in value any other introduction of species not heretofore in the country, made during the last quarter-century. During the years 1889, 1890 and 1891, some 380 species of plants not in commercial cultivation here were introduced into North America, partly from abroad and partly from our own flora. In 1891 alone, 219 distinct species were introduced.

Valuable as these new types are in themselves, all experience teaches that we are to expect better things from their cultivated and variable progeny. We can scarcely conceive what riches the future will bring.

3. *There is great progress in methods of caring for plants.* The manner of cultivating and caring for plants has changed much during recent years. It is doubtful if all this change represents actual progress in methods, but it indicates inquiry and growth, and it must eventually bring us to the ideal treatment of plants. Some of the change is simply a see-saw from one method to another, according as our knowledge seems to point more strongly in one direction than another. In one decade we may think lime to be an indispensable fertilizer, and in the next it may be discarded; yet we may eventually find that both positions are tenable. Yet there has been a decided uplift in methods of simple tillage and preparation of land and the science of fertilizing the soil; and, moreover, the application of this knowledge is widespread where it was once local or rare. And the application of machinery and mechanical devices to almost every horticultural labor cannot have escaped the attention of the most careless observer.

Among specific horticultural industries, the recent evolution of the glass house has been remarkable. In 1806 the greenhouse was still a place in which to keep plants green, and M'Mahon felt obliged to disapprove of living rooms over it to keep the roof from freezing, because they are ''not only an additional and unnecessary expense, but they give the building a heavy appearance.'' The first American greenhouse of which we have a picture, with a wooden roof and heavy sides, was built in 1764. Glass houses increased in numbers very slowly until the middle of this century, and they can only now be said to be popular. Twenty years ago a glass house was a luxury or an enterprise suited only to large concerns, and the management of it was to most intelligent people an impenetrable mystery. At the present time, even the humblest gardener, if he is thrifty, can afford a greenhouse. In fact, the glass house is rapidly coming to be an indispensable adjunct to nearly all kinds of progressive gardening. . . .

The first days of the commercial forcing of plants are still within the memory of many of this audience; and it is only within the present decade that great attention has been given in this country to the forcing of tomatoes, cucumbers, carnations, and many other plants. The business is yet in its infancy. The greenhouse has also exerted a marked influence upon the plants which are grown in them. There has now appeared a list of varieties of various plants which are especially adapted to the purposes of forcing; and this phenomenon is probably the most important and cogent proof of contemporaneous evolution.

If one were asked off-hand what is the most conspicuous recent advancement in horticulture, he would undoubtedly cite the advent of the sprays for destroying insects and fungi. These are not only eminently effective, but they were perfected at a time when dismay had overtaken very many of our horticulturists, and they have inspired new hope everywhere, and have stimulated the planting of fruit and ornamentals. I fancy that the future historian will find that the advent of the spray in the latter part of this century marked an important epoch in agricultural pursuits. Yet this epoch is not disconnected from the era before it. It is but a natural outcome or consequence of the rapid increase of insect and fungous enemies, which increase, in turn, is induced by the many disturbing influences of cultivation itself. When we devise effective means of checking the incursions of our foes, therefore, we are only keeping pace with the initial progress fostered by the origination of new varieties and the quickening commercial life of our time. Yet the era of spraying is none the less a mark of great achievement, and we have not yet seen the good of which it will ultimately prove to be capable. But a greater achievement than this must be made before we shall have reached the ideal and inevitable method of combating external pests; we must learn to so control natural agencies that one will counteract another. Nature keeps all her forces and agencies in comparative equilibrium by pitting one against another in the remorseless struggle for existence. The introduction of insect parasites and predaceans, entomogenous fungi, colonization of insectivorous birds, and the use of strategy in cultivation and in the selection of immune species and varieties, and the planning of rotations and companionships of plants, will eventually be so skillfully managed that most of our enemies will be kept under measurable control. A short rotation is now known to be the best means of combating wireworms and several other pests. The first great success in this direction in America is the introduction of the Australian vedalia, or lady-bug, to devour the most pestiferous of the orange-tree scales on the Pacific coast. This experiment is pregnant of greater and more abiding results than all the achievements of the sprays. But in your generation and mine, men must shoulder their squirt-guns as our ancestors shouldered their muskets, and see only the promise of time when they shall be beaten into pruning-hooks and plowshares and there shall come the peace of a silent warfare!

4. *There is great progress in the methods of handling and preserving horticultural products.* I need not tell the older men in this audience that there has been progress in the methods of handling fruits. When they were boys, apples and even peaches were taken to market loose in a wagon-box. We have all seen the development of the special-package industry, beginning first with rough bushel baskets or rude crates, then a better made and smaller package, which was to be returned to the consignor, and finally the trim and tasty gift packages of the present day. . . .

Perhaps we owe to a Frenchman the first distinct exposition, some eighty years ago, of a process of preserving perishable articles in hermetically sealed cans; but the process first gained prominence in the United States, and it became known as canning. In 1825, James Monroe signed patents to Thomas Kensett and Ezra Daggett to cover an improvement in the art of preserving, although Kensett appears to have practiced his method somewhat extensively as early as 1819. Isaac Winslow, of Maine, is supposed to have been the pioneer in canning sweet-corn, in 1842. About 1847 the canning industry began to attract general attention, and in that year the tomato was first canned. The exodus to California in 1849 stimulated the industry by creating a demand for unperishable eatables in compact compass. North America now leads the world in the extent, variety, and excellence of its canned products, and much of the material is the product of orchards and gardens. . . .

5. *There is a corresponding evolution in the horticulturist.* The rapidity with which education and general intelligence have spread in recent years is patent to every one. The rural classes have risen with the rest, but among the agricultural pursuits horticulture has probably shown the greatest advance in this respect . . . Downing rejoiced in 1852 that there were ''at least a dozen societies in different parts of the Union devoted to the improvement of gardening, and to the dissemination of information on the subject.'' Since that time a dozen national

horticultural societies of various kinds have come into prosperous existence, and there are over fifty societies representing states, provinces, or important geographical districts, while the number of minor societies runs into the hundreds. Over fifty states, territories, and provinces have established agricultural schools and experiment stations, all supported by popular sentiment. The derision of ''book farming'' is well nigh forgotten. Subjects which a few years ago were thought to be ''theoretical'' and irrelevant are now matters of common conversation. In short, a new type of man is coming onto the farms. This uplift in the common understanding of the science of cultivation, and of the methods of crossing and skillful selection, is exerting a powerful accelerating influence upon the variation of cultivated plants. But the most important and abiding evolution is that of the man himself; and I expect that the rising intellectual status will ultimately lead people to the farm rather than away from it. We are just now living in a time of conspicuous artificialism; but the farm must be tilled, and it must be inviting. When agriculture cannot pay, something is wrong with the times.

*

From *The Survival of the Unlike*, Liberty Hyde Bailey (1858-1954). New York: The Macmillan Company, 1896; sixth edition, 1911. One of the outstanding scientific minds in the field of horticulture, Bailey left his home in Michigan in 1888 to accept a professorship at Cornell University, which was to be his base for the rest of his professional life. In 1904 he became the first dean of the New York State College of Agriculture and director of its experiment station at Geneva, where he was also to establish the Bailey Hortorium herbarium. At the start, Bailey helped move the horticulture field further into modern science, through his interests in hybridization, plant pathology, plant breeding, and nomenclature. An evolutionist who first read Darwin's *Origin of the Species* as a teenager, Bailey, who was at one time the illustrious botanist Asa Gray's assistant, investigated plant origins, and promoted the study of plants in their natural environment, not as mere specimens for research in a laboratory, which was more commonly practiced then. He also collected plants on several continents into his eighties. Bailey wrote an astounding number of books—over sixty—in addition to his teaching and research. One of them,

Hortus (now in its third edition), an inventory and classification of all the plants cultivated in the U.S., Canada, Puerto Rico, and Hawaii is the most authoritative reference work on North American horticulture.

A life-long educator in the broadest sense of the word, Bailey believed in making scientific knowledge accessible to non-specialists. He supported nature study and botany in the schools, extension services in the countryside, wrote training manuals for teachers of agriculture, and others for the gardener and farmer, and he lectured widely on sociological issues, on forests, flowers, and trees. He wrote poetry, too. In 1908 President Theodore Roosevelt appointed him Chairman of the Country-Life Commission, set up to study and propose legislation to improve rural social and commercial life. What is exemplary in Bailey's activities is his linkage of social and economic relationships in the garden or farm to the larger community, and commerce and experimentation to ecology. Bailey worked in the best scientific tradition which articulates issues in a manner that leads to greater understanding of the nature of human life in the universe.

Bailey lived to be ninety-six, his life spanning the period of Reconstruction and the years just after World War II. His thinking was forced to confront the changes in horticulture, forestry, agriculture, and education, the rise of industrialization, urbanization and capitalism in a young country struggling to absorb such transformations. In the labor of his life and work, Bailey left a legacy which suggests that it is ever more urgent to consider human issues in relation to technology, and with the greatest philosophic and scientific care.

Hamburgers and Houseplants

Roger B. Swain

Marvel for a moment at the common-ness of hamburgers and houseplants. Both the philodendron and the all-beef patty are now staples of American life. No one pulls the shades at night, not because modesty has been forgotten, but because shade pulling has become both impossible and unnecessary—so dense are the flowerpots on the windowsills, so thick are the leaves against the glass. Humidity is up, headroom is down. Trip over the potted palm beside the sofa and risk being throttled by verdant macrame on the way down. Plants threaten to take over all but the darkest corner of every room, and yet we go on accumulating new ones, an unusual maidenhair fern one week, a cute little peperomia the next.

When we aren't buying houseplants, we are buying hamburgers. Millions of them. Blue-cheese burgers at business lunches, Big Macs with the kids. College students have an Elsie's Burger if they miss dinner, a triple cheeseburger at the Grill to get through the night. Once upon a time we ate tunafish sandwiches, peanut butter and jelly, cream cheese and olive. Now we eat hamburgers. We want them fast; we want them cheap. In return, we will tolerate jingles, billboards, and yellow arches.

We all know how common houseplants and hamburgers are. Few of us realize what they have in common. Houseplants are being treated as appliances. A fully furnished apartment comes with an air conditioner, a microwave oven, and a parlor palm. You can buy all these at K-Mart, and this gives the impression that, like other appliances, the indoor greenery originated in Chicago, Detroit, or West Bend. It did not. The Christmas cactus came from Brazil; the anthurium, from Colombia; the flaming sword, from French Guiana. Plant after plant is the descendant of some specimen collected by a plant hunter in tropical South America. *Aphelandra, Billbergia, Codonanthe, Dieffenbachia*—even a partial list would run through the alphabet and back.

Anyone who stops to think about the cultural requirements of our houseplants might deduce their tropical origin. Few would suspect it about hamburgers. On the menu there is always a picture of a Black Angus or Hereford steer, belly deep in western grass. Hamburgers are an American product all right, but not necessarily a North American one. The beef in the next hamburger you eat may well have come from Latin America.

In 1978, when the price of beef increased 35 percent in five months, the U.S. government decided to increase the amount of imported beef. Imported beef is much cheaper than beef grown in the United States. The 1978 wholesale price of beef imported from Central America was $1.47 per kilogram, compared to $3.30 for grass-fed beef grown in the United States. Although the amount of imported beef came to less than 1 percent of the total beef eaten in this country, government economists calculated that the imports would cut five cents off the price of every hamburger.

The government economists did not mention what increasing our consumption of imported beef would do to houseplants. The herds of Brahman cattle whose beef is shipped to the United States to be made into hamburgers and other processed meats are being raised on the same ground our houseplants came from. From Mexico to Brazil, tropical rainforests are being cut down to make new pastures. In some instances, the forest is simply doused with herbicide and set afire when the foliage dries out. In others, axes, chain saws, and bulldozers do the job. In any case, seldom is any of the wood even saved, so great is the pressure to get grass started and cattle herds established. Approximately 20,000 square kilometers of tropical rain forest in Latin America is being destroyed every year. Put another way, it will take less than six years to clear an area the size of Pennsylvania. One-quarter of all the forests in Central America have been destroyed in the last twenty years. Even the great forests of the Amazon are imperiled by Brazil's determination to become the world's biggest exporter of beef.

Boxcar statistics fail to capture the drama of felling even a single forest giant. As the chain saw begins to cut into a supporting buttress, spewing a plume of bright red sawdust, the parrots, the toucans, the oropendolas, and the howler monkeys who have been feeding in the tree's crown flee noisily. As the vibrations and exhaust reach them, the bats hanging upside down in the tree's interior awake from their day's sleep. Higher up the trunk, stingless bees pour out of a wax tube that marks the entrance to their nest. Out on a limb, thousands of ants rush about in search of the intruder. In the crown, nearly a hundred feet from the ground, the *Anolis* lizards, several species of frogs, a tree boa, and a sloth all sense that something is amiss, but they are too small or slow to do anything about it.

With all the buttresses on one side cut away, the sawyer begins the backcut. In only a moment the huge tree begins to lean. The sawyer, doing what none of the tree's inhabitants can do, flees to safety. Lianas, some as thick as a man's leg and as sinewy, hang from the tree and link it to adjacent smaller ones. For a moment it seems as though they might keep it from falling. But the tree's crown has too many epiphytes growing in it, too much moss, too many ferns, orchids, and bromeliads. The very luxuriance of the tree's canopy will speed its death. Lianas drawn tight snap the lesser trunks. The great tree, joined by its neighbors, crashes to the ground. It does not even bounce. When a tornado hits a cathedral, it is a tragedy. When such a tree falls, no one mourns. Whether its inhabitants are killed by the impact, or by desiccation, or incinerated in the fires that will shortly sweep through is unimportant.

Who knows what new medicines are being consumed by the flames, what oils, resins, dyes, spices, and insecticides; what unique genetic material that might someday be used for breeding; what plants that might someday grace our homes? Five out of six tropical organisms have never been identified, but that is not important.

What is important is cows. Slow, stupid, introduced beasts who know nothing of the grandeur that once occupied the ground on which they stand. It takes four years for them to reach full size; then they are slaughtered and their carcasses are reduced to hamburgers.

In less than a decade, the soil is too poor to grow grass, heavy rains have washed out the nutrients, erosion has scarred the land. Even heavy applications of fertilizer will not restore it. Scrub growth on which the cattle will not feed takes over. This is no problem. The rancher simply moves on to another piece of primary rain forest and starts again.

What can we do? Obviously, we can cut down on the amount of beef we eat. During World War I, the hamburger was renamed the Liberty Burger. Let's rename it once more. Call it a ''rain forest burger'' and eat fewer of them.

*

From *Field Days: Journal of an Itinerant Biologist*, Roger B. Swain (1949-   ). New York: Charles Scribner's Sons, 1983. It is always a pleasure to read the civilized writer who finds mystery and joy everywhere in his world. Swain transforms complexities of science into the most lucid reflections on the inter-connectedness of plant, animal, and human lives. Science editor of *Horticulture* magazine, and author of *Earthly Pleasures*, he continues the admirable tradition of nature/science writing which keeps in its heart a philosophical modesty.

WILD CARROT • BIRD'S NEST QUEEN ANNE'S LACE

FRANCES T. DANA

WHEN THE DELICATE FLOWERS OF THE WILD carrot are still unsoiled by the dust from the highway, and fresh from the early summer rains, they are very beautiful, adding much to the appearance of the roadsides and fields along which they grow so abundantly as to strike despair into the heart of the farmer, for this is, perhaps, the ''peskiest'' of all the weeds with which he has to contend. As time goes on the blossoms begin to have a careworn look and lose something of the cobwebby aspect which won them the title of Queen Anne's lace. In late summer the flower stalks erect themselves, forming a concave cluster which has the appearance of a bird's nest. I have read that a species of bee makes use of this ready-made home, but have never seen any indications of such an occupancy.

This is believed to be the stock from which the garden carrot was raised. The vegetable was well known to the ancients, and we learn from Pliny that the finest specimens were brought to Rome from Candia. When it was first introduced into Great Britain is not known, although the supposition is that it was brought over by the Dutch during the reign of Elizabeth. In the writings of Parkinson we read that the ladies wore carrot leaves in their hair in place of feathers. One can picture the dejected appearance of a ballroom belle at the close of an entertainment.

*

From *How to Know the Wild Flowers*, Frances T. Dana (1862-1952). New York: Charles Scribner's Sons, 1893; revised edition, 1897. One of the most popular nature books of its time, this guide for the New England area reflects a blend of personal experience, historical information, literary flavor, and folklore missing in such books now. The chapters are organized by color, a format which influenced the organization of later flower identification books. Katharine S. White remarked of *How to Know the Wild Flowers*, which she used as a child, and continued to consult for decades afterward, ''I shall always be grateful to Mrs. Dana for her sensible and unscientific identification scheme.''

On Top of the World

Lester Rowntree

*I*T IS QUITE TIME THAT SOMEONE WROTE SOMEthing about the alpines of California. About them and their companions and about their behavior when and if domesticated. Some of them have not yet been grown in gardens, but others, especially those species which have hopped the Oregon border or come over from the Rockies, are well known to growers of alpines.

Somehow the word has gone out that all California plants are tender, —because California, to many people, means the warm sunny winters and dry heat of its southern end. However, only a small though much advertised portion of the state is a place of palms and mockingbirds and pepper trees. The fact that much of California's area lies above the 4000 foot altitude is lost sight of. But after you have spent six or eight weeks above 9000 feet, in places bedight with the beauty of alpines, your idea of California plants is that they are a hardy race, lovers of wind and snow and sun and water, getting from 30 to 50 inches of rain in a year and blooming, at the end of July, at the foot of snowbanks 30 feet deep.

This group bears investigation and should be drawn upon for garden use in cold countries. Some species were brought into cultivation long ago in Europe and have lately been revived with much éclat as ''new'' plants. Many of them, though little known to Americans, are being grown successfully by English gardeners whose passionate questing for new plant material is renowned. California alpines did much better for me in the East than they do in my present garden; they liked, there, the assurance that friendly cold and snow were coming and that when the snow finally went it was safe for them to launch out into an orgy of growth.

I find that camping near the mountain crests and crawling over them in search of plants and seeds is a rich and liberating experience. To stand (on one of the rare windless days when you *can* stand) on the bald summit of a mountain, or to cling (when the wind *is* blowing) to a topmost peak and look out across the sublime desolation of miles of jagged red-brown rock or yellow crags or pearl-gray glacial boulders shining with silver sheen,—that leaves a memory worth gloating over. The thought of days on those same summits when devastating thunder storms raged over my defenseless head and I made my usual and completely faithless vow never again to venture so high, is best put aside as speedily as possible.

This high region is a place of violent contrasts. It can be so very quiet or so alarmingly noisy, so peaceful or so disturbing. The summits change suddenly from alluring domes of soft lavenders, pinks and golds, to dull ominous gray and black, and from inspiring to terrifying.

These are heights which no machine but the human body can climb. They are the most untouched region of California. Hunters generally keep below timber line and only quiet fishermen come to these silent blue lakes held so neatly in their rocky hollows. These summits are above the destructive potentialities of real estate agents or even of sheep and cattle. There is a glorious feeling of remoteness and permanence here. The air will never be polluted by carbon monoxide, the floor never strewn with pie plates and tin cans, the peace never desecrated by shrieking crowds.

Even the garrulous Clark crow is left behind, though his chatter comes faintly from below, where in the last stands of dwarfed straggly white-bark pine, *Pinus albicaulis,* his handsome black, gray and white foliage repeats all the color tones of granite and snow and shadow, as he flies quarrelsomely between the windswept derelicts.

The sleek glacial domes shine like ice in the sun and the rougher, duller ones catch the light to enhance the brilliancy of orange, bright green, and scarlet lichens and embedded stony streaks of green and brown and purple. Along the jagged horizons billowy white clouds like glorified and well-popped corn, pile one above another and form an ever-changing palisade.

This was the workshop of colossal glaciers. They ground across the mountains, polishing the resisting domes and at last, their work ended, retreated to the slopes of the highest peaks, while gradually, century by century, the scene of their labors became today's alpine flower fields.

The long watershed of the Sierra reaches its highest point about the middle of California. The western slope faces a moisture-laden air current coming from the Pacific. This wind, after discharging fog or rain upon the seaward slope of the Coast Ranges moves east across the Great Valley and strikes the Sierra part way up its slope.

If, standing on the crest of the mountains, you could see both sides at once, the contrast between them would show up very strikingly,—a contrast which begins almost as soon as you have reached the highest point and begun to go down the eastern side. Here all moisture-loving plants desert you except those beside the running streams, the air becomes noticeably dry and the growth is mainly species of high arid regions.

Iris missouriensis, Western blue flag, makes sheets of blue, acre upon acre, where it can find water, and its dry stalks and leaves are soft and fragrant mattresses, usually placed conveniently near a river and a willow thicket, which afford water to fill the canteens, excellent swimming within reach and privacy for one's bedroom.

Dwarf chrysothamnus and ericameria species and varieties, like chunky diminutive goldenrods, give color to the higher slopes in late summer, while bushes of the same genera make great mounds of gold on the lower reaches where no other bloom is in sight. Elsewhere for mile upon mile the traveler passes through colonies of sunflower-like wyethias, and *Argemone platyceras,* the big white prickly poppy, is at home on the desert mesas at the eastern foot of the mountains, massed across the light stony soil like a low and prickly steel-blue-leaved *Romneya coulteri.*

There is a monotony about the growth covering the eastern side of the Sierra, where comparatively few species monopolize the landscape. Seas of silver-gray desert sage, *Artemisia tridentata,* are broken by

Piñon pine, *Pinus monophylla* and California juniper, *Juniperus californicus.* Hot dry air comes across from the mountains and high valleys of Nevada. This is cattle and sheep country and much of the limited native flora has given way before the foreign fodder plants which eventually go wherever these grazing animals go. As the season advances the sheep are driven higher and higher up the mountains, keeping fairly near the passes, and at last reach their utmost altitude and gorge themselves fat on the best of the alpines.

On top of the Sierra you are in the Boreal or Arctic-Alpine life zone reaching from timber line to the mountain tops, which means, in this latitude, from 9000 to 14,500 feet.

Here are precipitous slopes covered with loose shale where at every step forward you seem to slip back a step. Along the smooth rock domes cracks of various widths run this way and that; sometimes the entire dome is a network of cracks, from a tiny fissure to a crevice eight inches wide, the whole looking as rough as newly ploughed ground. Though from a distance these slopes and domes appear bare and stripped of all plant life, closer inspection shows alpines growing quite happily in both loose shale and tight crevice.

Sometimes the fracture is so slight that you wonder the seed could find lodgment, and yet the root will have penetrated the rock for a long way. Some creepers put out short fibrous roots from their running stems, but many alpines depend entirely upon their tap roots for moisture and their first response to the early summer growing impulse is to lengthen this tap root, or if they employ auxiliaries, to wriggle another thread-like tentacle into the home crevice. These plants live in very intense light without strong heat, and seem to delight in it, in the iron they find in their granite abodes, in the extremes of temperature and in the mulch of gravel which is washed down from the slope above, half covering the low tough stems and closely huddled leaves. . . .

I have often been struck by the similarity of behavior between alpines, desert plants and those coastal plants which in the teeth of the gales cling close to ocean bluffs. There is a resemblance in the severity of the natural conditions and in the methods which the plants have adopted to combat or outwit them. In each of the three situations grow low-statured plants, with blooms oversized in proportion to the foliage and generally bright-colored as a result of the strong light in which they live. In each case the roots are long and prefer sand or gravel to soil. Often some subterfuge (especially in plants of the desert) has been resorted to in order to meet a need imposed by the surroundings. The desert and high mountain plants both have a short period for growth, their hurried progress to maturity caused in the first case by impending drought, in the second by oncoming cold. *Prunus fasciculata,* some lyciums, and *Heliotropium curassavicum* are instances of species found on both desert and seacoast. Many seaside gardeners can make some of the true alpines quite comfortable and in the coastal gardens of southern California desert plants often find things to their liking.

*

From *Hardy Californians,* Lester Rowntree (1879-1979). New York: The Macmillan Company, 1936. Born into an English Quaker family which moved to the U.S. in 1887, Rowntree settled in California in 1929. From then on she wrote, collected, photographed, and studied plants, also touring the U.S., Canada, and Mexico by car. Rowntree lived alone in deserts, chaparral, and mountains, becoming an expert in the native plants of California. She also started a seed business, and wrote more than a hundred articles on her discoveries, and another book, *Flowering Shrubs of California.* In her own way, Rowntree, besides being a literary stylist, was a twentieth-century plant hunter, of that breed of fiercely independent women born in the Victorian age and self-educated, who cultivated a special, solitary life in nature. In her late seventies, unable to roam around any longer on her botanical excursions, Rowntree began writing children's books. She lived to be a hundred.

OUR VANISHING VEGETABLE HERITAGE

KENT WHEALY

THE DIVERSITY AND QUALITY AND NUMBER of garden varieties now being offered commercially is almost beyond belief. Gardeners in the United States and Canada are truly blessed. But it is quite possible that half of everything available non-commercially today could be extinct within the next few years! The major forces threatening this diversity include: plant patenting legislation; takeovers of seed companies by multinational corporations; plant breeding for machines instead of gardeners; the profit-motivated hybrid bias of most seed companies; and increasing bankruptcies of small businesses. These events and trends, which have brought such a massive amount of plant material to the very brink of destruction, must be examined in order to determine how to neutralize this threat.

Plant patenting legislation was first passed in England in 1975. At that time England became a member of the International Union for the Protection of New Varieties of Plants (UPOV), which is a Geneva-based organization that promotes and coordinates plant patenting laws around the world. Proponents of the legislation argue that it is necessary to keep unscrupulous competitors from pirating newly developed varities and offering them under other names. Opponents say it stifles the free flow of plant material between breeders, which is essential if dynamic breeding programs are to be maintained, and allows breeders to make slight genetic manipulations to plant material, which they did not originally develop, and then ''lock up'' that material for 18 years.

Enforcement of the legislation quickly became a legal nightmare because it is almost impossible to prove in court that one plant is identical to another. But European lawmakers plunged ahead and phased in a system of ''legal'' and ''illegal'' vegetables designed to facilitate enforcement. They published a ''Common Catalogue'' listing all of the vegetables permissible to sell in Common Market countries and established stiff fines for anyone selling varieties not on the list. Dr. J. K. A. Bleasedale of England's Wellesbourne Station described the Common Catalogue as a ''self-inflicted wound'' and confided that the Catalogue was inspired by commercial interests and was intended to clear the European market for the patented varieties. In July of 1980 the legislation took full effect and 2126 vegetable varieties became illegal to sell in England and the other Common Market countries which belong to UPOV. Dr. Erna Bennett, formerly with the Crop Ecology and Genetic Resources branch of the United Nations' Food and Agriculture Organization (FAO) in Rome, estimated that by 1991 fully three-fourths of all the vegetable varieties now grown in Europe will be extinct because of attempts to enforce plant patenting laws.

The situation, as it continued to develop in England during those years, was reported in the quarterly newsletters of the Henry Doubleday Research Association (HDRA). Lawrence D. Hills, Director of the HDRA, spearheaded the forces in England that opposed plant patenting and has tried, valiantly but unsuccessfully, to change the legislation. He was able to stir up enough national publicity that OXFAM made a grant of 300,000 Pounds Sterling to establish a gene bank at Wellesbourne. The gene bank, built as a government facility, was dedicated six years after the situation first became apparent. The dedication was a bittersweet event because much of the vegetable material, which Lawrence D. Hills and his colleagues had hoped to save, was already extinct. They are currently establishing Vegetable Sanctuaries in the kitchen gardens of several stately homes in England, where the varieties they have been able to salvage will be permanently maintained. They have also sponsored expeditions to collect peasant-varieties in various European countries which have recently joined UPOV, hoping to lessen the destruction.

In January of 1979, amendments to strengthen and extend the Plant Variety Protection Act of 1970 were introduced on behalf of the American Seed Trade Association (ASTA) and its 600 member companies. The amendments sought to standardize U.S. patent coverage with European laws so that the United States could join UPOV. The hearings for these amendments were unpublicized and the ASTA and the USDA expected no public awareness on the issue and no trouble running them through. They were wrong. Before the hearings even started and continuing through the entire next year, gardeners who were members of several grass-roots organizations working with genetic preservation generated more mail against the legislation than any agricultural issue in memory. Opponents used the various hearings on the amendments to try to educate legislators about the threats facing genetic diversity and to expose the bills as destructive, European-inspired, special-interest legislation. But the final battle was lost due to unbelievable political acrobatics on one of the last frantic days of the Carter administration. The amendments were passed into law on a voice vote during a lame duck session of the United States Senate. The furor over the legislation died down all too quickly when there was no immediate move to install a system of legal and illegal varieties as had happened in Europe.

At that point opponents of the legislation hoped that the newly created public awareness about genetic vulnerability would at least result in increased support for the National Seed Storage Laboratory (NSSL) and for various collection programs. Unfortunately, that has not been the case. To say that germ plasm research and preservation programs in the U.S. have been given low priority would be a gross understatement. The NSSL did not receive a budget increase during its first 15 years of existence. The USDA has not had even one full-time plant explorer since 1970. The U.S. government only allocates a pathetic $40,000 per year to collect the rapidly vanishing genetic resources on which the future of U.S. agriculture will depend. And all this at a time when scientists around the world are voicing increased alarm as they watch the wholesale destruction of the centers of diversity for the world's food crops, caused by the introduction of the Green Revolution's hybrids and the newly patented varieties which are being marketed in third world countries. The U.S. government is making a catastrophic mistake by not immediately initiating a crash program for plant collection worldwide.

Plant patenting legislation has definitely made seed companies attractive investments for multinational corporations. During the first week after patenting legislation was passed in England, one company, RHM, bought out 84 seed companies. When RHM's buying spree was finally complete, over 100 seed companies had merged. Shell Oil of Great Britain has bought out 74 seed companies since the passage of the legislation in England. Royal Dutch Shell became the world's largest seed and agrichemical company, almost overnight. Seed company takeovers in the United States have also reached epidemic proportions: Atlantic Richfield (ARCO) took over Desert Seed Co.; Celanese bought out Joseph Harris Co.; Ciba-Geigy (of Switzerland) purchased Funk's Seed; ITT now owns the W. Atlee Burpee Co.; Amfac took over Gurney's Seed & Nursery and Henry Field Seed & Nursery; Sandoz (of Switzerland) purchased Northrup King Co.; Upjohn bought out Asgrow Seed Co.; and Monsanto purchased DeKalb Hybrid Wheat. And these are just a few of the more than 60 recent North American seed company takeovers.

Multinational agrichemical conglomerates view seeds as a logical lateral extension of their financial interests. They are already manufacturing pesticides, fungicides and chemical fertilizers. With their newly purchased seed companies, they are now able to give commercial growers a package deal—seeds which will grow well with their chemicals. Some agrichemical firms have even started selling pelleted seeds, which wraps each individual seed in a small capsule of pesticides and fertilizers. Such tactics point out an obvious conflict of interest which occurs when major agrichemical corporations are allowed to buy out seed companies. In the past, excellent breeding programs have produced food crops which are resistant to a multitude of diseases and even to pests. But it is doubtful that such corporations, whose very existence depends on selling pesticides and chemical fertilizers, will spend any time or money to develop disease- or pest-resistant crops. And yet plant patenting legislation is allowing these same corporations to lock up valuable breeding materials for 18 years. Agrichemical and pharmaceutical corporations should be prohibited by law from owning seed companies.

The tremendous consolidation now going on within the U.S. seed industry also threatens to destroy most of the plant material available to gardeners. When a large corporation buys out a small, regional, family-owned seed company, it invariably drops the former owner's collection of standard varieties and replaces them with the more profitable hybrids and patented seeds. The new corporate owners are only concerned with profits and usually switch immediately to generalized varieties which will grow reasonably well anywhere in the country, thus assuring the greatest sales in the company's new nationwide market. No thought is given to preservation or the fact that the collection of seeds being dropped is probably the reason that company was successful in the first place. Often these regionally-adapted collections represent the life's work of several generations of seedsmen within these families. Plants in these collections often are extremely well adapted to local weather, diseases and pests. We cannot allow this irreplaceable genetic wealth to be destroyed just for the short-term profits of a corporation which may not even own that company next year.

Such losses might be viewed with less alarm, if the varieties being dropped had been superseded by superior ones as was often the case during the first half of this century. But the garden seeds currently being dropped from the catalogues are the best home garden varieties we will ever see. Almost all of the vegetable breeding being done today is for commercial applications and such varieties seldom suit the needs of the home gardener. Most commercial breeding strives for an extremely concentrated harvest period, so that machines can do the picking all at one time. Fruits must have tough skins and solid flesh to withstand mechanical harvesting and then endure cross-country shipping. Varieties are bred for eye-appeal, so they will look good and sell good in grocery stores and in seed catalogues. Some are specifically developed to be stored for extended periods in refrigerated, controlled environments. And most are bred to produce well under optimum weather conditions and with inputs of chemical fertilizers and pesticides.

As long as our food crops are being bred for machines and large commercial growers, the varieties being introduced will continue to stray ever farther from the needs of the home gardener. Gardeners are most concerned with *flavor*. If that fantastic flavor is there, appearance means nothing. Fresh garden produce is only "shipped" from the backyard to the kitchen table, so skin and flesh can be as tender as possible. Gardeners want varieties that can be harvested all season long, so they can enjoy fresh produce right up until frost. Many of the older varieties have remained popular because their long keeping ability in fruit cellars allows gardeners to enjoy the fruits of their labor until the next spring. Gardeners need locally-adapted varieties which will grow well in their unique and increasingly changeable weather, and withstand local diseases and pests.

Home garden varieties such as these are the ones which are currently being dropped from the seed catalogues. Far from being obsolete or inferior, these varieties are the cream of our vegetable crops. Each is the result of millions of years of natural selection, thousands of years of human selection and usually almost a decade of intensive and costly plant breeding and testing. Only the very best make it to the catalogues and each is unique and irreplaceable. But they are being allowed to die out due to the economics of the situation with no systematic effort being made by government agencies or lay organizations to store and maintain them. The survival of these home garden varieties represents the vegetable gardener's *right* to determine the quality of the food which that family consumes. If home gardeners allow their vegetable heritage to die out, they will be locking themselves forever into a position of dependence on the seed companies and the varieties that their owners choose to offer.

In the spring of 1981, the decision was made to attempt an inventory of the entire U.S./Canadian seed industry. Mail-order vegetable seed catalogues, no matter how small or obscure, were gathered from throughout the United States and Canada. Early estimates mistakenly concluded that the inventory would be completed in one year and would include 120 seed companies and 3000 non-hybrid varieties. *The Garden Seed Inventory* has taken over three years to finally complete and includes 239 companies and nearly 6000 non-hybrid varieties.

For the first time it is possible to accurately assess which varieties are being dropped and how quickly. *The Garden Seed Inventory* became increasingly more fascinating and more frightening as it grew towards completion. Fascinating because, when viewing the entire garden seed industry in detail, the amount of plant material available is incredible! Frightening because it is now apparent that over *48% of all non-hybrid garden seeds are available from only one source* out of 239 companies! This study shows that: 2792 varieties (48.3% of the total) are available from only one source; another 642 varieties (11.1%) are available from two sources; so a total of 3434 varieties (59.4%) are available from only one or two sources.

	Companies Inventoried	Number of Varieties	Lost During That Year	Percentage of the Total
End of 1982	138	Incomplete	117	Incomplete
End of 1983	184	Incomplete	237	Incomplete
End of 1984	239	5785	263	4.5%

These losses do not truly reflect the overall decrease in availability. Many of the varieties, which are now available from one or two sources, were available from three to six (or more) sources when this study began. And most of those companies have dropped the varieties in 1984. In other words, it appears that the sources of supply for these seeds have already disappeared. Although many of these varieties have not yet been dropped *completely,* they will be as soon as those few companies sell out their remaining supplies of the seeds. An almost unbelievable amount of loss is possible within the next few years. Hopefully an immediate and systematic effort can still rescue most of these endangered seeds. But there is no guarantee that any variety offered by a small number of sources will still be available in next season's seed catalogues.

There has been only one other complete U.S. inventory of commercially available food plants. In 1903 the USDA published *American Varieties of Vegetables* for the years 1901 and 1902 by W. W. Tracy, Jr. It included variety names and sources, but no descriptions. This earlier inventory has been studied in depth and then compared to printouts of what is being kept in the National Seed Storage Laboratory. Only three percent of everything available commercially in 1901 and 1902 survives today in that government collection! It is depressing to see the huge lists of garden varieties available at the turn of the century and realize that almost all of them have been lost forever. Imagine everything that would still be alive today if the 1901/1902 USDA inventory had been updated annually and if endangered varieties had been systematically procured and maintained. But even though disastrous mistakes have been made in the past, there is no excuse for losing anything from now on. At this point we are just picking up the remaining pieces, but we must at least do that and do it quickly. Time is running out and we will never be given this chance again.

It is ironic that we presently have access to such a vast array of the best garden varieties ever developed, and yet so much of this invaluable and irreplaceable resource is in immediate danger of being lost forever. We are truly at a crossroads. It is still not too late to rescue from extinction what remains of our vanishing vegetable heritage. Just try to imagine what it would cost, in terms of time and energy and money, to develop this many excellent varieties. But they are already here. All we have to do is save them. We are the stewards of this sacred genetic wealth and we better start acting like it. If we don't, generations yet unborn will curse our stupidity and deplore the fact that we valued power and money more than we valued their survival.

*

From *The Garden Seed Inventory: An Inventory of Seed Catalogs—Listing All Non-Hybrid Vegetable and Garden Seeds Still Available in the United States and Canada,* edited by Kent Whealy (1946-). Decorah, Iowa: Seed Saver Publications, 1985. In 1975 Whealy founded the Seed Savers Exchange, an activist non-profit organization dedicated to keeping heirloom and endangered garden seeds from extinction. Roger B. Swain rightly calls Kent Whealy a modern Noah "in the midst of rising waters of uniformity." SSE's thousands of members across the United States and Canada save and offer seeds that otherwise are not available commercially. They include those brought by early immigrants to rural areas of the country, traditional Indian crops, and varieties dropped from catalogues. In its brief history SSE has made an enormous effort to protect the genetic diversity of seeds through publications, the maintenance of a Central Seed Collection of rare vegetable varieties, and by multiplying the supply of seeds in its own Preservation Garden. The organization has in its inventory more than 2000 beans, 600 tomatoes, 200 squash, 100 corns, and much more. The compilation of material available in another volume, *Seed Savers Exchange: The First Ten Years,* gives an encouraging view of the kinds of independent, grass roots projects people are involved in around the country —starting small seed businesses, tracking down heirloom vegetables, developing regional seed banks, and historical garden restorations. Such efforts recall eighteenth-century agricultural pursuits in the service of the common good.

The Changing Rose

Katharine S. White

In THIS COLD WINTER OF 1960—COLD, THAT IS, in the Maine coastal town from which I write—I have been thinking about the fragrance of flowers, a subject that has occupied my mind and nose all year, but one that the garden-catalogue writers, except for the rose growers, tend to neglect. Even the rose men, because they are stuck with a great many scentless varieties, do not give it the emphasis they might. My own nose is not a very good organ, because I am a heavy smoker, but nevertheless I value fragrance and find it one of the charms of a garden, whether indoors or out. The flowers I enjoy most that are in bloom indoors just now are my two big pots of freesias, a white and a yellow; their delicate scent is there for the sniffing, but it does not overwhelm the room, as some lilies do. Colette once wrote that the ideal place for the lily is the kitchen garden, and remembers that in the garden of her childhood "it was lord of all it surveyed by virtue of its scent and its striking appearance," but she goes on to say that her mother would sometimes call from her chair, "Close the garden gate a little, the lilies are making the drawing room un-inhabitable!" The young Colette was allowed to pick these lilies by the armful and

> . . . bear them away to place on the altar for the Hail Mary celebration. The
> church was hot and stuffy and the children burdened with flowers. The un-
> compromising scent of the lilies made the air dense and disconcerted the
> hymn singing. Some of the congregation hurriedly left the building, while
> others let their heads droop and slumbered, transported by a strange
> drowsiness.

We all know this phenomenon—the somnolent Easter Day service in a
lily-laden church. Outdoors, for my taste, lilies cannot be too sweet,
and I especially love the strong Oriental scent of the auratums.

Fragrance, whether strong or delicate, is a highly subjective matter,
and one gardener's perfume is another gardener's stink. My tastes are
catholic. I very much like the pungent late-summer flowers—the
marigolds, calendulas, and chrysanthemums, even the old-fashioned
single nasturtiums that have not been prettied up by the hybridizers.
These ranker autumn flowers, some of whose pungency comes from
the foliage, are what Louise Beebe Wilder, in her book *The Fragrant
Path* (1932), calls "nose twisters"; the very word "nasturtium"
means "nose twister" in Latin. It is my habit to keep two little vases
filled with small flowers on our livingroom mantelpiece all summer; by
September, these are often filled with nose twisters—French marigolds,
miniature Persian Carpet zinnias, calendulas, and a few short sprays
from the tall heleniums, all in the tawny and gold shades of autumn.
But to some people the aromatic scents of these flowers and their leaves
are unbearable. In fact, one friend of mine cannot tolerate them at all,
and her pretty nose will wrinkle with disgust when she is in the room
with them. If I know she is coming to the house in September, I hastily
change my bouquets to the softer tones and sweeter scents of the late-
blooming verbenas, annual phlox, and petunias.

I know next to nothing about fragrance. A year of trying to learn
about it has left me as ignorant as ever, beyond a few simple facts that
everybody knows, such as that a moist, warm day with a touch of sun
will bring out fragrance, that hot sun and drought can destroy it, that
frost sometimes releases it, and that rain will draw out the good
chlorophyll scents of grass and foliage. The commonest complaint one
hears today from the amateur gardener is that modern flowers, particularly roses, are losing their fragrance, thanks to the hybridizers'

emphasis on form and color, and it had seemed to me, too, that many flowers smell less sweet than they used to. Sweet peas: The ones I grow are sweet, of course, but I remember them as sweeter still in my aunts' flower garden of long ago. Iris: It is rare to find a fragrant flower among the hybrids we now grow on our terrace, but a gardening friend with a particularly alert nose remembers the old-fashioned ''flag lilies'' of his childhood as very fragrant. Lilacs: The common single farmyard lilac for me has the headiest spring scent of all, and some of the double modern French hybrids are said to be as fragrant, yet the double lilacs we grow here are distinctly less sweet than our common lilacs (*Syringa vulgaris*), probably because one of their ancestors was the only wild lilac that has no scent at all. Pansies: Oh, the list of lost sweet smells could go on and on.

These vexing doubts have given me courage to write around, asking questions of the scientists and horticulturists and commercial growers whom I dared to bother with my inquiries. A few of them have answered helpfully, a few evasively, but most of them mysteriously. The only consensus I can gather is that fragrance is not now a strong incentive among the growers and breeders. Color and form and hardiness are the thing, because that is what the public demands. This may be so, but it seems to me that the least the seedsmen and nurserymen can do for those of us who value fragrance is to tell us in their catalogues more often than they now do when a flower is particularly sweet-scented. Take the case of the large white single hybrid petunia called Snowcap, which my friend with the alert nose notes as beautifully fragrant in his garden, despite the fact that it is a modern grandiflora. You may see Snowcap's handsome portrait in color in Vaughan's 1960 catalogue, and it is listed in ''Park's Flower Book'' for 1960 and described there as the ''largest pure white.'' Neither cataloguer appears to think its scent worth mentioning, even though fragrance is rare in the large modern petunias. The Joseph Harris Company now sells Snowcap only to wholesale customers, probably because this year the firm has two even more beautiful large single white petunias to offer its retail customers—Seafoam and Snowdrift. These two are F_1 (first-generation) hybrids, so it could be they have no perfume. But perhaps, like Snowcap, which is also F_1, they have—who knows? Certainly not the catalogue reader.

The fragrance of the rose is probably more mourned when it is missing than that of any other flower, but it apparently would be inaccurate to say that modern roses are less fragrant than old-fashioned roses. Bertram Park, an English rose authority, writes in his *Guide to Roses*:

> Nothing irritates me more than the question "Why have modern roses lost their fragrance?". . . There are two or three hundred species of roses . . . from which our modern roses have descended; of these only a half a dozen or so are fragrant. In spite of this handicap, the hybridists have succeeded in bringing out fragrance in modern roses.

The truth seems to be that, not counting the species roses, there are quite a few old roses without scent or with very little scent, and we all know there are plenty of new ones. There is a difference, however, in the fragrance of the old and the new. Each type of ancient European rose had its distinctive and beloved scent—damask, gallica, musk, alba, centifolia, and so on—whereas the scent of modern roses has become mixed by an infusion of many strains. This may be one cause of the mutterings about today's hybrids. I suspect, though, that the chief basis for complaint about their loss of scent derives from the prevalence today of the floribundas, many of which are still far more floriferous than they are sweet-smelling. We grow them for other reasons than scent. Even so, each year the rose men develop a few new fragrant floribundas. As a catalogue reader, I suggest that home gardeners would complain less were the rose men only forthright, coming straight out in their descriptions of roses with "Unscented" or "Very faint fragrance," if this is the fact, and never failing to mention perfume when it is present. If none is spoken of in the description of a rose, I now tend to assume that it has none, but this may be unfair. For example, Sutter's Gold, a modern yellow, which I grew last summer and which has one of the most delightful perfumes I know, is described in several catalogues this year without a hint of this great asset. I am also wary when no scent is mentioned because of a ludicrous experience I had with white roses. For years, we had growing here that favorite of our parents, a Frau Karl Druschki, a white hybrid perpetual without any scent at all. Finally I tired of Frau Karl's lack of fragrance, so I did not grieve when a very cold winter killed the old lady off. To succeed her I chose a white hybrid tea that I saw highly touted in the Jackson & Perkins catalogue. No scent, at least to my nose. The next year, I bought another, which J. & P. said was even greater. Still no scent.

Neither was advertised as fragrant, but the praise was so loud and the pictures were so handsome that I simply failed to notice the omission. This year I see that the firm presents yet another ''great'' new white rose—the White Queen—but this time I shall be more cautious. Because there is not a word in the catalogue about the Queen's fragrance or lack of it, I shall avoid her and order instead Neige Parfum, which the J. & P. cataloguer says has ''a delicious lemon-verbena aroma.'' Another white hybrid tea I want to try is Conard-Pyle's Blanche Mallerin, a French rose that is ''nicely perfumed,'' and I certainly must order from Will Tillotson, for my bed of old-fashioned shrub roses, a Mme Hardy, said in the catalogue to be the ''finest white damask'' and said by a rose-growing friend to have a unique perfume—a mixture of sharp almond and violet. Unique indeed! Fragrance is next to impossible to describe, and comparisons help very little; perhaps this is why the cataloguers duck it so often. What is sharp almond to one may smell like doughnuts to another. (A favorite catalogue adjective for scent is ''fruity.'' What fruit, I always wonder.) As Colette said of peonies, whose fragrance someone had compared to that of a rose, ''The peony smells of peonies; that is to say, of cockchafers.''

*

From *Onward and Upward in the Garden*, Katharine S. White (1892-1977). New York: Farrar, Straus and Giroux, 1979. Ever since this book appeared, it has been celebrated as one of the classics of American garden literature. Katharine S. White was an editor at the *New Yorker* for thirty-six years, where she published all her garden writing. Not surprisingly, her discussions of seed and nursery catalogues took on the high moral tone of serious book reviewing that previously had been reserved for literary criticism.

Fiercely opinionated, practical, and unmoved by the latest flower fashions, she wrote in wonderfully careful prose of the destinies of plants and people in American life, from the perspective of her Maine garden. White's very first article revealed the breadth of her garden world: ''I read for news, for driblets of knowledge, for aesthetic pleasure, and at the same time I am planning the future, and so I read in dream.''

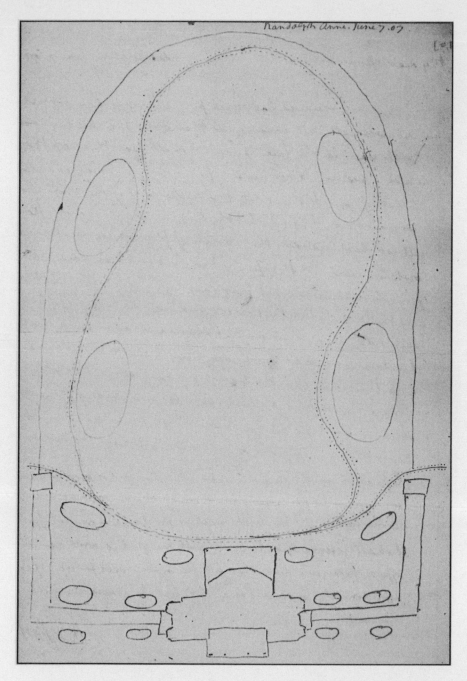

Thomas Jefferson's 1807 drawing of his ''Roundabout Walk'' at Monticello. The flower beds on the east and west lawns close to the house were planted in April of that year. Courtesy of The Massachusetts Historical Society.

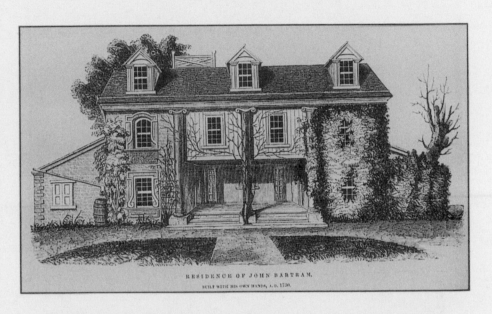

RESIDENCE OF JOHN BARTRAM.

BUILT WITH HIS OWN HANDS, A.D. 1730.

A 1730 view of the house John Bartram built himself on a slope
overlooking the Schuylkill River, outside of Philadelphia. Courtesy of
Dumbarton Oaks, Trustees for Harvard University.

The catalpa tree, Plate 49, from Volume I of Mark Catesby's
The Natural History of Carolina, Florida, and the Bahama Islands.
Courtesy of Dumbarton Oaks, Trustees for Harvard University.

Elizabeth Lawrence in her garden.
Courtesy of Duke University Press.

Ernest H. Wilson in China
Courtesy of Hunt Institute for
Botanical Documentation,
Carnegie Mellon University,
Pittsburgh, PA.

Liberty Hyde Bailey in 1941.
Courtesy of Hunt Institute for
Botanical Documentation,
Carnegie Mellon University,
Pittsburgh, PA.

The 1885 cover of Peter Henderson and Company's catalogue
of seeds and plants. Courtesy of Dumbarton Oaks, Trustees
for Harvard University.

One of the engravings from Frank Scott's *The Art of Beautifying Suburban Home Grounds of Small Extent* of 1870. Courtesy of Dumbarton Oaks, Trustees for Harvard University.

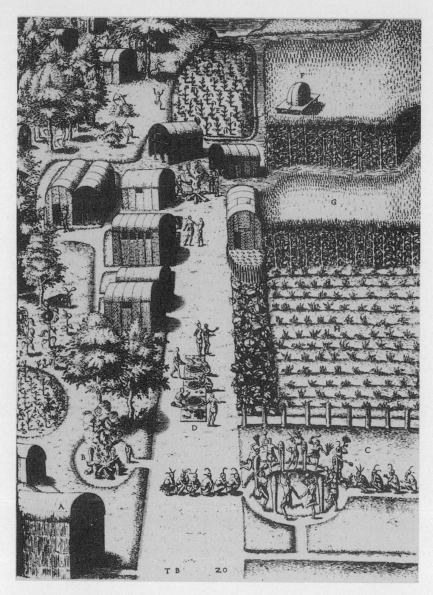

The Indian village of Secoton in Virginia, in an engraving by
Theodore de Bry, published in Thomas Harriot's *A Briefe and
True Report of the New Found Land of Virginia* (Frankfurt,
1590). Among the earliest British illustrations of the New World,
it was based on a drawing by John White who accompanied Sir
Walter Raleigh to Roanoke Island in the 1580s. Courtesy of Rare
Books and Manuscripts Division, The New York Public Library,
Astor, Lenox and Tilden Foundation.

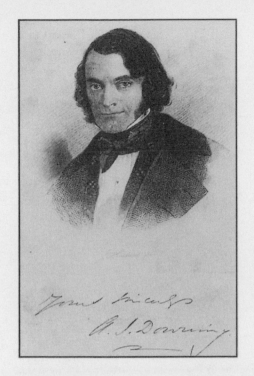

Andrew Jackson Downing.
Courtesy of Dumbarton Oaks,
Trustees for Harvard University.

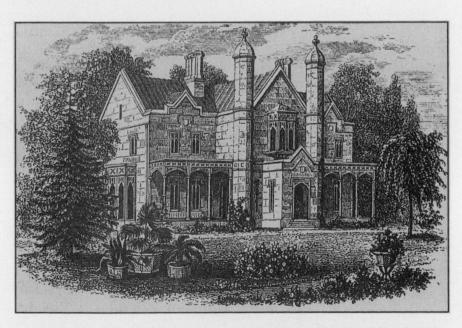

Downing's Newburgh residence in the Hudson Valley, one of the
illustrations in his *Treatise*. Courtesy of Dumbarton Oaks,
Trustees for Harvard University.

Beatrix Farrand. Courtesy of Dumbarton Oaks, Trustees for Harvard University.

The Lovers' Lane Pool at the east end of the gardens at Dumbarton Oaks, Washington, D.C. Courtesy of Dumbarton Oaks, Trustees for Harvard University.

Michael Pollan, author
of *The Botany of Desire.*
(Judith Belzer)

The gardens at Seed Savers Heritage Farm in Decorah, Iowa. Photo by Ian
Adams, courtesy of the Seed Savers Exchange.

III

TRAVELERS AND THE TRAVELS OF PLANTS

Selected Letters

John Bartram

FROM PETER COLLINSON TO JOHN BARTRAM

London, Jan. 20, 1734-5.

*M*Y GOOD FRIEND JOHN BARTRAM:

I now do myself a further pleasure to consider thy curious entertaining letters of November 6. I am only afraid, in doing me a pleasure, so much time was lost which would turn to a more profitable account in thy own affairs.

Thee writes for some botanical books; and indeed I am at a loss which to recommend, for, as I have observed, a complete history of plants is not to be found in any author. For the present, I am persuaded the gentlemen of the Library Company, at my request, will indulge thee the liberty, when thee comes to town, to peruse their botanical books: there is Miller's *Dictionary,* and some others.

Please to remember those Solomon's Seals, that escaped thee last year.

The great and small Hellebore are great rarities here, so pray send a root or two of each next year. Please to remember all your sorts of lilies, as they happen in thy way; and your spotted Martagons will be very acceptable.

The Devil's Bit, or Blazing Star, pray add a root or two, and any of the Lady's Slippers.

My dear friend, I only mention these plants; but I beg of thee not to neglect thy more material affairs to oblige me. A great many may be put in a box 20 inches or 2 feet square, and 15 or 16 inches high;—and a foot in earth is enough. This may be put under the captain's bed, or set in the cabin, if it is sent in October or November. Nail a few small narrow laths across it, to keep the cats from scratching it. . . .

Pray what is your Sarsaparilla? The May-apple, a pretty plant, is what I have had for some years sent me per Doctor Witt. It flowers well with us; but our summers are not hot enough to perfect its fruit.

The pretty humble beautiful plant, with a spike of yellow flowers, I take to be a species of Orchis or Satyrion. What sort of root it has thee hath not mentioned. If it is taken up with the earth about the roots, it will certainly flower the first, if not the second year. I wish thee'd send me two or three roots, if it is plenty.

The Ground Cypress is a singular pretty plant. If it bears berries or seeds, pray send some; and if its bears flowers or seeds, pray send some specimens in both states.

Pray send me a good specimen or two of the shrub, three feet high, that grows by the water courses. The shrub that grows out of the sides of rocks, sometimes five or six feet high, bearing red berries hanging by the husks, is called Euonymus, or Spindle tree. We have the same plant, with a small difference; grows plenty in England.

Your wild Senna, with yellow flowers, is a pretty plant. Send seeds of both this and Mountain Goat's Rue.

Thee need not collect any more of the White Thorn berries, that has prodigious long, sharp thorns. It is what we call the Cock-spur Thorn. I had a tree last year, that had at least a bushel of berries. But haws of any other sort of Thorns will be very acceptable.

Pray send me a root or two of cluster-bearing Solomon's Seal. It is in all appearance a very rare plant,—as is the Panax.

Pray send a root or two of Joseph Breintnall's Snake-root. Pray send a root of the grassy leaves, that bears pretty little blue flowers,—that's good against obstructions of the bowels, [probably *Sisyrinchium*, L.]

When it happens in thy way, send me a root or two of the little tuberous root called Devil's Bit, which produces one or two leaves yearly.

I only barely mention these plants; not that I expect thee to send them. I don't expect or desire them, but as they happen to be found ac-cidentally: and what is not to be met with one year, may be another. . . .

It happens that your late ships, in the autumn, come away before a great many of our seeds are ripe, and the spring I don't approve as the best season to send them; but as it rarely happens otherwise, I have taken a method to send some in paper, and some in sand. After thee has picked out the largest, which must be instantly set, for very probably they were chilled coming over. When it is my case, as it often happens, taking the following method, I have raised a great many pretty plants out of your earth. I lay out a bed five or six feet long by three feet wide; then I pare off the earth an inch or two deep, then I loosen the bottom, and lay it very smooth again, and thereon, (if I may use the term), I sow the sand and seed together as thin as I can, then I sift some good earth over it about half an inch thick. This bed ought to be in some place that it may not be disturbed, and kept very clear from weeds; for several seeds come not up till the second year. I have put some hard-shelled Almonds of my own growth, and some soft-shelled from Portugal: they are easily distinguished.

The almond makes a fine pie, taken whilst a pin can be run through them; for you eat husk, shell, and kernel, altogether. They must be first coddled over a gentle fire, and then put in crust. I query whether young peaches would be as good, before the shell is hard.

I have put in the sand some vine cuttings, and some of the great Neapolitan Medlar, which we always graft on white thorns, and so must you. As soon as these cuttings come to hand, soak them all over in water for twenty-four hours, and then plant the vines (the earth being well loosened) as deep as only the uppermost bud of the cutting may be level with the earth. Water them in dry weather. These seldom fail growing. The grafts, after soaking, may be laid in the earth, or in a moist place, till grafted, which should be soon.

I hope thee will take these two long rambling epistles in good part. They are writ, a bit now and then, as business will permit. Let me hear from thee at thy leisure, which will much oblige thy real friend,

P. Collinson.

Send a quantity of seed of the Birch or Black Beech; it seems to be new. Send me a good root of the Swallow-wort, or Apocinon, with narrow leaves and orange-coloured flowers; and of the pretty shrub called Red Root, and of the Cotton-weed or Life-everlasting, and some more seed of the perannual Pea, that grows by rivers; this year, or next, or next after, as it happens. Pray send me a walking-cane, of the Cane-wood.

MARK CATESBY TO JOHN BARTRAM

London, May 20, 1740.

Mr. Bartram:—

Your kind remembrance of me, in the three plants you sent me with those of Mr. Collinson, encourages me to give you further trouble, though not without an intention of retaliation.

As I have the pleasure of reading your letters, I see your time is well employed; therefore, in what I propose, I shall be cautious of desiring anything that may much obstruct your other affairs. But, as you send yearly to our good friend Mr. P. Collinson, the same conveyance may supply me; which I shall confine to as narrow a compass as may be, for I find my taste is agreeable with yours, which is, that I regard most, those plants that are specious in their appearance, or use in physic, or otherwise. The return that I propose to make you, is my book; but it will be first necessary to give you some account of it. The whole book, when finished, will be in two folio volumes, each volume consisting of an hundred plates of Animals and Vegetables.

This laborious work has been some years in agitation; and as the whole, when finished, amounts to twenty guineas, a sum too great, probably, to dispose of many, I chose to publish it in parts: viz., twenty plates with their descriptions, at a time, at two guineas. By this easy method, I disposed of many more than I otherwise should. Though I shall set a due value on your labours, the whole book would be too considerable to send you at once; therefore, I propose to send you, annually, a Part (i.e., twenty plates with their descriptions), for what you send me. . . .

Your obliged friend and servant,

M. Catesby.

CADWALLADER COLDEN TO JOHN BARTRAM

Coldengham, January 27th, 1746-7.

Dear Mr. Bartram:—

It is so long that I have lost the pleasure of my wonted correspondence with you, that I am afraid of my having fallen under your censure; and which would give me more concern, than the censure of some great men in the world. But if you knew the true reason of my discontinuing to write, as usual, you would be so far from blaming me, that you would pity me.

I was unexpectedly engaged in the public business, and when I entered upon it, I expected it would only have been for one single piece of service; but one drew on another, and I was kept more months from my family, than I expected to have been weeks from them. . . .

It gives me much pleasure to think that your name and mine continue together, in remembrance of our friendship. I do not know the plant, of which you send me the description from Gronovius. It is none of them I described to him; and therefore I suppose you have sent it to him, and that he has honoured it with your name.

It was not possible for me to comply with your desire, of sending you a plant of the *Arbor vitae,* for it was the 14th of December before I returned home from New York.

All my botanical pleasures have been stopped this summer, while I was at Albany. We durst not go without the fortifications without a guard, for fear of having our scalps taken; and while I was at New York, I was perpetually in company, or upon business, so that I shall be a very dull correspondent. However, I designed to have sent you something of our transactions, by Mr. Franklin, at his return from Boston; but he stayed so long, that I left New York before he returned; and I was at last exceedingly hurried, in leaving that place. If I had stayed one day longer, the river had become impassable.

Now, dear Mr. Bartram, take pity on me, and let me have some share of that pleasure which you receive from your correspondents. I have not a line from any, but a short one from Mr. Collinson, of the 3d of August. I expected to have heard from Gronovius, by a ship expected from Amsterdam, and by which I wrote to him; but I do not hear that she is arrived. I sowed some of the seed of the *Arbor vitae,* but it failed as yours did. Perhaps they may germinate next year.

Can you give me no hopes of seeing you, in your rambles next summer, in search of new knowledge of things? Pray, make my compliments to the good woman, your spouse, and be assured,

That I am your affectionate, humble servant,

Cadwallader Colden.

JOHN BARTRAM TO CAROLUS LINNAEUS

[Not dated, 1752 or 3.]

Respected and Worthy Friend:—

I received, about two months past, a letter from thee dated August the 10th, 1750. I was exceedingly pleased to receive so kind a letter from one that so deservedly bears so superior a character for learning; but was very much concerned that I could not have had it sooner than above two years after it was wrote; and much the same misfortune happened to several pamphlets thee sent to Dr. Colden and Mr. Clayton, which our worthy friend Benjamin Franklin showed me last week, which he had just received, and intended to send according to direction, by the next post.

I travelled, in 1751, most part of the autumn, and found several new species of plants, and shrubs, which I should have sent to thee, if I had known they would have been acceptable.

We have four or five beautiful species of Jacoboea [*Lilium*], that you have not in Europe. One species grows in our marshes, another on flat stiff ground, another on cold shady banks, by the rivers, another on loose slaty soil on the great mountains; and most of these species are much valued by the Indians, and back inhabitants, for the cure of the same diseases that the ancients used their Jacoboea for, though not one of them knew the name of the plant.

I hope thee hath received the *Medicina Britannica.* I hope to send thee some specimens next fall. We are all surprised that we have not one letter from Peter Kalm.

JOHN BARTRAM TO PHILIP MILLER

April the 20th, 1755.

Worthy Friend Philip Miller:—

I have received thy kind letter of February the 19th, 1755, which gave me much satisfaction; and some uneasiness, that so many years have elapsed wherein we might have reciprocally communicated our observations to each other: and although thee had incomparably the advantage over me, yet, notwithstanding, I love to peep into the abstruse operations of nature. Perhaps I might, by thy familiar instruction, have made some remarks that might have been satisfactory. But, for the time to come, I hope we may double our diligence, if the war with France do not obstruct our endeavours.

The Catalogue of Shrubs and Trees is very acceptable, or any other books in Natural History. I have thy first and second book of the Gardener's Dictionary,—one sent me by Lord Petre, the other by Dr. Dillenius.

I design to take particular care to send those seeds thee mentioned, which I can procure; and if thee will please to send by the first opportunity, it may come to me soon enough to send, next fall, any other curiosity thee pleases to mention: for time is so far spent, past our meridian, that the affair calls for diligence.

I design to collect specimens of our Pines, just when they are in flower, and the young cone just impregnated, which is to ripen, not this ensuing fall, but the next; when it immediately dischargeth its seed, before it is well dry; whereas other trees keep their cones shut for several years, containing perfect ripe seeds, and then discharge them. Pray, do all your European Pines set their cones on the same spring's shoot, and perfect them the succeeding year—or the second year's wood, as, by your draught, the Scotch Pine doth? Although the species of Pines, and Fir, may, many of them, be distinguished by their cones, in Europe, they are no certain distinguishing character in America, except Lord Weymouth's Pine. . . .

I take thy offer very kindly, to assist me in understanding Linnaeus's system, which I am acquainted with in some degree; having several books of his setting forth, which Dr. Gronovius, my good friend, hath sent me; and Mons. Dalibard sent me his Catalogue of Plants growing near Paris; and Hill hath nearly translated Linnaeus's Characters. But I find many plants that do not answer to any of his Genera, and are really new.

I have an account that he hath published, lately, two books containing all our North American plants which Kalm observed, when he was with us. I showed him many, that he said were new Genera, and that Linnaeus must make many alterations, when he was by him more truly informed of their true characters, as I should soon see when they were printed. I long to see these books,—to see if they have done me justice, as Kalm promised me. Dr. Gronovius promised to send them to me, as soon as they came to his hand.

I shall be much obliged to thee for thy Figures of Plants, as soon as finished. I love to see nature displayed, in all its branches.

I shall be glad to assist thee with any new plant, or shrub—either dead or alive—in substance, or a particular description; as thee pleases to inform me after what manner it will answer thy intention the best.

JOHN BARTRAM TO THOMAS DALIBARD

[Not dated.]

To Monsieur Dalibard, à Paris:—
Our very worthy friend, Benjamin Franklin, Esq., whom I have the

pleasure (as well as honour) to be intimately acquainted with, showed me a letter wherein thee mentioned a book thee designed to send me, which will be very acceptable, for I love Botany, and Natural History, exceedingly.

I shall be well pleased to correspond with one so curious, and shall make use of all opportunities to oblige; and as an introduction, I have sent a little parcel of seeds, and specimens, which I gathered. But as you are possessed of so large a part of North America, I suppose it will be difficult to send you any plant that you have not, although I believe we have several which you want; but the difficulty is, to know which they are. If I had a catalogue either of what you have, or what you want, I will endeavour to supply you, which I suppose must be carried on by the good offices of Benjamin Franklin here, or my first correspondent in London, the generous Mr. Peter Collinson, who is ready to oblige all men.

BENJAMIN FRANKLIN TO JOHN BARTRAM

                                                    Paris, May 27, 1777.

My Dear Old Friend:—

The communication between Britain and North America being cut off, the French botanists cannot, in that channel, be supplied as formerly with American seeds, &c. If you, or one of your sons, incline to continue that business, you may, I believe, send the same number of boxes here, that you used to send to England; because England will then send here, for what it wants in that way. Inclosed, is a list of the sorts wished for here. If you consign them to me, I will take care of the sale, and returns, for you. There will be no difficulty, in the importation, as the matter is countenanced by the ministry, from whom I received the list.

My love to Mrs. Bartram, and your children. I am ever, my dear friend,

                Yours most affectionately,

                                                    B. Franklin.

*

From *Memorials of John Bartram and Humphry Marshall,* edited by William Darlington (Bartram: 1699-1777). Philadelphia: Lindsay and Blakiston, 1849. The gentle Quaker John Bartram is one of the most remarkable figures in the early history of American science. In 1728 he bought a 102-acre farm on the Schuylkill River outside of Philadelphia, and soon established what was to become the first botanical garden on the American continent. One of the few native-born Americans of this time who explored for plants, he was equally interested in plant physiology, rocks and minerals, birds, insects, and animals. Self-taught, he studied Latin in order to read botanical books. Over the years Bartram collected in and studied the complete ecological systems of the area that spread all the way from upper New York State to Florida, and as far west as the Ohio River. Bartram planted the findings from his travels, kept safe in a pouch made from a cow's bladder, in his garden, later supplying interested parties in England and on the continent, in addition to many at home in the colonies. In 1765 he was appointed botanist to King George III.

Bartram wrote a narrative of one of his journeys, *Observations . . . Travels from Pensilvania to Onondago, Oswego, and the Lake Ontario, in Canada,* and was still roaming about at seventy in Florida with his son William who was to take up the legacy in his own right. But the real portrait of John Bartram that remains is to be found in his extensive correspondence. Here one finds an extraordinary account of the exchanges in the natural sciences that were carried on between the most knowledgeable people in America and Europe in the eighteenth century, all of whom constituted an international scientific circle. Much of this orbit was centered in Philadelphia where Bartram helped found the American Philosophical Society in 1769. A year before his death the Declaration of Independence would be written. The letters published here show the range of Bartram's correspondence reporting the travels of plants and information and books. Nowhere is this more apparent than in the thirty-five years of letters he sent to the London Quaker merchant Peter Collinson for whom Bartram collected. Other Englishmen he developed ties to included Mark Catesby who produced the exquisite color plates in his *Natural History of Carolina, Florida, and the Bahama Islands,* based on his visits to the South in 1712 and 1722, and Philip Miller whose *Gardener's Dictionary* was then one of the most admired English reference books. Bartram also corresponded with the brilliant Swedish scientist Linnaeus who developed a system for classifying all plants and animals, transforming the natural sciences of his day. He called Bartram ''the greatest natural botanist in the world.'' In France there was a link to the botanist Dalibard, in Germany the physician-botanist Dillenius, and in Holland the noted scholar Gronovius who had published *Flora Virginica* by the early American botanist John Clayton. And of course, there were the Americans themselves Bartram kept up with, receiving or conveying the latest news, Benjamin Franklin who urged his friend to write a natural history book (Bartram did contribute a preface to his *Poor Richard Improved* in 1749), and Cadwallader Colden, the noted botanist, surveyor, and author of a major study on the Iroquois Indians, who resided in the Hudson Valley near Newburgh with his learned daughter Jane, the first woman botanist in America.

John Bartram, in his own exemplary way of living in science, contributed so much to his young country at a time when virtually every act of intellectual life, commerce, and politics was an experiment. Long after the exquisite creation of Moghul gardens in the East, after Michelangelo had painted the Sistine Chapel, and just about the time Diderot was about to invent the modern novel, and the Americans democracy, at the dawn of the Industrial Revolution plain John Bartram, enraptured by the illimitable knowledge of things, was bending down to get a closer peek at a species of lily he had not seen before in the New World.

The Bounteous Kingdom of Flora

William Bartram

How harmonious and soothing is this native sylvan music now at still evening! inexpressibly tender are the responsive cooings of the innocent dove, in the fragrant Zanthoxylon groves, and the variable and tuneful warblings of the nonpareil, with the more sprightly and elevated strains of the blue linnet and golden icterus: this is indeed harmony, even amidst the incessant croaking of the frogs: the shades of silent night are made more cheerful, with the shrill voice of the whip-poor-will* and active mocking-bird.

My situation high and airy: a brisk and cool breeze steadily and incessantly passing over the clear waters of the lake, and fluttering over me through the surrounding groves, wings its way to the moon-light savannas, while I repose on my sweet and healthy couch of the soft *Tillandsia usnea-adscites,* and the latter gloomy and still hours of night pass rapidly away as it were in a moment. I arose, strengthened and cheerful, in the morning. Having some repairs to make in the tackle of my vessel, I paid my first attention to them; which being accomplished,

---

Caprimulgus rufus, called chuck-will's-widow, from a fancied resemblance of his notes to these words: it inhabits the maritime parts of Carolina and Florida, and is more than twice the size of the night hawk or whip-poor-will.

my curiosity prompted me to penetrate the grove and view the illu-
mined plains.

What a beautiful display of vegetation is here before me! seemingly
unlimited in extent and variety: how the dew-drops twinkle and play
upon the sight, trembling on the tips of the lucid, green savanna,
sparkling as the gem that flames on the turban of the eastern prince.
See the pearly tears rolling off the buds of the expanding Granadilla;*
behold the azure fields of cerulean Ixea! what can equal the rich golden
flowers of the *Canna lutea,* which ornament the banks of yon serpentine rivulet, meandering over the meadows; the almost endless varieties
of the gay Phlox, that enamel the swelling green banks, associated with
the purple *Verbena corymbosa,* Viola, pearly Gnaphalium, and silvery
Perdicium? How fantastical looks the libertine Clitoria, mantling the
shrubs, on the vistas skirting the groves! My morning excursion
finished, I returned to my camp, breakfasted, then went on board my
boat, gently descended the noble river, and passed by several openings
of extensive plains and meadows, environing the east lake, charming
beyond compare. At evening I came to at a good harbour, under the
high banks of the river, and rested during the night amidst the fragrant
groves, exposed to the constant breezes from the river: here I made
ample collections of specimens and growing roots of curious
vegetables, which kept me fully employed the greatest part of the day;
and in the evening arrived at a charming spot on the east bank, which I
had marked on my ascent up the river, where I made some addition to
my collections; and the next day I employed myself in the same manner, putting into shore frequently, at convenient places, which I had
noticed; and in the evening arrived again at the upper store, where I
had the pleasure of finding my old friend, the trader, in good health and
cheerful, and his affairs in a prosperous way. There were also a small
party of Indians here, who had lately arrived with their hunts to purchase goods. I continued a few days at this post, searching its environs
for curious vegetable productions, collecting seeds and planting growing roots in boxes, to be transported to the lower trading house.

Now, having procured necessaries to accommodate me on my
voyage down to the lower store, I bid adieu to my old friend and
benefactor, Mr. Job Wiggens, embarked alone on board my little for-

---

Passiflora incarnate, called May-Apple.

tunate vessel, and set sail. I chose to follow the eastern-most channel of the river to the Great Lake, because it ran by high banks and bluffs of the eastern main the greatest part of the distance, which afforded me an opportunity of observing a far greater variety of natural subjects, than if I had taken the western or middle channel, which flowed through swamps and marshes.

At evening I arrived at Cedar Point, my former safe and pleasant harbour, at the east cape of the Great Lake, where I had noticed some curious shrubs and plants; here I rested, and on the smooth and gentle current launch again into the little ocean of Lake George, meaning now, on my return, to coast his western shores in search of new beauties in the bounteous kingdom of Flora.

I was however induced to deviate a little from my intended course, and touch at the enchanting little Isle of Palms. This delightful spot, planted by nature, is almost an entire grove of Palms, with a few pyramidal Magnolias, Live Oaks, golden Orange, and the animating Zanthoxylon. What a beautiful retreat is here! blessed unviolated spot of earth, rising from the limpid waters of the lake: its fragrant groves and blooming lawns invested and protected by encircling ranks of the *Yucca gloriosa.* A fascinating atmosphere surrounds this blissful garden; the balmy Lantana, ambrosial Citra, perfumed Crinum, perspiring their mingled odours, wafted through Zanthoxylon groves. I at last broke away from the enchanting spot, and stepped on board my boat, hoisted sail, and soon approached the coast of the main, at the cool eve of day: then traversing a capacious semicircular cove of the lake, verged by low, extensive grassy meadows, I at length by dusk made a safe harbour, in a little lagoon, on the sea shore or strand of a bold sandy point, which descended from the surf of the lake. This was a clean sandy beach, hard and firm by the beating surf, when the wind sets from the east coast. I drew up my light vessel on the sloping shore, that she might be safe from the beating waves in case of a sudden storm of wind in the night. A few yards back the land was a little elevated, and over-grown with thickets of shrubs and low trees, consisting chiefly of Zanthoxylon, *Olea americana, Rhamnus frangula,* Sideroxylon, Morus, Ptelea, Halesia, Querci, *Myrica cerifera,* and others. These groves were but low, yet sufficiently high to shelter me from the chilling dews; and being but a few yards distance from my vessel, here I fixed my encampment. A brisk wind arising from the lake, drove away the clouds of mosquitoes into the thickets. I now, with difficulty and industry, collected a sufficiency of dry wood to keep up a light during the night, and to roast some trout which I had caught when descending the river: their heads I stewed in the juice of Oranges, which, with boiled rice, afforded me a wholesome and delicious supper: I hung the remainder of my broiled fish on the snags of some shrubs over my head. I at last, after reconnoitring my habitation, returned, spread abroad my skins and blanket upon the clean sands by my fire-side, and betook myself to repose.

How glorious the powerful sun, minister of the Most High in the rule and government of this earth, leaves our hemisphere, retiring from our sight beyond the western forests! I behold with gratitude his departing smiles, tinging the fleecy roseate clouds, now riding far away on the eastern horizon; behold they vanish from sight in the azure skies!

All now silent and peaceable, I suddenly fell asleep. At mid-night I awake; when, raising my head erect, I find myself alone in the wilderness of Florida, on the shores of Lake George. Alone indeed, but under the care of the Almighty, and protected by the invisible hand of my guardian angel. . . .

The morning being clear, I set sail with a favourable breeze, coasting along the shores; when on a sudden the waters became transparent, and discovered the sandy bottom, and the several nations of fish, passing and repassing each other. Following this course I was led to the cape of the little river, descending from Six Mile Springs, and meandering six miles from its source through green meadows. I entered this pellucid stream, sailing over the heads of innumerable squadrons of fish, which, although many feet deep in the water, were distinctly to be seen. I passed by charming islets of flourishing trees, as Palm, Red Bay, Ash, Maple, Nyssa, and others. As I approached the distant high forest on the main, the river widened, floating fields of the green Pistia surrounded me, the rapid stream winding through them. What an alluring scene was now before me! A vast basin or little lake of crystal waters, half encircled by swelling hills, clad with Orange and odoriferous Illicium groves, the towering Magnolia, itself a grove, and the exalted Palm, as if conscious of their transcendent glories, tossed about their lofty heads, painting, with mutable shades, the green floating fields beneath. The social prattling coot enrobed in blue, and the squealing water-hen, with wings half expanded, tripped after each other, over the watery mirror.

I put in at an ancient landing place, which is a sloping ascent to a level grassy plain, an old Indian field. As I intended to make my most considerable collections at this place, I proceeded immediately to fix my encampment but a few yards from my safe harbour, where I securely fastened my boat to a Live Oak, which overshadowed my port.

After collecting a good quantity of fire-wood, as it was about the middle of the afternoon, I resolved to reconnoitre the ground about my encampment. Having penetrated the groves next to me, I came to the open forests, consisting of exceedingly tall straight Pines (*Pinus palustris*) that stood at a considerable distance from each other, through which appeared at N.W. an almost unlimited plain of grassy savannas, embellished with a chain of shallow ponds, as far as the sight could reach. Here is a species of Magnolia that associates with the *Gordonia lasianthus*; it is a tall tree, sixty or eighty feet in height; the trunk is straight; its head terminating in the form of a sharp cone; the leaves are oblong, lanceolate, of a fine deep green, and glaucous beneath; the flowers are large, perfectly white and extremely fragrant: with respect to its flowers and leaves, it differs very little from the *Magnolia glauca*. The silvery whiteness of the leaves of this tree, had a striking and pleasing effect on the sight, as it stood amidst the dark green of the *Quercus dentata, Nyssa sylvatica, Nys. aquatica, Gordonia lasianthus,* and many others of the same hue. The tall aspiring *Gordonia lasianthus,* which now stood in my view in all its splendour, is every way deserving of our admiration. Its thick foliage, of a dark green colour, is flowered over with large milk-white fragrant blossoms, on long slender elastic peduncles, at the extremeties of its numerous branches, from the bosom of the leaves, and renewed every morning; and that in such incredible profusion, that the tree appears silvered over with them, and the ground beneath covered with the fallen flowers. It at the same time continually pushes forth new twigs, with young buds on them, and in the winter and spring, the third year's leaves, now partly concealed by the new and perfect ones, are gradually changing colour, from green to golden yellow, from that to a scarlet, from scarlet to crimson; and lastly to a brownish purple, and then fall to the ground. So that the *Gordonia lasianthus* may be said to change and renew its garments every morning throughout the year; and every day appears with unfading lustre. And moreover, after the general flowering is past, there is a thin succession of scattering blossoms to be seen, on some parts of the tree, almost every day throughout the remaining months, until the floral season returns again. Its natural situation, when growing, is on the edges of shallow ponds, or low wet grounds on rivers, in a sandy soil, the nearest to the water of any other tree, so that in droughty seasons its long serpentine roots which run near or upon the surface of the earth, may reach into the water. When the tree has arrived to the period of perfect magnitude, it is sixty, eighty, or an hundred feet high, forming a pyramidal head. The wood of old trees when sawn into plank is deservedly admired in cabinet-work or furniture; it has a cinnamon coloured ground, marbled and veined with many colours: the inner bark is used for drying a reddish or sorrel colour; it imparts this colour to wool, cotton, linen, and dressed deer-skins, and is highly esteemed by tanners.

The *Zamia pumila,* the *Erythryna corallodendrum,* and the *Cactus opuntia,* grow here in great abundance and perfection. The first grows in the open pine forests, in tufts or clumps, a large conical strobile disclosing its large coral red fruit, which appears singularly beautiful amidst the deep green fern-like pinnated leaves.

The *Erythryna corallodendrum* is six or eight feet high, its prickly limbs stride and wreathe about with singular freedom, and its spikes of crimson flowers have a fine effect amidst the delicate foliage.

The *Cactus opuntia* is very tall, erect, and large, and strong enough to bear the weight of a man: some are seven or eight feet high: the whole plant or tree seems to be formed of great oval compressed leaves or articulations; those near the earth continually increase, magnify and indurate as the tree advances in years, and at length lose the bright green colour and glossy surface of their youth, acquiring a ligneous quality, with a whitish scabrous cortex. Every part of the plant is nearly destitute of aculea, or those fascicles of barbed bristles which are in such plenty on the common dwarf Indian Fig. The cochineal insects were feeding on the leaves. The female of this insect is very large and fleshy, covered with a fine white silk or cottony web, which feels always moist or dewy, and seems designed by nature to protect them from the violent heat of the sun. The males are very small in comparison to the females, and but very few in number: they each have two oblong pellucid wings. The large polypetalous flowers are produced on the edges of the last year's leaves, are of a fine splendid yellow, and are succeeded by very large pear-shaped fruit, of a dark livid purple when ripe: its pulp is charged with a juice of a fine transparent crimson colour, and has a cool pleasant taste, somewhat like that of a pomegranate. Soon after eating this fruit the urine becomes of the same crimson colour, which very much surprises and affrights a stranger, but is attended with no other ill consequence; on the contrary, it is esteemed wholesome, though powerfully diuretic.

On the left hand of those open forests and savannas, as we turn our eyes southward, south-west and west, we behold an endless wild desert, the upper stratum of the earth of which is a fine white sand, with small pebbles, and at some distance appears entirely covered with low trees and shrubs of various kinds, and of equal height, as dwarf Sweet Bay (*Laurus borbonia*), *Olea americana, Morus rubra, Myrica cerifera,* Ptelea, *Aesculus pavia, Quercus ilex, Q. glandifer, Q. maritima, foliis cuneiformibus obsolete trilobis minoribus, Q. pumila, Rhamnus frangula, Halesia diptera,* & *tetraptera,* Cassine, *Ilex aquifolium, Callicarpa johnsonia, Erythryna corallodendrum, Hibiscus spinifex,* Zanthoxylon, *Hopea tinctoria,* Sideroxylum, with a multitude of other shrubs, many of which were new to me, and some of them admirably beautiful and singular. One of them particularly engaged my notice, which, from its fructification, I took to be a species of Cacalia. It is an evergreen shrub, about six or eight feet high; the leaves are generally somewhat cuneiform, fleshy, and of a pale whitish green, both surfaces being covered with a hoary pubescence and vesiculae, that when pressed feels clammy, and emits an agreeable scent; the ascendent branches terminate with large tufts or corymbes of rose coloured flowers, of the same agreeable scent; these clusters of flowers at a distance, look like a large Carnation or fringed Poppy flower, (*Syngenesia polyg. Aequal. Linn.*), *Cacalia heterophylla, foliis cuneiformibus, carnosis, papil. viscidis.*

Here is also another species of the same genus, but it does not grow quite so large; the leaves are smaller, of a yet duller green colour, and the flowers are of a pale rose; they are both valuable evergreens.

The trees and shrubs which cover these extensive wilds are about five or six feet high, and seem to be kept down by the annual firing of the deserts, rather than the barrenness of the soil, as I saw a few large Live Oaks, Mulberry trees, and Hiccories, which evidently have withstood the devouring flames. These adjoining wild plains, forests, and savannas, are situated lower than the hilly groves on the banks of the lake and river; but what should be the natural cause of it I cannot even pretend to conjecture, unless one may suppose that those high hills, which we call bluffs, on the banks of this great river and its lakes, and which support those magnificent groves and high forests, and are generally composed of shells and sand, were thrown up to their present height by the winds and waves, when the bed of the river was nearer the level of the present surface of the earth; but then, to rest upon such a supposition, would be admitting that the waters were heretofore in greater quantities than at this time, or that their present channels and receptacles are worn deeper into the earth.

I now directed my steps towards my encampment, in a different direction. I seated myself upon a swelling green knoll, at the head of the crystal basin. Near me, on the left, was a point or projection of an entire grove of the aromatic *Illicium floridanum*; on my right, and all around behind me, was a fruitful Orange grove, with Palms and Magnolias interspersed; in front, just under my feet, was the enchanting and amazing crystal fountain, which incessantly threw up, from dark, rocky caverns below, tons of water every minute, forming a basin, capacious enough for large shallops to ride in, and a creek of four or five feet depth of water, and near twenty yards over, which meanders six miles through green meadows, pouring its limpid waters into the great Lake George, where they seem to remain pure and unmixed. About twenty yards from the upper edge of the basin, and directly opposite to the mouth or outlet of the creek, is a continual and amazing ebullition, where the waters are thrown up in such abundance and amazing force, as to jet and swell up two or three feet above the common surface: white sand and small particles of shells are thrown up with the waters, near to the top, when they diverge from the centre, subside with the expanding flood, and gently sink again, forming a large rim or funnel round about the aperture or mouth of the fountain, which is a vast perforation through a bed of rocks, the ragged points of which are projected out on every side. Thus far I know to be matter of real fact, and I have related it as near as I could conceive or express myself. . . .

The sun passing below the horizon, and night approaching, I arose from my seat, and proceeding on arrived at my camp, kindled my fire, supped and reposed peaceably. Rising early, I employed the fore part of the day in collecting specimens of growing roots and seeds. In the afternoon, I left these Elysian springs and the aromatic groves, and briskly descended the pellucid little river, re-entering the great lake. The wind being gentle and fair for Mount Royal, I hoisted sail, and successfully crossing the N. west bay, about nine miles, came to at Rocky Point, the west cape or promontory, as we enter the river descending towards Mount Royal; these rocks are horizontal slabs or flat masses, rising out of the lake two or three feet above its surface, and seem an aggregate composition or concrete of sand, shells, and calcareous cement, of a dark gray or dusky colour. The stones are hard and firm enough for buildings, and serve very well for light hand mill-stones; and when calcined afford a coarse lime: they lie in vast horizontal masses upon one another, from one to two or three feet in thickness, and are easily separated and broken to any size or form, for the purpose of building. Rocky Point is an airy, cool, and delightful situation, commanding a most ample and pleasing prospect of the lake and its environs; but here being no wood, I re-embarked and sailed down a little farther to the island in the bay, where I went on shore at a magnificent grove of Magnolias and Oranges, desirous of augmenting my collections. I arose early next morning, and after ranging the groves and savannas, returned, embarked again, and descending, called at Mount Royal, where I enlarged my collections; and bidding adieu to the gentleman and lady who resided there, and who treated me with great hospitality on my ascent up the river, arrived in the evening at the lower trading house.

*

From *Travels Through North and South Carolina, Georgia, East and West Florida,* William Bartram (1739—1823). Philadelphia: James and Johnson, 1791. William Bartram accompanied his "curious" father John on many collecting trips in the colonies. A few decades later, the elder Michaux and his son would explore the plant kingdom together, but unlike them the Bartrams never published any strictly scientific books. They simply traveled, looked about, collected, and remembered in the grand storytelling tradition of old travelers. On one of their trips around Georgia they discovered the beautifully fragrant flowering tree which they named after their good friend Benjamin Franklin (*Franklinia alatamaha*)—a tree that has not been seen in the wild since 1803.

The gentle, starry-eyed young Bartram had a spirit of innocence and child-like wonder which comes sparkling through his *Travels,* one of the great lyrical books of its time and an American classic. It grew out of his 1773-77 journey to collect in the South for the London physician Dr. John Fothergill who had one of the most remarkable gardens then. *Travels* magically criss-crossed the genres of natural history, ethnology, geography, literature, and travel commanding a veritable feast for the senses through its radiant prose. Bartram's own fine drawings added to its charm. *Travels* is unsurpassed as an account of the eighteenth-century American imagination confronting a new world, its flowers, birds, fishes and alligators, its Indians and hardy settlers. Less appreciated in its own time at home, *Travels* was immensely influential for Romantic writers abroad, its rhapsodic images of nature insinuating themselves effortlessly, as only inspiration can, into the poetry of Samuel Taylor Coleridge's ''The Rime of the Ancient Mariner'' and ''Kubla Khan'' and William Wordsworth's ''Ruth.''

Bartram set the tone for his ode to life at the very start of the book, infusing nature with a fervent religiosity:

> This world, as a glorious apartment of the boundless palace of the sovereign Creator, is furnished with an infinite variety of animated scenes, inexpressibly beautiful and pleasing. . . .

In his writing he showed how this is so. Marvelously.

In a Charleston Garden

François André Michaux

I LEFT CHARLESTON, AND WENT TO RESIDE IN a small plantation about ten miles from the town, where my father had formed a botanic garden. It was there he collected and cultivated, with the greatest care, the plants that he found in the long and painful travels that his ardent love for science had urged him to make, almost every year, in the different quarters of America. Ever animated with a desire of serving the country he was in, he conceived that the climate of South Carolina must be favourable to the culture of several useful vegetables of the old continent, and made a memorial of them, which he read to the Agricultural Society at Charleston. A few happy essays confirmed him in his opinion, but his return to Europe did not permit him to continue his former attempts. On my arrival at Carolina I found in this garden a superb collection of trees and plants that had survived almost a total neglect for nearly the space of four years. I likewise found there a great number of trees belonging to the old continent, that my father had planted, some of which were in the most flourishing state. I principally remarked two *Ginkgo bilobas,* that had not been planted above seven years, and which were then upward of thirty feet in height; several *Sterculia platanifolia,* which had yielded seed upward of six years; in short, more than a hundred and fifty *Mimosa illibrissin,* the first plant of which came from Europe about ten inches in diameter. I set several before my return to France, this tree being at that time very much esteemed for its magnificent flowers. The Agricultural Society at Carolina are now in possession of this garden: they intend keeping it in order, and cultivating the useful vegetables belonging to the old continent, which, from the analogy of the climate, promise every success. I employed the remainder of the autumn in making collections of seed, which I sent to Europe; and the winter, in visiting the different parts of Low Carolina, and in reconnoitring the places where, the year following, I might make more abundant harvests, and procure the various sorts that I had not been able to collect during the autumn.

On this account I must observe, that in North America, and perhaps more so than in Europe, there are plants that only inhabit certain places; whence it happens that a botanist, in despite of all his zeal and activity, does not meet with them for years; whilst another, led by a happy chance, finds them in his first excursion. I shall add, in favour of those who wish to travel over the southern part of the United States for botanical researches, that the epoch of the flower season begins in the early part of February; the time for gathering the seeds of herbaceous plants in the month of August; and on the 1st of October for that of forest trees.

*

From *Travels to the West of the Alleghany Mountains, in the States of Ohio, Kentucky, and Tennessea,* François André Michaux (1770-1855). London: B. Crosby and Company, 1805. The younger Michaux first came to America in 1795 as a boy of fifteen, accompanying his famous father André on collecting expeditions for Louis XVI, and with the help of Crèvecoeur who was then French Consul in New York. The first to write a comprehensive flora of North America, and already a seasoned collector from his travels in the Middle East, the elder Michaux shipped plants, animals, and birds to France and stocked forests there with American trees such as oak, hickory, and maple. A few years earlier, nearly ten years ahead of the Lewis and Clark trip, André Michaux was on his way west for the American Philosophical Society, with directives prepared by an eager-to-explore Thomas Jefferson, but political complications in the post-French Revolution years cut short the adventure. François André

Michaux returned on his own in 1801 to sell the nurseries his father had set up near Hackensack, New Jersey, and at Charleston. The Charleston garden was significant in American horticultural history for the European and Asian species first brought there. Today the gardens at Middleton Place in South Carolina still have plantings of camellias and crape myrtle believed to have been given to the Middleton family by the elder Michaux who introduced them to this country.

François André's *Travels* is filled with carefully detailed observations from his botanizing trip down the Ohio River, including an interesting account of failed experiments with 25 different kinds of grape vine (among the successes were Madeira and an iffy Burgundy) in Kentucky in 1802. His major three-volume work, *North American Sylva,* was published in 1817-18, and illustrated by the great botanical artist Redouté. The new biography of the father and son by Henry and Elizabeth Savage, *André and François André Michaux*, applauds them as pioneers in forest conservation in this country.

The Spontaneous Productions of Nature

Thomas Nuttall

THE FOREST TREES OF AMERICA, BEING A SUB-
ject of such great extent and importance, I felt, consequently, very diffi-
dent of undertaking their study, after what has been already done so
well by my predecessor M. Michaux. Yet, in offering a new edition of
the *American Sylva* in English, it appeared requisite, in keeping pace
with the progress of discovery, that all the forest trees of the extended
dominion of the United States, should, in some way or other, be
included; and, I confess, the magnitude of the task appeared, at first,
sufficiently appalling, when we reflect on the vast territory now
claimed by the United States. Beginning with the arctic limits of all ar-
borescent vegetation, in the wilds of Canada, which we cannot, with
propriety, exclude, forming as it does the boreal boundary of the North
American forest; we then follow the extended shores of the Atlantic,
until, towards the extremity of East Florida, and its Keys or Islands, we
have attained the very confines of the tropical circle and make a near
approach to the island of Cuba and the Bahamas: turning westward, we
pass over the wide forests of the Mississippi, pursue the western
streams, through vast woodless plains, until we attain the long crests of
the "Rocky Mountains" or Northern Andes. Here, in these alpine
regions, we meet with a total change in the features of the forest;

resiniferous evergreens, of the family of the Pines, now predominate, and attain the most gigantic dimensions. All the species, and they are numerous, have peculiar traits, and form so many curious and distinct species, of which little is yet known more than their botanical designation. Other remarkable forest trees, also imperfectly known, inhabit this great range of mountains, which continues uninterruptedly into the interior of Mexico in its southern course; while on the north, following the sources of the Missouri and the Oregon, and after thus dividing the waters which flow into the Atlantic and Pacific, it is, at length, merged in the "Shining Mountains," which send off their distant tributaries to the Arctic Ocean.

The plains of the Upper Platte, those of the Oregon and of Northern California, a region bereft of summer rains, forming extensive barren steppes, like those of Siberia, present no forests, scarcely an alluvial belt along the larger streams of sufficient magnitude to afford even fuel for the camp fire of the wandering hunter or the erratic savage. The scanty drift wood, borne down from the mountains, the low bitter bushes of the arid plain, even the dry ordure of the bison, is collected for fuel, and barely suffices to prepare a hasty meal for the passing traveller; who, urged by hunger and thirst, hurries over the desert, a region doomed to desolation, and, amidst privations the most appalling, lives in the hope of again seeing forests and green fields in lieu of arid plains and bitter weeds, which tantalized our famished animals with the fallacious appearance of food, like the cast-away mariner raging with thirst, though surrounded with water as fatal to the longing appetite as poison.

Towards the shores of the Pacific, and on the banks of the Oregon, we again meet with the aggreable features of the forest.

> Majestic woods, of every vigorous green,
> Stage above stage, high waving o'er the hills;
> Or to the far horizon wide diffus'd,
> A boundless deep immensity of shade.

Transported in idea to the borders of the Hudson or the Delaware, we recline beneath the shade of venerable Oaks and spreading Maples; we see, as it were, fringing the streams, the familiar Cotton-wood and spreading Willows. On the higher plains, and ascending the hills and mountains to their summits, we see a dark forest of lofty pines; we hear the light breeze sigh and murmur through their branches as it did to the poets of old. But the botanist, in all this array, fails to recognise one solitary acquaintance of his former scenes: he is emphatically in a strange land; a new creation, even of forest trees, is spread around him, and the tall Andes and wide deserts rise as a barrier betwixt him and his distant home. . . .

Thirty-four years ago, I left England to explore the natural history of the United States. In the ship Halcyon I arrived at the shores of the New World; and after a boisterous and dangerous passage, our dismasted vessel entered the Capes of the Delaware in the month of April. The beautiful robing of forest scenery, now bursting into vernal life, was exchanged for the monotony of the dreary ocean, and the sad sickness of the sea. As we sailed up the Delaware my eyes were rivetted on the landscape with intense admiration. All was new!—and life, like that season, was then full of hope and enthusiasm. The forests, apparently unbroken, in their primeval solitude and repose, spread themselves on either hand as we passed placidly along. The extending vista of dark pines gave an air of deep sadness to the wilderness.

—these lonely regions, where, retired
From little scenes of art, great Nature dwells
In awful solitude, and nought is seen
But the wild herds that own no master's stall.

The deer brought to bay, or plunging into the flood from the pursuit of the Indian, armed with bow and arrow, alone seemed wanting to realize the savage landscape as it appeared to the first settlers of the country.

Scenes like these have little attraction for ordinary life, but to the naturalist it is far otherwise; privations to him are cheaply purchased, if he may but roam over the wild domain of primeval nature, and behold

Another *Flora* there, of bolder hues,
And richer sweets, beyond our garden's pride.

How often have I realized the poet's buoyant hopes amidst these solitary rambles through interminable forests. For thousands of miles my chief converse has been in the wilderness with the spontaneous productions of Nature; and the study of these objects and their contemplation has been to me a source of constant delight.

This fervid curiosity led me to the banks of the Ohio, through the dark forests and brakes of the Mississippi, to the distant lakes of the northern frontier; through the wilds of Florida; far up the Red River and the Missouri, and through the territory of Arkansa; at last over the

> Vast savannahs, where the wandering eye,
> Unfixt, is in a verdant ocean lost.

And now across the arid plains of the far west, beyond the steppes of the Rocky Mountains, down the Oregon to the extended shores of the Pacific, across the distant ocean to that famous group of islands where Cook at length fell a sacrifice to his temerity. And here for the first time, I beheld the beauties of a tropical vegetation; a season that knows no change; but that of perpetual spring and summer: an elysian land, where Nature offers spontaneous food to man. The region of the Bread fruit; the Tarrow (*Colocasia esculenta*) which feeds the indigent mass of the population; the Broussonetia, a kind of Mulberry tree, whose inner rind, called *tapa,* affords an universal clothing. The low groves produce the Banana, the Ginger, the Turmeric, the inebriating *Kava* (*Piper methysticum*), a kind of Arrow root, resembling the potato (*Tacca*), and the Saccharine Tee root (*Dracaena terminalis*), at the same time the best of portable fodder. The common timber for constructing houses, boats, various implements, and the best of fuel, is here the produce of a Mimosa (*Acacia heterophylla*). For lights and oils, the *too tooe* kernels (*Aleurites triloba*) produce an excellent and inexhaustible supply; the cocoa-nut and the fragrant *Pandanus* afford delicious food, cordage and mats, and the very reeds, reduced in size, which border the rivulets, are no other than the precious sugar-cane of commerce.

Leaving this favoured region of perpetual mildness, I now arrived on the shores of California, at Monterey. The early spring (March) had already spread out its varied carpet of flowers; all of them had to me the charm of novelty, and many were adorned with the most brilliant and varied hues. The forest trees were new to my view. A magpie, almost like that of Europe (but with a yellow bill), chattered from the branches of an Oak, with leaves like those of the Holly (*Quercus agrifolia*). A thorny Gooseberry, forming a small tree, appeared clad with pendulous flowers as brilliant as those of a Fuchsia. A new Plane tree spread its wide arms over the dried up rivulets. A Ceanothus, attaining the magnitude of a small tree, loaded with sky-blue withered flowers, lay on the rude wood-pile, consigned to the menial office of affording fuel. Already the cheerful mockingbird sent forth his varied melody, with rapture imitating the novel notes of his neighbouring songsters. The scenery was mountainous and varied, one vast wilderness, neglected and uncultivated; the very cattle appeared as wild as the bison of the prairies, and the prowling wolves (*Coyotes*) well fed, were as tame as dogs, and every night yelled familiarly through the village. In this region the Olive and the Vine throve with luxuriance and teemed with fruit; the Prickly Pears (*Cactus*) became small trees, and the rare blooming Aloe (*Agave americana*) appeared consigned without care to the hedge row of the garden.

After a perilous passage around Cape Horn, the dreary extremity of South America, amidst mountains of ice which opposed our progress in unusual array, we arrived again at the shores of the Atlantic. Once more I hailed those delightful scenes of nature with which I had been so long associated. I rambled again through the shade of the Atlantic forests, or culled some rare productions of Flora in their native wilds. But the "oft told tale" approaches to its close, and I must now bid a long adieu to the "new world," its sylvan scenes, its mountains, wilds and plains, and henceforth, in the evening of my career, I return, almost an exile, to the land of my nativity!

*

From *The North American Sylva,* Vol. I (being the fourth volume of Michaux and Nuttall's *North American Sylva*), Thomas Nuttall (1786-1859). Philadelphia: Robert P. Smith, Publisher, 1852. An Englishman who arrived in the U.S. in 1808, when the younger Michaux was still here, Nuttall soon found himself in Philadelphia where he met William Bartram, Bernard M'Mahon and Benjamin Smith Barton who had already written *Elements of Botany,* the first U.S. textbook on the subject. Taking along André Michaux's *Flora Boreali-Americana* (in Latin), Nuttall began collecting for his patron Barton, in the new territories opened up by the Lewis and Clark expedition only five years earlier. In the thirty years that he resided in the U.S., Nuttall traveled and collected specimens in every area of the country, often on foot —the Atlantic and Pacific coasts, Oregon Trail, the Columbia River Valley, and the Great Lakes. His *Journal of Travels Into the Arkansa Territory Dur-*

ing the Year 1819 is a wonderfully intelligent account of wilderness life. Nuttall himself appears as a character in two classics of the frontier, Washington Irving's *Astoria* and Richard Dana's *Two Years Before the Mast.* A renowned botanist of his day, Nuttall accepted a position as curator of the Botanic Garden in Cambridge, and taught at Harvard University for a decade, from 1823. He published his authoritative *Genera of North American Plants* and *North American Sylva* which added to Michaux's discoveries, and greatly advanced the scientific knowledge of his day. An enthusiastic all-around naturalist who knew more about the different natural wonders of the country, and traveled it more widely, than any of his contemporaries, Nuttall also studied its geology, minerology, and shells, and wrote an outstanding three-volume reference work on ornithology. Emerson called *The Land Birds,* its first part, a book that "everyone who lives in the country ought to read." Nuttall was a true lover of nature, whose writing shows a special attachment to the American land.

The Franciscan Missionaries in Southern California

Victoria Padilla

THE BEGINNINGS OF HORTICULTURE IN CALI-
fornia lie amid the thorny, rock-strewn wastes of the peninsula to its
south, for the first settlers came to Baja California to establish outposts
in the name of God and the King of Spain. These were the Jesuits who
in 1697 obtained permission to extend their proselytizing endeavors to
this most westerly province of Mexico. They founded thirty-two stations and sixteen missions, and brought with them not only the pro
mise of salvation and a knowledge of a more abundant living, but seeds
for the first gardens to be planted on the West Coast.

Of all the missionary establishments in Baja California, none could
equal San Xavier. As the land is outstanding for its inhospitable
weather and the infertility of its soil, it is astonishing to learn what was
planted by these zealous men. Around the Mission of San Xavier were
gardens, orchards, and fields in which grew wheat, maize, rice,
squashes, melons, cotton, citrons, plantains, figs, grapes, dates,
pomegranates, oranges,olives, and deciduous fruits. Flowers must have
been raised, too, being necessary for the decoration of the church. "In
fact," so an early writer tells us, "almost all productions of both
temperate and torrid zones throve side by side with astonishing exuberance." The success of the plantings was based largely on the

endeavors of Padre Juan de Ugarte, whose achievements at San Xavier were not only to earn him the title of the "First Great Agriculturist of the Californias," but were also to serve as an inspiration to those friars who were to spread their missions from San Diego to Sonoma. From San Xavier came many of the seeds, cuttings, and plants used in the first mission gardens of Alta California. Important, too, was Padre Ugarte's knowledge of irrigation, which he passed on to the Franciscans, for in a semi-arid land with only seasonal rainfall this information was of vital importance.

The Jesuits maintained their supremacy in Baja California for almost one hundred years, but in 1767, with their expulsion from Spain, their control passed into the hands of the Franciscans under the direction of Padre Junipero Serra. Padre Serra and his missionaries had been in Baja California for a year when Spain was suddenly aroused from her lethargy regarding her holdings in the north. The Russians, with their eye on the land that was reputed to be near to the terrestrial paradise, were sending reconnoitering parties to Alaska. Because of these explorations and also the long-felt need for a refitting point on the California coast for the galleons from Manila, the Spanish government instructed Serra to go north and establish three missions—one in San Diego, one in Monterey, and one at some midway point, thus extending the dominion not only of Spain but also of the Catholic Church. Serra formed two expeditions, one to proceed by water and one by land. Having heard of the fertility of Alta California from their Jesuit predecessors, who had made several excursions to the north, the Franciscans took care to include in their provisions seeds and cuttings of fruits, flowers, and vegetables from both the old world and the new, as well as the necessary implements with which to till the soil.

On May 15, 1769, the main overland party, headed by Padre Serra and the gallant soldier, Gaspar de Portolá, left on its northward journey. The trip comprised forty-five days of extreme hardship, but when Serra scanned the pleasant terrain around San Diego, he felt that it had been worthwhile. Nature was kind to these first migrants, for the spring that year had been both late and rainy. There were pleasant *arroyos* with running streams lined with live oaks, willows, cottonwoods, and alders. Green pasture lands and valleys abounded in leafy wild grapes and roses in bloom—roses similar to their beloved Rose of Castile. In fact, Padre Serra and his men believed that there could be no spot more ideal for the location of their first mission; and on July 16, 1769, it was formally dedicated. Soon a garden was planted, fruit trees set out, fields cleared, and vegetable seeds sown. The site chosen, unfortunately, was not good, and in a few years the padres were compelled to move their mission to a more favorable location. Little remains of the garden that was originally planted around Mission San Diego de Alcalá, though it was once famous for its olives and pomegranates. A visitor to the old mission today can see a few remnants of some olive trees said to be planted by the Franciscans, but that is all.

There were nine missions founded in southern California—nine original gardens from which came the seeds and plants that beautified the homesites of the first settlers. The original plan was to have the missions one day's journey apart, but this scheme was not strictly followed. In 1771, the greatest mission of them all, San Gabriel Arcángel, was established, to be followed in 1776 by San Juan Capistrano, in 1782 by San Buenaventura, in 1786 by Santa Bárbara, in 1787 by La Purísima Concepción, in 1797 by San Fernando, in 1798 by San Luis Rey de Fráncia, and in 1804 by Santa Inés.

To their mission gardens, the Franciscans brought from Mexico all the garden and orchard seeds and plants which they thought would grow. Although in their early years they experienced difficulties with the untilled soil, as well as drought and flood, pests and Indian uprisings, they had not been unaware of the problems they had to face. Probably in no other land have missionaries been so blessed with the comforts of a genial climate, a fertile land, and willing workers. The padres were the first farmers of California, and it was they who taught the natives how to cultivate the earth and to raise their foodstuffs. Early accounts record that the missionaries grew lemons, oranges, figs, dates, olives, pomegranates, limes, and grapes successfully, as well as peaches, pears, cherries, apples, walnuts, almonds, plums, quinces, apricots, raspberries, and strawberries. Some of the fruits still grown in the state are direct lineal descendants of those planted by the padres, notably the Mission grape, Mission fig, and Mission olive. Most of the fruit trees, it is believed, were introduced before 1800. The Franciscans also discovered that cotton, flax, hemp, and other textile plants could be grown to good advantage. They raised an assortment of vegetables, and every year the harvest of wheat, corn, beans, lentils, and garbanzos proved to be increasingly bountiful. The missionaries knew little about agricultural methods and their implements were primitive, but they were ambitious projectors and excellent managers and executed their plans with surprising success.

In the mission at Santa Barbara is an interesting volume bound in sheepskin which was evidently used as a guide by the padres in their horticultural activities. Published in Madrid in 1767 and edited by Alonso de Herrera, it deals with all aspects of farming and gardening. Copies of this book were distributed to the missions; the Santa Barbara edition had been used by Fray Antonio Jayme in 1797 when he was active in Soledad Mission. The work, consisting of 494 pages, is divided into six discourses, each pertaining to a special phase of agriculture. Of particular interest is the sixth discourse, which treats flowers and trees and could well serve as a clue to some of the plants introduced into California by the Franciscans. Among the trees described are the pistachio, dogwood, cypress, laurel, jujube, carob, blackthorn, juniper, and oak. Bulbous plants, such as lilies, hyacinths, daffodils, and jonquils, are listed, as well as many of the favorites of long ago—the cornflower, larkspur, peony, marigold, sweet William, gillyflower, violet, carnation, Marguerite, honeysuckle, jasmine, rose, and buttercup.

So busy were the padres, however, keeping records of conversions and vital statistics that they made little note of the trees, shrubs, and plants they raised. Our only descriptions of mission gardens are those written by travelers who visited them. One of the first to write of what he saw was the English navigator, George Vancouver, who in 1793 visited the mission at Ventura. The padres at this mission were enthusiastic plantsmen, and their gardens early became renowned for their beauty and their harvests. Of them Vancouver wrote:

> . . . the garden of Buena Ventura far exceeded anything I had before met with in this region, both in respect of the quality, quantity, and variety of its excellent productions, not only indigenous to the country, but appertaining to the temperate as well as the torrid zone; not one species having yet been sown, or planted, that had not flourished, and yielded its fruit in abundance, and of excellent quality. These have principally consisted of apples, pears, plums, figs, oranges, grapes, peaches, and pomegranates, together with the plantain, banana, cocoa nut, sugar cane, indigo, and a great variety of the necessary and useful kitchen herbs, plants and roots. All these were flourishing in the greatest health and perfection though separated from the sea-side only by two or three fields of corn, that were cultivated within a few yards of the surf. The grounds, however, on which they were produced, were

supplied, at the expense of some labour with a few small streams, which as occasion required, were conducted to the crops that stood most in need of water.
Here also grew great quantities of the Indian fig, or prickly pear. . . .

Another visitor of distinction was George Simpson of the Hudson's
Bay Company, who traveled in California in 1838 and 1841. He
marveled at the floral display at Mission Santa Barbara, commenting
on the jonquils, marigolds, lilies, wallflowers, violets, hollyhocks, and
other flowers then in bloom. Although the missions were in their
decline when Edwin Bryant made his journey throughout the state in
1846, he was nonetheless impressed by the gardens of Mission San
Fernando, writing:

> There are two extensive gardens, surrounded by high walls; and a stroll
> through them afforded a most delightful contrast from the usually un-
> cultivated landscape we have been traveling through for so long a time. Here
> were brought together most of the fruits and many of the plants of the
> temperate and tropical climates. Although not the season of flowers
> [January], still the roses were in bloom. Oranges, lemons, figs, and olives
> hung upon the trees, and the blood-red tuna, or prickly pear, looked very
> tempting. Among the plants I noted the American aloe (*Agave americana*)
> which is otherwise called maguey.

The mission that evoked the highest praise was the one dedicated to
the Archángel Gabriel, which at the height of its glory occupied practically the entire San Gabriel Valley. In 1771 it was formally dedicated in a spot chosen near an *arroyo* lined with blackberries, roses,
grapevines, willows, and cottonwoods, and was less than a league distant from a large forest of oaks. The site was considered the most
charming in the entire province. Although so blessed, the mission was
not without its days of travail and bloodshed, but by 1784 it had
become well enough established that the *padre principe* began to consider the planting of fruits and farm products. Accordingly, he sent one
of his loyal retainers, Corenino Agina, to Mexico to procure seeds, cuttings, and grafts of fruits and other plants that would do well in the new
mission. The stalwart Spaniard returned after traveling through the
wilds of Sinaloa, bringing with him oranges, lemons, limes, olives, figs,
pecans, grapes, and other fruits and seeds. The pear seems to have been
a favorite in the early days.

To Padre José Salvidea, who took over the command of the mission in 1805, goes the credit of making it the center of agriculture in California and the richest of the missions. Hugo Reid, who had purchased a rancho close by wrote:

> He it was who planted the large vineyards, intersected with fine walks, shaded by fruit trees of every description, and rendered still more lovely by shrubs interspersed between; who laid out the orange garden, fruit and olive orchards, built the mill and dam; made fences of tunas round the fields, made hedges of rose bushes, planted trees in the Mission square with a flower garden and hour-dial in the center; brought water from long distances. . . .

Padre Salvidea was the father of California viticulture, and from his "Vina Madre" of 150,000 vines went cuttings to supply the other missions with their grapes. His orange groves, too, were among the first to be planted, marking the beginning of the great citrus industry of California. In 1812 the mission harvested the largest wheat crop to be garnered by any mission—32,618 bushels. Alfred Robinson, visiting the mission in 1829, commented on the extensive gardens and the fruit growing in abundance.

Because of the difficulty of obtaining sufficient water, the mission fathers did not cultivate large flower gardens. Nonetheless, they were men of tender sensibilities and they endeavored to recreate in this faraway and lonesome country the gardens of their homeland. Guadalupe Vallejo, niece of General Vallejo and member of one of the most noted families of old California, tells us that the gardens "were more extensive and contained a greater variety of trees and plants than most persons imagine." A tinkling fountain was a part of each garden, as were shaded walks for periods of meditation and prayer, plantings of lilies to be used for the altar, hedges of the Rose of Castile, and always a palm or two.

It is not possible to arrive at an exact listing of the purely ornamental trees, plants, and shrubs which the Franciscans introduced into California. A notable effort to arrive at such an accounting was made in the 1920s by George W. Hendry, of the University of California, who analyzed the adobe-brick content taken from various missions. Seeds and leaves of grasses and vegetables were found, as well as those of lilies, the Castilian rose, musk rose, jasmine, lavender, pennyroyal, tamarind, anise, and other herbs. Found in every mission in the south was the nopal or prickly pear (*Opuntia tuna*), remnants of which can still be seen. This sturdy cactus grew in great hedges, often reaching a height of twenty feet and a thickness of twelve, its purpose being to enclose lands under cultivation and so protect them from beasts and marauders.

What other plants grew on mission grounds? References have been made to the hollyhock, oleander, carnation, nasturtium, four-o'clock, sweet pea, portulaca, French marigold, calla, Madonna lily, and the Matilija poppy that was first grown in the gardens at Santa Barbara. The padres made use of other natives in their gardens. They planted the wild cherry (*Prunus ilicifolia*) around their buildings and it became a popular plant with the first American settlers. Mission San Fernando was said to have had a fine garden of native plants.

A familiar sight in every mission garden was the pepper tree (*Schinus molle*) that was first grown at Mission San Luis Rey. The widely used castor bean (*Ricinus communis*), whose seeds were brought from Mexico, was known as *Palma Christi* because of its five-fingered leaves. *Nicotiana glauca,* the tobacco plant from the Argentine, was also a favorite, as was the European giant reed (*Arundo donax*), which was grown chiefly for windbreaks and for the making of mats. Besides the date palm, the Franciscans raised the Mexican fan palm (*Washingtonia robusta*) and the native fan palm (*Washingtonia filifera*), the seeds of which were brought by the padres from the California desert and planted in their gardens.

The work of the Franciscans did not extend beyond the cactus hedges enclosing their mission lands, although seeds and cuttings of their plants were distributed to the settlers who asked for them. The padres were primarily men of God and their powers ended with their proselytization of the Indians, though within the bounds of the missions they were complete masters. In 1822, however, the death knell sounded for these outposts of Spain and the Catholic Church. Mexico in that year attained her independence and, fearful of any situation that might jeopardize her standing, issued an edict that the California missions be secularized. Although the full impact of this decree was not felt until 1834, the missions, shorn of their prestige, began slowly to deteriorate. By 1839 San Diego had already fallen into decay, its vineyard unpruned and the soil untilled. In 1843 San Juan Capistrano was reported to have been a brothel. In 1852 the last baptism was recorded in San Gabriel, but the Mother Mission was by then but an unhappy relic of times past. In 1834 a blight had fallen on her 163,000 vines, and her orange grove, then the only one in California and boasting of 2333 trees, was in decline. "All now is in ruins," wrote William Brewer in 1861. "Long lines of prickly pear hedges, now all ruined, told of ancient enclosures and vineyards, but now a waste. Immense labor had once wrought this lovely valley into a veritable paradise, but now it is desolate again."

One by one the mission bells were silenced, the fountains stilled, the garden paths choked with weeds, and the flower beds left to perish. The avenues of fig, olive, and citrus, which the padres had carefully tended in order that they might have shade during the long days of summer, were cut down too often by American squatters for firewood. Throughout Padre Serra's rosary of missions desolation was to prevail in most instances for more than half a century.

Although the sphere in which they worked was limited, the Franciscans left an indelible imprint on the land they had sought to cultivate. For three quarters of a century their missions had been the only developed areas in an otherwise primitive region. It was they who planted the first orange grove and gathered the first grapes for wine: it was they who showed that the olive would flourish and bear fruit. They introduced the palm and the pepper tree into California gardens, as well as many other plants closely associated with the "Golden State." The influence of the padres did not die with their missions; left behind was a heritage more valuable than the gold discovered later in the mountains. The padres proved that California's greatest treasure lay in a soil capable of producing crops that would bring more wealth than all the minerals within the hills. They did reveal that the "Garden of the Hesperides" was not entirely a myth.

*

From *Southern California Gardens,* Victoria Padilla (1905-1986). Berkeley: University of California Press, 1961. Padilla provides groundbreaking scholarship for a geographic region whose horticultural life is much less documented than that of the East Coast. Her book is an enthusiastic historical survey of early influential nurseries and central figures in the trade, detailing the worldwide importance of the Southern California seed industry. It also gives a good sketch of California flora, imported and native.

A prominent figure in Southern California horticulture, she helped to found The Bromeliad Society in 1950. She wrote three books on bromeliads, and from 1960 through 1980 was editor of the *Journal of the Bromeliad Society.*

FIRST IMPRESSIONS

DAVID DOUGLAS

AUGUST 19TH 1825. TOWARDS AFTERNOON left in a small canoe with one Canadian and two Indians, in company with a party of men going on a hunting excursion to southward, on a visit to the Willamette River, one of the southern branches of the Columbia. The distance I was enabled to go was about 56 miles. The river is large, nearly as large as the Thames. Thirty-six miles from the Columbia are very fine falls, about 43 feet high, across the whole river, in an oblique direction; when the river is low they are divided into three principal channels, all of which have a perpendicular pier; when the water is high it rushes over in an unbroken sheet. This season in July, which is the time it is at its greatest height, it rose 47 feet. From the Columbia to the Falls there is but little or no current; gorged back by the waters of that river. The banks are covered with *Pseudotsuga menziesii, A. balsamea,* oak and poplar. The soil is by far the richest I have seen. Above the Falls, as far as I went, at many places the current is rapid. I had considerable difficulty in making the portages at the Falls, having to haul the canoe up with ropes; this laborious undertaking occupied three hours, and one hour on my return. This at one time was looked on as the finest place for hunting west of the Rocky Mountains. The beaver now is scarce; none alive came under my notice. I was much gratified in viewing the deserted lodges and dams of that wise economist. . . .

Collected the following plants and obtained seeds of several very important plants already collected: among them *Nicotiana quadrivulvis,* correctly supposed by Nuttall to exist on the Columbia; whether its original habitat is here in the Rocky Mountains, or on the Missouri, I am unable to say, but am inclined to think it must be in the mountains. I am informed by the hunters it is more abundant towards them and particularly so among the Snake Indians, who frequently visit the Indians inhabiting the head-waters of the Missouri by whom it might be carried in both directions. I have seen only one plant before, in the hand of an Indian two months since at the Great Falls of the Columbia, and although I offered him 2 ozs. of manufactured tobacco he would on no consideration part with it. The natives cultivate it here, and although I made diligent search for it, it never came under my notice until now. They do not cultivate it near camps or lodges, lest it should be taken for use before maturity. An open place in the wood is chosen where there is dead wood, which they burn, and sow the seed in the ashes. Fortunately I met with one of the little plantations and supplied myself with seeds and specimens without delay. On my way home I met the owner, who, seeing it under my arm, appeared to be much displeased; but by presenting him with two finger-lengths of tobacco from Europe his wrath was appeased and we became good friends. He then gave me the above description of cultivating it. He told me that wood ashes made it grow very large. I was much pleased with the idea of using wood ashes. Thus we see that even the savages on the Columbia know the good effects produced on vegetation by the use of carbon. His knowledge of plants and their uses gained him another finger-length. When we smoked we were all in all.

Returned on the 30th of August. From that time till Thursday, September 1st, employed drying, arranging, putting up seeds, and making up my notes. Early on Thursday went on a journey to the Grand Rapids to collect seeds of several plants seen in flower in June and July. Went up in a canoe accompanied by one Canadian and a Chief (called Chumtalia) of the tribe inhabiting the north banks of the river at the Rapids. I arrived on the evening of the second day and pitched my tent a short distance from the village. I caused my Canadian to drench the ground well with water to prevent me from being annoyed with fleas, although I was not altogether exempt from them, yet it had a good effect. I found my Indian friend during my stay very attentive and I received no harm or insult. He accompanied me on some of my journeys. (They were only a few years since very hostile. The Company's boats were frequently pillaged by them and some of their people killed.) My visit was the first ever made without a guard. On Saturday morning went on a journey to the summit near the Rapids on the north side of the river, with the chief's brother as my guide, leaving the Canadian to take care of the tent and property. This took three days, and was one of the most laborious undertakings I ever experienced, the way was so rough, over dead wood, detached rocks, rivulets, &c. that very little paper could be carried. Indeed I was obliged to leave my blanket (which, on my route is all my bedding) at my first encampment about two-thirds up. My provision was 3 oz. tea, 1 lb. sugar, and four small biscuits. On the summit all the herbage is low shrub but chiefly herb plants. The second day I caught no fish, and at such a great altitude the only birds to be seen were hawks, eagles, vultures, &c. I was fortunate enough to kill one young white-headed eagle, which (then) I found very good eating. On the summit of the hill I slept one night. I made a small fire of grass and twigs and dried my clothes which were wet with perspiration and then laid myself down on the grass with my feet to the fire. I found it very cold and had to rise four times and walk to keep myself warm. Fortunately it was dry and a keen north wind prevented dew. On Monday evening at dusk I reached my tent at the village much fatigued and weak and found all things going on smoothly. Made a trip to the opposite side two days later, also to the summit of the hills, which I found of easier ascent, the only steep part near the top. My food during my stay was fresh salmon, without salt, pepper, or any other spice, with a very little biscuit and tea, which is a great luxury after a day's march.

Last night my Indian friend Cockqua arrived here from his tribe on the coast, and brought me three of the hats made on the English fashion, which I ordered when there in July; the fourth, which will have some initials wrought in it, is not finished, but will be sent by the other ship. I think them a good specimen of the ingenuity of the natives and particularly also being made by the little girl, twelve years old, spoken of when at the village. I paid one blanket (value 7s.) for them, the fourth included. We smoked; I gave him a dram and a few needles,

beads, pins, and rings as a present for the little girl. Faithful to his pro-
position he brought me a large paper of seeds of *Vaccinium ovatum* in a
perfect state, which I showed him when there, then in an unripe state. I
have circulated notices among my Indian acquaintances to obtain it for
me.

*

From *Journal,* David Douglas (1799-1834). London: William Wesley and
Son, 1914. The Douglas fir, and Mount Douglas, a Rocky Mountain peak, are
named after this rugged Scottish plant explorer who came to the U.S. in 1823
to collect for the London (later called Royal) Horticultural Society. With the
help of the Hudson's Bay Company he soon sailed for the West Coast, wandering around British Columbia and Oregon the next few years. Douglas's unsen-
timental journal entries give a grim picture of hardship and deprivation
brought on by hunger and cold and natural disasters, sometimes by conflict
with Indians. He suffered the loss of specimens and arduous journies by foot
through often deadly terrain. This was a time in U.S. history when the territories of California, Nevada, Utah, Arizona, New Mexico, and Texas were
under Mexican rule. In a wilderness largely unmapped, Douglas believed
himself on occasion to be the first white man confronting a certain landscape.
This great explorer managed to discover and introduce countless species of
plants from the Pacific Northwest to the Mexican lands, including the sugar
pine, red-osier dogwood, and black oak. He gave numerous trees, particularly
conifers, to the British landscape. Soon he would give his life. The heroic
Douglas came to an unfortunate, early end in Hawaii, on his way back to
England, when he accidentally fell into a pit used to trap bulls, and was
mauled to death.

THE PRINCESS KURUME

ERNEST H. WILSON

WE HAVE THE HONOR TO ANNOUNCE THAT Princess Kurume, reigning beauty of the Azalea Kingdom, is in town and will hold court throughout Easter. Further, I have to declare the Princess' intention of becoming a permanent resident, also, that in each succeeding year her court will be held continuously from Christmas to Easter. The doors are open to all. Her handsome debonair Chinese cousin, under the pseudonym of Indian azalea, has been long a favorite in the floral courts of America and Europe and so, too, have other relatives, but endowed with radiant beauty this youthful, winsome Princess is bound to capture and hold the stronghold of public affection and esteem. She first came to these shores as a baby in 1916 and in 1920 a few favored folk were permitted to peep at this charming damsel in conservative Boston, Massachusetts. The effect was magical, all who saw forthwith became her devotees. Her first lover in this part of the world, her sponsor and guardian, I immediately found myself a mere atom in her universe. A crown of gold was by unanimous consent placed on her head and with loud acclamation she was proclaimed mistress royal of her clan. Pleasing speeches were made and nice things said of me for the part I had played in prevailing upon her to leave her island home of the Rising Sun to grace these western shores. Her conquest was too spontaneous and complete for jealousy to wing dart. Hard-headed nurserymen fell in love with her at first sight even as I had done, and she was surrounded by chaperons intent upon providing for her well-being and proper education into western modes of life. I relinquished my trust and went abroad not disconsolate, however, since I knew she was in safe hands.

Since that epoch-making date Princess Kurume has, except on rare occasions, remained in the seclusion of educational cloisters. Her education completed the pleasant task of announcing the coming of age of this royal debutante has fallen to me.

More than royal is this lovely Princess, for is she not descended from Ninigi, grandson of the Sun-goddess, Amaterasu? History tells that her ancestors sprang from the soil on which Ninigi alighted when he came down from heaven to found the Empire of Japan. If skeptics there be they have but to visit Mt. Kirishima, in south Japan, where they themselves can see in wondrous beauty the kinsfolk of this damsel in countless thousands embellishing the slopes of this sacred and still active volcano. How many generations of the Princess' family displayed their beauty to the sun, the moon and the stars, to the birds of the air and the four-footed friends that walk the earth we do not know. But about a century ago a wandering pilgrim of the genus Homo became enraptured with them and lovingly carried a few away to his home in the town of Kurume and a new era in the family history dawned.

I was first introduced to the Kurume family in 1914 when, at the invitation of my lamented friend, the late Mr. H. Suzuki, the foremost Japanese horticulturist of his time, I accompanied him on a visit to the nursery district of Hatagaya, a few miles north of Tokyo. There in a garden I saw thousands of tiny plants bearing white and colored flowers of nearly every hue. With the courteous consent of the owner I secured a set of fragments and dried them for the Arnold Arboretum. In 1917, at my suggestion, Mr. John S. Ames secured a number of small plants from this collection and these were the first ever brought into the eastern States. They were midgets, indeed, but grew amazingly and flowered profusely and soon became one of the floral delights of the Ames Estate, a joy to the owner and his friends.

What I saw in 1914 whetted my appetite and I was hungry to see and learn more about these delightful plants. Opportunity came in 1918, and to my great good fortune my friend, Suzuki, was able to accompany me to the headquarters of the family, the city of Kurume. This city is on the island of Kyushu, situated some 800 miles south by west of Tokyo and is quite an important place. But the fame of its azaleas will make it universally known. There we arrived on a fine May morning, to find the azaleas in the pink of perfection. I went prepared to see a display of blossoms, but the entrancing beauty of myriad delicately colored flowers clothing a multitude of shapely grown plants surpassed my most sanguine expectations. The gardens of two leading specialists were veritable fairy-lands and I gasped with astonishment when I realized that garden-lovers of America and Europe knew virtually nothing of this wealth of beauty. Most of the plants were trained into low standards, each about 20 inches high with flattened or convex crowns some 24 inches through, and were monuments to the patience and cultural skill of the Japanese gardener. Other shapes there were but this was the favorite and most effective. The flowers, each about one-half to three-quarters of an inch across and borne in clusters of from two to several at the end of the twigs, were in such profusion as to almost completely hide the leaves. If a fault could be found, it was that the flowers were too numerous! Some have bizarre-colored flowers but such I do not favor. A great many have the calyx petaloid and the flowers are hose-in-hose. The stamens, always five, and pistil are perfect and there is no malformation as in ordinary double-flowers. The anthers are light to dark, varying with the color shades, tip the straight filaments and add not a little to the pleasing appearance of the flowers. They are, in truth, the roguish eyes of laughing, dimpled and blushing blossoms.

At Kurume the azaleas are grown in a number of gardens but the oldest and best collection is that of Mr. Kijiro Akashi, who for more than forty years has assiduously devoted himself to the development of these charming azaleas. He has raised from seeds and perpetuated by cuttings nearly all the kinds in cultivation. In his garden is the finest of all collections, and the loving pride with which this grand old gardener pointed out to us the particular merits of this or that pet can be appreciated only by those whose lives have been lived in close companionship with plants. In this garden I made a selection in duplicate of fifty of the best kinds. Making the selection was much easier than the persuading later of Mr. Akashi to part with them, though, with true old-time Japanese politeness, he had offered me any or all that he had.

He loved his plants and I fully understand his diffidence when the time to part with them actually came.

I think that Kurume azaleas are the loveliest of all azaleas. Small of stature but sturdy they are rich in attractive features. The branches are very numerous and twiggy, clothed with small neat rich green leaves and crowned with clusters of small slightly fragrant flowers, which on different individuals embrace all the delicate shades of color familiar to us in sweet peas. The individual flower suggests the frilled petticoat of a dainty lady. In many the calyx, green and inconspicuous in ordinary flowers, grows to the same size and has the same color as the corolla and here we get two frilled petticoats, one over the other, of exquisite grace and finish. Such arrangement is called hose-in-hose, that is one flower within another. These hose-in-hose flowers have none of the ugliness usually associated with the double flowers and, moreover, last in perfection much longer than the ordinary sorts.

The colors so pure and exquisite, are of every hue and shade—pure pink to rose-color, cerise, lavender, vermilion, salmon, bright red to scarlet, crimson and the richest magenta; others the purest white.

At Kurume the plants are often trained as low standards with a compact umbrella-shaped crown; less commonly they are dense and globose, or open and irregular in form. They are extremely floriferous, and in season the blossoms often completely hide the leaves. The leaves are of two forms and they vary considerably in size, in shades of green, in their autumn-coloring and in their degree of persistence. In a great measure these variations are correlated with the color of the flowers, and experts in Japan can with ease distinguish each variety by its foliage and general appearance. . . .

As to the origin and history of these plants, Mr. Akashi kindly furnished me with the details. They were originated by a Japanese gentleman named Motozo Sakamoto, who lived in the city of Kurume about one hundred years ago. The parent stock came from sacred Mt. Kirishima, but whether brought from there by Sakamoto or given to him by some pilgrim is uncertain. At any rate, he cultivated several varieties and raised and selected seedlings, including one he named "Azuma-kagami" from which it is claimed have descended all the pink-colored forms. After his death, Sakamoto's collection passed into the hands of K. Akashi. The original plant "Azuma-kagami" is still healthy. I photographed it but failed to purchase it, though I tried hard to do so. Mr. Akashi showed us a gold medal awarded to him for an exhibit of thirty plants, in a dozen kinds, of Kurume azaleas at the Panama Pacific Exposition, San Francisco, in 1915. The plants were afterwards sold, and Akashi's pride in the gold medal seemed a little saddened when he thought of the loss of those thirty plants.

Next it was determined to visit Mt. Kirishima, the place tradition says the parents of the plants came from. I had visited this mountain early in March, 1914, and remembered that an azalea grew there and that I had gathered leafless specimens. We spent a night near the base of Kirishima and starting early the next morning soon reached an altitude of 3000 feet above sea-level, where forests abruptly give place to grassland and saw before us the mountain slopes dotted with blossoming azalea bushes in quantity. They grow in volcanic soil on wideswept grassy slopes and among rocks. In size the bushes are from nearly prostrate to a yard high, and hardly two plants have flowers of the same shade of color. We gathered specimens of forms with pink, salmon, mauve to rich magenta-colored flowers and at a little higher altitude red-flowered forms and an occasional white one. We found much variation in the size and shape of the flowers and leaves and also that the anthers varied in color. The evidence was complete in every detail, and no shadow of doubt as to the origin of the wondrous race of azaleas we had seen in Kurume remained in our minds.

To a place so sacred as Kirishima pilgrimages have been made by the Japanese from immemorial time. With their profound love for flowers some of the pilgrims would certainly take back as souvenirs living plants of this charming azalea. Naturally it was named for the mountain, and in the course of time was distributed widely in the gardens of Japan. It is easily understood that a plant bearing flowers of an unusual color would be that selected as a souvenir by the average pilgrim. It is such forms that reached gardens first, and so we find the red *obtusa,* the magenta *amoena,* the white *alba* to be the earliest known.

The reader may think it strange that a race of azaleas so rich in forms and of such decorative value should have remained so long unknown to us, yet the explanation is simple. Interior Kyushu is little known to the Western world, and even to those Japanese whose homes are on the other islands. The feudal system of government which until comparatively recently obtained in Japan created and preserved this aloofness. Further, Kurume is remote from the horticultural centers of

Osaka and Yokohama, from whence we have drawn the bulk of our garden plants and where business is made of growing for export. Nagasaki is much nearer, but in the days of early explorers, intercommunication was difficult and, for foreigners, impossible. And so it has resulted that the product of Sakamoto's hobby, richly developed by Akashi, has remained hidden from the outside world until now. During the last fifteen years the fame of the Kurume azaleas has reached Osaka, Tokyo and other places, and growers have obtained stocks and are propagating them apace. Unfortunately, every grower and enthusiast names the plants according to his fancy and the result in a few years will be chaos. And this is helped by the fact that every slight sport or variant is kept and named and no attempt at selection made. I do not see how it is possible to improve upon the strain grown in Kurume unless yellow could be injected. What is needed is rigorous selection and the reduction of the named forms to fifty or less. In the past seedling selection and preservation of sports by vegetative propagation have been the sole means employed in the evolution of the race of Kurume azaleas, but now attempts at hybridizing them with the large flowered "Indian" and "Ledifolia" types are in progress. This may result in a new race, but whether it will be as lovely and fascinating as the present one is doubtful.

Just how hardy this race will prove remains to be seen, but I am of the opinion that under the genial influence of the Gulf Stream from Cape Cod southward many places will be found where they will be at home and flourish in perfection. They root readily from cuttings and in conservatories may be had in blossom from Christmas until Easter. Good-natured, adaptable, at home in any surroundings, brightening and cheering us with a glow of color and beauty—the divine Princess Kurume is assured of a lasting welcome in the land of her adoption. Proud am I of being the fortunate one to introduce this exquisite damsel to the gardens of eastern North America.

*

From *Plant Hunting,* Vol. II, Ernest H. Wilson (1876-1930). Boston: The Stratford Company, 1927. Wilson was one of the last of the great, bold plant hunters. It was the noted Veitch nursery in his native England that first sent him to the Orient in 1899, in search of Abbé David's famed dove tree. This was an era when some men hunted tigers and others, none the less adventurous, hunted plants, and somewhere in this age of glamour and empire and tourism, there is a story to be written about the politics of horticulture. Wilson clearly loved his work, and seemed to take a special interest in the personalities of plants, referring to the "arrogant gladiolus" and "my lady acacia." He risked his life in the province of Szechuan to bring back the Regal lily. Wilson collected so many species in China he was called "Chinese" Wilson, but he also visited Japan, India, Sikkim, South and Central Africa, Australia, and New Zealand. In 1909 he joined Charles S. Sargent at the Arnold Arboretum in Massachusetts, eventually succeeding him as keeper.

Wilson wrote many books on his travels, *A Naturalist in Western China, Aristocrats of the Trees, Cherries of Japan,* and the two-volume *Plant Hunting* which opens rather dashingly with these words: "From 1899 when I paid my first visit to China until 1922, when I sailed home from Cape Town in South Africa, I wandered about the world in search of plants." The books are filled with his photographs, then a new research tool, which document a more peaceful occupation in this period of history framed by the Boxer Rebellion in China and later World War I in Europe. Wilson introduced more than a thousand species to the West, including several rhododendrons, cotoneaster, meadow rue, Chinese dogwood, and paperbark maple. Many of the tropical plants he brought back influenced hothouse cultivation.

The ebullient Wilson who had traveled deep into remote, dangerous terrain and across formidable mountain passes, to bring back plants which were to change the shape of the modern garden, died a simple death in a car accident on a Massachusetts highway, not far from his American home.

New Acquisitions to the American Flora

Frederick Pursh

Among the numerous useful and inter-esting objects of natural history discovered on the vast extent of the New Continent, none claim our attention in a higher degree than the vegetable productions of North America. Her forests produce an endless variety of useful and stately timber trees; her woods and hedges the most ornamental flowering shrubs, so much admired in our pleasure grounds; and her fields and meadows a number of exceedingly handsome and singular flowers (many of them possessing valuable medicinal virtues), different from those of other countries. All these are more or less capable of being adapted to an European climate, and the greater part of easy cultivation and quick growth; which circumstances have given them, with much propriety, the first rank in ornamental gardening.

A country so highly abundant in all the objects of my favourite pur-suits, excited in me, at an early period of life, a strong desire to visit it, and to observe in their natural soil and climate the plants which I then knew; and to make such discoveries as circumstances might throw in my way. This plan I carried into execution in the year 1799; when I left Dresden, the place where I had received my education, and em-barked for Baltimore in Maryland, with a determination not to return to Europe until I should have examined that country to the utmost extent of my means and abilities. In 1811, after an absence of nearly twelve years, I returned to Europe, with an ample stock of materials towards a Flora of North America. . . .

My first object, after my arrival in America, was to form an acquaintance with all those interested in the study of botany. Among these I had the pleasure to account one of the earliest, and ever after the most valuable, the Rev. Dr. Mühlenberg of Lancaster, in Pennsylvania, a gentleman whose industry and zeal for the science can only be surpassed by the accuracy and acuteness of his observations; I only regret, that his extensive and interesting materials towards a Flora of the United States, in which he has been engaged for a number of years, should not before this have been communicated to the public.

I next visited the old established gardens of Mr. Marshall, author of a small *Treatise on the Forest-trees of North America.* This gentleman, though then far advanced in age and deprived of his eye-sight, conducted me personally through his collection of interesting trees and shrubs, pointing out many which were then new to me, which strongly proved his attachment and application to the science in former years, when his vigour of mind and eye-sight were in full power. This establishment, since the death of Mr. Marshall, (which happened a few years ago), has been, in some respects, kept up by the family, but is now very much on the decline, only a few old established trees being left as a memento of what formerly deserved the name of a respectable botanic garden.

Near Philadelphia I found the botanic garden of Messrs. John and William Bartram. This is likewise an old establishment, founded under the patronage of the late Dr. Fothergill, by the father of the now living Bartrams. This place, delightfully situated on the banks of the Delaware, is kept up by the present proprietors, and probably will increase under the care of the son of John Bartram, a young gentleman of classical education, and highly attached to the study of botany. In Mr. William Bartram, the well known author of *Travels Through North and South Carolina,* I found a very intelligent, agreeable, and communicative gentleman; and from him I received considerable information about the plants of that country, particularly respecting the habitats of a number of rare and interesting trees. It is with the liveliest emotions of pleasure I call to mind the happy hours I spent in this

worthy man's company, during the period I lived in his neighbourhood.

Not far from the latter place are also the extensive gardens of
William Hamilton, Esq., called the Woodlands, which I found not only
rich in plants from all parts of the world, but particularly so in rare and
new American species. Philadelphia being a central situation, and extremely well calculated for the cultivation of plants from all the other
parts of North America, I found this collection particularly valuable for
furnishing me with a general knowledge of the plants of that country,
preparatory to more extensive travels into the interior, for the
discovery of new and unknown subjects. Mr. John Lyon, who had the
management of these gardens, was then about to give them up: having
the offer of being appointed his successor, I embraced it, and accordingly in 1802 I entered upon the situation. During my stay in this place,
which was until 1805, I received and collected plants from all parts of
North America; and when Michaux's *Flora Boreali-Americana* appeared, which was during that time, I was not only in possession of
most of his plants, but had then a considerable number not described
by him.

Within this period I had also formed a connection with Dr. Benjamin
S. Barton, Professor of Botany in the University of Pennsylvania, &c.
whose industrious researches in all the different branches of natural
history are so well known to the literary world. He likewise, for some
time previous, had been collecting materials for an American Flora. As
I was now very anxious to explore the more remote parts of the country, particularly the interesting ranges of the Alleghany Mountains, I
was enabled, by the kind assistance of this gentleman, to take a more
extensive range for my botanical excursions, which during my stay at
the Woodlands had been confined within a comparatively small compass, the necessary attention to the duties of that establishment not permitting me to devote more time to them.

Accordingly, in the beginning of 1805, I set out for the mountains
and western territories of the Southern States, beginning at Maryland
and extending to the Carolinas, (in which tract the interesting high
mountains of Virginia and Carolina took my particular attention), and
returning late in the autumn through the lower countries along the
sea-coast to Philadelphia. The following season, 1806, I went in like
manner over the Northern States, beginning with the mountains of

Pennsylvania and extending to those of New Hampshire, (in which tract I traversed the extensive and highly interesting country of the Lesser and Great Lakes), and returning as before by the sea-coast.

Both these tours I principally made on foot, the most appropriate way for attentive observation, particularly in mountainous countries; travelling over an extent of more than three thousand miles each season, with no other companions than my dog and gun, frequently taking up my lodging in the midst of wild mountains and impenetrable forests, far remote from the habitations of men. The collections and observations made in the course of these journeys, all of which I communicated to Dr. Barton, were considerable, in respect to the discovery of many new and interesting subjects of natural history in general. But the knowledge which I thereby acquired of the geography, soil, and situation of the plants of that country, (points of the greatest interest to the practical botanist), was of the greatest importance to me.

Soon after my return from the last-mentioned journey, I had the pleasure to form an acquaintance with Meriwether Lewis, Esq., then Governor of Upper Louisiana, who had lately returned from an expedition across the Continent of America to the Pacific Ocean, by the way of the Missouri and the great Columbia rivers, executed under the direction of the Government of the United States. A small but highly interesting collection of dried plants was put into my hands by this gentleman, in order to describe and figure those I thought new, for the purpose of inserting them in the account of his Travels, which he was then engaged in preparing for the press. . . .

The collection of plants just spoken of was made during the rapid return of the expedition from the Pacific Ocean towards the United States. A much more extensive one, made on their slow ascent towards the Rocky Mountains and the chains of the Northern Andes, had unfortunately been lost, by being deposited among other things at the foot of those mountains. The loss of this first collection is the more to be regretted, when I consider that the small collection communicated to me; consisting of about one hundred and fifty specimens, contained not above a dozen plants well known to me to be natives of North America, the rest being either entirely new or but little known, and among them at least six distinct and new genera. This may give an idea of the discerning eye of their collector, who had but little practical knowledge of the Flora of North America, as also of the richness of those extensive regions in new and interesting plants, and other natural productions. Several of them I have had an opportunity of examining in their living state, some being cultivated from seeds procured by Mr. Lewis, and others since my arrival in England from seeds and plants introduced by Mr. Nuttall.

Here I cannot refrain from drawing the attention of future botanists travelling those regions, to two highly interesting plants, of which I have only seen imperfect specimens. The first is what Mr. Lewis in his journals calls "the Osage Apple," or "Arrowwood of the Missouris." This is a tree, or rather shrub, with leaves resembling those of a pear-tree, but broader in proportion; they are alternate, and have a recurved thorn near their base; the flowers are of separate sexes, and appear in axillary, peduncled, globular catkins, which produce a depressed globular fruit, in size and colour resembling an orange, in interior structure approaching near to the genus Morinda. This shrub, on account of its fruit and handsome foliage, must be highly ornamental: the wood, being excessively hard, is preferred by the natives to any other for making their arrows; and as it does not spontaneously grow in their neighbourhood, they travel annually to a considerable distance South-west, to procure it. About the village of the Osage Indians a few trees have been planted, from which one has been introduced into one of the gardens at St. Louis on the Mississippi. Perfect seeds from the last-mentioned tree were given by Mr. Lewis to Mr. M'Mahon, nursery and seedsman, at Philadelphia, who raised several fine plants from them, and in whose possession they were when I left America. The other plant alluded to is called by Mr. Lewis "A bulbous Rush, which serves the Indians for bread." Of this I have only seen the root, which is of a yellowish-brown colour, about the thickness of a finger, and jointed; on each joint, which are about three inches asunder, several tubers of about an inch and a half are produced, of an oblong ovate shape, tapering into a point towards the end; these tubers are filled with an exquisite white and fine farina, resembling starch; these roots are used in the same manner as those of *Psoralea esculenta*. I take this to be a larger species of tuberous *Cyperus*.

While I was thus engaged in describing and figuring those new acquisitions to the American Flora, another opportunity offered to augment my resources. Mr. Aloysius Enslen, who had been sent to America by Prince Lichtenstein of Austria, as a collector of new and interesting subjects of natural history, returned to Philadelphia from his extensive travels through the Western Territories and Southern States. This gentleman, with whom I had previously been on terms of intimate friendship, was now in possession of an extremely valuable collection of living and dried plants, to which I had unrestrained access. To his liberality I am indebted for many new and scarce specimens, which filled up a desideratum in my collection, particularly in the plants of Lower Louisiana and Georgia.

At the same time I had frequent opportunities of seeing the herbarium and collection of living plants of Mr. John Lyon, a gentleman through whose industry and skill more new and rare American plants have lately been introduced into Europe than through any other channel whatever.

By these and several other connections, which it is unnecessary to mention here, added to my own occasional excursions through the different parts of the United States, I was put in possession of an extensive herbarium, containing plants from all the different parts of North America; which when summed up would nearly double the number of those described in Michaux's excellent *Flora.* As that work was then extremely scarce in America, I determined to publish a Compendium of it, executed on the plan of Hoffmann's *Flora Germanica,* which work I had no doubt would be acceptable to the botanist, and particularly so to the cultivator. I communicated my design to Messrs. Bradford and Inskeep, booksellers at Philadelphia, who gave me every encouragement towards the prosecution thereof.

While I was engaged in arranging my materials for this publication, I was called upon to take the management of the Botanic Garden at New York, which had been originally established by the arduous zeal and exertions of Dr. David Hosack, Professor of Botany, &c. as his private property, but has lately been bought by the Government of the State of New York for the public service. As this employment opened a further prospect to me of increasing my knowledge of the plants of that country, I willingly dropped the idea of my intended publication for that time, and in 1807 took charge of that establishment.

Here I again endeavoured to pay the utmost attention to the collection of American plants, as the establishment was principally intended for that purpose. In this I was supported by my numerous botanical connections and friends, among whom I must particularly mention

John Le Conte, Esq. of Georgia, whose unremitting exertions added considerably to the collection, particularly of plants from the Southern States.

The additions to my former stock of materials for a Flora were now considerable, and in conjunction with Dr. D. Hosack I had engaged to publish a periodical work, with coloured plates, all taken from living plants, and if possible from native specimens, on a plan similar to that of Curtis's Botanical Magazine; for which a great number of drawings were actually prepared. But at this period I was attacked by a serious and obstinate intermitting fever, which made a change of air and climate absolutely necessary to me; I therefore, in 1810, took a voyage to the West Indies, visiting the islands of Barbadoes, Martinique, Dominique, Guadaloupe, and St. Bartholomew's, from which I returned in the autumn of 1811 in a perfect state of recovered health. The vessel in which I returned landed at the town of Wiscasset in the province of Maine. This being a country I had never visited before, I examined its vegetation with all possible attention; and although the season was too far advanced for making any new discoveries, I gained considerable information respecting the geography of plants, a point I always considered highly interesting to the science. During my journey towards New York, I had an opportunity of visiting Professor Peck of Cambridge College near Boston, and seeing his highly interesting collection of plants, collected on a tour to the alpine regions of the White Hills of New Hampshire. As the season was too far advanced when I was in that country to suffer me to think of ascending those mountains, this collection was highly gratifying to me.

On my return to New York, I found things in a situation very unfavourable to the publication of scientific works, the public mind being then in agitation about a war with Great Britain. I therefore determined to take all my materials to England, where I conceived I should not only have the advantage of consulting the most celebrated collections and libraries, but also meet with that encouragement and support so necessary to works of science, and so generally bestowed upon them there.

*

From *Flora Americae Septentrionalis,* Vol. I, Frederick Pursh (1774-1820). London: White, Cochrane and Company, 1814. The gifted, controversial Pursh was one of a number of foreign travelers who made timely contributions to early American horticulture. He had worked in the Royal Botanic Garden of Dresden before coming to the U.S. where he seems easily to have made the acquaintance of the leading men in the botanical field of his day. Like David Douglas, he visited Michaux's New Jersey nursery. He also traveled extensively on collecting trips. For a few years he was in charge of one of the most important gardens of the period, Dr. Hosack's Elgin Botanic Garden which, in the pastoral days of 1811, was established on the site of what is now Rockefeller Center. Pursh tells his own story quite well, and indeed his achievements are not to be undervalued. His two-volume *Flora* offered the first account of North American plants that included the glories of the Pacific Northwest. Nevertheless, he apparently helped himself to the Lewis and Clark specimens and drawings deposited with him, and Nuttall criticized Pursh for making use of his research without crediting him.

The Flowering Cherry Trees Are Planted in Washington

David Fairchild

And now the moment has come to tell the story of the Japanese flowering cherry trees planted on the Speedway and around the Tidal Basin in Washington. I am often asked how they came there, for they have become a national institution; they appear on rosy picture postals and each spring they create a special fiesta as increasing thousands come to view their pink perfection.

Back in 1905 when Marian and I bought "In the Woods," one of our chief preoccupations had been to have a place where we could grow Japanese flowering cherry trees, and the first plants to arrive there were cherries from my friend H. Suzuki of the Yokohama Nursery Company. It was all an experiment in those days. Doubt of their hardiness had been expressed by so many horticultural experts that I tried to coddle them by planting them in sheltered spots.

The strange and happy coincidence which sent our gardener Mori to us just at this time, with a letter of introduction from Professor Tomari, was of real benefit to the cherries. Mori cleared places here and there among the cedars and made what he called a "sakura-no" or field of cherries, and later a "sakura-michi," cherry path. Mori also translated the Japanese names into English; there were, for example, the Tiger's Tail, the Milky Way, and The Royal Carriage Turns Again to Look and See.

Curiously enough, there is an important psychological difficulty which attaches to the name ''cherry'' tree in countries like ours where the cherry is a popular and abundant fruit. This was brought home to me by a question fired at me by Franklin K. Lane, when he was in the Cabinet of President Wilson. He arrived when I was showing our cherry trees to the Japanese Ambassador and his staff, and, with his usual brusque joviality, Mr. Lane remarked, ''Cherry trees? Cherry trees? Do they produce good cherries?'' In defense of our beloved trees, I retorted, ''Must a rose or dogwood produce a fruit for us to eat?'' Marian tactfully suggested that if we called them ''cherry-blossom trees'' we would avoid much of this misunderstanding, and I think she is right.

When it had become evident that the trees would do well, Marian and I wanted to do something towards making them better known in Washington. We therefore sent to Japan for more trees, mainly of the drooping type which seemed to be the most hardy, and the following spring, through Miss Susan B. Sipe, the indefatigable teacher of ''Nature Study'' in the public schools, we invited a boy from each school in the District of Columbia to come out and get a tree for his particular school yard.

It was a wonderful day in the spring of 1908 when the boys came single file through the woods. The buds on the oaks were red with young growth, and hepaticas and blood-roots and dog-tooth violets were coming up under the dead leaves on the ground. Each boy was shown how to dig and plant his tree; we gave them a little talk on tree culture, and then they went back on the special car which the Street Car Company had provided for their transportation.

At the same time we discussed how the barrier of conservatism in the Department of Parks could be broken through and a ''sakura-no'' be made on the Speedway, which had just been created. I was to give an illustrated lecture at the Franklin School the next afternoon after the children had planted cherry trees in the school grounds, and I invited Miss Eliza R. Scidmore, then the most noted writer on Japan, to be present. I secured some views of the new, unplanted Speedway, which I threw on the screen at the close of the lecture saying that the Speedway would be an ideal place for a ''Field of Cherries,'' and quoted Miss Scidmore, the great authority on Japan, who was there as the distinguished guest of the occasion. The next day *The Washington Star* had an item: ''Celebrate Arbor Day. Pupils Plant Japanese Flowering Cherry Trees. Mr. Fairchild described the beautiful flora of Japan and aroused the enthusiasm of his audience by telling them that Washington would one day be famous for its flowering cherry trees.''

Mrs. Taft, at that time the First Lady of the Land, was much interested in all that concerned the beauty of Washington, so Miss Scidmore took our suggestion to her, with the result that the Park Department was asked to buy any available trees and to plant them along the Speedway. I think that it was the Ellwanger and Barry Nursery who supplied the first lot. Miss Scidmore consulted me regarding the importation of a large number from the Yokohama Nursery Company. She wanted bigger trees than Marian and I had imported, insisting that it was important to make a show as soon as possible, but I cautioned her not to order large trees, because of the difficulties in making them live as well as the extra expense involved.

Some time later Major Cosby, head of the Office of Public Buildings and Parks, wrote us that he had been notified by the Mayor of Tokyo that he was sending two thousand cherry trees as a gift to Mrs. Taft, to aid in her plans. As Major Cosby had no agent in Seattle through whom to arrange for their entry, I offered the services of our importing agent there, and the Office of Plant Introduction handled the shipment across the continent into Washington.

I had been worried about the trees, fearing that they might prove too large, but I had not dreamed of any difficulty with the Quarantine authorities; this was in the early days of the existence of the Quarantine and it had not yet assumed the role which it now plays. The crates arrived January 7, 1910, and immediately came under the inspectors' eyes, with the result that almost every sort of pest imaginable was discovered, and I found myself in a hornets' nest of protesting pathologists and entomologists, who were all demanding the destruction of the entire shipment.

Ghastly as it seems, the trees were all burned.

Public interest had been aroused and much expectancy encouraged, so that the handling of the newspapers was no easy matter, particularly as Commander Hobson chose just this moment to speak on the floor of Congress in a derogatory way of the Japanese. This, added to the disgust of Miss Scidmore, the annoyance of Major Cosby, the criticism of the pathologists and entomologists, and the astonishment of my Japanese friends, combined to give me many sleepless nights. My only comfort was the knowledge that the trees had been so large, and their roots had been so cut, that I felt sure the greater number of them would have perished in the raw soil of the Speedway.

The entire matter was finally hushed up. I wondered, of course, just what kind of impression the affair had made in Tokyo, but it was not until years afterwards, in Geneva, that Miss Scidmore told me of a meeting in Mayor Osaki's office at which it was suggested that if the American public felt towards the Japanese as Commander Hobson's speech seemed to indicate, the matter of the flowering cherries had better be dropped. Fortunately, more generous counsels prevailed, and on February 2, 1912, the Mayor of Tokyo wrote to the Superintendent of Public Buildings and Parks of Washington saying that he was sending another two thousand trees. In this letter he said:

> Although a small token of the very high esteem in which the people of this city hold your great country, it gives them boundless pleasure to think that the trees may in a measure add to the embellishment of your magnificent capital. As for the first lot of trees which we sent you three years ago, we are more satisfied that you dealt with them as you did, for it would have pained us endlessly to have them remain a permanent source of trouble. The present trees have been raised under the special care of scientific experts and are reasonably expected to be free from the defects of their predecessors.

When this second shipment arrived in March, 1912, many of the same quarantine inspectors who had examined the previous one were on hand and Dr. L. O. Howard, Chief of the Bureau of Entomology, stated that no shipment could have been cleaner and freer from insect pests.

It has always seemed a pity to me that the official planting on the Speedway was not made the occasion for an elaborate ceremonial, for I do not know of any greater or more lasting instance of international friendliness than that shown by the Japanese when they sent their favorite trees to flower in the heart of our Capital. The first tree was planted in the presence of Mrs. Taft, the Japanese Ambassador, Major Cosby and Miss Scidmore, but little was published in the papers about the affair.

Several years passed and the cherries around the Speedway came into

bloom, adding to our feeling that there should be an attempt on the part
of the city of Washington to return the courtesy of the Japanese. About
this time a great friend of Count Okuma, Mr. Kuwashima, visited
America. Swingle had met him in Japan, and we three were often
together when he reached Washington. The thought of some return
courtesy was discussed, and finally it was arranged that several
hundred dogwood trees, a large quantity of dogwood seed and some
plants of our mountain laurel should be sent from the Department of
Agriculture to Count Okuma for presentation to the city of Tokyo.

In 1918 I received the followed letter from Mayor Tojiri of Tokyo:

> The dogwoods which your government sent here in 1915 and 1917 blos-
> somed in the spring quite beautifully with popular admiration as the picture
> in forwarding by the same mail it seems that they suit to our climate very well
> and I hope they will do better in the future. I thank you very much for the
> Kalmias which were sent by your government. Then we shall take the best
> care for them and I hope they will do just as well as the dogwoods.

On receipt of the photograph of the American pink dogwood flowering in Tokyo, we felt that we should send pictures of the Japanese cherries flowering in Washington. This was done, and at the same time
duplicate sets were sent to Mrs. Taft and to Doctor Takamine of New
York, who had been an enthusiastic collaborator in the project.

I never dared to imagine the popular enthusiasm which these
Washington trees have caused throughout the country. Through them
there must have filtered into the consciousness of hundreds of
thousands an appreciation of the nobility of a people who can love these
trees as do the Japanese. A national holiday is declared in Japan when
the cherry trees come into bloom.

For keenest enjoyment, I visit the flowers when the dew is on them,
or in cloudy weather, or when the rain is falling; and I must be alone or
with someone who cares for them as I do. For those who are satisfied
with the distant view of a plant, the cherries may not seem as impressive as the hawthorns or flowering crab apples. The cherries are
more delicate and one must stand beneath their branches and see the
dainty blossoms against the blue or gray of the sky fully to appreciate
them.

I used to roam among our trees at dawn and gaze at the individual
flowers through the darkness of my enlarging camera before the

dewdrops had vanished from their petals. I seemed a Lilliputian wandering among their soft, velvety surfaces. As normal pictures did not reproduce this feeling, I decided to see whether by enlarging them I could give the impression which the actual flowers made upon my mind.

Of course I had my favorites among the twenty-five varieties scattered over our hillside. Alas, their names became involved in a nomenclatorial tangle.

However, some of the most beautiful varieties have survived with their names intact. The Murasaki, for example, with its deep purplish-pink, semi-double flowers which covered the ground with a carpet of pink petals as they fell, is still called Murasaki. But my Naden has become Shogetsu, though its extremely double blooms still hang on long flower stems and it still seems to have the most delicate shell-pink color of them all. Choshu, which is now recognized as the Kanzan, has immense double flowers of the deepest pink and was one of the latest of all to bloom; Ussussumi, now Shiro-Fugen, has deep sepia-colored foliage, and the flowers when half-opened are among the most charming blossoms in the world. The Amanogawa, Milky Way, with its strikingly fastigiate form, and its upright branches like garlands of delicate pink stretching upwards into the blue sky, never failed to thrill me, and as a tree for the small garden it deserves to be widely planted. The Asagi and the Ukon, strange, greenish-flowered varieties, were not so impressive on the tree, but Marian loved their strange exotic character and used them often as cut flowers in the house.

The trees I have just mentioned are more or less short-lived, cultivated varieties of the single species *Prunus serrulata,* whereas *Prunus yedoensis,* with its more vigorous growth and longer life, belongs to an entirely different class. I did not get the latter in my first introductions from Japan in 1902 and 1906, but later I ordered several in the collection for the Chevy Chase Land Company, for I had seen a remarkable tree of this species which Professor Sargent was growing in the Arnold Arboretum. These trees grew with amazing rapidity and have charmed all who pass them on Connecticut Avenue, near Chevy Chase Lake. This is the cherry which has been extensively planted in and around Tokyo, and nearly a thousand of the trees sent to Washington from the city of Tokyo were of this variety.

But of all the flowering cherries of Japan, those of the small-leaved species, which Ingram calls the Spring Cherries because they flower earlier than those just mentioned, are the ones which have always fired my imagination as an introducer of plants. There are two distinct forms: the weeping cherry, *Prunus subhirtella pendula,* and the erect type, *Prunus subhirtella ascendens,* either of which may appear when you plant seeds. I can assert this from personal experience, for the birds scattered the seeds of my trees of the weeping type and thousands of seedlings of this lovely tree grew wild in our woods. About one in ten of these seedlings had the weeping habit so characteristic of the parent.

When the drooping cherry trees began to show lavender tips in early April, they seemed like chiffon veils spread over the threadlike tracery of the bare branches. As the flowers opened, the color faded to a ghostly gray. Not only were they the first of the trees to come out in the spring, but from the very start they showed unusual vigor. It is now twenty-five years since little Mori planted the cherries and today the trunks are about a foot and a half in diameter at their bases and fully twenty-five feet in height. Compared with the double-flowered *Prunus serrulata* species, they give the impression of greater hardiness and the promise of far greater age. During the great drought of 1930, when so many trees in Washington suffered, they did not seem affected, although a good many of the shorter-lived cherries either died or were severely injured.

It is a great pity that most of the old specimens scattered throughout the Atlantic States were grafted high on Mazzard (*Prunus avium*) stock and are dying when they should be coming into their glory. When grafted low, beneath the ground, they soon get off onto their own roots, and there is every reason to feel confident that they will live for a century or more in America, as they do in their native country.

The October-bloomer, *Prunus subhirtella* var. *autumnalis,* blooms in the spring as well as in the fall, and is an ideal tree of just the right shape for a large city yard. Its scattering show of bloom in autumn after all other flowers were gone, and the fact that, at any time through the winter, branches taken into the house would bloom, never failed to surprise and charm us. It, too, will probably prove a long-lived tree in America.

Only the barest beginning has been made in a study of these enchanting trees. Hidden away among the ruins of those old feudal gardens of ancient Japan, there are priceless forms as yet unknown to us, while still lovelier and hardier and longer-lived varieties may yet be created to brighten the springtime of our gardens.

As trees, the cherries of Japan are not to be compared with oaks, elms or maples. The double sorts require the treatment of any orchard tree but should not often be pruned. Dead wood must be removed and branches that are too long should be pinched back in June, but otherwise they are best left alone unless attacked by some fungus, when spraying must be resorted to.

I am loath to leave these cherry-blossom trees behind; as loath to leave them in this book as I was to leave them when we sold our place "In the Woods." I will sentimentally close this chapter with a poem written by Frances Hodgson Burnett in Japanese characters on her place-card at dinner one evening. I had told her of my distress that we had sold our cherry trees and would never see them bloom again.

> Only in dreams of spring
> Shall I see again
> The flowering of my cherry trees.

*

From *The World Was My Garden: Travels of a Plant Explorer,* David Fairchild (1869-1954). New York: Charles Scribner's Sons, 1939. It would be difficult to find an American plant explorer who traveled so much and made as great a contribution in his field as David Fairchild. Throughout his life, beginning in the late 1890s, he visited every corner of the globe—India, Africa, South America, Europe, the Near East and Middle East, Malaysia, Australia, the Caribbean, Central America, the Orient. The title of his best-selling autobiography, *The World Was My Garden,* seems an understatement. Notwithstanding, Fairchild is a splendid writer, with a sharp eye for detail, making his copiously illustrated book a social, anthropological, and historical document of travel and custom before the jet age, extras beyond its immense horticultural value.

Head of the Office of Seed and Plant Introduction for the U.S. Department of Agriculture for twenty-five years, Fairchild helped bring many tropical plants into this country, and was especially influential in the early years of the citrus industry. His introduction gardens in the South were research centers from which he dispersed plants for the first time to different parts of the country. Unlike E. H. Wilson, whom he had known, Fairchild did not collect ornamental plants exclusively, but made a great effort to develop and study new food crops and economic species which could be used for commercial products. He was surprised to learn that Wilson brought back from his expeditions only seeds and bulbs, while he and his own staff were very successful with cuttings and scions of plants.

Because it is so good a personal history of how and when certain plants immigrated to America, Fairchild's narrative complements his contemporary Liberty Hyde Bailey's long view of the nineteenth century. The genteel, modest Fairchild, who was married to the daughter of Alexander Graham Bell, also wrote *Garden Islands of the Great East* and *The World Grows Round My Door*. Miami's Fairchild Tropical Garden, the largest tropical botanical garden in the continental U.S., was named after the man who brought so many wonders to Florida, and made his own home there.

IV

THE PLAY OF ART AND NATURE

Cemeteries Into Parks

Ann Leighton

THE CONJOINING OF GARDENS, PARKS, AND cemeteries may seem far-fetched in a study of the making of nineteenth-century American gardens, but it resembles what Cotton Mather called the practice by one individual of both religion and medicine, a "divine conjunction."

As early as the beginning of the nineteenth century, it had become evident, particularly in old cities, that the conventional plan of burying the dead in congested areas would no longer suffice. In England, where burial places were hallowed ground in churchyards, the problem had become acute. New burials took place on top of older ones, and eventually the space became too crowded for either public health or private solace. Captain Hall described the typical English burial ground as "a soppy churchyard, where the mourners sink ankle-deep in a rank and offensive mould, mixed up with broken bones and fragments of coffins," and doubted that any virtue could be derived from "the recollections of coughs, colds and rheumatism out of number, caught whilst half a dozen old fellows with longtailed threadbare black coats are filling up a grave for which they themselves might seem the readiest tenants."

Americans seemed to have had a special fondness for cemeteries as places to visit, to court in, and to show foreign guests. On an October afternoon in 1827 Captain Hall was taken to visit the cemetery in New Haven. His impressions were favorable.

> [W]e drove out of town to the Grave-yard, one of the prettiest burying places I ever saw. It occupies . . . twenty acres laid out in avenues and divided by rows of trees into lots for the different inhabitants. These connecting lanes or roads are not gravelled but laid down in grass as well as the intermediate spaces which are spotted over with handsome monuments of all sizes and forms, giving a lively instead of a gloomy air to the whole scene.
>
> There is certainly some improvement in this compared with the practice of huddling together so many graves in the confined space round the places of worship in a populous city.

In the New England towns, the best spot with the loveliest view was set aside for a burying ground. But burial of the dead remained a personal matter, as witness the small family cemeteries on the outskirts of gardens and fields down the rural East Coast, from Maine farms to Virginia plantations. As Mrs. Trollope noted, "*In Virginia and Maryland* almost every family mansion has its little grave-yard, sheltered by locust and cypress trees," although she also added, "and one mansion on the Delaware, near Philadelphia, has the monument which marks the family resting-place, rearing itself in all the gloomy grandeur of black and white marble, exactly opposite the door of its entrance."

Partly because of the macabre journalistic onslaught on old London cemeteries, and partly as a result of commonsense village-into-city forecasts in America, there was a move toward improving American cemeteries to the point of making them attractive even to the living— in fact, of treating them as parks. As with many of the social reforms for which Americans became famous in the nineteenth century (such as democratic government, universal public education, prison reform, and public health measures), the initial impulse came from Boston.

In Boston the first graveyards had been established to receive and commemorate the distinguished fathers of the new colony, the governors and magistrates in family lots surmounted by long rectangular stone monuments, like coffins or stone tables on which family names could be inscribed, or by tombs like small houses dug into the hillside. Simple, impressive, but doomed to be overcrowded. In Boston also, the medieval custom of burial under churches had been followed where church affiliation had been established by the Church of England. Heroes of both sides at Bunker Hill lie today in the Old North Church.

In 1825, Dr. Jacob Bigelow of Boston, already famous for his contributions to medicine, education, and horticulture, was approached by a group of concerned philanthropic citizens about a new idea for a parklike cemetery. Bigelow's own history of the ensuing project tells us that his "attention had been drawn to some gross abuses in the rites of sepulture as they then existed under churches and in other receptacles of the dead." At this time, he says, his own "love of country, cherished by the character of earlier pursuits," had led him to

> desire the institution of a suburban cemetery in which the beauties of nature should, as far as possible, relieve from their rupulsive features the tenements of the deceased; and in which, at the same time, some consolation to survivors might be sought in gratifying, as far as possible, the last social and kindred instincts of our nature.

Within a year, Dr. Bigelow called a meeting of "a few gentlemen" at his house, where he submitted to them a plan for a cemetery composed of family burial lots, separated by and interspersed with trees, shrubs, and flowers, in a wood or landscape garden. This was approved and a committee appointed to "look out for a tract of ground suitable for the desired purpose." Several proposed sites were unattainable, because of their high price or from "the reluctance of the owners to acquiesce in the use proposed." After nearly three years, a tract in Cambridge and Watertown known as Stone's Woods, though "more familiarly to Harvard College as 'Sweet Auburn,' " became available. It was owned by Mr. George W. Brimmer, "a gentleman whose just appreciation of the beautiful in nature had prompted him to preserve from destruction the trees and other natural features of that attractive spot."

In 1830 Dr. Bigelow proposed to enlist sufficient subscribers to purchase the whole area for an "ornamental cemetery." Mr. Brimmer generously offered to accept only what the land had cost him and became one of the "most active members of the first Committee or Board of Managers."

Divine conjunctions being what they were in Boston in the early days, Dr. Bigelow had been chosen corresponding secretary of the newly incorporated Massachusetts Horticultural Society the year before the land was acquired. "At that time," wrote Dr. Bigelow, "there was no ornamental rural cemetery, deserving of notice, in the United States, and none even in Europe, of a plan and magnitude corresponding to those which Mount Auburn" was to possess. However,

> the subject was new, the public were lukewarm, and in many cases the prejudices and apprehensions of the community were strongly opposed to the removal of the dead from the immediate precincts of populous cities and villages to the solitude of a distant wood.

Dr. Bigelow realized the value of a "young, active and popular society" in overcoming these prejudices. The Horticultural Society, young and destitute, found itself officially raising the money to pay Mr. Brimmer. "To accommodate the wishes of the horticulturists, an experimental garden for the cultivation of flowers, fruits, etc." was allowed for in the allotment of the ground. After a year of exploratory visits to Sweet Auburn and several explanatory leaflets, a scheme was proposed, "in behalf of the Horticultural Society," to purchase land from the patient Mr. Brimmer "as soon as one hundred subscribers for cemetery lots at sixty dollars each should be obtained." By the spring of 1831, the Horticultural Society closed the deal for the "experimental Garden and Cemetery" (note the order) and asked that the establishment, including the garden and cemetery, be supplied a definite name. Mount Auburn it became.

As Mount Auburn was to be a rural beautification achievement, incorporating the natural advantages of the site to make a place of recreation for the living as well as of repose for the dead and of comfort for mourners, it would take a man of many parts to accomplish the project. Dr. Bigelow was easily the best-qualified man of the day in Boston—a practicing physician, a botanist, popular with his fellows, and an artist.

Landscaping for the project rejects the usual grid and develops a loosely woven net of avenues and paths, draped over the rising ground and incorporating ponds in the lowland area. Virgil, in his *Georgics*, recommended following the contours of the land for plowing (very likely many of the lot purchasers could quote this passage by heart). From the enormously impressive Egyptian entrance gate, said to have been designed by Dr. Bigelow (who seems to have been credited with the design of everything, horticultural or architectural, in the cemetery), there is an open space on the right of the entrance for a lawn, which lies before the granite Gothic chapel, also popularly attributed to Dr. Bigelow. (As we are not writing a guidebook to the cemetery, beyond attesting to the idea of Dr. Bigelow as a genius, we must leave correcting attributions to others.) To the left of the entrance stretches a large expanse, uncut by paths, which, because it is bordered by Garden Avenue, must have been set aside for the experimental garden, though this never transpired ''for want of specific funds'' for its support ''and various other causes.'' At the top of the highest hill is a tower (another of Dr. Bigelow's supposed designs, not unlike a simplified Qutb Minar in Delhi), which was named for Washington. A sphinx, originally commissioned by Dr. Bigelow, awaited an appointed place and function until it finally became the monument to honor the Civil War dead in 1872. Four large statues were commissioned to stand near the Gothic chapel. The first was of Justice Joseph Story of the United States Supreme Court and was paid for by his friends. Three others—of John Winthrop, James Otis, and President John Adams— were paid for by the board.

Mount Auburn became such a showplace that by 1839 a guide for visitors was issued, called *The Picturesque Pocket Companion*. Perhaps the experimental garden never evolved because the whole area became a garden. It was claimed the soil was not suitable for an experimental garden. In any case, the Horticultural Society in no way felt betrayed and years later realized a handsome sum—about forty times the sum paid Mr. Brimmer—in settlement of its withdrawal from the agreement.

By 1849 the relationship between cemeteries and parks was pointed up by Andrew Jackson Downing in *The Horticulturist*. He hailed as ''one of the most remarkable illustrations of the popular taste in this country . . . the rise and progress of our public cemeteries.'' Twenty years earlier, he said, they had been nothing better than common graveyards, except for a few—like the burial ground at New Haven, where Downing, unlike Captain Hall, found little to praise, ''only a few willow trees'' to break ''the monotony of the scene.'' However, when Mount Auburn was made a rural cemetery, eighteen years before Downing wrote his assessment, the idea of ''the charming natural site, finely varied in surface, . . . admirably clothed by groups and masses of forest trees . . . tastefully laid out . . . monuments . . . the whole highly embellished,'' took the public mind by storm. ''Travelers made pilgrimages to the Athens of New England solely to see the realization of their long cherished dream of a resting place for the dead, at once sacred from profanation, dear to the memory, and captivating to the imagination.''

In 1849 Downing asserted that scarcely a city of note in the whole country did not have its rural cemetery.

> The three leading cities of the north, New York, Philadelphia, Boston, have, each of them, besides their great cemeteries—Greenwood, Laurel Hill, Mount Auburn—many others of less note . . . any of which would have astonished and delighted their inhabitants twenty years ago.

Here he makes a point that was to change American cities for all time.

> The great attraction of these cemeteries is not in the fact that they are burial places . . . all these might be realized in a burial ground planted with straight lines of willows and sombre avenues of evergreen. The true secret of the attraction lies in the natural beauty of the sites, and in the tasteful and harmonious embellishment of these sites by art. . . . Hence to an inhabitant of the town a visit to one of these spots has the united charm of nature and art—the double wealth of rural and moral associations. . . . Indeed, in the absence of great public gardens, such as we must surely one day have in America, our rural cemeteries are doing a great deal to enlarge and educate the popular taste in rural embellishment.

Interestingly, Downing continued, although these three leading examples are all laid out in admirable taste, with the greatest variety of trees and shrubs to be found in the country, and kept in a manner seldom equaled in private places, they differ in their essential characters. Greenwood in Brooklyn is large, grand, dignified, and parklike, laid out in a broad and simple style and commanding ocean views. Mount Auburn is richly picturesque in varied hill and dale and owes its charm mainly to a variety of sylvan features. Laurel Hill near Philadelphia is a charming pleasure ground, filled with beautiful and rare shrubs and flowers, "at this season a wilderness of roses, as well as fine trees and monuments." In a footnote, Downing protested the "hideous iron-mongery" beginning to disfigure cemeteries with elaborate fences, gates, and, most deplorably, coats of arms.

But this last was only a footnote; after describing the roses and monuments he began to try to persuade his readers. He directed them to understand the influence these beautiful cemeteries constantly exercise on the public by considering how rapidly parklike burial settings had increased in fifteen years. The numbers of visitors they attracted was an indication of the extent to which they had aroused public interest. Laurel Hill, four miles from Philadelphia, had counted 30,000 visitors in one year; double that must have visited Greenwood; Mount

Auburn must certainly have had an equal number. Rural cemeteries, in the absence of public gardens, were filling their place to a certain degree. Downing suggested that public gardens established in a liberal and suitable manner near large cities would be equally successful, that they would rapidly educate the public taste, and that the progress of horticulture as a science and as an art would be equally benefited.

Downing added,

> The passion for rural pleasures is destined to be the predominant passion of all the more thoughtful and educated portion of our people, and any means of gratifying their love for ornamental or useful gardening will be eagerly seized by hundreds of thousands of our countrymen.

We are here watching the birth of an American park, Central Park to be its name.

> Let us suppose a joint stock company, formed in any one of our cities, for the purpose of providing its inhabitants with the luxury of a public garden. A site should be selected . . . [to] have a varied surface, a good position, sufficient natural wood, with open space and good soil enough for the arrangement of all those portions which required to be newly planted.

Downing envisaged its bright future. In 50 to 100 acres, an example can be afforded of laying out grounds, thus teaching practical landscape gardening. A collection of all the hardy trees and shrubs that grow in this climate, each distinctly labeled, will insure that the most ignorant visitor can learn something of trees. A botanical arrangement of plants and a lecture room would allow for educational activities. A magnificent wooded drive could be laid out, and (in the same sentence) suitable ices and other refreshments could be served, as in the German gardens, which, along with the finest music and the most rigid police, would tempt the better classes to such a resort. In fact, it would be ''the greatest promenade of all strangers and citizens, visitors or inhabitants of the city of whose suburbs it would form a part.''

The park could be supported by a small admission fee and by subscription. Only shareholders, like those who own lots in a cemetery, would be allowed to bring in their horses and carriages—a privilege that would tempt hundreds to subscribe. No traveler could leave the city without seeing such a public garden, the city's most interesting feature.

Two points remained in Downing's argument. If the road to Mount Auburn was lined with coaches carrying thousands and tens of thousands, then a garden full of varied instruction, amusement, and recreation should be ten times more visited. And if hundreds of thousands in New York pay to see stuffed boa constrictors at Barnum's Museum on Broadway and will incur the expense of going six miles to see Greenwood, surely one could safely estimate that many more would resort to a public garden.

Besides being profitable, the garden would civilize and refine the national character, foster the love of rural beauty, and increase the knowledge of and taste for rare and beautiful trees and plants. If only one of the three cities that first opened cemeteries would set an example, the practice of making such public spaces would become widespread. The true policy of republics, Downing argued, is to foster the taste for great public libraries, sculpture and picture galleries, parks and gardens that *all* may enjoy.

So, thanks to Mr. Downing, within a very few years Central Park was established in New York City.

*

From *American Gardens of the Nineteenth Century*, Ann Leighton (1902?-1985). Amherst: The University of Massachusetts Press, 1987. As the author of *Early American Gardens* and *American Gardens in the Eighteenth Century*, in addition to the nineteenth-century study from which this excerpt is taken, Leighton has written the most comprehensive volumes of American garden history available to date. These books demonstrate the painstaking work of a tireless scholar, in the wealth of detail and opinion based on original research, and the visual documentation of countless historical illustrations. As if that were not enough of a task, they also feature annotated appendices chronicling plants growing in seventeenth-century New England, and those most frequently cultivated in eighteenth- and nineteenth-century American gardens. Regretfully, Leighton did not live to write a twentieth-century history of gardens. The sheer joy and exuberant, personal style that characterize her writing make these histories indispensable for people she thought of as "reading gardeners." Notwithstanding, that was too modest an audience profile. Leighton's commonsensical, rich interpretations of social history and culture extend her work across specialized borders, into the more expansive field of American studies.

NOTES FROM A GARDEN BOOK

THOMAS JEFFERSON

JEFFERSON TO WILLIAM HAMILTON

Washington July 1806.

YOUR FAVOR OF THE 7TH CAME DULY TO hand and the plant you are so good as to propose to send me will be thankfully recd. The little *Mimosa julibrisin* you were so kind as to send me the last year is flourishing. I obtained from a gardener in this nbhd [neighborhood] 2 plants of the paper mulberry; but the parent plant being male, we are to expect no fruit from them, unless your [trees] should chance to be of the sex wanted. At a future day, say two years hence I shall ask from you some seeds of the *Mimosa farnesiana* or *nilotica*, of which you were kind enough before to furnish me some. But the plants have been lost during my absence from home. I remember seeing in your greenhouse a plant of a couple of feet height in a pot the fragrance of which (from it's gummy bud if I recollect rightly) was peculiarly agreeable to me and you were so kind as to remark that it required only a greenhouse, and that you would furnish me one when I should be in a situation to preserve it. But it's name has entirely escaped me & I cannot suppose you can recollect or conjecture in your vast collection what particular plant this might be. I must acquiese therefore in a privation which my own defect of memory has produced. . . .

Having decisively made up my mind for retirement at the end of my present time, my views and attentions are all turned homewards. I have hitherto been engaged in my buildings which will be finished in the course of the present year. The improvement of my grounds has been reserved for my occupation on my return home. For this reason it is that I have put off to the fall of the year after next the collection of such curious trees as will bear our winters in the open air.

The grounds which I destine to improve in the style of the English gardens are in a form very difficult to be managed. They comprise the northern quadrant of a mountain for about ⅔ of its height then spread for the upper third over its whole crown. They contain about three hundred acres, washed at the foot for about a mile, by a river of the size of the Schuylkill. The hill is generally too steep for direct ascent, but we make level walks successively along it's side, which in it's upper part encircle the hill & intersect these again by others of easy ascent in various parts. They are chiefly still in their native woods, which are majestic, and very generally a close undergrowth, which I have not suffered to be touched, knowing how much easier it is to cut away than to fill up. The upper third is chiefly open, but to the South is covered with a dense thicket of Scotch broom (*Spartium scoparium Lin.*) which being favorably spread before the sun will admit of advantageous arrangement for winter enjoyment. You are sensible that this disposition of the ground takes from me the first beauty in gardening, the variety of hill & dale, & leaves me as an awkward substitute a few hanging hollows & ridges, this subject is so unique and at the same time refractory, that to make a disposition analogous to its charcter would require much more of the genius of the landscape painter & gardener than I pretend to. I had once hoped to get Parkins to go and give me some outlines, but I was disappointed. Certainly I could never wish your health to be such as to render travelling necessary; but should a journey at any time promise improvement to it, there is no one on which you would be received with more pleasure than at Monticello. Should I be there you will have an opportunity of indulging on a new field some of the taste which has made the Woodlands the only rival which I have known in America to what may be seen in England.

Thither without doubt we are to go for models in this art. Their sunless climate has permitted them to adopt what is certainly a beauty of the very first order in landscape. Their canvas is of open ground, variegated with clumps of trees distributed with taste. They need no more of wood than will serve to embrace a lawn or a glade. But under the beaming, constant and almost vertical sun of Virginia, shade is our Elysium. In the absence of this no beauty of the eye can be enjoyed. This organ must yield it's gratification to that of the other senses; without the hope of any equivalent to the beauty relinquished. The only substitute I have been able to imagine is this. Let your ground be covered with trees of the loftiest stature. Trim up their bodies as high as the constitution & form of the tree will bear, but so as that their tops shall unite & yield dense shade. A wood, so open below, will have nearly the appearance of open grounds. Then, when in the open ground you would plant a clump of trees, place a thicket of shrubs presenting a hemisphere the crown of which shall distinctly show itself under the branches of the trees. This may be effected by a due selection & arrangement of the shrubs, & will I think offer a group not much inferior to that of trees. The thickets may be varied too by making some of them of evergreens altogether, our red cedar made to grow in a bush, evergreen privet, pyrocanthus, Kalmia, Scotch broom. Holly would be elegant but it does not grow in my part of the country.

Of prospect I have a rich profusion and offering itself at every point of the compass. Mountains distant & near, smooth & shaggy, single & in ridges, a little river hiding itself among the hills so as to shew in lagoons only, cultivated grounds under the eye and two small villages. To prevent a satiety of this is the principal difficulty. It may be successively offered, & in different portions through vistas, or which will be better, between thickets so disposed as to serve as vistas, with the advantage of shifting the scenes as you advance on your way.

You will be sensible by this time of the truth of my information that my views are turned so steadfastly homeward that the subject runs away with me whenever I get on it. I sat down to thank you for kindnesses received, & to bespeak permission to ask further contributions from your collection & I have written you a treatise on gardening generally, in which art lessons would come with more justice from you to me.

FROM THE *WEATHER MEMORANDUM BOOK* 1776-1820

1807
Apr. 11. Nursery. begun in bed next the pales, on the lower side,
     where Genl. Jackson's peaches end to wit within 2. f. of the
     4th. post from the S. E. corner.

No. 1. *Quercus coccifera.* Prickly Kermes ⎫
     oak, 3. cross rows.   ⎪
2. *Vitus agnus castus.* Chaste-trees. *Faux* ⎬ seeds recd.
     poiorier. 9. rows.   ⎪ from Doctr
3. *Cedrus libani.* Cedar of Lebanon, 2.   ⎬ Gouan at
     rows.   ⎪ Montpelier.
4. *Citisus laburnum* of the Alps. 2. rows. ⎪
5. *Lavathera albia,* the shrub Marshmallow. ⎭
     2. rows.

Apr. 15. 16. 18. 30. planted & sowed flower beds as above
               [Round and oval flower beds—ed.]

April 16. planted as follows.

	N. E. clump	S. E. clump	S.W. clump	N.W. clump
13. Paper mulberries	2	2	5	4
6. Horse chestnuts	3	3		
2. Taccamahac poplars	1	1		
4. Purple beach			2	2
2. *Robinia hispida*	1	1		
2. Choak cherries	1	1		
3. Mountain ash *Sorhus aucuparia*	- - - -	- - - -	1	2
2. Xanthoxylon			1	1
1. Red bud	1			

          the above were from Maine except 5 horse chestnuts from
     nursery & the Redbud

planted same day 1. Fraxinella in center of N.W. shrub ⎫
          circle   ⎬ from
     * 1. Gelder rose in dº. of N.E. dº.   ⎬ Maine's
       1.   dº.   in dº. of S.E. dº.   ⎭
       1. Laurodendron in margin of S.W. dº. from the
          nursery

planted also 10. willow oaks in N.W. brow of the slope, to wit from
          the N. Pavilion round to near the setting stones as S.W. end
          of level.
          and 12. Wild crabs from the S. to the N. pavilion near the
          brow of the slope.

* *Viburnum opulus rosea.*

Apr. 17.   planted 2. *Robinia hispida* & 2. choak cherries on the S.W.
slope.
20. Weymouth pines on the slope by the Aspen thicket.
In the Nursery. began at the N.W. corner & extended rows
from N.W. to NE. & planted
1st. row abt. 2. f. from the pales }
2d. d°. 18 I. from that   } 100. paccans.
3d. d°....................................Gloucester hiccory nuts from Roanoke.
4th. d°.   d°. from Roanoke. 79 in all. 6. d°. from
Osages. 2. scarlet beans.
5th. a bed of 4. f wide, 3 drills, globe artichoke. red.
6th. a d°......d°..green

Apr. 18.   7th. a bed. Cooper's pale green asparagus. 5 rows. [?]
feet long, a seed every 6. I.
at N.E. end of same bed 14. Ricara beans very forward.
8th. a bed 26. f. long. 2. rows & about 8 f. of a 3d. say
60 f. Missouri great Salsafia. 120 seeds 6. I. apart.

The following is the list of the flowers planted & sowed [in the round and oval flower
beds on the east and west lawns near the house—ed.]

Dianthus chinensis   China pink
Caryophyllus Sweet William [Single carnation]
barbatus Single carnation [Sweet William]
Glaucium   Yellow horned Poppy
Ixia chinensis
Jeffersonia binata.
Lathyrus latifolius. Everlasting pea
Flowering pea of Arkansa. From Capt. Lewis.
Lavatera thuringica.
Lilly. The yellow of the Columbia. It's root a food of the natives.
Lobelia cardinalis Scarlet Cardinal's flower.
Lychnis chalcedonica. Scarlet Lychnis
Papaver rhoeas flor. plen. Double Poppy
Physalis alkekengi. European winter cherry

50 Ranunculuses, double............
24. *Polyanthus tuberosa.*   Double
5. Double pink hyacinths ⎱
10. Double yellow d°.
6. Double white d°.   } in one bed } roots
6. Double blue d°.   ⎰
20. Tulips
6. *Amaryllis formosissima*
24. Double anemones.................

Apr. 19.   planted 9. *Philapelphius coronarius,* Mock orange in the 4.
circular beds of shrubs at the 4. corners of the house.

20. planted among the old cherry trees in the 3d. & 4th. rows
    4. cherry trees from Col°. Coles, to wit Carnations May-
    dukes.

21. planted the following trees from Timothy Matlack, see his
    list of Mar. 14. description.

h. (almond row) N.E. ⎧ N°. 1. Carolina Canada peach.
    of Vineyard   ⎪   clingstone.
                     ⎪   2. two Oldmixon peaches.
                     ⎨   3. the Mammoth peach.
                     ⎪   clingstone.
                     ⎪   4. the Oldmixon freestone
                     ⎩   peach (supposed Madeira)

g. (Apricot row) d°. ⎧   5. the lady's favorite. lately
                     ⎪   imported from France.
                     ⎨   6. The Italian Redstone im-
                     ⎪   ported by Rob[ert] Mor-
                     ⎪   ris.
                     ⎩   7. the Moore park Apricot.
f. (Quince row) d°.   8. the Italian white freestone.
                             importd. by Rob. Morris.

Note. They were in the places of dead trees. N°. 1. 2. 3.
4. run from S.W. to N.E. 7. 5. 6. d°. in this order.

m. (Pear row) Sickel's pear, no N°. blank.
        N°. 11. the Richmond pear.
    6. plants of Purple Syrian grape from Twickenham.
        upper row of S.W. vineyard at the N.E. end.
Apr. 24. sowed liburnum in the 6. circular beds of shrubs. also put
        into each 1. or 2. seeds of the honeysuckle of Lewis's river.
    27. planted 11. Kentucky coffee seeds in the upper row of the
        nursery contind N. E. by 2. f. from pales, also some seeds
        of a tree from Kentucky, said to be handsome, but name for-
        gotten by Mrs Lewis. also Clematis or Virgin's bower seeds
        about the 3. springs on & near the road from the river up
        to the house & at the Stone spring.
    29. planted a sod of Peruvian grass 15 I. square in the North
        corner of the Nursery.
    30. planted 6. scarlet Alpine strawberry roots from Mc.Mahon
        on the lower side of the Peruvian tussock, within a few inches.

JEFFERSON TO CHARLES WILLSON PEALE

Poplar Forest, August 20, 1811.

. . . I have heard that you have retired from the city to a farm, and that you give your whole time to that. Does not the museum suffer? And is the farm as interesting? Here, as you know, we are all farmers, but not in a pleasing style. We have so little labor in proportion to our land that, although perhaps we make more profit from the same labor, we cannot give to our grounds that style of beauty which satisfies the eye of the amateur. Our rotations are corn, wheat, and clover, or corn, wheat, clover and clover, or wheat, corn, wheat, clover and clover; preceding the clover by a plastering. But some, instead of clover substitute mere rest, and all are slovenly enough. We are adding the care of Merino sheep. I have often thought that if heaven had given me choice of my position and calling, it should have been on a rich spot of earth, well watered, and near a good market for the productions of the garden. No occupation is so delightful to me as the culture of the earth, and no culture comparable to that of the garden. Such a variety of subjects, some one always coming to perfection, the failure of one thing repaired by the success of another, and instead of one harvest a continued one through the year. Under a total want of demand except for our family table, I am still devoted to the garden. But though an old man, I am but a young gardener. . . .

From *Thomas Jefferson's Garden Book,* annotated by Edwin Morris Betts (Jefferson: 1743-1826). Philadelphia: The American Philosophical Society, 1944; 1981 edition. A twenty-two-year-old Thomas Jefferson opened his *Garden Book* in 1766 with a note of joy, ''Purple hyacinth begins to bloom.'' He was to continue writing in this book—recording dates of planting, harvesting, duration of blooms, the purchase of seeds and price of goods, farming and landscaping plans, gifts of plants and seeds to and from friends, even bird sightings and weather—until two years before his death, in 1826. Here Jefferson left the best account of gardening in his time, perfected in his fifty years at Monticello. Jefferson experimented with growing sesame, olives, sugar maples, dry rice, and tried techniques of rotating crops, mixing herbs and vegetables, manuring, and contour ploughing. He grew the latest varieties of flowers, fruits and vegetables, importing many from the continent.

When Lewis and Clark, sent by Jefferson to expand the Western territories, triumphantly returned from their expedition, they brought him peas, dwarf cedar, corn, and snowberry which he planted at Monticello. He sent on currants and gooseberries to Bernard M'Mahon, and zoological specimens to the famous painter Charles Willson Peale who had set up the first natural history museum in the country before he retired to his Belfield Farm whose artistic gardens he frequently painted. To William Hamilton, a third friend in the horticultural center that characterized Philadelphia and its environs, Jefferson gave the Osage apple and Aricara tobacco for ''The Woodlands,'' one of the great private estates and gardens in America, known for its rare and unusual plants and trees.

Jefferson admired Hamilton's showplace as a rival to the English natural landscapes that attracted him. On a 1786 tour of England's great houses and countryside, accompanied by his friend John Adams, Jefferson had taken along one of the most influential of English garden books, Thomas Whately's *Observations on Modern Gardening.* Of his trip Jefferson, then Minister to France, wrote to a friend at home praising the English style of landscape: ''My inquiries were directed chiefly to such practical things as might enable me to estimate the expense of making and maintaining a garden in that style.''

Monticello was to be the scene of Jefferson's ideal garden world, reflecting both the theory and practice of horticulture in his very kitchen and flower gardens, orchards and vineyard. The region itself would be the theme of his remarkable *Notes on the State of Virginia* in which he catalogued the trees, plants, and fruits to be found there. He did the same in his *Garden Book,* his account of April 1807, excerpted here, demonstrating that affairs of state could not stop a president who needed the private world of his garden, away from the public world of government. ''The greatest service which can be rendered any country is to add a useful plant to its culture,'' he thought.

There was a deep connection between Jefferson's life as an intellectual and statesman, and his work as a gardener. His example follows the Roman concept of a ''cultured'' individual, and so it is not coincidental that agriculture, which then subsumed horticulture, always embraced the notion of ''culture'' itself. Versed in philosophy, science, government, law, architecture, husbandry, art, literature, religion, Jefferson was a sophisticate at home in the capital of Washington, and in European cities, but he preferred rural life. ''Nature, at once everywhere and nowhere, was the Jeffersonian City of God,'' observed historian Daniel Boorstin. In a larger sense, Jefferson is a brilliant study in the natural history of the imagination. Jefferson was equally experimental in political thought and garden practice. He helped to create the liberal imagination, embodied in the Declaration of Independence which he wrote. More significantly, he showed how politics, too, can be a matter of taste.

Essay on Landscape Gardening

Andrew Jackson Downing

Although music, poetry, and painting, sister fine arts, have in all enlightened countries sooner arrived at perfection than Landscape Gardening, yet the latter offers to the cultivated mind in its more perfect examples, in a considerable degree a union of all these sources of enjoyment; a species of *harmony*, in a pleasing combination of the most fascinating materials of beauty in natural scenery: *poetic* expression in the babbling brook, the picturesque wood, or the peaceful sun-lit turf: and the lovely effects of landscape *painting*, realized in the rich, varied, and skillfully arranged whole.

The object of this charming art, is to create in the grounds of a country residence a kind of polished scenery, producing a delightful effect, either by a species of studied and elegant *design*, in symmetrical or regular plantations: or by a combination of beautiful or picturesque forms, such as we behold in the most captivating passages of general nature.

The *practice* of Landscape Gardening has grown out of that love of country life, and the desire to render our own property attractive, which naturally exists to a greater or lesser degree in the minds of all men. In the case of large landed estates, the capabilities of Landscape

Gardening may be displayed to their full extent, as from five to five hundred acres may be devoted to a park or pleasure-grounds. But the principles of the art may be applied, and its beauties realized to a certain degree, in the space of half an acre of ground—wherever grass will grow, and trees thrive luxuriantly.

Two distinct modes of the art widely differing in themselves, have divided, for some time, the admiration of the world. One is the Ancient, formal or Geometric Style: the other the Modern, Natural, or Irregular Style. The first, characterized by regular forms and right lines, the last by varied forms and flowing lines.

A recurrence to the history of Gardening as well as to the history of the fine arts, will afford abundant proof that in the first stage, or infancy of these arts, while the perception of their ultimate capabilities is yet crude and imperfect, mankind has in every instance been completely satisfied with the mere exhibition of *design* or *art*. Thus in Sculpture, the first statues were only attempts to imitate rudely the *form* of a human figure, or in painting, to represent that of a tree: the skill of the artist in effecting an imitation successfully, was sufficient to excite the astonishment and admiration of those who had not yet made such advances as to enable them to appreciate the superior beauty of *expression*.

In laying out gardens, the practice from all antiquity (until in late times the superiority of natural beauty was discovered) has been to display the skill of the designer in arranging all the materials of nature, in artificial, regular, or symmetrical forms. Walks and roads straight, beds square and round, trees smoothly clipped and shorn into different figures, these were the predominant characteristics of the Ancient or Geometric Style. That person who possessed in his grounds a luxuriant and graceful elm, its branches elegantly sweeping the earth, and forming a varied outline against the sky, saw no more than nature everywhere afforded: but he, whose garden exhibited a cypress or a yew cut by the shears into a four-sided pyramid of verdure, had at least achieved something which nature has not been able to do, and commanded a sort of respect for the excellence or novelty of his art. This taste rendered more or less elegant, continued throughout all Europe until about the year 1700. The lavish expenditure in the royal and princely gardens of the courts of Europe, in the decoration and embellishment of their gardens, gave a new impulse as well as a sublime grandeur, to the art. The finest example of this style is perhaps that of Versailles, the garden of the extravagant Louis XIV, and the most distinguished artist its designer, Le Nôtre. Its water works, *jets-d'eau,* etc., alone, are stated to have been played off seven or eight times a year at an expense of more than two thousand dollars per hour. Sculpture of every description, mural and verdant, was scattered in profusion through the superb gardens of this period; statues and busts of celebrated heroes and statesmen, fountains of all descriptions, urns and vases almost without number: and the whole, especially on so grand a scale, had a most imposing and magnificent effect.

Any person who will analyze the kind of beauty aimed at in the ancient style, will we think, at once perceive its characteristics to be *uniformity* and the display of *symmetric art.* Almost any one may succeed in laying out and planting a garden in right lines, and may give it an air of stateliness and grandeur, by costly decorations; and even now, there are perhaps thousands who would express greater delight in walking through such a garden, than in surveying one where the finest natural beauties are combined. The reason of this is indeed sufficiently obvious.

Every one, though possessed of the least possible portion of taste, readily appreciates the cost and labour incurred in the first case, and bestows his admiration accordingly; but we must infer the presence of a cultivated and refined mind, to realize and enjoy the more exquisite beauty of natural forms.

As however cultivation progressed in Europe, the taste for this style began to be weakened by several causes. In the first place, a large portion of the lands coming under the plough, fine natural woods were gradually cut off, and wild landscape beauties, once so common as to be unheeded, became sufficiently rare to be more prized and admired. The increased admiration of landscape painting, poetry, and other fine arts, by imbuing many minds with a love of beautiful and picturesque nature, also tended to create a change in the taste. Gradually, men of refined sensibilities perceived that besides mere beauty of FORM, natural objects have another and much higher kind of beauty—namely, the beauty of EXPRESSION.

With the recognition of this principle commenced a new era in Ornamental Gardening. The defects of the Geometric School, were freely pointed out and discussed, by writers of cultivated sensibility and taste, and an entire revolution suddenly took place in the public mind. With a higher perception of the capacities of Landscape Gardening, gradually grew up another class of artists, who, laying aside the prejudice which allowed men to see beauty in Gardens, only through the manifestation of design, derived from the study of nature, new elements to interest the mind as well as elevate the art. One of these, looking around him for materials, observes the spirit and expression of natural objects, the varied forms of ground and water, and the character of trees individually and in composition. He perceives that there is an expression of dignity and majesty in an old oak, of gracefulness and luxuriance in a fine sweeping elm, or of the spirited and picturesque in the larch, which confer or create a character in scenes in which they are happily introduced: and, laying down the shears of the old gardeners, he feels that there is a grace and beauty in their free and unshorn luxuriance, infinitely above that of the tree, clipped according to the rules of a formal art. Undulating surfaces of ground have an expression superior to the tame level; and there is a more delightful variety in a walk of half a mile in length, which winds naturally here and there, over a diversified surface, bordered occasionally with luxuriant groups of trees, open spaces of fine lawn, and dense thickets of shrubbery, or underwood, than in a straight level avenue over the same distance, whose sides present but one continuous line of trees seen at the same moment, and presenting but one single and monotonous view. Losing by degrees his reverence for avowed and uniform art, he learns to appreciate those flowing, smooth, and continuous lines, which characterize objects the most graceful and delicate around us; in short that, instead of endeavouring to distort Nature, we should rather strive to heighten her beauties and remove all her defects.

"Although," as Loudon remarks, "it is impossible to doubt that beautiful scenery was admired, by minds of refinement, in all times and places, and that the wealthy would frequently endeavour to create it," yet it is no less true that to England belongs the honour of having first established the principles of modern Landscape Gardening. Lord Bacon in his *Essay on Gardens*, attempted during the reign of James I to effect some change in the method of laying out places. "As for the making of knots," says he, "or figures with divers coloured earth; they be but toys; I do not like images cut out in juniper or other garden stuff; they are for children."

Some of the English writers on this subject assert, that Milton's beautiful descriptions in *Paradise Lost* had much influence in awakening a taste for natural beauty. His conception of the garden was not only totally at variance with the generally entertained notions of such a spot, but it evinced a mind full of exquisite natural beauty, as well as the most sublime poetry.

Addison and Pope, however, undoubtedly have the merit of completely overthrowing the formal, and substituting in the minds of the British public a taste for the natural style. The celebrated essay by Addison, ''On the Causes of the Pleasures of the Imagination arising from the works of Nature, and their superiority over those of Art,'' was written in 1712. And the widely-read article ''On Verdant Sculpture,'' by Pope, appeared in the *Guardian* in the succeeding year. In the former, the superiority of the beauty of natural expression is most effectively shown, and the philosophical principles of Landscape Gardening suggested; in the latter, the absurdities of the ancient style are pointed out in a masterly manner.

Kent was the first artist who, fully entering into the spirit of these reformers in taste, fairly put in execution on a large scale what they suggested in theory. ''Painter enough,'' says Horace Walpole, ''to taste the charms of landscape, bold and opinionative enough to dare and dictate, and born with a genius to strike out a great system; from the twilight of imperfect essays, he realized the compositions of the greatest masters in painting.'' The effect of these practical illustrations of the beauties of the new style was astonishing, and the taste soon spread in a most rapid manner throughout England.

It has been asserted by continental authors, that the English borrowed their ideas of the natural style from the Chinese. But the assertion is destitute of foundation. The gardens of the Chinese, as illustrated by Sir William Temple in a work about that period, though characterized by great irregularity, are full of littlenesses and puerile conceits, far below the standard of natural beauty aimed at by the English.

Among other authors whose works were devoted to the improvement of Landscape Gardening in the modern or natural style, we shall mention the following principal ones in addition to those already quoted, for the benefit of the reader who wishes to pursue the subject further than we are able to lead him. Mason's *Essay on Design in Gardening*, first published in 1768. Whately's *Observations on Modern Gardening*, 1770. *The English Garden*, a poem, by W. Mason, in 1782. Price's *Essays on the Picturesque*, and on the use of studying pictures with a view to the improvement of real Landscape,

1794. Horace Walpole's *History of Modern Gardening*, published in 1782. Repton's *Observations on the Theory and Practice of Landscape Gardening*, in 1795. Among French authors we will only refer to Girardin, whose work *De la Composition des Paysages*, was published in 1783, and the Abbé De Lille, the author of an exquisite poem on this subject, "*Les Jardins*," in 1820.

As the modern style owes its origin mainly to the English, so it has also been developed and carried to its greatest perfection in the British Islands. The law of primogeniture, which has there so long existed, in itself contributes greatly to the continual improvement and embellishment of those vast landed estates which remain perpetually in the hands of the same family. Magnificent buildings added to by each succeeding generation, who often preserve also the older portions with the most scrupulous care, wide-spread parks, clothed with a thick velvet turf, which amid their moist atmosphere preserves during a great part of the year an emerald greenness—studded with noble oaks and other forest trees which number centuries of growth and maturity—these advantages in the hands of the most intelligent and the wealthiest aristocracy in the world, have indeed made, as it were, an entire landscape garden of "merry England." Among a multitude of splendid examples of these noble residences, we will only refer the reader to the celebrated Blenheim, the seat of the Duke of Marlborough, where the lake alone (probably the largest piece of artificial water in the world) covers a surface of two hundred acres: Warwick Castle, a venerable pile, (portions of which have been built a thousand years), standing on a hill from whence the eye, though ranging over a wide-spread landscape, only beholds the park and wooded demesne of one proprietor: and Woburn Abbey, the grounds of which are full of the choicest specimens of trees and plants, and where the park, like that of Ashbridge, Chatsworth, and several other private residences in England, is only embraced within a circumference of from ten to twenty miles.

On the continent of Europe, though there are a multitude of examples of the modern style of landscape gardening, which is there called the *English* or *natural* style, yet in the neighbourhood of many of the capitals, especially those of the south of Europe, the taste for the geometric or ancient style of gardening still prevails to a considerable extent—partially no doubt because that style admits, with more facility, of those classical and architectural accompaniments of vases, statues, busts, etc.—the passion for which pervades a people rich in ancient and modern sculptural works of art. Indeed many of the Italian gardens are more striking from their profusion of statues, busts, and other mural ornaments, interspersed with fountains and *jets-d'eau*, than from the beauty or rarity of their vegetation or from their arrangement.

In the United States, it is highly improbable that we shall ever witness such splendid examples of landscape gardens as those abroad, to which we have alluded. Here the rights of man are held to be equal; and if there are no enormous parks and no class of men whose wealth is hereditary, there is, at least, what is more gratifying to the feelings of the philanthropist, the almost entire absence of a very poor class in the country; while we have, on the other hand, a larger class of independent landholders, who, in many respects, are intelligent and well educated, than any other country in the civilized world can at present boast.

The number of individuals among us who possess wealth and refinement sufficient to enable them to enjoy the pleasures of a country life, and who desire in their private residences so much of the beauties of landscape gardening and rural embellishment, as may be realized without any enormous expenditure of means, is every day increasing. And although, until lately, a very meagre plan of laying out the grounds about a residence, was all that we could lay claim to, yet the taste for elegant rural improvements is advancing now so rapidly, that we have no hesitation in affirming that in half a century more, there will exist a greater number of beautiful villas and country seats of moderate extent in the Atlantic States, than in any country in Europe, England alone excepted. With us, a feeling, a taste, or an improvement, is contagious; and once fairly appreciated and established in one portion of the country, it is disseminated with a celerity that is indeed wonderful, to every other portion.

In so far as regards the literature and practice of Landscape Gardening as an art, in North America, almost every thing is yet before us, but little that we can refer to, having yet been done. Almost all the improvements in the grounds of our finest country residences, have been carried on under the direction of the proprietors themselves, suggested by their natural good taste, in many instances improved by the study of European authors or by a personal inspection of the finest places abroad. The only American work yet published which treats directly of Landscape Gardening, is the *American Gardener's Calendar*, by Bernard McMahon of Philadelphia. The only practitioner of the art, of any note, was the late M. Parmentier of Brooklyn, Long Island.

M. André Parmentier was the brother of the celebrated Horticulturist, the Chevalier Parmentier, Mayor of Enghien, Holland. He emigrated to this country about the year 1824—and in the Horticultural Nurseries which he established at Brooklyn, he gave a specimen of the natural style of laying out grounds, combined with a scientific arrangement of plants, which excited public curiosity, and contributed not a little to the dissemination of a taste for the natural mode of landscape gardening. . . .

In an infant state of society, in regard to the fine arts, much will be done in violation of good taste; but here, where nature has done so much for us, there is scarcely a large country residence in the Union, from which useful hints in Landscape Gardening, may not be taken. A natural group of trees, an accidental pond of water, or some equally simple object, may form a study more convincing to the mind of a true admirer of natural beauty, than the most carefully drawn plan, or the most elaborately written description.

*

From *A Treatise on the Theory and Practice of Landscape Gardening,* Andrew Jackson Downing (1815—1852). New York: Wiley and Putnam, 1841. Downing was one of the most significant voices in the development of American domestic architecture and rural taste in the middle of the nineteenth century, and for decades afterwards. Influenced by English gardening styles, chiefly by the naturalism of Uvedale Price, Humphry Repton, and John C. Loudon, later by art critic John Ruskin, he filtered their ideals through his innate sense of what was desirable in an American setting. But situated in the Hudson Valley at Newburgh, Downing's greatest inspiration was the glorious landscape he lived in, not far down the river from where Thomas Cole was creating the Hudson River School of painting from the same Romantic wilderness views.

Downing's first book, the *Treatise* laid out the principles of his design approach, appearing in more than fifteen editions for forty years after its publication. Subsequent books, *Cottage Residences* and *The Architecture of Country Houses*, were enormously influential around the country as primary texts for the design and landscaping of country homes, providing alternatives to the

Gothic Revival style. In essence, the first American "how-to" books of their kind, they celebrated rural home life as the repository of moral values and sentiment necessary for the cultivation of the American character. Written with the intent to refine and elevate American taste, these books filled with handsome engravings, treated the house in relation to the grounds, offering a wealth of architectural detail for exterior design, choice of furniture for interior decoration, and landscaping advice in the picturesque mode. Another book, *The Fruits and Fruit Trees of America*, established Downing who liked to call himself a "rural architect," as an authority on fruits. In 1846 he became editor of *The Horticulturist* which he was to make a prominent gardening periodical at mid-century. Here he elaborated on his architectural and horticultural themes, and all manner of culture, also agitating for the creation of public parks.

All this while Downing was running his nursery business, advising on country homes up and down the Hudson, and planning new designs for the grounds of the Capitol, White House and Smithsonian Institution. He had virtually invented the professions of landscape architect and architecture critic, and in all likelihood he would have become a major figure in the design of Central Park. But America lost this powerful, enthusiastic arbiter of taste when at thirty-six he was lost in the fire of the steamer Henry Clay on his beloved Hudson River.

THE LAWN

FRANK SCOTT

Whether we look, or whether we listen,
We hear life murmur, or see it glisten;
Every clod feels a stir of might,
　An instinct within it that reaches and towers,
And, groping blindly above it for light,
　Climbs to a soul in grass and flowers.

Lowell

On each side shrinks the bowery shade,
Before me spreads an emerald glade;
The sunshine steeps its grass and moss,
That couch my footsteps as I cross.

Alfred B. Street

A SMOOTH, CLOSELY SHAVEN SURFACE OF grass is by far the most essential element of beauty on the grounds of a suburban home. Dwellings, all the rooms of which may be filled with elegant furniture, but with rough uncarpeted floors, are no more incongruous, or in ruder taste, than the shrub and tree and flower-sprinkled yards of most home-grounds, where shrubs and flowers mingle in confusion with tall grass, or ill-defined borders of cultivated ground. Neatness and order are as essential to the pleasing effect of ground furniture as of house furniture. No matter how elegant or appropriate the latter may be, it will never look well in the home of a slattern. And however choice the variety of shrubs and flowers, if they occupy the ground so that there is no pleasant expanse of close-cut grass to relieve them, they cannot make a pretty place. The long grass allowed to grow in town and suburban grounds, after the spring gardening fever is over, neutralizes to a certain degree all attempts of the lady or gentleman of the house to beautify them, though they spend ever so much in obtaining the best shrubs, trees, or flowers the neighbors or the nurseries can furnish. It is not necessary to have an acre of pleasure ground to secure a charming lawn. Its extent may always be proportioned to the size of the place; and if the selection of flowers and shrubs and their arrangement is properly made, it is surprising how small a lawn will realize some of the most pleasing effects of larger ones. A strip twenty feet wide and a hundred feet long may be rendered, proportionally, as artistic as the landscape vistas of a park.

And it needs but little more to have room to realize by art, and with shadowing trees, the sparkling picture that the poet, Alfred B. Street, thus presents in his ''Forest Walk.''

> A narrow vista, carpeted
> With rich green grass, invites my tread:
> Here showers the light in golden dots,
> There sleeps the shade in ebon spots,
> So blended that the very air
> Seems net-work as I enter there.

To secure a good lawn, a rich soil is as essential as for the kitchen garden. On small grounds the quickest and best way of making a lawn is by turfing. There are few neighborhoods where good turf cannot be obtained in pastures or by road-sides. No better varieties of grass for lawns can be found than those that form the turf of old and closely fed pastures. Blue-grass and white clover are the staple grasses in them, though many other varieties are usually found with these, in smaller proportions.

The ground should be brought to as smooth slopes or levels as possible before laying the turf, as much of the polished beauty of a perfected lawn will depend on this precaution. If the ground has been recently spaded or manured, it should be heavily tramped or rolled before turfing, to guard against uneven settling. A tolerably compact soil makes a closer turf than a light one. Marly clay is probably the best soil for grass, though far less agreeable for gardening operations generally than a sandy loam. After compacting the soil to prevent uneven settling, a few inches on top must be lightly raked to facilitate laying the turf, and the striking of new roots. Before winter begins all newly laid turf should be covered with a few inches of manure. After the ground settles in the spring this should be raked off with a fine-toothed rake, and the lawn then well rolled. The manure will have protected the grass from the injurious effect of sudden freezing and thawing in the winter and early spring, and the rich washings from it gives additional color and vigor to the lawn the whole season. The manure raked from the grass is just what is needed to dig into the beds for flowers and shrubs, or for mulching trees. This fall manuring is essential to newly set turf, and is scarcely less beneficial if repeated every year. Cold soap-suds applied from a sprinkling-pot or garden-hose when rains are abundant, is the finest of summer manure for grass. If applied in dry weather it should be diluted with much additional water. The old rhyme—

> Clay on sand manures the land,
> Sand on clay is thrown away

is eminently true in relation to the growth of grass. The clay should always be applied late in autumn.

If grounds are so large that turfing is too expensive, the soil should be prepared as recommended above for turfing, and seeded as early in the spring as the ground can be thoroughly prepared and settled. If the surface has been prepared the preceding autumn, then it will be found a good practice to sow the grass seed upon a thin coating of snow which falls frequently early in March. Seed can be sown more evenly on snow, because better seen, than on the ground.

A variety of opinions prevail concerning the best grasses for seeding. It will be safe to say that for lawns timothy and red clover are totally unsuited, and that the grasses which make the best pastures in the neighborhood, will make the best lawns. The following mixture for one bushel of seed is recommended in Henderson's *Manual of Floriculture,* viz:

> 12 quarts Rhode Island Bent Grass.
> 4 quarts creeping Bent Grass.
> 10 quarts Red-top.
> 3 quarts Sweet Vernal Grass.
> 2 quarts Kentucky Blue Grass.
> 1 quart White Clover.

We have seen very successful lawns made with equal parts, *by weight,* of Kentucky blue grass, red-top, and white clover seed. The quantity required is about a half bushel to each one hundred feet square.

When rains are frequent, *no lawn can be brought to perfection if cut less often than once a week,* and two weeks is the longest time a lawn should remain uncut, except in periods of total suspension of growth by severe drought. Where shrubs and flowers are placed properly, there will always be clear space enough to swing a lawn scythe or roll a lawn machine. Only in the most contracted yards should there be nooks and corners, or strips of grass, that an ordinary mower cannot get at easily, and without endangering either the plants or his temper. Places that are so cluttered with flowers, trees, and shrubs that it becomes a vexatious labor for a good mower to get in among them, are certainly not well planted. Good taste, therefore, in arrangement, will have for its first and durable fruits, *economy,* a product of excellent flavor for all who desire to create beauty around their homes, but who can ill afford to spend much money to effect it, or to waste any in failing to effect it. The advice to plant so as to leave sufficient breadth to swing a scythe wherever there is any lawn at all, is none the less useful, though the admirable little hand-mowing machines take the place of the scythe; for a piece of lawn in a place where a scythe cannot be swung, is not worth maintaining.

Rolling mowers by horse or hand power have been principally employed on large grounds; but the hand machines are now so simplified and cheapened that they are coming into general use on small pleasure grounds, and proprietors may have the pleasure of doing their own mowing without the wearisome bending of the back, incident to the use of the scythe. Whoever spends the early hours of one summer, while the dew spangles the grass, in pushing these grass-cutters over a velvety lawn, breathing the fresh sweetness of the morning air and the perfume of new mown hay, will never rest contented

again in the city. It is likely that professional garden laborers will buy
these machines and contract cheaply for the periodical mowing of a
neighborhood of yards, so that those who cannot or do not desire to do
it for themselves may have it done cheaply. The roller is an essential
implement in keeping the lawn to a fine surface, and should be
thoroughly used as soon as the frost is out of the ground; for it will then
be most effective to level the uneven heaving and settling of the earth.
After heavy rains it is also useful, not only in preserving a smooth surface, but in breaking down and checking the vertical tendency of grass
that is too succulent.

The season after seeding many persons are discouraged by the luxuriance of the weeds, and the apparent faint-heartedness of the grass.
They must keep on mowing and rolling patiently. Most of these forward weeds are of sorts that do not survive having their heads cut off
half a dozen times; while good lawn grasses fairly laugh and grow fat
with decapitation. Weeds of certain species, however, will persist in
thrusting their uninvited heads through the best kept lawns. These are
to be dealt with like cancers. A long sharp knife, and busy fingers, are
the only cure for them.

*

From *The Art of Beautifying Suburban Home Grounds of Small Extent,* Frank
Scott (1828-1919). New York: D. Appleton and Company, 1870. Scott
dedicated this book to his former teacher Downing, regarding it as a continua-
tion of the now deceased landscape architect's interest in the cultivation of
rural taste. Scott, having his own Victorian view of the "home-picture,"
however, planned his book not for the wealthy but those who worked in towns
and cities. The businessman who made up the rising industrial population
needed suitable home-grounds, and that he defined as "a fine lawn and large
trees." Scott pictured townships of streets, roads and streams dotted with
suburban homes set among groves, with nearby pastures, fields, and
woodlands. The benefits of capitalism plus domestic tranquility amidst nature
came together in a new iconography of success. That was to be the cornerstone
of the American dream—owning your own home.

Scott's book aimed to help the suburban homeowner to learn about
"decorative gardening," turning nature into art. He offered advice on dividing
land into lots, how to plant trees, shrubs, grass, and flower beds (preferring the

showy canna and castor-bean in carpet bed effect). But more significantly for American culture, Scott advocated a move away from fenced in private grounds hidden behind walls, high fences, and belts of tree or shrubbery. He had a different idea of what characterized American space: an open front lawn to allow neighbors to admire each other's ornamental plantings. In the difference between Scott's and Alice Morse Earle's ideal front yard it is possible to trace transformations in the concept of the public and the private realm in American society. The politics of style is always an aspect of horticulture.

Scott marked a real shift in attitude away from the English manner of landscape gardening for country estates created in the manner of private parks, and later an influence on the design of American cemeteries and public parks. He had something in his approach of the enlightened developer and town planner who, alas, in the hundred years since the publication of his book, has run wild. Indeed, after opening the first architect's office in Toledo, Ohio in 1852, a few years later Scott joined his father and brother in the real estate business. He also wrote several pamphlets, ''Property Without a Price'' and ''Ancient and Modern Utopias,'' and the book *Portraitures of Julius Caesar.* Somehow they all seem to connect in Scott's vision of a modern community.

Italian Garden-Magic

Edith Wharton

Though it is an exaggeration to say that there are no flowers in Italian gardens, yet to enjoy and appreciate the Italian garden-craft one must always bear in mind that it is independent of floriculture.

The Italian garden does not exist for flowers; its flowers exist for it: they are a late and infrequent adjunct to its beauties, a parenthetical grace counting only as one more touch in the general effect of enchantment. This is no doubt partly explained by the difficulty of cultivating any but spring flowers in so hot and dry a climate, and the result has been a wonderful development of the more permanent effects to be obtained from the three other factors in garden-composition—marble, water and perennial verdure—and the achievement, by their skillful blending, of a charm independent of the seasons.

It is hard to explain to the modern garden-lover, whose whole conception of the charm of gardens is formed of successive pictures of flower-loveliness, how this effect of enchantment can be produced by anything so dull and monotonous as a mere combination of clipped green and stone work.

The traveler returning fron Italy, with his eyes and imagination full of the ineffable Italian garden-magic, knows vaguely that the enchantment exists; that he has been under its spell, and that it is more potent, more enduring, more intoxicating to every sense than the most elaborate and glowing effects of modern horticulture; but he may not have found the key to the mystery. Is it because the sky is bluer, because the vegetation is more luxuriant? Our midsummer skies are almost as deep, our foliage is as rich, and perhaps more varied; there are, indeed, not a few resemblances between the North American summer climate and that of Italy in spring and autumn.

Some of those who have fallen under the spell are inclined to ascribe the Italian garden-magic to the effect of time; but, wonder-working as this undoubtedly is, it leaves many beauties unaccounted for. To seek the answer one must go deeper: the garden must be studied in relation to the house, and both in relation to the landscape. The garden of the Middle Ages, the garden one sees in old missal illuminations and in early woodcuts, was a mere patch of ground within the castle precincts, where "simples" were grown around a central well-head and fruit was espaliered against the walls. But in the rapid flowering of Italian civilization the castle walls were soon thrown down, and the garden expanded, taking in the fish pond, the bowling green, the rose arbor and the clipped walk. The Italian country house, especially in the center and the south of Italy, was almost always built on a hillside, and one day the architect looked forth from the terrace of his villa, and saw that, in his survey of the garden, the enclosing landscape was naturally included: the two formed a part of the same composition.

The recognition of this fact was the first step in the development of the great garden art of the Renaissance: the next was the architect's discovery of the means by which nature and art might be fused in his picture. He had now three problems to deal with: his garden must be adapted to the architectural lines of the house it adjoined; it must be adapted to the requirements of the inmates of the house, in the sense of providing shady walks, sunny bowling greens, parterres and orchards, all conveniently accessible; and lastly it must be adapted to the landscape around it. At no time and in no country has this triple problem been so successfully dealt with as in the treatment of the Italian country house from the beginning of the sixteenth to the end of the eighteenth century; and in the blending of different elements, the subtle transition from the fixed and formal lines of art to the shifting and irregular lines of nature, and lastly in the essential convenience and livableness of the garden, lies the fundamental secret of the old garden-magic.

However much other factors may contribute to the total impression of charm, yet by eliminating them one after another, by *thinking away* the flowers, the sunlight, the rich tinting of time, one finds that, underlying all these, there is a deeper harmony of design which is independent of any adventitious effects. This does not imply that a plan of an Italian garden is as beautiful as the garden itself. The more permanent materials of which the latter is made—the stonework, the evergreen foliage, the effects of rushing or motionless water, above all the lines of the natural scenery—all form a part of the artist's design. But these things are as beautiful at one season as at another; and even these are but the accessories of the fundamental plan. The inherent beauty of the garden lies in the grouping of its parts—in the converging lines of its long ilex walks, the alternation of sunny open spaces with cool woodland shade, the proportion between terrace and bowling green, or between the height of a wall and the width of a path. None of these details was negligible to the landscape architect of the Renaissance: he considered the distribution of shade and sunlight, of straight lines of masonry and rippled lines of foliage, as carefully as he weighed the relation of his whole composition to the scene about it.

Then, again, any one who studies the old Italian gardens will be struck with the way in which the architect broadened and simplified his plan if it faced a grandiose landscape. Intricacy of detail, complicated groupings of terraces, fountains, labyrinths and porticoes, are found in sites where there is no great sweep of landscape attuning the eye to larger impressions. The farther north one goes, the less grand the landscape becomes and the more elaborate the garden. The great pleasure-grounds overlooking the Roman Campagna are laid out on severe and majestic lines: the parts are few; the total effect is one of breadth and simplicity.

It is because, in the modern revival of gardening, so little attention has been paid to these first principles of the art that the garden lover should not content himself with a vague enjoyment of old Italian gardens, but should try to extract from them principles which may be applied at home. He should observe, for instance, that the old Italian garden was meant to be lived in—a use to which, at least in America, the modern garden is seldom put. He should note that, to this end, the grounds were as carefully and conveniently planned as the house, with broad paths (in which two or more could go abreast) leading from one division to another; with shade easily accessible from the house, as well as a sunny sheltered walk for winter; and with effective transitions from the dusk of wooded alleys to open flowery spaces or to the level sward of the bowling green. He should remember that the terraces and formal gardens adjoined the house, that the ilex or laurel walks beyond were clipped into shape to effect a transition between the straight lines of masonry and the untrimmed growth of the woodland to which they led, and that each step away from architecture was a nearer approach to nature.

The cult of the Italian garden has spread from England to America, and there is a general feeling that, by placing a marble bench here and a sun-dial there, Italian ''effects'' may be achieved. The results produced, even where much money and thought have been expended, are not altogether satisfactory; and some critics have thence inferred that the Italian garden is, so to speak, *untranslatable*, that it cannot be adequately rendered in another landscape and another age.

Certain effects, those which depend on architectural grandeur as well as those due to coloring and age, are no doubt unattainable; but there is, nonetheless, much to be learned from the old Italian gardens, and the first lesson is that, if they are to be a real inspiration, they must be copied, not in the letter but in the spirit. That is, a marble sarcophagus and a dozen twisted columns will not make an Italian garden; but a piece of ground laid out and planted on the principles of the old garden-craft will be, not indeed an Italian garden in the literal sense, but, what is far better, *a garden as well adapted to its surroundings as were the models which inspired it.*

This is the secret to be learned from the villas of Italy; and no one who has looked at them with this object in view will be content to relapse into vague admiration of their loveliness. As Browning, in passing Cape St. Vincent and Trafalgar Bay, cried out:

> Here and here did England help me: how can I help England?—say,

so the garden lover, who longs to transfer something of the old garden-magic to his own patch of ground at home, will ask himself, in wandering under the umbrella pines of the Villa Borghese, or through the box parterres of the Villa Lante: What can I bring away from here? And the more he studies and compares, the more inevitably will the answer be: ''Not this or that amputated statue, or broken *bas relief*, or fragmentary effect of any sort, but a sense of the informing spirit—an understanding of the gardener's purpose, and of the uses to which he meant his garden to be put.''

*

From *Italian Villas and Their Gardens*, Edith Wharton (1862-1937). New York: The Century Company, 1904. Wharton's first book, *The Decoration of Houses* which she co-authored in 1897, influenced the interior design of private houses at the end of the last century. Before she was to write her celebrated novels, *The House of Mirth*, *Ethan Frome*, and *The Age of Innocence* for which in 1920 she became the first woman novelist to receive a Pulitzer Prize, Wharton wrote a second book on design, *Italian Villas and Their Gardens*. Here she drew upon an impressive knowledge of architectural and garden history, comparing drawings, paintings and other documents to analyze a particular garden through the centuries, with special attention to the French, Italian, and English features that have transformed landscape architecture. Wharton was chiefly concerned with the relationship of the house to the grounds, and like Downing, treated the full perspective. (Interestingly, her novel *Hudson River Bracketed* took its name from a style of architecture created by him in the 1840s.) Wharton had a real feeling for texture, stonework, water, and setting, making her book, lavishly ilustrated with color paintings by Maxfield Parrish, a work of sensual erudition. The volume also gives a lucid first-hand account of what Italian gardens in the regions of Rome, Florence, Milan, and Venice looked like nearly one hundred years ago.

It is enlightening to read her on the social history of the garden, most pointedly in the example of the Anglicanization of the Tuscan garden in her time. English colonies near Florence, still under the influence of Humphry Repton and Capability Brown, contributed to the disappearance of the graceful Tuscan parterres, terraces, and vineyards by putting in their place the English-style landscape of an open lawn dotted with specimen trees, and exotic plants then in fashion.

Wharton at one time had a much admired all-blue garden at her Pavillion Colombe outside Paris. In America her own villa and garden, where summers she entertained the likes of Henry James, Stanford White, and President Theodore Roosevelt in the first decade of this century, was an English-Italianate house in Lenox which she called The Mount. The Berkshire estate, now home to theatre and art events, like many former homes of celebrated Americans is undergoing restoration.

Inspiration from Tropical Scenery for Park Planting

Frederick Law Olmsted

Panama, September 26, 1863.

My Dear Mr. Pilat:

I have never had a more complete satisfaction and delight of my love of nature than I had yesterday in crossing the isthmus. You will remember that I always had a reaching out for tropical effect. . . . I wished that we could have seen five years ago what I saw yesterday, and received then the same distinct lesson which I did yesterday, and of which I certainly had some sort of prophetic feeling, and desire to avail myself in some of our study of the park planting. The groundwork was not extraordinary to us, the topographical characteristics not differing essentially from those of the park; yet the scenery excited a wholly different emotion from that produced by any of our temperate-zone scenery, or rather it excited an emotion of a kind which our scenery sometimes produces as a quiet suggestion to reflection, excited it instantly, instinctively and directly. If my retrospective analysis of this emotion is correct, it rests upon a sense of the superabundant creative power, infinite resource, and liberality of Nature—the childish playfulness and profuse careless utterance of Nature.

This is what I felt most strongly, and, after my excitement was somewhat tempered, I naturally fell to questioning how it was produced, and whether, with materials that we can command in the temperate regions, we could to any marked degree reproduce it. I think that I was rather blindly and instinctively feeling for it, in my desire to give "tropical character" to the planting of the island, and luxuriant jungled variety and density and intricate abundance to the planting generally of the lake border and the Ramble and the River Road. Of course, it is the very reverse of the emotion sought to be produced in the Mall and playgrounds region—rest, tranquillity, deliberation and maturity. As to how it is caused—I mean how the intensity of it which I yesterday experienced is occasioned by any details which I can select in tropical scenery—it is unnecessary to ask, if we can assume that these details do naturally contribute to it. Taking it for granted that they do, what is there here that we have not something similar to, or that by management we can bring something that we have to resemble?

First, we have nothing that will resemble cocoanut or date palms (none of our established materials) or bamboo. These are the most striking things we see. But does this esthetic effect of the tropical scenery depend directly upon them? In the center of the isthmus we passed considerable intervals where palms were absent from the foreground. The tropical picture was much less complete as merely a picture of the tropics, but the sense of the luxuriance of nature produced was not less complete. Indeed, I think the association of the palm with the open, flat monotonous desert, and with many scenes of barrenness, as on the rocky, parched and sterile coast of Cuba, makes it not absolutely essential, but only favourable to this impression. The banana or plantain is a great help and is of the greatest possible value, but it appears only occasionally, and is also not indispensable though more desirable than any other of the family. On the high grounds, especially, there was often nothing of which we have not a typical representative in our scenery; the great difference being that we have no scenery in which there are not qualities which are altogether absent here, and we have no scenery in which those qualities which are common to both are seen in anything like the same profusion and combination. I frequently thought, looking at any ten or twenty square feet of which I saw before me, and omitting the palms, it would only be necessary to assemble various bits of scenes to have a complete scene resembling and producing in considerable degree the moral effect of a scene before me. Palms or palm-like trees were never out of sight, though sometimes, as I said, absent from the foreground. Well, it was then a great satisfaction to find that the trees most markedly different from our common temperate-zone trees, at a little distance, could not be distinguished from what we were trying to get and what we know it to be possible to get on the island. It is true, nature uncontrolled, except by a most rare accident possibly, never quite gives us the palm, or palm-like tree in our distances,—but she sometimes comes near it. By selection and special treatment, we can then produce trees, which, seen at a distance of a couple of hundred feet, shall lead a man to say, ''I have seen such trees before only in the tropics.''

This is what we are aiming for on the island. Wherein are we wrong? As far as the palm-like effect is concerned, only in not pushing our plan far enough. The length of stem and smallness of head is more than I had supposed, often more marked than I had supposed, I mean at a distance, the trunk frequently is imperceptible, and you see the head apparently floating unsupported. The trees growing in this way are not palms, or not all palms, but in their foliage so nearly like the Ailanthus that at no great distance (as a landscape painter would depict them) you would not know them apart, at least an average observer would not. Another of our prominent trees on the island, the Aralia, is, if I mistake not, itself in several varieties, actually present and frequent and not unimportant in the minor scenery of the isthmus. I saw these two trees (something resembling the Ailanthus and the Aralia) on the shore of lagoons and rivers and on islands in these, not a few hundred yards away, not differing at all from those on our island, except as they stretched themselves higher toward heaven and had smaller bunches of plumes at the top. I saw also great lengths of shore, where the immediate border of the water consisted wholly of shrubs and grass or herbage, which would in the middle distance of a picture be perfectly represented by a copy of a bank, very densely grown (horizontally over the water) of our Holly-leaved Barberry and beds of Sweet Flag and Tiger Lily with vines running through and over them. These vines are thinly leaved with leaves like Kalmia, but longer, and a blossom like a white Convolvulus. The only noticeably frequent blossom or flower at all conspicuous was not to be distinguished a few rods off from the Convolvulus, sometimes white and sometimes purple. A speck of scarlet was sometimes seen in the herbage, but I could not catch the form. There were also great broad leaves of the color of the Skunk Cabbage and others which I could not distinguish from the Paulownia. A small tree was sometimes seen also having exactly the effect of the Paulownia four to five years old in rich soil. These then are all details which (seen across water) we can very well produce.

Other plants, of the general density, form, size and best color of the *Berberis aquifolia*, including some of the broader leaf and greater pliancy, are mixed with that. The Forsythia and the Oriental Magnolias represent closely other shrubs which I saw distinctly by the roadside. I saw also, as it seemed to me, our Wild Raspberry, the fragrant variety, one purple dark leaf of the same form (a single shrub of Purple Barberry would meet the effect in a bank). I saw also our common rushes and the Cat-tail Flag, but without seed-stems. Of many scenes, there was no other marked detail. Of trees which I could distinguish in the general body of foliage, there were besides those spoken of, what I suppose to be Tamarinds, not essentially differing in landscape effect from our Honey-locust, and one resembling in its structure our Sycamore, with a thinly scattered foliage of leaves like the *Magnolia grandiflora*; I almost think it is that, grown very large and straggling under tropical heat. There were glaucous-leaved small trees which the *Magnolia glauca* would tolerably replace and all the varieties of Magnolia, generally growing in clusters and not large, much the most marked of these not differing from our great-leaved Magnolia when young and in rich soil. Young shoots of this growing as it would if from a stool with the different stems cut down one or two every year, and none growing over five years, would give what was of most value of the great-leafed trees not palms and not of the Paulownia character. I saw no great-leafed trees more than twenty feet high, always excepting palms. As a general rule, in the landscape, these and whatever trees there were, were lost completely (as individuals) in the intricacy of whatever went to make up the mass of luxuriance, but especially under the all-clothing garment of vines and creepers.

You know how we see a single tree—most frequently a *Juniperus virginiana*—lost completely under the Cat-briar. Frequently—generally —the whole forest is lost in the same way here. You often see nothing but the foliage of the vines, and this is generally so small and delicate in detail that you distinguish nothing individual except in the immediate foreground. Palms and everything are lost under it. As far as I could make out, the largest and highest trees were completely covered with a most delicate vine with a close narrow long leaf, gray-green in color, or more likely with a small white or gray blossom, which gave that effect. When growing over shrubs or small trees, a hundred feet distant, it was not essentially different in landscape effect from the Clematis as we often see it showered over a Sumach.

If you could have large spreading trees like the Chestnut or Sycamore growing on a steep hillside, and completely cover them with Clematis as the Sumach is covered, only here and there little branches and twigs of the other trees I have mentioned pushing up through, you would have the effect of the tropical forest much as I saw it yesterday across the Chagres River. There are all sorts of other vines. I saw, I suppose, the yellow jessamine (of Georgia) and the Trumpet Creeper, but the Virginia Creeper would at a distance answer better the purpose of what was more common. But also there were many more delicate in structure and smaller leaf, but larger and more cord-like in trunk. Very often it seemed as if hundreds of cords ($\frac{1}{2}$ inch) were stretched from every part of the great spreading tops of trees, fifty to a hundred feet to the ground. All large trees seem to have strained themselves to the utmost to get their foliage away from the smothering density of the ground-growth, the smaller trees and shrubs, but not to have been able to get away from the vines and creepers. Thus there is often, as it were, an upper and a lower growth, of which the Cocoanut Palm growing out of a jungle, but itself overgrown by creepers, is the extreme type. There are parts of the Ramble where you will have this result in a considerable degree after a few years, the lower stratum being a few shrubs that will endure the shade and the upper low-spreading topped, artificially dwarfed trees assisted by vines. I don't doubt that in the interior of these forests you would find spots where the ground-growth was killed by density of shade and the trunks only supported a canopy or extended parasol, rendered complete and impervious by the vines and by the absence of shade above. The theory of adaptation of varieties thus accounts for the palm-like growth of so many tropical trees and shrubs or sub-trees. Our Sassafras as it grows in the Sassafras grove in the Ramble, is a perfectly tropical tree in character. But for the tropical or tropic-like scenery, you must get the utmost possible intricacy and variety and can have no breadth or mass of color or simple continuity of outline.

The country is very rocky but except where there are cliffs or precipices (where stone is being quarried, generally by the railroad company) all the rock is covered by verdure. The most beautiful thing in itself is the young (or small variety) Banana, or what I suppose to be that. Is there nothing which would give something of that exquisite

transparent glaucous-green which by strawing and all manner of practical winter protection, you could get on the lakeshore? You get no
conception of its beauty when it is grown as an object by itself in a tub
under glass. It wants a little play of light, derived from its own motion
and that of other foliage reflected on it. I assume, as I said at starting,
that as a general rule, these things which I have mentioned as the most
obvious parts (except those clearly out of our power to produce) which
combine to constitute tropical scenery all help to that emotion, the root
of which seems to be a profound sense of the Creator's bountiful-
ness. . . .

> Very truly yours,
>
> Fred. Law Olmsted.

*

From *Forty Years of Landscape Architecture: Central Park*, edited by
Frederick Law Olmsted, Jr. and Theodora Kimball (Olmsted: 1822-1903).
Cambridge: The MIT Press, 1973. After the untimely death of Downing,
Olmsted was next in line to build on his legacy, eventually even joining in
partnership with Calvert Vaux who had come to America to work with Downing. Olmsted's career was a sensitive response to the rapid changes the country
was undergoing in the second half of the nineteenth century, particularly the
growth of cities and suburban areas, and new developments in transportation
and technology. Perhaps more significantly, there was a shifting awareness in
modern consciousness that reflected the way the country now thought of itself.
One aspect of this feeling was the great desire for a public park in the European
style. This was to be New York City's Central Park, with Olmsted becoming
Superintendent and Architect-in-Chief. Olmsted conceived of his role in a
perspective that went beyond that of landscape gardener, preferring to coin the
term "landscape architect" which more appropriately described the totality of
his design in relation to his social views. Olmsted was more influential than
anyone in the field before him, creating parks, cemeteries, parkways,
campuses, railroad stations, estates, and suburban centers all over the country,
and in Canada. He designed the park systems of Boston, Buffalo, Milwaukee
and Louisville, Detroit's Belle Isle Park, and the Riverside community near
Chicago, also Montreal's Mount Royal Park, and the Biltmore estate in North
Carolina. He worked on the Capitol grounds in Washington and the Chicago
World's Fair. Following an abiding interest in conservation he drew up plans

for the preservation of Yosemite Valley and Niagara Falls.

But even before he had accomplished so much in the world of landscape architecture, Olmsted had started a farm, for a while went into publishing, and traveled extensively here and abroad, writing several books on his experiences. *Walks and Talks of an American Farmer in England* (dedicated to Downing) described his enthusiasm for English country houses and public parks, and other books, *A Journey in the Seaboard Slave States* and *A Journey Through Texas* supported the abolition of slavery and vast social reforms in the tumultuous years before the Civil War. During the war itself Olmsted served as General Secretary of the U.S. Sanitary Commission. In 1857 when he applied for the position to design Central Park his application was seconded by respected figures of the day, including William Cullen Bryant, Washington Irving, Asa Gray, Albert Bierstadt, and Horace Greeley. Olmsted went on to transform over 800 acres, between 59th St. and 110th St. in the center of Manhattan, into a park that would offer beauty and recreation to all classes of society. It was the centerpiece to his progressive politics. Later Olmsted would become one of the founders of the Metropolitan Museum of Art and the Museum of Natural History, both of which faced his park.

The letter excerpted here, addressed to Ignaz Pilat, chief landscape gardener of Central Park, reflects his aesthetics of landscape design, especially the precarious balance between the exotic and the natural environment in the choice of plant material and overall effect. More profound, however, is the religious feeling Olmsted brought to his relationship with nature as the artwork of a supreme Creator, this moral imperative being very much a part of the American experience since its beginnings. There was another equally valuable attribute in Olmsted's philosophy: the heritage of civic responsibility joined to individual effort that was so much an aspect of his vision of landscape architecture as a social act. Quite simply, Olmsted was one of the magnificent men of America's nineteenth century.

THE LOVERS' LANE POOL

BEATRIX FARRAND

IT WILL DOUBTLESS BE REALIZED BY THOSE standing at the edge of Lovers' Lane Pool that the change in level from the steps opposite the orangery to the pool itself amounts to a very considerable number of feet—approximately 55. The whole arrangement surrounding the Lovers' Lane Pool is, again, entirely controlled by the natural slopes of the ground and the desire to keep as many of the native trees as possible unhurt and undisturbed. The big walnut at the south end of the pool has been gracefully framed by the surrounding levels, and the pool itself so placed that it does not interfere with the roots of either the big silver maple (*Acer saccharinum*) to the north of the pool or the boundary trees to the east.

The Lovers' Lane Pool and the seats surrounding its south end were never intended for a large audience; probably at most fifty people could be comfortably seated. These seats have been adapted from the well-known open-air theatre on the slopes of the Janiculum Hill at the Accademia degli Arcadi Bosco Parrasio. The shape of the theatre at Dumbarton was copied from the one in Rome, but the slopes surrounding the Dumbarton theatre are far steeper than those on the Italian hillsides and therefore the seats are considerably raised from one level to another. In order to give seclusion to this little theatre, it has been surrounded by cast-stone columns, also baroque in design and taken in their essential ideas from Italian gardens of the baroque period. The cast stone columns are connected with a split natural-wood lattice in long horizontal rectangles. These trellises are covered by both deciduous and evergreen creepers, such as honeysuckle, ivy, and jasmine; and on the east trellis, where protection is needed from the very close easterly boundary, the heavy-growing kudzu has been amply used. The ground cover under the seats is of *Vinca minor* and this also surrounds the pool. The Lovers' Lane Pool was designed in its outline to give added perspective to the length available, to act as a sounding board for those using the small stage at the north end of the pool, as well as to act as a reflecting mirror to the overhanging silver maples on the north.

Outside the trellis, it is protected by some few plants of privet, both the Japanese and *amurense*, and a few plants of bamboo; and, on the west side of the pool, a weeping willow breaks the steep slope of the bank north of where the seats end.

PLANT LIST: LOVERS' LANE POOL

Trees, shrubs and vines surrounding the pool

Tsuga canadensis, Canadian hemlock
Acer saccharinum, Silver maple
Fagus sylvatica 'Purpurea' [*Fagus sylvatica* 'Atropunicea'], European purple-leaved beech
Juglans regia, Persian walnut
Liriodendron tulipferia, Tulip poplar
Prunus sp., Cherry
Salix babylonica, Weeping willow
Buxus sempervirens 'Suffruticosa,' Edging box
Ligustrum amurense, Amur privet
Ligustrum japonicum, Wax-leaf privet
Lonicera japonica, Japanese honeysuckle
Bambusa sp., Bamboo

On the trellis

Hedera sp., Ivy
Jasminum sp., Jasmine
Lonicera sp., Honeysuckle
Pueraria lobata, Kudzu vine

On the brick wall

Vinca minor, Periwinkle

Ground cover, perennials, and spring bulbs around the pool

Crocus sp., Crocus
Vinca minor, Periwinkle
Viola sp., Violet

Spring bulbs and perennials underneath the beech tree

Crocus sp., Crocus
Eranthis hyemalis, Winter aconite
Erythronium sp., Dog-tooth violet
Fritillaria sp., Guinea-hen flower
Galanthus nivalis, Common snowdrop
Hepatica sp., Liverleaf
Narcissus sp., Daffodil
Osmorhiza sp., Sweet cicely
Podophyllum peltatum, Mayapple
Trillium sp., Trillium
Triteleia sp., Triteleia
Viola sp., Violet

Trees and shrubs on the bank outside the east wall of the Fountain Terrace

Acer saccharinum, Silver maple
Crataegus cordata [*Crataegus phaenopyrum*], Washington thorn

Platanus occidentalis, Buttonwood
Pyrus lecontei 'Kieffer', Kieffer pear
Buxus sempervirens, Common box
Cydonia sinensis, Chinese quince
Jasminum nudiflorum, Winter jasmine
Ligustrum amurense, Amur privet

*

From *Beatrix Farrand's Plant Book for Dumbarton Oaks*, edited by Diane Kostial McGuire (Farrand: 1872-1959). Washington, D.C.: Dumbarton Oaks, 1980. Farrand was the only woman among the founders of the American Society of Landscape Architects in 1899. Indeed it was hardly a profession women aspired to in her day so unique it was, and long before this remarkable woman who liked to call herself by the English term "landscape gardener" could even vote in her own country, she had landscaped many of its great estates and universities. The recent publication of *Beatrix Farrand's American Landscapes* (by Balmori, McGuire and McPeck) through its careful scholarship has helped to articulate her prominent place in the history of American landscape architecture.

As a young woman Farrand, who was Edith Wharton's niece and advised her on The Mount grounds, studied botany and horticulture under the tutelage of Charles S. Sargent at the Arnold Arboretum. She traveled in Europe where she visited great gardeners (William Robinson and Gertrude Jekyll) and great gardens. Her own work combined the English naturalistic landscape and the Italian formal garden. In a more than fifty-year career she worked on private estates in New York, New England, and England, the most distinguished among them, now mostly disappeared as gardens are wont to do, the Abby Aldrich Rockefeller Garden in Seal Harbor, Maine, still maintained. Farrand's own garden was at her nearby home in Bar Harbor where for decades she nurtured carefully-labeled plants, amassed an extensive library of rare landscape architecture books and prints, and planned for a center of design and horticultural research. When it no longer seemed possible to realize this dream according to her high standards, in the mid-1950s Farrand dismantled her garden and library so that nothing remained.

What the new interest in Farrand has made clear is how much her landscaping, once linked largely to the era of country estates, inspired the look of American campuses. Farrand landscaped buildings at Princeton University for more than thirty years, at Yale University for two decades, working also at Oberlin College, the University of Chicago, and the California Institute of

Technology. She designed a White House garden during Woodrow Wilson's presidency, and in her seventies, served as consultant to the Santa Barbara Botanic Garden.

Farrand's greatest challenge was the garden at Dumbarton Oaks in Washington, D.C. which she refined over a twenty-five-year period, from 1921 to 1947. Her *Plant Book* is the kind of special garden document seldom available to the non-professional, for here Farrand set down in a straight-forward manner the treatment of each section of the garden, the list of plants used, and their maintenance, which was an integral part of her landscaping approach. At Dumbarton Oaks one can study her elegant garden detail, in the arrangement of walkways, the choice of stone and sculpture, how water and walls outline a border. Moving from the formality of garden settings close to the house to the more free-flowing naturalism beyond it, the full sweep of her landscaping becomes apparent, in the texture of plants and their breathy foliage, in the shapes and seduction of trees, their smells, especially the quivering odorous boxwood that unifies the pathways, and the metamorphosing color of seasons. One returns again and again to a luxurious garden as one rereads a great book whose structure never fails to protect its ungraspable beauty.

Urban Landscapes

Garrett Eckbo

Landscape elements include all forms of planting and vegetation, all adjustments, refinements or designed developments in ground forms, rock groupings, and water patterns, all construction other than completely enclosed buildings or primarily utilitarian engineering structures—walks, terraces, patios, steps, walls, screens, arbors, shelters, play areas, etc. These are the elements used to develop and refine spaces between, around, or within buildings and vehicular circulation elements, when they occur either intentionally or through accidents of nonintensive land use. The extent and qualitative treatment of landscaped pedestrian open space is a barometer of community concern with the character of its physical surroundings. Bacon's famous line, ''Men tend to build stately sooner than to garden finely,'' might be paraphrased today as ''men tend to build densely sooner than to garden at all.''

Trees, rather than buildings, are the best measure of the civilized landscape. A community in which many mature trees survive and more are planted regularly demonstrates a sense of time, history, and continuity on the land which is directly contrary to our normal speculative scramble and the normal real estate drive for higher and better use which regards all green open space as raw land waiting for the magic wand of progress (construction) to touch it. It takes ten years or longer to produce a reasonably mature tree in most parts of the country; few urban land users anticipate a tenure longer than five years. This is not progress, growth, development, or vitality. It is insanity, a squirrel cage in which most of us chase madly round and round only to find the same old ugly city in the end. Those sections in which fine old trees do survive—the better residential districts, institutional grounds, parks—are the showplaces of the city. These are the sections to which the tourists are sent to offset the slums and the blighted areas.

Tree men spend their lives searching for trees which will accommodate themselves to the impossible conditions of urban living—soot, dust, smog, heat, glare, carbon monoxide, barren dry soil covered with paving, no space in which roots or top can flourish. The ideal urban tree is narrow, neat, and inoffensive, somewhat like the ideal urban citizen of these conformist days. Its roots will not push and swell enough to disrupt sidewalks and utilities, its top will not be so broad and dense as to cover signs or windows. It will not drop leaves, twigs, flowers, or fruit enough to make a troublesome mess. The natural cycle of growth and decay which produces the rich humus of the forest floor has no place in our centers of civilization. Now we are even searching for trees that will grow in containers. What a contradiction in terms!

Trees are nature's air conditioners. They moderate the climate, reducing extremes of heat, wind, aridity, and glare. It has been said that an adequate number of trees in and around Los Angeles would filter out the smog. Likewise trees moderate the visual landscape. Most construction can become acceptable in the landscape, both visually and functionally, if it is so spaced that it can be framed and balanced with adequate groups of trees. Rare is the piece of architecture that is self-sufficient without the counterpoint of natural vegetation. Trees are the friends of man. The environment which is good for trees is good for people, and that which is bad for trees is likewise bad for people. Trees and people should band together against the unwholesome ugliness of most city living. The flight to the suburbs is a symptom of this need. If, instead of forcing trees and people to conform to the demands of today's cities, we were to redesign those cities to conform to the needs of trees and people, the millennium might be near.

*

From *Urban Landscape Design,* Garrett Eckbo (1910–2000). New York: McGraw Hill Book Company, 1964. A landscape architect with a deeply humanistic approach, Eckbo posed an alternative to the rise of impersonal, high-tension urbanization in the development of cities and suburbs after World War II. He envisioned more environmentally sound public spaces for people. In a long career he has designed numerous parks, gardens, campuses, shopping malls, and parkways, shaping a California style in American landscape design. Much of his work can be seen on the West Coast, in the Southwest, and in Asia, including the El Paso International Airport, Botanic Gardens at Denver and Memphis, the University of New Mexico-Alberquerque, the Fresno Mall, and Delhi's Lodi Park. At one time he headed the Department of Landscape Architecture at the University of California-Berkeley. Eckbo's numerous writings, among them the influential *Landscape for Living* and *The Art of Home Landscaping,* outline a philosophy of design which he views as mediator "between architecture and ecology."

RESTORATION OF A POET'S GARDEN

JANE BABER WHITE

FOUR YEARS AGO, ON THE ADVICE OF A FRIEND, I went to see the remnants of a little garden in the heart of Lynchburg, Virginia. The garden I saw was that of Anne Spencer, a Harlem Renaissance poet of international renown whose poems have been published in the United States as well as South America and Europe. Anne was educated at the Virginia Seminary in Lynchburg and worked as a high school librarian for 24 years. Her husband, Edward, was Lynchburg's first parcel postman. The Spencers' home served as an intellectual oasis for notable black scholars and entertainers, such as Martin Luther King, Jr., James Weldon Johnson, George Washington Carver, and Marian Anderson.

Anne frequently worked on her poetry into the late evening hours in her garden cottage, "Edankraal," a charming one-room sanctuary built for her by her husband. Edward constructed the chimney, floor, and terrace using slabs of greenstone given to him by his friends at a local quarry. The stained glass used for the front window and the Gothic arches used to make trumpet-vine supports on the sides of the front porch were also gifts from friends and neighbors.

Anne created a traditional cottage garden to complement Edankraal. Although she had no formal training in landscape design and few opportunities to observe the construction of a garden firsthand, she seemed to have a talent for designing gardens. She decided to divide the long (45-by-125-foot) space behind the house into "rooms" by using an arbor and a pergola. This design proved to be not only attractive but also effective in directing the flow of traffic through the garden.

Edward added his own clever touches to the garden, including a lattice fence at the entrance, which he built with wood from the original back porch of the main house. He also constructed three large purple martin houses, which towered above the garden.

Friends often traveled from afar to see the garden at its peak of bloom. One frequent visitor, W. E. B. Du Bois, presented the Spencers with "Prince Ebo," a cast-iron African head, which they imbedded in the concrete edge of their pond and was used to spout water.

An amateur horticulturist, Anne kept abreast of the latest plant introductions and sometimes traveled long distances to purchase new cultivars. Her love for plants was so strong, in fact, that almost every poem she wrote derived from the garden in some way. For example, nasturtium was a favorite subject. Other features of nature, such as blades of grass, the sky, or earthworms, also figured prominently in her poetry. In 1976, the Spencers' house, along with the garden, was declared a Virginia Historic Landmark and placed on the National Register of Historic Places.

When I went to see the garden, it was in shambles. A peony was poking its head out from under the smothering weight of honeysuckle vines, the little English boxwood was broken, and the cast-iron head no longer spouted water. Yet I could tell, just from the feeling of the place, that Anne Spencer had loved the garden which she tended for more than 70 years.

Anne's son, Chauncey, who is now 81 and lives across the street from the family home, gave me a tour of the property. As we talked, he pulled out old photographs of the garden as it looked in the 1920s and in later years. As a landscape designer, I knew then that this little jewel of an abandoned garden deserved to be—indeed *had* to be—restored, and that I knew how to do it.

It was difficult to know where to begin. Although the garden area was relatively small, there were so many things to consider—for example, historical accuracy, as well as selection of a time period on which to concentrate restoration efforts. Then there was maintenance of the garden once it was restored, not to mention the practicality of the operation itself; existing flowers, trees, and shrubs would have to be salvaged, and the garden structures (of which there were many) would have to be re-built.

But the greatest obstacle of all was money. The Friends of Anne Spencer Foundation, consisting of a small group of local citizens, had already encountered many financial problems in restoring and maintaining the historic house. It was obvious the garden restoration would have to be a separate undertaking.

The financial obstacle was overcome thanks to a generous offer made by the Hillside Garden Club. A local club affiliated with the Garden Club of Virginia, Hillside has been involved in garden restorations for almost 60 years. Not only did the Club adopt the restoration of the garden as a project and agree to provide financial backing, Club members also offered to contribute ''old garden flowers'' from their own gardens to supplement those salvaged from Anne Spencer's garden.

After several months of visiting the garden, studying old photographs, and reading about Anne Spencer's life and poetry, we drew up a restoration plan. It was Fall 1983, and we were finally ready to begin.

Before we could bring in the bulldozer, however, we needed to salvage plants and structures. The lacy wrought-iron trim atop the bordering fence was removed in one-foot pieces, cleaned, and stored. English boxwood, peonies, daylilies, and roses were rescued and moved to the vegetable garden area on my property.

The ''bulldozer'' (actually a front-end loader) moved in cautiously to avoid damaging the old dogwood trees, the colorful lattice fence at the garden entrance, and other garden landmarks. We worked along the garden's perimeters with burlap, boxes, and a shovel, constantly on the lookout for another rose, a clump of unknown bulbs, a hunk of greenstone, or an old brick that might need rescuing. Three days and 25 truckloads of debris later, the land was bare, except for a few trees and the fish-pond, and the garden was bathed in light once again.

One of the first things to be restored was Edward Spencer's underground water line, which terminated at the pond. ''Prince Ebo'' began to spout water again, and a large concrete semicircular bench was placed at the pond's edge.

Next came the boundary fence, which was restored using the same framework of iron water pipe, with a double-pipe ''post'' and two-by-four-inch mesh screening between posts. The lacy iron trim, salvaged earlier, was re-attached all along the top. This unusual fence had originally bordered Randolph-Macon Woman's College and had been given to Edward by the College, where he frequently delivered mail on his parcel post route.

Chauncey Spencer took on the task of restoring the purple martin houses. Attaching the 150-pound structures atop the 21-foot iron poles, which were already imbedded in concrete, was not an easy task. In the end, it took three ''floors'' of scaffolding and an elaborate system of pulleys to mount the houses.

Restoration of the grape arbor and wisteria pergola came next. An Eagle Scout candidate, along with his leaders and fellow Scouts, spent many weekends designing and reconstructing both structures with the help of old photographs.

Although the garden paths were grass at one time, for practical purposes they were restored using crushed gravel edged with brick. Three high school masonry students completed the job in record time, incorporating a few irregularities that now add to the restored charm of the garden. A secondary path leading to the garden from the house was laid in large flagstone, a gift from the city of Lynchburg. Flagstone was also used to create a terrace under the pergola, where a statue of Minerva looks out over the garden.

Finally, in the spring of 1984, eight months after the area was cleared, it was time to replant the garden. Those of us involved in the actual digging were delighted with the beautiful rich soil, which required no additional treatment. According to Chauncey, his parents had brought truckloads of leaves into the garden and had worked them into the soil to enrich it. Decades of gardening using organic techniques had produced an 18-inch-thick layer of soil that was totally unlike the red clay typical of the region.

The rose garden came first. There were approximately 35 plants, many with unusual configurations—for example, huge gnarled roots with 10-foot stems protruding. We sawed and pruned, and finally put every one of the original plants in the ground at random to see what would happen. Miraculously, all the roses survived. With the help of a local heritage rose expert, Carl Cato, all but one (a lovely spring-blooming yellow climber) have been identified. These include Climbing Crimson Glory (1946), Climbing American Beauty (1909), Blaze (1932), Betty Prior (1935), American Pillar (1902), Aloha (1949), Mothersday (1949), and Mme. Gregoire Staechelin (1927).

We replanted all of Anne Spencer's bulbs in a little wooded area. Now, each spring, visitors are greeted with a profusion of snowdrops, daffodils, and narcissus. Scilla, tiger lilies, and Quaker-ladies that had been smothered for years have also ''reappeared'' to join the others. The local Sweet Briar College Alumnae Club donated additional bulbs to the restoration project.

Next, we tackled the two long, narrow borders that run the length of the garden. On one side, we planted old-fashioned purple and white lilacs to form a hedge. We then underplanted the lilacs with periwinkle and bulbs. Along the other border, we planted a full array of mixed old-fashioned perennials and annuals, based on old photographs of the garden: poppies, peonies, iris, dayliles, hollyhocks, rose-of-Sharon, daisies, phlox, chrysanthemums, coral bells, and foxglove, to name just a few.

The central axis leading from the grape arbor to the pond was planted with more than 100 little English boxwood. We decided to use the slow-growing boxwood instead of replanting the privet hedge, since the former is easier to maintain.

We replanted the grape arbor with two cultivars of grape that were known to exist in the early twentieth century: Concord and Niagara. Several months later, we were thrilled to discover a poem by Anne Spencer entitled ''Grapes: Still-Life,'' in which she describes the ''green-white Niagara'' and the ''purpling Concord.''

In 1985, the Hillside Garden Club received the coveted Commonwealth Award from the Garden Club of Virginia in recognition of the Club's efforts. Hillside was also given additional funds to restore the driveway as well as the colorful lattice fence at the garden entrance. Now, 12 years after Anne Spencer's death, the garden has been completely restored, thanks to the contribuions and expertise of many community friends, volunteers, and donors.

I often wonder whether Anne Spencer would be happy with the way her garden has been restored. Although she was undoubtedly used to scholars interpreting her poetry, her garden was never as closely scrutinized as her writing during her lifetime. Perhaps the following verse from ''Any Wife to Any Husband: A Derived Poem'' reveals the garden's true meaning for the gifted poet from Lynchburg:

> This small garden is half my world
> I am nothing to it—when all is said,
> I plant the thorn and kiss the rose,
> but they will grow when I am dead.

*

From ''Restoration of a Poet's Garden,'' Jane Baber White, in *American Horticulturist,* Volume 66, No. 10, October 1987; Virginia. Landscape designer and life-long resident of Lynchburg, White reconstructs a fortuitous sequence of events demonstrating how a community can work together successfully to bring back to life a long-forgotten garden. Such restoration projects have been occurring more and more around the country in the last dozen or so years. Virginia, home to Williamsburg, Mt. Vernon and Monticello, has a longer tradition of historical restoration than any other state. Nonetheless, the garden of Anne Spencer (1882-1975) retains a special significance in the broader historical perspective. Regrettably, so little documentation is available to trace the contribution of blacks to American garden history, and beyond that to ethno-botany, and *materia medica.* What of the seeds the slaves brought from Africa? On a larger and more obvious scale is the lack of attention to their work establishing the great plantation gardens of the South. And, what of black rural gardens?

Anne Spencer's life in the garden was of a very private, artistic order. Her biographer J. L. Greene points out, in *Time's Unfading Garden,* how central its metaphors and imagery were to her poetry which has been anthologized in such diverse volumes as *The Book of American Negro Poetry* and *The Norton Anthology of Modern Poetry*, over a period of fifty years. Spencer, a child two decades after the Civil War, at home more in her Lynchburg garden than in the town itself, understood nature as a form of utterance. *Earth, I thank you / for the pleasure of your language.*

When the article excerpted here appeared in the *American Horticulturist,* the poet's son received a letter from a man in prison, who wrote: ''A question I've often asked, since I've been a horticultural ornamental student [is]: Surely there were or are some black gardeners that had treasures of wisdom. . . ?'' Garden history is only one of the many histories of the world diminished by their exclusions.

V

REFLECTIONS IN A GARDEN WORLD

The Bean-Field

Henry David Thoreau

MEANWHILE MY BEANS, THE LENGTH OF whose rows, added together, was seven miles already planted, were impatient to be hoed, for the earliest had grown considerably before the latest were in the ground; indeed they were not easily to be put off. What was the meaning of this so steady and self-respecting, this small Herculean labor, I knew not. I came to love my rows, my beans, though so many more than I wanted. They attached me to the earth, and so I got strength like Antaeus. But why should I raise them? Only Heaven knows. This was my curious labor all summer,—to make this portion of the earth's surface, which had yielded only cinque-foil, blackberries, johnswort, and the like, before, sweet wild fruits and pleasant flowers, produce instead this pulse. What shall I learn of beans or beans of me? I cherish them, I hoe them, early and late I have an eye to them; and this is my day's work. It is a fine broad leaf to look on. My auxiliaries are the dews and rains which water this dry soil, and what fertility is in the soil itself, which for the most part is lean and effete. My enemies are worms, cool days, and most of all woodchucks. The last have nibbled for me a quarter of an acre clean. But what right had I to oust johnswort and the rest, and break up their ancient herb garden? Soon, however, the remaining beans will be too tough for them, and go forward to meet new foes.

When I was four years old, as I well remember, I was brought from Boston to this my native town, through these very woods and this field, to the pond. It is one of the oldest scenes stamped on my memory. And now tonight my flute has waked the echoes over that very water. The pines still stand here older than I; or, if some have fallen, I have cooked my supper with their stumps, and a new growth is rising all around, preparing another aspect for new infant eyes. Almost the same johnswort springs from the same perennial root in this pasture, and even I have at length helped to clothe that fabulous landscape of my infant dreams, and one of the results of my presence and influence is seen in these bean leaves, corn blades, and potato vines.

I planted about two acres and a half of upland; and as it was only about fifteen years since the land was cleared, and I myself had got out two or three cords of stumps, I did not give it any manure; but in the course of the summer it appeared by the arrow-heads which I turned up in hoeing, that an extinct nation had already dwelt here and planted corn and beans ere white men came to clear the land, and so, to some extent, had exhausted the soil for this very crop.

Before yet any woodchuck or squirrel had run across the road, or the sun had got above the shrub oaks, while all the dew was on, though the farmers warned me against it,—I would advise you to do all your work if possible while the dew is on,—I began to level the ranks of haughty weeds in my bean-field and throw dust upon their heads. Early in the morning I worked barefooted, dabbling like a plastic artist in the dewy and crumbling sand, but later in the day the sun blistered my feet. There the sun lighted me to hoe beans, pacing slowly backward and forward over that yellow gravelly upland, between the long green rows, fifteen rods, the one end terminating in a shrub oak copse where I could rest in the shade, the other in a blackberry field where the green berries deepened their tints by the time I had made another bout. Removing the weeds, putting fresh soil about the bean stems, and encouraging this weed which I had sown, making the yellow soil express its summer thought in bean leaves and blossoms rather than in wormwood and piper and millet grass, making the earth say beans instead of grass,—this was my daily work. As I had little aid from horses or cattle, or hired men or boys, or improved implements of husbandry, I was much slower, and became much more intimate with my beans than usual. But labor of the hands, even when pursued to the verge of drudgery, is perhaps never the worst form of idleness. It has a constant and imperishable moral, and to the scholar it yields a classic result. A very *agricola laboriosus* was I to travelers bound westward through Lincoln and Wayland to nobody knows where; they sitting at their ease in gigs, with elbows on knees, and reins loosely hanging in festoons; I the home-staying, laborious native of the soil. But soon my homestead was out of their sight and thought. It was the only open and cultivated field for a great distance on either side of the road; so they made the most of it; and sometimes the man in the field heard more of travellers' gossip and comment than was meant for his ear: ''Beans so late! peas so late!''—for I continued to plant when others had began to hoe,—the ministerial husbandman had not suspected it. ''Corn, my boy, for fodder; corn for fodder.'' ''Does he *live* there?'' asks the black bonnet of the gray coat; and the hard-featured farmer reins up his grateful dobbin to inquire what you are doing where he sees no manure in the furrow, and recommends a little chip dirt, or any little waste stuff, or it may be ashes or plaster. But here were two acres and a half of furrows, and only a hoe for cart and two hands to draw it,—there being an aversion to other carts and horses,—and chip dirt far away. Fellow-travellers as they rattled by compared it aloud with the fields which they had passed, so that I came to know how I stood in the agricultural world. This was one field not in Mr. Coleman's report. And, by the way, who estimates the value of the crop which Nature yields in the still wilder fields unimproved by man? The crop of *English* hay is carefully weighed, the moisture calculated, the silicates and the potash; but in all dells and pond holes in the woods and pastures and swamps grows a rich and various crop only unreaped by man. Mine was, as it were, the connecting link between wild and cultivated fields; as some states are civilized, and others half-civilized, and others savage or barbarous, so my field was, though not in a bad sense, a half-cultivated field. They were beans cheerfully returning to their wild and primitive state that I cultivated, and my hoe played the *Rans des Vaches* for them.

Near at hand, upon the topmost spray of a birch, sings the brown-thrasher—or red mavis, as some love to call him—all the morning, glad of your society, that would find out another farmer's field if yours were not here. While you are planting the seed, he cries,—''Drop it, drop it,—cover it up, cover it up,—pull it up, pull it up, pull it up.'' But this was not corn, and so it was safe from such enemies as he. You may wonder what his rigmarole, his amateur Paganini performances on one string or on twenty, have to do with your planting, and yet prefer it to leached ashes or plaster. It was a cheap sort of top dressing in which I had entire faith.

As I drew a still fresher soil about the rows with my hoe, I disturbed the ashes of unchronicled nations who in primeval years lived under these heavens, and their small implements of war and hunting were brought to the light of this modern day. There lay mingled with other natural stones, some of which bore the marks of having been burned by Indian fires, and some by the sun, and also bits of pottery and glass brought hither by the recent cultivators of the soil. When my hoe tinkled against the stones, that music echoed to the woods and the sky, and was an accompaniment to my labor which yielded an instant and immeasurable crop. It was no longer beans that I hoed, nor I that hoed beans; and I remembered with as much pity as pride, if I remembered at all, my acquaintances who had gone to the city to attend the oratorios. The nighthawk circled overhead in the sunny afternoons—for I sometimes made a day of it—like a mote in the eye, or in heaven's eye, falling from time to time with a swoop and a sound as if the heavens were rent, torn at last to very rags and tatters, and yet a seamless cope remained; small imps that fill the air and lay their eggs on the ground on bare sand or rocks on the tops of hills, where few have found them; graceful and slender like ripples caught up from the pond, as leaves are raised by the wind to float in the heavens; such kindredship is in Nature. The hawk is aerial brother of the wave which he sails over and surveys, those his perfect air-inflated wings answering to the elemental unfledged pinions of the sea. Or sometimes I watched a pair of hen-hawks circling high in the sky, alternately soaring and descending, approaching and leaving one another, as if they were the imbodiment of my own thoughts. Or I was attracted by the passage of wild pigeons from this wood to that, with a slight quivering winnowing sound and carrier haste; or from under a rotten stump my hoe turned up a sluggish portentous and outlandish spotted salamander, a trace of Egypt and the Nile, yet our contemporary. When I paused to lean on my hoe, these sounds and sights I heard and saw any where in the row, a part of the inexhaustible entertainment which the country offers.

On gala days the town fires its great guns, which echo like popguns to these woods, and some waifs of martial music occasionally penetrate thus far. To me, away there in my bean-field at the other end of town, the big guns sounded as if a puff ball had burst; and when there was a military turnout of which I was ignorant, I have sometimes had a vague sense all the day of some sort of itching and disease in the horizon, as if some eruption would break out there soon, either scarlatina or canker-rash, until at length some more favorable puff of wind, making haste over the fields and up the Wayland road, brought me information of the "trainers." It seemed by the distant hum as if somebody's bees had swarmed, and that the neighbors, according to Virgil's advice, by a faint *tintinnabulum* upon the most sonorous of their domestic utensils, were endeavoring to call them down to the hive again. And when the sound died quite away, and the hum had ceased, and the most favorable breezes told no tale, I knew that they had got the last drone of them all safely into the Middlesex hive, and that now their minds were bent on the honey with which it was smeared.

I felt proud to know that the liberties of Massachusetts and of our fatherland were in such safe keeping; and as I turned to my hoeing again I was filled with an inexpressible confidence, and pursued my labor cheerfully with a calm trust in the future.

When there were several bands of musicians, it sounded as if all the village was a vast bellows, and all the buildings expanded and collapsed alternately with a din. But sometimes it was a really noble and inspiring strain that reached these woods, and the trumpet that sings of fame, and I felt as if I could spit a Mexican with a good relish,—for why should we always stand for trifles?—and looked round for a woodchuck or a skunk to exercise my chivalry upon. These martial strains seemed as far away as Palestine, and reminded me of a march of crusaders in the horizon, with a slight tantivy and tremulous motion of the elm-tree tops which overhang the village. This was one of the *great* days; though the sky had from my clearing only the same everlastingly great look that it wears daily, and I saw no difference in it.

It was a singular experience that long acquaintance which I cultivated with beans, what with planting, and hoeing, and harvesting, and threshing, and picking over, and selling them,—the last was the hardest of all,—I might add eating, for I did taste. I was determined to know beans. When they were growing, I used to hoe from five o'clock in the morning till noon, and commonly spent the rest of the day about other affairs. Consider the intimate and curious acquaintance one makes with various kinds of weeds,—it will bear some iteration in the account, for there was no little iteration in the labor,—disturbing their delicate organizations so ruthlessly, and making such invidious distinctions with his hoe, levelling whole ranks of one species, and sedulously cultivating another. That's Roman wormwood,—that's pigweed,—that's sorrel,—that's piper-grass,—have at him, chop him up, turn his roots upward to the sun, don't let him have a fibre in the shade, if you do he'll turn himself t'other side up and be as green as a leek in two days. A long war, not with cranes, but with weeds, those Trojans who had sun and rain and dews on their side. Daily the beans saw me come to their rescue armed with a hoe, and thin the ranks of their enemies, filling up the trenches with weedy dead. Many a lusty crest-waving Hector, that towered a whole foot above his crowding comrades, fell before my weapon and rolled in the dust.

Those summer days which some of my contemporaries devoted to the fine arts in Boston or Rome, and others to contemplation in India, and others to trade in London or New York, I thus, with the other farmers of New England, devoted to husbandry. Not that I wanted beans to eat, for I am by nature a Pythagorean, so far as beans are concerned, whether they mean porridge or voting, and exchanged them for rice; but, perchance, as some must work in fields if only for the sake of tropes and expression, to serve a parable-maker one day. It was on the whole a rare amusement, which, continued too long, might have become a dissipation. Though I gave them no manure, and did not hoe them all once, I hoed them unusually well as far as I went, and was paid for it in the end, "there being in truth," as Evelyn says, "no compost or laetation whatsoever comparable to this continual motion, repastination, and turning of the mould with the spade." "The earth," he adds elsewhere, "especially if fresh, has a certain magnetism in it, by which it attracts the salt, power, or virtue (call it either) which gives it life, and is the logic of all the labor and stir we keep about it, to sustain us; all dungings and other sordid temperings being but the vicars succedaneous to this improvement." Moreover, this being one of those "worn-out and exhausted lay fields which enjoy their sabbath," had perchance, as Sir Kenelm Digby thinks likely, attracted "vital spirits" from the air. I harvested twelve bushels of beans.

But to be more particular, for it is complained that Mr. Coleman has reported chiefly the expensive experiments of gentlemen farmers, my outgoes were,—

For a hoe	$0 54
Ploughing, harrowing, and furrowing	7 50, Too much
Beans for seed	3 12½
Potatoes ''	1 33
Peas ''	0 40
Turnip seed	0 06
White line for crow fence	0 02
Horse cultivator and boy three hours	1 00
Horse and cart to get crop	0 75
In all	$14 72½

My income was, (*patrem familias vendacem, non emacem esse oportet,*) from

Nine bushels and twelve quarts of beans sold	$16 94
Five '' large potatoes	2 50
Nine '' small	2 25
Grass	1 00
Stalks	0 75
In all	$23 44
Leaving a pecuniary profit, as I have elsewhere said, of	$ 8 71½

This is the result of my experience in raising beans. Plant the common small white bush bean about the first of June, in rows three feet by eighteen inches apart, being careful to select fresh round and unmixed seed. First look out for worms, and supply vacancies by planting anew. Then look out for woodchucks, if it is an exposed place, for they will nibble off the earliest tender leaves almost clean as they go; and again, when the young tendrils make their appearance, they have notice of it, and will shear them off with both buds and young pods, sitting erect like a squirrel. But above all harvest as early as possible, if you would escape frosts and have a fair and salable crop; you may save much loss by this means.

This further experience also I gained. I said to myself, I will not plant beans and corn with so much industry another summer, but such seeds, if the seed is not lost, as sincerity, truth, simplicity, faith, innocence, and the like, and see if they will not grow in this soil, even with less toil and manurance, and sustain me, for surely it has not been exhausted for these crops. Alas! I said to myself; but now another summer is gone, and another, and another, and I am obliged to say to you,

Reader, that the seeds which I planted, if indeed they *were* the seeds of those virtues, were worm-eaten or had lost their vitality, and so did not come up. Commonly men will only be brave as their fathers were brave, or timid. This generation is very sure to plant corn and beans each new year precisely as the Indians did centuries ago and taught the first settlers to do, as if there were a fate in it. I saw an old man the other day, to my astonishment, making the holes with a hoe for the seventieth time at least, and not for himself to lie down in! But why should not the New Englander try new adventures, and not lay so much stress on his grain, his potato and grass crop, and his orchards,—raise other crops than these? Why concern ourselves so much about our beans for seed, and not be concerned at all about a new generation of men? We should really be fed and cheered if when we met a man we were sure to see some of the qualities which I have named, which we all prize more than those other productions, but which are for the most part broadcast and floating in the air, had taken root and grown in him. Here comes such a subtle and ineffable quality, for instance, as truth or justice, though the slightest amount or new variety of it, along the road. Our ambassadors should be instructed to send home such seeds as these, and Congress help to distribute them all over the land. We should never stand upon ceremony with sincerity. We should never cheat and insult and banish one another by our meanness, if there were present the kernel of worth and friendliness. We should not meet thus in haste. Most men I do not meet at all, for they seem not to have time; they are busy about their beans. We would not deal with a man thus plodding ever, leaning on a hoe or a spade as a staff between his work, not as a mushroom, but partially risen out of the earth, something more than erect, like swallows alighted and walking on the ground:—

> And as he spake, his wings would now and then
> Spread, as he meant to fly, then close again,

so that we should suspect that we might be conversing with an angel. Bread may not always nourish us; but it always does us good, it even takes stiffness out of our joints, and makes us supple and buoyant, when we knew not what ailed, to recognize any generosity in man or Nature, to share any unmixed and heroic joy.

Ancient poetry and mythology suggest, at least, that husbandry was once a sacred art; but it is pursued with irreverent haste and heedlessness by us, our object being to have large farms and large crops merely. We have no festival, nor procession, nor ceremony, not excepting our Cattle-shows and so called Thanksgivings, by which the farmer expresses a sense of the sacredness of his calling, or is reminded of its sacred origin. It is the premium and the feast which tempt him. He sacrifices not to Ceres and the Terrestrial Jove, but to the infernal Plutus rather. By avarice and selfishness, and a grovelling habit, from which none of us is free, of regarding the soil as property, or the means of acquiring property chiefly, the landscape is deformed, husbandry is degraded with us, and the farmer leads the meanest of lives. He knows Nature but as a robber. Cato says that the profits of agriculture are particularly pious or just, (*maximeque pius quaestus*) and according to Varro the old Romans ''called the same earth Mother and Ceres, and thought that they who cultivated it led a pious and useful life, and that they alone were left of the race of King Saturn.''

We are wont to forget that the sun looks on our cultivated fields and on the prairies and forests without distinction. They all reflect and absorb his rays alike, and the former make but a small part of the glorious picture which he beholds in his daily course. In his view the earth is all equally cultivated like a garden. Therefore we should receive the benefit of his light and heat with a corresponding trust and magnanimity. What though I value the seed of these beans and harvest that in the fall of the year? This broad field which I have looked at so long looks not to me as the principal cultivator, but away from me to influences more genial to it, which water and make it green. These beans have results which are not harvested by me. Do they not grow for woodchucks partly? The ear of wheat, (in Latin *spica*, obsoletely *speca*, from *spe*, hope,) should not be the only hope of the husbandman; its kernel or grain (*granum*, from *gerendo*, bearing,) is not all that it bears. How, then, can our harvest fail? Shall I not rejoice also at the abundance of the weeds whose seeds are the granary of the birds? It matters little comparatively whether the fields fill the farmer's barns. The true husbandman will cease from anxiety, as the squirrels manifest no concern whether the woods will bear chestnuts this year or not, and finish his labor with every day, relinquishing all claim to the produce of his fields, and sacrificing in his mind not only his first but his last fruits also.

*

From *Walden*, Henry David Thoreau (1817-1862). Boston: Ticknor and Fields, 1854. Thoreau lived in his cabin at Walden Pond from 1845 to 1847, and out of that transcendental existence came one of the great books of American literature. His writing chronicles an exemplary life in which it is possible to study how the history of a man is inseparable from the history of nature. Little appreciated in his lifetime, he had only published one other book, *A Week on the Concord and Merrimack Rivers*, while his massive journal would have to wait for later generations of readers. Thoreau hardly went anywhere far from his beloved Concord, where the first battle of the American Revolution was fought, but his ideas traveled around the world. *Walden* is a basic work in the literature of the self as text, but more to the point, it shows how the theme of consciousness marks the beginning and the end of a life lived in nature.

Thoreau the natural man was simply one aspect of Thoreau the political man. If Walden joined the contemplation of nature to political thought, his "Civil Disobedience" went even farther, later inspiring such diverse historical changes as those led by Gandhi, Martin Luther King, Jr., Viet Nam war protesters and anti-nuclear groups. It is a measure of historical irony that, as a recent *New York Times* article reported, Walden Pond, now neighbor to the town dump, is ravaged yearly by recreationers, and the current owner of *The Atlantic,* which once published him, plans an office park close by. Of course, Thoreau has always sparked controversy as a mere presence in history, and liking him or not can be considered a matter of taste. Eleanor Perényi, not one to beat around a berry bush, holds Thoreau, who preferred a bog to a well-tended garden, partly responsible for "the slovenliness of the American backyard."

Broom and Wisteria

Allen Lacy

That field, perhaps ten acres of former woodland its owner cleared several years ago in hope of selling it to some developer who has yet to show up, lies between my house and the drugstore where I buy out-of-town newspapers, so I pass it several times a week, and always on Sundays. In any season it's a pleasant sight. It slopes gently toward the hedgerows that define the neighborhood bicycle path, and its unknown owner had the good sense to leave some fine oaks standing instead of converting them to cordwood when he brought in the bulldozer and the chain saws.

In compliance with town ordinances, most of the field gets mowed by the Fourth of July, so its vegetation runs chiefly to grasses and butterfly weed and black-eyed Susans, punctuated by patches of poison ivy that turn a glorious if deadly scarlet every fall. But in early May, part of that field always slows me down on the way to the drugstore and sometimes brings me to a halt. Just when the daffodils have quit and the azaleas are blooming like crazy in the front yards of half the split-levels within 350 miles, the field offers a sight that to my mind is worth most of the azaleas in town (and all its hydrangeas)—a strip of land some fifty feet wide, where the owner has held back the tractor that annually mows the rest of his property. Here, at the field's western edge, he has allowed a fine colony of self-sown Scotch broom (*Cytisus scoparius*) to develop, perhaps five hundred plants. Attractive all year round, because the stems of Scotch broom remain brilliant green even in the dreariest part of winter, these volunteer shrubs radiate a special, almost pyrotechnic cheer in May, when they burst into deep golden bloom. But what makes the field where they grow especially lovely is that when the broom comes into blossom, it is accompanied and complemented by the soft blue haze of another volunteer—wisteria vines (*Wisteria floribunda*, I think) that scramble over the dry, sandy slope and clamber to the tops of the nearby oaks.

Sometimes in May I do more than admire. I plunge into the sea of green and golden broom, dodge bumblebees seeking nectar, try to keep from tripping on the wisteria vines, and snip off a few branches of broom and some clusters of wisteria to bring home. Technically my act is theft, but I've always thought St. Augustine went on just a little too much about those stolen pears in his *Confessions*. There's plenty of both wisteria and broom in that field, and having arrived there on their own, they're really weeds. And if some ecologist took it into his head to chide me for disturbing the balance of nature, I'd chide right back. Neither Scotch broom nor *Wisteria floribunda* is native to our shores. Broom's name leaves its origins no mystery, and this particular wisteria is a Japanese import, although there are native American species. Certainly neither plant could be called an endangered species. "Endangering species" would be more apt. Broom, in its preferred habitat of sparse soil, spreads as quickly as a small-town rumor. Wisteria has engulfed whole pine forests in the Tidewater and Piedmont regions of Virginia, though it can't be mentioned in the same breath with kudzu, another import, which with some assistance from the manufacturers of polyester has just about toppled King Cotton in Mississippi and Alabama. I think I'm fairly sound on most environmental issues. I wouldn't dream of picking a lady's slipper orchid, much less digging it up and bringing it home. The one time I allowed myself to "rescue" a Turk's-cap lily from a roadside I felt remorse for a month. But picking some broom and wisteria from a vacant field troubles me not a jot.

A free, loose, and informal bouquet of wisteria and broom on a table flooded by the bright morning light of late spring offers an invitation to observe each plant for itself and then to attend to their differences and similarities. It also teaches something about the differences between poetry and science—and about their hidden common ground.

It will not do at all to speak of wisteria's ''blue haze.'' To speak this way is to speak from a distance; we may be approximately correct but as far off the mark as congratulating ourselves for missing a plane connection by only a few minutes or referring to someone as being slightly pregnant. Blue is too simple a name for a cluster of wisteria blossoms, taken in hand like a bunch of grapes, slowly turned, and seen up close. I take one such cluster from the vase. It has forty-nine individual florets and buds, arranged in a spiral along its pendant stem. The twelve blossoms at the top, fully open, are multicolored, and none of their colors is blue at all. Each blossom has five petals. The topmost, which stands erect, is grayish-mauve, but overlaid with gold along a vertical crease at its center. Semitransparent, when held to the light it fades toward whiteness. The two middle petals, pointing outward and downward, are a deep violet purple, as are the bottommost set they protect, which point outward and slightly downward, are fused together at their bottom edge, and conceal within themselves stamens and pistil, the organs of generation. Below the twelve blossoms at the top of the cluster are nine others that have partially opened and are noticeably a darker purple. Below these, and darker still, seventeen buds show signs of swelling. Still lower, there are twenty-one small, tight buds, each one tinier in its turn down the spiral, each deepening from purple toward black. The final bud is a mere speck, no larger than the period that ends a sentence. Nothing here is blue; the blue is a trick of the eye and of distance. Furthermore, a cluster of wisteria has properties that utterly elude the eye. I shut my eyes, bring it to my face, and breathe deeply of a fragrance that I compare to that of violets and ripe grapes, though the comparison is crude.

At first glance, broom lacks the mathematical symmetry of wisteria's downward spiral. Its blossoms follow no apparent sequence, seeming to appear almost at random up and down the stem. There are blossoms open at the top of the stem, here and there in the middle, and at the bottom—and they are everywhere interspersed with swollen buds. Each blossom emerges from a point on the stem where it is accompanied by a pair of trifoliate leaves and a tiny bud that will bloom only when its larger companion has shattered and fallen. (The paired buds give broom a very long flowering season, well over a month.) All the petals of broom are the same color—an intense, saturated golden-yellow.

The differences between broom and wisteria are plain. Broom is upright and perky and straightforward, as emphatic as a manifesto. Wisteria is drooping and languid and complex, as indirect as a hint. Seen up close, broom's color is just what it seems to be from a distance; wisteria is more than it first seemed to be.

But surprises follow when you look even more closely at broom. The paired blossoms and buds and their accompanying leaves also spiral around their stem. And each blossom, like those of wisteria, has a top petal pointing up, two middle petals, pointing out and flanking two lower petals that point outward and slightly upward and conceal stamens and pistil. Despite their differences, broom and wisteria are greatly similar one to the other.

Calling similar things by similar names is one of the most primordial of human acts, symbolized most profoundly in the story of Adam and Eve being given dominion in Eden by the commandment to give names to the other living things they found there. Classification of things lies at the root of language and thus of culture, and it reaches its most advanced development and expression in science. Having looked closely at broom and wisteria on a bright May morning, having noticed the similarities that lie beneath their differences, I need words to name these things. I reach for the nearest botanical book at hand. Published in 1926 by a firm that no longer exists, it is very much out of date, being entirely silent on matters of molecular biology. But it serves my particular needs as regards the similarities of broom and wisteria, whose flowers show them to be indisputably kin, if not exactly kissing cousins.

Their top petal, I learn, is called a ''standard.'' The middle petals are ''wings.'' The bottom petals, fused into one, are called the ''keel.'' I learn, furthermore, that both broom and wisteria are members of the vast numbers of genera and species that make up the legume family. Knowing this, I may also infer that, like all legumes, they have the power to transform nitrogen, to pluck it out of the atmosphere and fix it into the soil by interaction with certain bacteria. And thus I know that not only are those brooms and wisteria vines bringing beauty to that vacant field in May, they are also improving the fertility of the soil from which they spring. This knowledge is a matter of science.

But beneath the science there lies poetry. *Standards, wings, keel:* in naming the parts of these blossoms, we follow the path of metaphor into the poetic dimension that underlies all detailed observation and all science. We are comparing ultimately dissimilar things to one another, relating the parts of flowers to the banners that armies once carried before them into battle, to the means of flight in birds and butterflies, to the unseen, bottommost part of a ship slicing through the water.

And beneath the poetry? Here lies, I believe, finally a mystery. We cannot know the *Ding an sich*, the broom as it is in itself, the wisteria itself. These are instances of the unspeakable beauties of the things of this earth.

*

From *Home Ground: A Gardener's Miscellany*, Allen Lacy (1935-). New York: Farrar, Straus and Giroux, 1984. Lacy brings a gentleness and real love of plants to his work, and he is not afraid of sentiment. A philosophy professor with a self-effacing humor, he shows a deep sense of wonder in the question of being, whether plants or people. Not surprisingly, he has written about and translated Miguel de Unamuno, the Spanish inquirer into the mystery of existence. Lacy's *Farther Afield: A Gardener's Excursions* continues his research into the changing lives of the garden world.

And So To Bed

Richardson Wright

HEN THAT AMOROUS RESTORATION worthy, Samuel Pepys, finished the day's record in his diary, he gave a last fine flourish of the pen and ended with, ''And so to bed.''

Millions before his time and millions since have gone off to rest with as light a conscience as he, yet Samuel Pepys' phrase will go down to posterity as the last exultant remark one makes as he stifles a yawn and switches off the light. ''And so to bed'' has a finality to it. The day is done. There are no more things one wishes to do or has to do. There are no more people to talk to and nothing more to be said. Work and play, trouble and laughter, earnest endeavors and inconsequential flippancies—all are over. That day's finished. ''And so to bed!''

An amusing picture Pepys makes as he stumbles up the stairs. A young man (for the Pepys of the diary was in his thirties) often the worse for drink, and wearing the finery of his day—the silk suit with the gold buttons of which he was so proud, and the new periwig, that had aroused no comment when he first wore it, pushed to the back of his shaved pate. A candlestick is in his hand. One of the wenches of his household may be at his elbow. From the top of the stairs his sprightly French wife, in the petticoat that cost £5 and the patches that she favored, tells him in no uncertain terms what she thinks of him.

Whether sober or in his cups, whether bowed with the worries of the British Navy, of which he was secretary, or light-hearted over the last girl he had kissed, to Pepys going to bed was a ceremony. And so it was for many generations until, in our own era, people began to live on one plane. ''And so to bed'' meant going *upstairs* to bed.

Today, with innumerable people living in apartments or in bungalows, the act of ascending the stairs to one's rest is almost becoming obsolete. We merely walk into another room and tumble into the sheets. Going to bed has lost some of its fine old flavor. It has ceased being a luxury, and has become an efficient necessity.

My youth was spent in an old household in Philadelphia where going to bed still retained the atmosphere of quaint domesticalities. After dinner the family sat around and read or talked. Callers drifted in, chatted for a while, had their wine, and went home. At about half-past ten Bridget thumped up from her kitchen carrying the silver basket, which she deposited on the floor beside Grandmother's chair. Having bade a broguish good night, she disappeared. Then a yawn broke the conversation and bed was suggested. Grandmother went first, carrying the silver. The rest of the family trooped after her. Finally Grandfather, putting out the gas lights as he went along, began his slow progress up the wide stairs. He always seemed engrossed in deep thought. On the landing he stopped, compared his watch with the landing clock, wound it and stood there silently for a moment. Then he, too, mounted the last flight.

What he did in that silent moment before the clock always piqued my curiosity. One day I made so bold as to ask him. He was attending to a purely private affair, it seemed. That arrested position before the tall clock gave him a chance, so he explained, to say his prayer for a good death. It was the prayer of Launcelot Andrewes, the 16th century English mystic: ''Grant, O Lord, that the end of this life be Christian, without sin and without shame, and if it please Thee, without pain.''

That perhaps gives us the clue to the old ceremony of going to bed. The darkness and uncertainty of night were akin to the darkness and uncertainty of death. The thought of one evoked thought of the other. The terrors of night were real terrors. Dreams were things to tremble over. There were no Freuds in those days to explain them pleasantly or unpleasantly away. The Compline hymn went—

From all ill dreams defend our eyes
From nightly fears and fantasies.

Today any psychoanalyst will tell us what our dreams mean; if we fear the dark we have merely to push a button and its terrors are dispelled. Night is divested of its apparent uncertainties. It is all safe and sane and explainable. It is difficult to visualize a man of the present generation living in an apartment and saying a prayer for a good death as he passes from the living room into his bedroom. It is impossible to believe that he fears the night when he has a telephone and a light switch at his elbow. This one-plane living has divested the act of going to bed not only of its picturesqueness but its faith as well. The mere act of ascending to a safe place and the sense of security that it gives are forgotten.

After one has lived for a while in a modern, convenient and thoroughly efficient apartment, he begins to realize that he is paying a heavy price for his luxuries. He is missing a lot of those domestic habits that go to make up the picturesqueness of life in a house. A house with an upstairs and a down requires attention. It presupposes responsibilities. There is a fire to bank for the night. There are windows and doors to lock. There is the business of going down to the kitchen to raid the icebox for a pre-bed snack or an apple. There is the cat to put out. There is the final glance at the thermometer and a look up at the sky to see what weather lies ahead. Then comes the procession up the stairs. That, sirs, is the way to go to bed. And if, perchance, at the foot of the stairs is a table where you pick up your candle to light your way, then your joy can be complete.

Perhaps it is because of these things that more and more people are taking houses in the country where, for the summer season at least, they can enjoy the habits of living a little less efficiently, where things aren't all explained away, where life is lived closer to the uncertainties of Nature, and going upstairs to bed is a ceremony.

*

From *The Gardener's Bed-Book*, Richardson Wright (1887-1961). Philadelphia: J. B. Lippincott Company, 1929. The editor of *House and Garden* for over forty years, Wright was an influential figure on the garden scene. He was also a former war correspondent in Siberia and Manchuria, and a *New York Times* literary critic, and one-time drama critic. Chairman of the International Flower Show in New York for two decades, Wright published over two dozen books, which include *Russia: An Interpretation*, *Truly Rural*, *Hawkers and Walkers in Early America*, *The Bed-Book of Travel*, and *The Story of Gardening*. Wright's personal style evokes an uncomplicated genteel world of bygone days. His classic *The Gardener's Bed-Book* softly chronicles the little comedies of manners that take place in flower beds, on rural roads, and in country houses, all part of the changing American social and ecological landscape.

WOMAN'S PLACE

ELEANOR PERÉNYI

There are the husband's apple and pear trees, twined by the wife's clematis; his cabbage beds fringed with her pinks and pansies; the tool-house wreathed with roses; his rougher labor adorned by her gayer fancy, all speaking loudly of their hearts and tastes . . . We trust the cottager's wife will love and care for the flowers and we are sure if she does that her husband's love and esteem for her will be heightened and strengthened.

From an English gardening magazine, 1848

A CHARMING SENTIMENT ON THE FACE OF IT, but what about that veiled threat at the end? Why should the cottager's love and esteem for his wife be contingent on her care for the flowers? And if he neglected the apple and pear trees—would she then be entitled to think less of *him*? It may come as a surprise that sexism should play any part in horticulture but the more you read of gardening history the more convincing the case for it becomes, and the less you are ready to see the cottager as a chivalrous male doing the hard work while indulging his wife in her "gayer fancy." Divisions of labor there have been, but not nearly as simple as that, while the whole business of women's supposed devotion to flowers may need another look.

At Woburn Abbey in the seventeenth century there was a famous lifelike statue of a woman weeding, and records of English estates show that from a very early period this chore was almost exclusively performed by females. It is, says my source (who is, naturally, a man), "a task at which they have always been pre-eminent," and this is an assessment with which male gardeners have long agreed. La Quintinie, who was in charge of Louis XIV's *potagers* and otherwise an adorable person, recommended the hiring of married men rather than bachelors (as was the usual custom), on the ground that wives would be available for weeding, as well as cleaning and scraping out pots. In the Orient, women weed the rice paddies in water up to their knees. In general, it is to be observed that men plow while women sow; prune fruit and nut trees but leave the harvest to women; and most men like working with vegetables (all, that is, but the weeding). Other crops appear to be largely in the hands of women. In that part of Turkey where tobacco is grown, I saw them patting together the raised beds, setting out seedlings, and of course weeding, while the male population sat under pergolas playing tric-trac. But why pick on Turks? In other parts of the world women are thought to be pre-eminent at hauling brushwood on their backs. Russian grannies sweep leaves in parks and streets.

Altogether, it is pretty obvious that relative physical strength isn't the determining factor in most cases of divided labor but rather which tasks men prefer to do and which they have decided to leave to women. The man in charge of our Hungarian vineyard was the envy of the neighborhood on account of his ten terrific daughters, who could and did get through twice the work of any male, and he didn't hesitate to lay it on them. In peasant societies nobody worries very much about overtaxing women's strength. I doubt if they do in any society. What men fear is competition and losing the services of women as drudges. Thus, La Quintinie must have known that women could be trained as well as men to perform a hundred more exacting and interesting horticultural tasks than scraping out pots.

This is all the more striking when you consider that it was women who invented horticulture in the first place, women who ventured into field and forest in search of wild plants, and women who domesticated them while men were still out chasing wild beasts. Women were the first gardeners; but when men retired from the hunting field and decided in favor of agriculture instead, women steadily lost control. No longer were they the ones to decide what was planted, how, or where; and accordingly the space allotted to them diminished too, until flowers and herbs were the only plants left under their direct management, while their former power passed into myth. The inventor of agriculture became the goddess of agriculture, her daughter the bringer of spring, when plants come to life; and each of these had a flower or flowers assigned to her—almost certainly by men and as a form of propitiation. For make no mistake: Men were always half in a terror of women's complicity with nature, and the power it had given them. The other face of the goddess belongs to the witch brewing her spells from plants, able to cure and also curse with her knowledge of their properties. In some societies this fear of women amounted to panic. It was believed that their mere presence could blight vegetation. Democritus wrote that a menstruating woman could kill young produce "merely by looking at it." On the one hand, the benign giver of life and fertility; on the other, the baneful caster of withering spells—it's a tall order and no wonder that men were inclined to confine such a dangerously two-faced influence to a safe place.

For that is how I have come to interpret the two-thousand-odd years of women's incarceration in the flower garden. The superstitious fear that women were in league with nature in some way that men were not was thus simultaneously catered to and kept in check. Flowers are of all plants the least menacing and the most useless. Their sole purpose is to be beautiful and to give pleasure—which is what one half of man wants from woman (the other, it is needless to say, asks for qualities more practical and down-to-earth)—and as such they are the perfect combination of tribute and demand. A gift of flowers to a woman implies that she is as deliciously desirable as the blossoms themselves; but there may be another and hidden message, contained in old-fashioned phrases like "shy as a violet," "clinging vine," not originally conceived as pejoratives, that tells more of the truth—which is that flowers are also emblems of feminine submission. In the western world, this is rarely explicit. In the Orient, where fewer bones are made about the position of women, two examples may be cited. The art of Japanese flower arrangement, *ikebanu*, whose masters are male, was originally imparted to women as a means of silent communication with stern samurai husbands to whom words, and especially plaintive words, would have been an intolerable presumption; whereas an iris and a pussy willow and perhaps a convolvulus, arranged in the right order, conveyed a world of meaning. In China, we find another example, one that borders on the atrocious: the bound foot, to be encountered as late as the 1920s. My Chinese amah's feet were bound, and filled me with fascinated horror. What unspeakable distortion lay inside that delicate little slipper that caused her to sway (seductively to men, that was the point) as she walked? She would never show me but I have seen photographs since, and learned that the hideously crushed mass of flesh and bone was compared by Chinese poets to a lotus bud.

With this in mind, one may feel that those paintings of Chinese gardens in which exquisitely clad ladies float about tending to potted peonies depict scenes less idyllic than they appear. What we are seeing is a sort of floral cage—one that in the Hindu and Moslem world was an actual prison. Purdah and the harem were mitigated for their captives by the presence of many beautiful flowers. The illiterate women in the Ottoman seraglio even devised a ''language of flowers'' (described with some scorn by Lady Mary Wortley Montagu in her letters from Turkey and later all the rage among European females with nothing better to do) to take the place of the written language forbidden them. But there was no escape from the famous tulip gardens of the seraglio. Call them what you will—and as everybody knows the word ''paradise'' derives from the Persian word for garden, an idea later expanded in Moslem usage to mean a heaven where male wants were attended to by ravishing and submissive houris—one of the principal functions of the Oriental garden from Turkey to China was the incarceration of women.

To equate European gardens with any such purpose might seem to carry feminist interpretation too far, and obviously the differences are great. Garden plans nevertheless suggest a similar if less drastic impulse on the part of men. The Roman atrium was a flower-filled enclosure chiefly for women's use, and it is in marked contrast to the pleasure grounds laid out by a rich Roman gentleman and intellectual like Pliny, who makes it perfectly clear that his were entirely for male diversion. Those pavilions for reading and sunbathing, dining with friends, those philosopher's walks, were for himself and his male companions. Possibly there was somewhere an inner courtyard where the women of the household could spend their leisure time, and more than likely it was filled with flowers, if only those that would be picked for the house; but except for his violet beds, he doesn't speak of flowers —or of women.

Medieval gardens repeat the pattern of the *hortus conclusus*, with the difference that they are more elaborate and better adapted to feminine comfort. Trellised walks, turf seats, tiny flower beds, all mark a female presence that is borne out in the illuminations and tapestries where we almost invariably see a lady stooping to pluck a strawberry, a rose, or at her ease with embroidery and lute. So plainly were they designed for women that they even convey an illusion of female supremacy at last—and it wasn't entirely an illusion. The mass folly of the Crusades occupied European men for the better part of two hundred years, and with her lord away at the wars the chatelaine did often manage his estate at home, and not badly either. She lived behind fortified walls nevertheless, and it isn't hard to conjecture that her garden was in the nature of a chastity belt, locking her in until the return of her lord and master. "A garden inclosed is my sister, my spouse; a spring shut up, a fountain sealed," says the Song of Solomon—to all of course but him. That feminine purity is only to be preserved within four walls is another ancient idea, and in the late Middle Ages it found indirect expression in those curious paintings of so-called Mary gardens, which show the Virgin seated in a castellated enclosure surrounded by richly symbolic fruits, vines and flowers. But the fortified walls came down with the return of something like peace and leisure, and the Renaissance garden with its magical perspectives, its cascades and fountains, was another story altogether—a celebration of humanism—except that in Italy at least it always had an odd little appendix attached, as it were, to the grand design: the *giardino segreto*.

Garden histories don't try to account for the *giardini segreti* except to note that flowers, largely absent in the rest of the garden, grew in them. To me it is at least plausible that these fossilized remnants of the medieval garden were for women, intended to be so, and that in fact they kept alive the tradition of the flower-filled feminine ghetto.

"Know that it doesn't displease but rather pleases me that you should have roses to grow and violets to care for," wrote a fifteenth-century French merchant to his wife, sounding the note to be heard again and again for the next three hundred years. From 1500 to 1800 was the great age of garden design: visions of what a garden should be shifted like scenery upon a stage, theories multiplied and books on the subject poured from the presses. But in England only two were in all that time specifically directed to women, and both assume her province to be flowers and herbs. Lawson's *Countrie Housewife* (1618) gives her a list of sixteen flowers for nosegays, five kinds of bulbs including "Tulippos," and twenty-six herbs. Charles Evelyn's *Lady's Recreation* (1707) discusses most of the same flowers while permitting a fountain and "an excellent contriv'd statue." He also allows her a wilderness where "being no longer pleas'd with a solitary Amusement you come out into a large Road, where you have the Diversion of seeing Travellers pass by, to compleat your Variety." Why she should be solitary and driven to watch travelers in the road he doesn't say. His whole tone, however, is one of a patronage that is echoed elsewhere. Sir William Temple (*Garden of Epicurus*, 1685): "I will not enter upon any account of flowers, having only pleased myself with seeing or smelling them, and not troubled myself with the care, which is more the ladies' part than the men's . . ." John Lawrence (*New System . . . a Complete Body of Husbandry and Gardening*, 1726) adds to patronage something like a scolding: "I flatter myself the Ladies would soon think that their vacant Hours in the Culture of the *Flower-Garden* would be more innocently spent and with greater Satisfaction than the common Talk over a Tea-Table where Envy and Detraction so commonly preside. Whereas when Opportunity and Weather invite them amongst their Flowers, there they may dress, and admire and cultivate Beauties like themselves without *envying* or *being envied*." Here the argument for keeping women shut up with flowers is almost entirely trivialized, The Virgin's bower is now a school for decorum.

What amazes me is the way female scholars have failed to notice the implications of statements like these. Eleanor Sinclair Rohde (*The Story of the Garden*, 1932), to whom I am indebted for many of my quotations, gives no hint that she catches their drift. She takes no umbrage at her adored Parkinson (or perhaps doesn't choose to understand him) when she quotes a passage like this from the *Paradisus*: "Gentlewomen, these pleasures are the delights of leasure [*sic*], which hath bred your love and liking to them, and although you are not herein predominant, yet cannot they be barred from your beloved, who I doubt not, will share with you in the delight as much as is fit." Not the cleanest prose in the world, and Mrs. Rohde construes it as a tribute to the central place of women in seventeenth-century gardening. I read it as the opposite: a warning to wives with ideas about garden layout to leave that area to their husbands, who know best but will, if not aggravated, allow a share in the result.

Whichever of us is right, history is on my side. Not until the twentieth century did any woman play a recognizable part in garden design. We know why, of course. The great gardens of the world have been reflections of men's intellectual and spiritual experience: visions of Arcadia, hymns to rationalism or the divine right of kings, Zen parables—and the well-known reasons for our failure to compose symphonies, paint masterpieces, conceive the Einstein theory, apply equally to our failure to produce a feminine incarnation of, say, Le Nôtre. One or two great gardens *were* made for women, who were queens or the equivalent; but as they were always in the prevailing fashion it isn't possible to tell to what extent they conformed to the client's particular wishes. In one case we know they didn't. Marie de Medici's ideas for the Luxembourg were resolutely opposed by her designer, the incomparable Boyceau, and he had his way (much to posterity's gain, it should be said). We know, too, that Marie Antoinette's *hameau*, arranged in what she imagined to be the English style, was done in a taste all her own, but that sad spot, so out of place at Versailles, doesn't say much in favor of feminine theories about design.

Malmaison might be a happier example. It, too, was laid out for a woman, and given the Empress Josephine's character, one can be sure she got what she wanted. Malmaison, however, isn't outstanding for its design but for the millions of roses that grew there, probably the greatest collection the world has ever seen; and this was generally true of all gardens made by or for women of which we have any record. Flowers were, and until the twentieth century remained, the theme. In the eighteenth, the Duchess of Beaufort grew exotics, as did Mme. de Pompadour in all the many ravishing gardens given her by Louis XV—she adored the white, highly scented tropicals, gardenias and jasmine especially, brought to her from all parts of the French empire. Lady Broughton specialized in alpines, and was one of the first to grow them outdoors in a rock garden; Lady Holland introduced dahlias to England and grew them in her greenhouses.

Here, a new note was introduced, for it was at about this time that women were allowed to embark on the study of botany—not too seriously and rather late in the day; and it is notable that various writers should have seen their studies in much the same light as pottering in the flower garden itself. J. C. Loudon, for one, recommended botany as "a charming and instructive female exercise," or a grade or two above the netting of purses, and in the hands of the upper-class young ladies who went in for it, that was about what these studies amounted to. In fact, they mostly consisted in the coloring of flower engravings, and counting stamens according to the newly introduced

Linnaean system of classification, which made everything wonderfully simple. Honorable exceptions there were, mostly royal. The dowager Princess of Wales founded the great botanic garden at Kew in 1761; and Queen Charlotte was accounted a passionate student, though how she found time for her researches in the course of bearing her sixteen children is a wonder. The Strelitzia or bird-of-paradise flower, however, is named for her (she was born Mecklenberg-Strelitz), as were four varieties of apple—hence, it is said, Apple Charlotte, the dessert.

Women in humbler positions, who might have contributed rather more to the science, did not fare so well. One of them was Jane Colden, the daughter of a lieutenant-governor of New York, who lived near Newburgh-on-Hudson and who ventured into the wilderness at a time when that was neither easy nor safe. By 1758 she had compiled a manuscript describing four hundred local plants and their uses, illustrated by herself. It was never published. During the Revolution it fell into the hands of a Hessian officer who was interested in botany. He took it back to Germany where it was preserved at the University of Göttingen. Evidently it was important enough to have been purchased at a later date by Sir Joseph Banks, the most influential botanist of his time; but he didn't try to have it published and it reposes in the British Museum to this day. Nor is any flower called Coldenia, the accolade regularly bestowed by botanists on those of their tribe who have made important contributions to science. (That those standards have been less than strict is, however, obvious even where men's names are concerned: The Montanoa, a species of shrub, appears to have been named for a Mexican bandit-politician. As applied to women, names seem chiefly to have been bows to rank: *Victoria amazonica*, that water-lily whose pad is the size of a dinner table, was of course named for the dear queen; while the *Cinchona,* from whose bark quinine is derived, was called after the Condesa de Cinchon, Vicerene of Peru, who in 1638 was cured of malaria by a decoction of what had previously been called Peruvian bark.)

Given the circumstances—circumscribed travel, the reluctance to admit that female minds could cope seriously with science—it isn't surprising that no woman made a name for herself in botany. That her accomplishments in the breeding and cultivating of plants should also be a well-kept secret is another matter. "In March and in April from morning till night / In sowing and seeding good housewives delight," sang Thomas Tusser (1524-80) in his rhyming calendar for gardeners.

Even in Tudor times England was famous for the beauty of its flowers, especially doubled varieties—columbines, primroses, violets, marigolds and campanulas—but also striped and unusual colors, which included sports such as a reddish lily-of-the-valley. Foreigners attributed these variations to the damp English climate which allowed for year-around planting, but also noted that the selection and cultivation were done by housewives rather than professionals—at that period well behind their French and Dutch colleagues. In the seventeenth century, the great age of English plantsmanship, when collectors like the Tradescants began to range the world, these accomplishments receded into the background—where they remained for another two hundred years. What the Victorians called "old-fashioned" flowers were really housewives' flowers, grown continously and in defiance or ignorance of fashion —including the landscape movement that destroyed so many of England's finest and most characteristic gardens and prohibited so much as a cowslip from showing its pretty head above ground. In the feminine domain called the cottage garden, which a modern state might designate as a preserve with plants whose removal would be punishable by law, grew such otherwise lost rarities as blue primroses, Parkinson's "stately Crown Imperial," and the fairy rose (not to be confused with the modern polyantha of that name), many violas and pinks long since vanished from cultivation in the gardens of the rich and those desiring to be à la page.

The cottage garden was rediscovered toward the end of the nine- teenth century—mostly by women like Mrs. Juliana Horatia Ewing, who founded a Parkinson Society "to search out and cultivate old flowers which have become scarce," and of course Gertrude Jekyll, who reintroduced the fairy rose. But although these gardens clearly pointed to the role of women as important conservators as well as breeders and cultivators of plant species, no one pursued the obvious conclusion that what had happened in the nineteenth century might also be presumed to have occurred in others as well. No writer I know of has, for example, enlarged the thesis that in the Dark Ages it was monks in monasteries who preserved such species as survived in those parts of Europe not fortunate enough to be conquered by the garden- loving Arabs (Spain, Sicily, etc.). Why not also nuns in nunneries? It is known that they grew flowers in profusion for the adornment of churches and herbs for simples, just as the monks did. Indeed it was one of their functions to school ladies in the uses of cooking and medicinal herbs (which then included flowers like marigolds, poppies, even roses and honeysuckle), especially the latter because it was the lady of the manor who compounded and administered medicines, though she wasn't of course honored with the title of physician, and the few venturesome women who did try to set themselves up as doctors were promptly squelched.

With all the vast amount of writing about gardens that has appeared in the last hundred years, much of it by women, you might expect somebody to have devoted a book to women's place in garden history. If anyone has, I haven't heard of it, and it must be admitted that the difficulties of research would be formidable. Where would the documentation come from? In England, the earliest herbal published by a woman was Elizabeth Blackwell's in 1737. The earliest essay on gardening itself is probably Lady Charlotte Murray's *British Garden* (1799); in America, Mrs. Martha Logan's *Gardener's Kalender* (known only through republication in a magazine around 1798). What the library stacks of other countries would yield I can't say; the pickings would presumably be even slimmer. Private correspondence would be a richer source, if one knew where to look. (There are, for instance, tantalizing hints in Mme. de Sévigné's letters that in the age dominated by Le Nôtre's geometry she had ideas about *la nature* that anticipated Rousseau's—as when she told her daughter that she had spent the morning on her country estate ''in the dew up to my knees laying lines; I am making winding *allées* all around my park . . .'') Novels by women could also be studied in this light. Jane Austen has a great deal about the theory and practice of gardening, especially in *Mansfield Park*, where a part of the plot hinges on Mr. Rushworth's determination to have Mr. Repton remodel his grounds, though in fact every novel has its gardens and each is made to say something about the character and social situation of the owner. (Elizabeth Bennet isn't entirely joking when she says she must date her falling in love with Mr. Darcy to her visit to his ''beautiful grounds at Pemberley.'')

Diaries and notebooks would be another source, not forgetting *The Pillow Book of Sei Shonagon*. In the remote past, the body of feminine knowledge was locked away under the anonymous heading of old wives' tales, a phrase I have always found offensive. Assume that ''old'' doesn't mean the woman gardener was a crone but refers to ''old times.'' The expression still implies a combination of ignorance and superstition peculiarly female—and never mind that a thirteenth-century church father like the Abbott of Beauvais testified that a decoction of heliotrope could produce invisibility or that St. Gregory the Great believed the devil hid in lettuce heads. Women will have shed their superstitions at about the same time men did, and what many an old wives' tale really refers to is orally transmitted information, as often as not the result of illiteracy, not inborn backwardness. Women weren't stupider than men; they lacked the means of expressing themselves, and instead of writing herbals or treatises on what is called (note this) husbandry, they told one another what experience had taught them about plants, medicines and many other things. This is also called folk wisdom, and it can be as discriminatory as the rest of human history: How many people know, for instance, that the subtly constructed tents of the Plains Indians were designed and set up entirely by women?

To remedy these deficiencies wouldn't be easy, but I wish somebody would try. The story could end well, too—up to a point. In the spring of 1980 a symposium was held at Dumbarton Oaks whose subject was "Beatrix Jones Farrand (1872-1959) and fifty Years of American Landscape Architecture." The setting was appropriate: Mrs. Farrand designed the beautiful garden at Dumbarton Oaks and many other famous ones as well. She was the only woman among the eleven original members of the American Society of Landscape Architects, founded in 1899, and the first to demonstrate that women could design gardens as well as plant flowers. (Jekyll, remember, worked in collaboration with the architect Edwin Lutyens.) She was a thorough professional and inaugurated a period of great brilliance for women as landscape architects. Ellen Biddle Shipman, another of them, told a reporter in 1938 that "until women took up landscaping, gardening in this country was at its lowest ebb. The renaissance was due largely to the fact that women, instead of working over their boards, used plants as if they were painting pictures and as an artist would. Today women are at the top of the profession."

That, alas, is no longer true. Not only are the gardens designed by those women for the most part in a sad state of neglect, the profession itself leaves something to be desired. It has, so it seems, gone back to the drawing boards. Many universities now separate courses in design and horticulture into different academic departments. We are where we were in earlier centuries when the designer and the plantsman lived in different worlds—an extraordinary step backward. Does it also represent a resurgence of male chauvinism, a return of the old idea that flowers and plants are a province less worthy than that of stone and water? Not overtly so perhaps. But the lack of interest in horticulture shown by liberated women, including liberated women architects, suggests that they recognize, however subconsciously, the link between flowering plants and old-style femininity as opposed to feminism, and if forced to choose between the two courses, as I gather the students more or less must, would opt for the "higher" (i.e., male-dominated) one of landscaping. If so, though we have come a long way from the statue of the female weeder and the cottager's wife, it isn't far enough.

*

From *Green Thoughts: A Writer in the Garden*, Eleanor Perényi (1918-). New York: Random House, 1981. In less than a decade after its publication this book has already secured a place for itself among those few truly regarded as the best of American garden books. If Alice Morse Earle's *Old Time Gardens* stands at one end of this century and Perényi's *Green Thoughts* at the other, then the very nature of a garden "classic" has changed from marvelously decorous writing to politically astute horticultural awareness. That Perényi reports on the historical and social issues involved in the cultivation and travel of flowers around the world is a measure of how broad an intellectual sweep the study of gardens and gardeners has today. *Green Thoughts,* deeply rooted in Perényi's more than thirty years of "amateur" gardening experience, abounds in bristling wisdom and good sense. A biographer of Liszt, and lover of formality in garden design, her book proves that the finest garden writing moves in the realm of the stylish literary essay. "A writer who gardens *is* sooner or later going to write a book about the subject," she admits, with an air of quiet joy in contributing to the history of garden lives, and thus of the world.

SUMMER 1945

LOUIS BROMFIELD

AUGUST 18: CAME ACROSS A QUOTATION from Thoreau in this week's *New Yorker*. It was written concerning museums but it might well be applied to this half-mad, materialist, decadent, industrial world in which we live: "One green bud of spring, one willow catkin, one faint trill from a migrating sparrow would set the world on its legs again. The life that is in a single green weed is of more worth than all this death."

One might add that all this is true and that it might save the world if the trill from a migrating sparrow could be heard above the clamor for higher wages, higher profits, election promises, water closets and automobiles, above all the outcry for materialistic things and standards by which man does *not* live, by which eventually he dies the death of the soul, of the spirit, of all understanding and growth, in the end, of decency itself. An age in which God is represented by the Holy Trinity of plumbing, overtime and assembly lines is not a great age, unless man learns to use these things for his freedom and the growth of his spirit rather than his brutalization.

In all the oceans of printer's ink used by columnists regarding the Atomic bomb I have seen no mention of its true and profound horror —that it is the symbol of the fact of utter destruction and negation to which so many brilliant minds have devoted their energies. It is appalling to reflect on how much of human thought, of spirit, of creative force either in the polished beauty of a turbine or the quiet still beauty of a garden, can be annihilated by a single Atomic bomb. The deepest horror of war is not the death of individual men but the destruction of so much that man has striven painfully and eagerly to build up in his slow, aspiring climb upward out of the steaming swamps of the primeval world. As in an ant-hill kicked over by the careless foot of a passerby, there will always be a few ants and a few men to cherish the impulse and the aspiration to carry on and build another ant-hill or another civilization elsewhere. That impulse and aspiration is the most profound justification for the existence both of the ant and of man himself. I have heard that a few scientists refused to lend their brilliant talents to the creation of the Atomic bomb. It is possible that in a century or two these men will be honored above those whose names and faces appear everywhere in the press today.

Perhaps it is that the world needs not a dictator or Communism or technology or any of the other materialistic doctrinaires of doctrines but another Jean Jacques Rousseau who with all the snobberies, and affectations and romanticism which followed in his trail like the tail of a comet had as much to do with revitalizing the European world of the tired, cynical, brilliant eighteenth century as the steelyminded Voltaire. Together they and their followers planted the seed of a revolution which revitalized the civilization of the world and brought man another step upward in the long, slow ascent of his development.

Reason, machines and guaranteed wages are not enough because man does not live by these things alone and if the spirit and nature itself are ignored, they lead him only into the blind alley of defeat and eventually of annihilation. Mankind can do without plumbing but not without Saint Francis of Assisi. It can survive without automobiles but scarcely without the leavening experience, wisdom and faith of Saint Augustin [*sic*—ed.]. Russia found that man could *exist* on the bare, materialistic skeleton of the Marxian system with its machines and lavishly decorated Moscow subway but he could not *live* without the writers and the actors and the dancers of the ballet, and in the end that he could not *live* without even the dubious splendors of the Orthodox Church. It is simply that in all life on this earth as in all good agriculture there are no short-cuts that by-pass Nature and the nature of man himself and animals, trees, rocks, and streams. Every attempt at a formula, a short-cut, a panacea always ends in negation and destruction. And the worst violation of all is the negation of the nature of man and his relation to the universe and eternity.

*

From *Malabar Farm*, Louis Bromfield (1896-1956). New York: Harper and Brothers, 1947. Bromfield wrote more than two dozen books—novels, plays, and autobiographical works—which include *The Farm*, *The World We Live In*, *Agricultural Economics*, and the Pulitzer Prize-winning *Early Autumn*. There is an easy, honest exchange between his fiction and non-fiction, unified by a profound Jeffersonian belief in democracy based on true agrarian ideals. Though he lived in Europe for more than twenty years after World War I, many of them in France, Bromfield eventually returned to his family roots in Ohio where he ran Malabar Farm on sound ecological principles. The politics of husbandry was always an integral part of his writing life. His nature and agricultural books of the forties and fifties partake of the solid tradition of activist writing. "I belong by nature, inclination, and perhaps even through atavistic forces, to rich green country with rainfall and four marked and distinct seasons," he reflected.

THE MOTH AND THE CANDLE

JOSEPH WOOD KRUTCH

THE MOTH WHO SINGES HIS WINGS HAS pointed many a moral but he does not "desire" the flame, not even in the dim way that the first scorpion to leave the water may have "desired" to succeed in his dangerous adventure. The moth accomplishes no purpose of his own and none appropriate to nature at large. He is merely the victim of a situation which can seldom have arisen before man put in his appearance long after moths and many other insects had developed a tropism which was usually harmless during millions of years.

A moth's wings beat faster when light falls upon his eyes, and when it falls more strongly on one eye than on the other, the wings on one side beat faster than those on the other. Irresistibly his flight curves toward the source and if he reaches it, he dies—a victim of one of the mistakes which nature sometimes makes because even she cannot foresee every eventuality.

But in the case of a certain moth which lives in the desert and of a certain candle which grows there the situation is different.

Almost anywhere in the Southwest you will find as a conspicuous feature of the landscape one or another of the yuccas with their large bundle of stiff, sword-sharp leaves and, in early summer, an incredibly tall spire of innumerable creamy white blossoms held high on a great spike which shot up suddenly from the middle of the sword cluster. Pass by again in the fall and the spire will be bearing handsome pods which split open as they dry and scatter innumerable shiny black seeds on the sand. Though a bit difficult to gather, the pods make a fine addition to a winter bouquet and those who gather them often notice that each is perforated by at least one hole from which some insect has obviously emerged.

Sometimes the collector will search for a ''perfect'' specimen, but perfect ones are not to be found. The ''infestation'' was necessary. Either the ovary from which the pod developed was ''infested'' or it didn't mature. Thereby hangs a tale as strange as any the desert has to tell and in certain important respects the most difficult to explain of all the strange tales which are told of the interdependence of insects and flowers. The hole was made by the larva of a moth, and just to make the question we are about to ask as neat as possible, it happens that certain species of yucca are still commonly called by the name which the Spaniards gave them: Our Lord's Candle.

Does *Pronuba yuccasella*, the moth in question, ''desire'' this particular candle? Please wait until you have heard the whole story before you answer.

Everybody—or at least everybody old enough to have been a child before directer methods of sex instruction came into fashion—knows about the bees and the flowers. If he did not lose all interest in the subject as he began to realize its remoter personal implications, he probably now knows at least in a very general way that many plants depend upon many insects and some, even, upon certain birds, to help them in what the eighteenth century liked to call ''their nuptial rites.'' Orchard growers tend bees principally to increase their yield of apples and plums and pears; Darwin wrote a classic on the pollination of orchids; the Smyrna fig would not fruit in California until the particular wasp which acts as marriage broker for it in the Near East was imported to perform his function here, etc., etc.

But in every known case except that of the moth and the candle it is a somewhat one-sided affair with all the ''intention'' being on the part of the flower. Though the insect may be lured by a scent which it likes—even by the stench of rotten meat in the case of certain tropical blossoms pollinated by flesh-eating flies—and though he may be rewarded with nectar or with edible pollen, he does not do anything directly calculated to fertilize the flower. Sometimes the flower is so constructed that, for instance, the insect cannot get at the nectar without brushing against the pollen-bearing anthers and then against a stigma which will ultimately conduct the gene-bearing protoplasm of the pollen down to the ovules below. But he does not deliberately fertilize the plant and it would not affect his chances of passing on the torch to his posterity if the flower were not fertilized. The plant uses the insect but there is no active cooperation on the insect's part.

Consider, on the other hand, what happens in the unique case of the yucca and its attendant moth. In the first place, though there are many species of yuccas, only a single one of them—and it does not grow in this region—appears to be capable of getting along without the moth upon which all the rest depend. Moreover, the moths, in their turn, are no less completely dependent upon the yuccas because their larva cannot feed upon anything except its maturing seeds. But this situation, which is odd without being unique, is not all. What *is* unique is the fact that the moth goes through a series of purposeful actions which have no other function except to fertilize a flower which could not be fertilized in any other way. If we naively interpreted its actions, we should find ourselves compelled to say that it "knows what it is doing."

The classic observation was made seventy-five years ago by the remarkable Missouri entomologist, Charles V. Riley, though the subject has been much studied and written about since Riley himself fully described the crucial, incredible event as he observed it on a cultivated species grown in the neighborhood of St. Louis. Several different insects frequent the flowers to eat the nectar or the pollen but perform no service in return. Meanwhile the female of the indispensable moth rests quietly in the half-closed blossoms.

When evening comes she goes in turn to several of the flowers just opening for their one night of perfect bloom. While the male, who has already done his duty, flutters uselessly about, she collects from the anthers a ball of the pollen which is surrounded by a sticky gum to prevent its accidental dispersal. After she has collected under her chin a mass somewhat larger than her head, she climbs the pistil of a different flower and into it she inserts her egg tube about a third of the way down from the top and injects several eggs. However, she "knows" that if she left it at that her larva would have nothing to feed on. Accordingly, she mounts the rest of the way up the pistil, deposits the pollen ball on the stigma, and moves her head back and forth to rub the pollen well in. She eats neither nectar nor pollen. She gets no immediate benefit from her action. It has no purpose other than to fertilize the flower.

The insect which does these remarkable things is nothing much to look at—a little inch-long moth, silvery white in color and, so far as anyone knows, quite conventional in behavior except during the one great moment when it is impelled to act as though it knew a great deal about the physiology of plants as well as about the life history of its own species.

Most of what happens after the fertilization of the flower follows a familiar pattern. The flowers wither and a few days later the wormlike larva can be found. In time it will bore its way out of the maturing pod, drop to the ground, spin a cocoon a few inches below the surface, and there transform itself into an adult completely equipped to repeat, next year, the whole complicated process. Since there are commonly not more than two larvae per pod, they eat only a few of the perhaps two hundred seeds which the pod produces. From the standpoint of the yucca it is a very good arrangement since the sacrifice of a few seeds is a small price to pay for a very efficient job of fertilization. The staggering question for anyone who has committed himself to ''explaining'' nature is simply this: How on earth was such a system of mutual cooperation for individual ends ever worked out?

Evidently the yucca and the yucca moth came to their mutual understanding a long time ago—certainly before the plant genus had evolved the many species now flourishing—because, with the one exception previously mentioned, they all seem to be signatories to the agreement; certainly, also, long enough ago for the Pronuba moth to have itself evolved into at least several distinguishable species, because those which visit certain yuccas are slightly different from those which visit others. On the other hand, moth and yucca have not always worked together, because the flower continues to secrete a nectar which now merely attracts useless insects of various sorts and presumably it learned to do that at a time before Pronuba got into the habit of paying a visit on business of her own for which no honeyed inducement is necessary.

Apparently, sometime during the millenniums when the two were engaged in a late phase of their evolution and separating themselves into the different species of moth and yucca, they must themselves have kept together. "Wherever thou goest I go," said the moth, because, again with the one single exception, where a yucca is native, so is a Pronuba. Attempt to grow the former outside its range and it may flower very nicely. But "no moth, no seed" seems to be the absolute rule.

William Trelease, student and monographer of the yucca genus, calls attention to the fact that "the mutual dependence seems absolute" and he then permits himself a cautious, scientific understatement when he remarks that the fact is "no doubt of the greatest suggestiveness," though "its meaning has escaped both botanists and zoologists."

Now the relatively simple one-sided arrangement which is so prevalent in the plant world is difficult enough to understand. Geology seems to demonstrate that the earliest flowering plants depended, as the conifers do today, upon the chance that some of their abundant pollen would be carried by the wind to the waiting ovaries. Then, since all organic matter is potentially edible by something, it is assumed that certain insects got into the habit of eating pollen, accidentally got some of it entangled in the hair on their bodies as many still do, and accidentally rubbed some of it off on the stigmas of the other flowers they visited. Since, for the plant, this was more effective than wind pollination and involved less waste of vital material, those plants which were most attractive to insects got along best. And as the degree of attractiveness accidentally varied, "natural selection" favored those which were most attractive, until gradually all the devices by which plants lure insects or birds—bright colored petals, nectar which serves the plant in no direct way, and perfume which leads the insect to the blossom; even the "guide lines" which sometimes mark the route to the nectar glands—were mechanically and necessarily developed.

Gardeners usually hate "bugs," but if the evolutionists are right, there never would have been any flowers if it had not been for these same bugs. The flowers never waste their sweetness on the desert air or, for that matter, on the jungle air. In fact, they waste it only when nobody except a human being is there to smell it. It is for the bugs and for a few birds, not for men, that they dye their petals or waft their scents. And it is lucky for us that we either happen to like or have become "conditioned" to liking the colors and the odors which most insects and some birds like also. What a calamity for us if insects had been color blind, as all mammals below the primates are! Or if, worse yet, we had had our present taste in smells while all the insects preferred, as a few of them do, that odor of rotten meat which certain flowers dependent upon them abundantly provide. Would we ever have been able to discover thoughts too deep for tears in a gray flower which exhaled a terrific stench? Or would we have learned by now to consider it exquisite?

The whole story, as it is usually told, of how flowers developed is thus a rather tall tale, as indeed the whole story of evolution is. But it does fall just short of the completely incredible even though we are likely to feel an additional strain when we begin to bring in the more remarkable features and find ourselves compelled to believe in the gradual blind development of the more intricate devices by which a flower is often adapted to some particular insect or bird and the exact correspondence between, say, the length of a given flower's tube and the length of the moth's proboscis or the hummingbird's bill which is going to reach down into it. But when we come to Pronuba and the yucca we get something more staggering still. That two different organisms should have simultaneously adapted themselves one to another is, if I understand the laws of probability, at least four times as improbable as that one should have adapted itself to the other. I am not saying I don't believe it did. On the whole I think I do, at least with one reservation. But sometimes I can't help saying to myself, ''A man who will believe that will believe anything.''. . .

The Mr. Riley who first told the world about Pronuba was a distinguished entomologist. He had the confidence of his professional brethren and textbook after textbook has repeated his tale. But is it just possible that he was overenthusiastic? How many other people have watched the performance and can vouch for it from their own experience?

Well, I confess that the shadow of such doubts crossed my own mind. Of the various references to Pronuba with which I was familiar, only one after Riley's own seemed on internal evidence to be indubitably firsthand. The most learned entomologist of this region where yucca flourishes confessed that he had never seen the performance and I didn't know anybody who had. Not too willingly—since I knew the difficulties, which include, besides the dilatoriness of the insect, darkness, a limited blooming season, and flowers lifted high above one's head—I decided to try to see for myself. And not to sustain any suspense which any reader may feel, I did. Three times Pronuba demonstrated before my eyes how she performed the crucial act, mounting the pistil of the recently opened flower and with prolonged purposefulness rubbing the pistil vigorously to get the pollen well in.

Partly to avoid the possibility that some amateur alienist might telephone a mental hospital that for several evenings a maniac had been standing for two hours and more peering at yucca flowers with a flashlight, I decided to make my observations well out into the desert and some twenty miles from town. And for poetic if not for strictly scientific reasons it was a good idea. It is one thing to read about what Pronuba does. It would be quite another to see her at work in a neighbor's back yard. But the performance belongs properly among the mysteries which one can only appreciate fully when the context is remote from the human and as exclusively as possible in that of almost timeless nature.

The moonless night was brilliant with stars. In the distance a coyote pack obligingly set up its chorus which is as wild a sound as one is likely to hear anywhere. And then, presently, there was Pronuba, even more insignificant looking than I had expected her to be, performing her delicate operation precisely, no doubt, as her ancestors had performed it millions of times during millions of springs. On the horizon the lights of town were just visible. In all that town few knew about, perhaps none had ever seen, the strange actions of this silent moth without whom the tall spires of flowers would never conceive their seeds and without whom, therefore, the whole race of yuccas would gradually die out. It was for the almost invisible moth, not for you or me or any aesthetically appreciative human spectator, that the great masses of flowers were lifted high.

As little Pronuba moved her head back and forth I remembered the question once asked by the American essayist Charles D. Stewart after he had described what looked like a remarkably purposeful action on the part of a spider who suddenly cut the main cable of his web and thereby sent flying an intruder of another species with designs upon an insect caught in the owner's web. "Is it God who is doing these things," Stewart asked, "or is it the spider?"

Fabre would have answered without hesitation, "God." Most biologists would reply with equal assurance, "Neither." But few are willing to admit what seems to me not wholly improbable—namely that the spider himself had something to do with it.

*

From *The Voice of the Desert*, Joseph Wood Krutch (1893-1970). New York: William Sloane Associates, 1954. One of the notable men of American letters, Krutch approached the things of this world—books, insects, plants, people—with a passion and reverence that brought to his philosophical reflections a ceaseless inquiry. He concerned himself with the search of the human spirit for a home in the modern universe, and tried to resolve for himself the growing separation between science and the humanities. Krutch wrote with equal precision about the New England landscape and the Southwest desert. He moved effortlessly from literary to theatre to nature books, writing and editing well over two dozen, among them *The Modern Temper*, *Modernism in Modern Drama*, *The Gardener's World*, *The World of Animals*. Ever the modern thinker reconciling necessity and pleasure, he wondered as others do, in the blank field at the border of a page, ''Does the gardener really need any excuse at all? Is the beautiful the good only because it supports the utilitarian, or is the utilitarian good only because it makes possible the cultivation of the beautiful?''

VI

*E*DUCATION OF THE *G*ARDENER

Compost and Its
Moral Imperatives

Michael Pollan

Soon after we bought this onetime dairy farm and I started reading books about gardening, I began entertaining a fantasy about turning over a shovelful of earth somewhere on the property and finding a thick vein of composted cow manure. To judge from everthing I'd read, a trove of this airy, cakelike, jet-black earth would do much more than ensure an impressive harvest; it would elevate me instantly to the rank of *serious* gardener. There isn't an American gardening book published in the last twenty years that doesn't become lyrical on the subject of compost. James Crockett called it "brown gold" in his *Victory Garden*, where he provides a recipe for making compost as complicated as one for a soufflé. The more literary garden writers, such as Eleanor Perényi and Allen Lacy, offer fervent chapters on the benefits and, strange as it sounds, the virtues compost confers. The gardening periodicals—*Organic Gardening* and *National Gardening* in particular—regularly profile heroic gardeners singled out less for the elegant design and lush growth of their perennial borders than for the steaming heaps of compost dotting their yards. In American gardening, the successful compost pile seems almost to have supplanted the perfect hybrid tea rose or the gigantic beefsteak tomato as the outward sign of horticultural grace. What I read about compost gave me my first inkling that gardening, which I had approached as a more or less secular pastime, is actually moral drama of a high order.

Before attempting to grasp the metaphysics of compost, the reader might want briefly to consider the stuff itself. Compost, very simply, is partially decomposed organic matter. Given sufficient time, moisture, and oxygen, any piles of leaves, grass clippings, flower heads, brush, manure, or vegetable scraps will, by the action of bacteria, decay into a few precious shovelfuls of compost. All of the elaborate theories, formulas, and mechanical devices for making compost are really just tricks for speeding this natural process. (A rotating steel drum on the market is said to produce compost in fourteen days; most books say it takes three months.)

Some gardeners, and even some garden writers, talk about compost as if it were fertilizer, but that is only part of the story, and it is somewhat misleading. It is true that compost contains nitrogen, phosphorus, and potash (the principal ingredients of fertilizer), but not in terribly impressive quantities. The real benefits of compost lie in what humus—its main constituent—does to the soil. Consider:

1. Compost improves the soil's "structure." Soil is made up of clay, sand, silt, and organic matter, in varying proportions. Too much clay or silt, and the soil tends to become compacted, making it difficult for air, water, and roots to penetrate. Too much sand, and the soil's ability to retain water and nutrients is compromised. An ideal, friable garden soil consists of airy crumbs in which particles of sand, clay, and silt are held together by humic acid. Compost helps these particles to form.

2. Compost increases the soil's water-holding capacity. One experiement I read about found that 100 pounds of sand will hold 25 pounds of water, 100 pounds of clay will hold 50 pounds, and 100 pounds of humus will hold 190 pounds. A soil rich in compost will need less watering, and the plants growing in it will better withstand drought.

3. Because it is so dark in color, compost absorbs the sun's rays and warms the soil.

4. Compost teems with microorganisms, which break down the organic matter in soil into the basic elements plants need.

5. Because it is made up of decaying vegetable matter, compost con-

tains nearly every chemical plants need to grow, including such trace elements as boron, manganese, iron, copper, and zinc, not often found in commercial fertilizer. Compost thus returns to the soil a high proportion of the things agriculture takes out of it.

And yet as important as these benefits are, they don't account for the halo of righteousness that has come to hover over compost and those who make it. There are many other sources of humus, after all. To understand compost's mystery, one probably needs to know somewhat less about soil science than about the reasons Americans garden. Which, to judge from the literature and my conversations with experienced gardeners, frequently have less to do with considerations of beauty than of virtue.

Much of the credit for compost's exalted status must go to J. I. Rodale, the founding editor of *Organic Gardening*, who, until his death in 1971, promoted the virtues of organic gardening with a zeal bordering on the messianic. As Eleanor Perényi tells his story in *Green Thoughts*, Rodale was a latter-day Jeremiah, calling on Americans to follow him out of the agricultural wilderness. This is how Perényi, ordinarily the most sober of garden writers, describes her own conversion:

> [Rodale's] bearded countenance glared forth from the editorial page like that of an Old Testament prophet in those days (since his death it has been supplanted by the more benign one of his son), and his message was stamped on every page. Like all great messages, it was simple, and to those of us hearing it for the first time, a blinding revelation. Soil, he told us, isn't a substance to hold up plants in order that they may be fed with artificial fertilizers, and we who treated it was such were violating the cycle of nature. We must give back what we took away.

The way to give back what we had taken, to redeem our relationship with nature, was through compost.

As Rodale himself was the first to admit, there was nothing particularly new about composting. Agriculture had relied on composted organic waste for thousands of years—until the invention, early in this century, of chemical fertilizers. By World War II, most American farmers had been persuaded that all their crops needed in order to thrive were regular, heavy applications of fertilizer. To the farmer, however, the temptations of fertilizer pose something of a Faustian dilemma. At first, yields increase dramatically. But the cost is high, for the chemicals in fertilizer gradually kill off the biological activity in the soil and ruin its structure. Eventually, few organic nutrients remain, leaving crops completely dependent on fertilizer—the soil has become little more than a device to hold plants upright while they gorge themselves on 5-10-5. And to make matters worse, the more fertilizer he uses, the more problems the farmer has with disease and insects, since chemical fertilizer seems to weaken a plant's resistance. After the war, the farmer in this predicament succumbed to a host of new chemical temptations—DDT, Temik, chlordane—and it wasn't long before he found himself deep in agricultural hell.

The home gardener, meanwhile, had been walking down pretty much the same ruinous road, buying more and more chemical fertilizer and then more and more pesticides. By the 1960s, the shelves of his garage were lined with the dubious products of America's petrochemical industry: Cygon, Sevin, kelthane, benomyl, malathion, folpet, diazinon. Where one might reasonably have expected to find the logo of Burpee or Agway there were now the wings of Chevron. Somehow gardening, this most wholesome and elemental of pastimes, had gotten cross-wired with the worst of industrial civilization.

This is the wilderness in which Rodale found the American gardener and confronted him with a stark moral choice: he could continue to use petrochemicals to manufacture flowers and vegetables, or he could follow Rodale, learn how to compost, and redeem the soil—and, the implication was clear, himself.

When Rodale first made his pitch, he was greeted with the degree of respect that is usually accorded prophets. Even as late as the 1960s, he was generally regarded as a crank. When he keeled over and died during a taping of the Dick Cavett show in 1971, the nation responded with a smirk. Johnny Carson told jokes about it for weeks. But as concern over pesticides and the environment deepened during the 1970s, Rodale's message won a wider hearing. Today his is the conventional wisdom in home gardening, and his ideas have even made inroads in American agriculture.

That Rodale should have found a quasi-religious movement—and that the compost pile should have emerged as a status symbol among American gardeners—makes perfect sense when you consider the attitudes Americans have traditionally held toward the land. The apotheosis of compost is really just the latest act in a long-running morality play about the American people and the American land. In the garden writer's paeans to compost you can still hear echoes of Jefferson's agrarian ideal, paraphrased here by Henry Nash Smith: "Cultivating the earth confers a valid title to it; the ownership of the land, by making the farmer independent, gives him social status and dignity, while constant contact with nature makes him virtuous."

At least in a metaphorical way, compost restores the gardener's independence—if only from the garden center and the petrochemical industry. With the whole of the natural cycle reproduced in his garden, the gardener no longer has to depend on anyone else (save, perhaps, the seed merchant) to grow his own food. And because it makes the soil more fertile, composting flatters the old American belief that improving the land strengthens one's claim to it.

This notion of the garden as a realization in miniature of the agrarian ideal seems to have first appeared in the nineteenth century, as Americans in large numbers began leaving the farm for the city. If America could no longer remain primarily a nation of farmers, at least town-dwelling Americans might, by gardening, cultivate some of the rural virtues. "The man who has planted a garden feels that he has done something for the good of the world," wrote Charles Dudley Warner, editor of the *Hartford Courant*, at mid-century. "He belongs to the producers. . . . It is not simply beets and potatoes and corn and string beans that one raises in his well-hoed garden, it is the average of human life." Around the same time, Thoreau planted his bean field at Walden, not so much in order to grow beans that he might eat or sell, but so that he might harvest tropes about the human condition. Improving the soil improved the man.

Americans had come to regard gardening as much more than a pastime, and in the decades prior to the Civil War, horticulture actually attained the status of moral crusade for a time. In an era characterized by "the restlessness and din of the railroad principle," wrote Lydia H. Sigourney in 1840, gardening "instills into the bosom of the man of the world, panting with the gold fever, gentle thoughts, which do good, like a medicine." Addressing the prosperous Bostonians who crowded the Massachusetts Horticultural Society each Saturday morning to hear inspirational talk about gardening and self-improvement, Ezra Weston declared in 1845 that "he who cultivates a garden, and brings to perfection flowers and fruits, cultivates and advances at the same time his own nature."

The hortatory rhetoric may sound foreign to us today, but what about the underlying assumptions? These, it seems to me, we share. No less than the nineteenth-century transcendentalists and reformers, we look to the garden today as a source of moral instruction. They sought a way to preserve the Jeffersonian virtues even in the city; we seek a way to use nature without damaging it. In much the same way that the antebellum garden became a proof of the agrarian ideal, we regard our own plots, hard by the compost pile, as models of ecological responsibility. Under both dispensations, gardening becomes, at least symbolically, an act of redemption.

So pious an attitude toward gardening undoubtedly would strike a European as absurd. You do not read much about compost in English garden literature. This is partly because the sort of people who write garden books in England are not usually the same sort of people who handle soil. But I think the deeper reason is that British gardeners have traditionally regarded themselves more as artists than as reformers. The issues in English garden writing are invariably framed in aesthetic, rather than moral, terms. Gertrude Jekyll, the influential turn-of-the-century garden designer and writer, borrowed the metaphors of art, not religion, to talk about gardening: she likened plants to a "box of paint" and held that we must "use the plants that they shall form beautiful pictures." *The Education of a Gardener*, by Russell Page, perhaps the most celebrated garden designer of recent times, follows the traditional form of an artist's autobiography, chronicling the artist's discovery of his gift, the development of a personal vision and style, and the various intersections of his life and art. Not a word about compost, self-improvement, or the state of the biosphere.

As might be expected, the gardens made by aesthetes are considerably more pleasing to the eye than those made by moralists. It is no accident that Americans have yet to produce many world-famous gardens or landscape architects, or to found a style of garden design that anyone else would want to copy. I'm not saying we don't have beautiful gardens in this country—we do—but how many of these are derivative of European or Oriental styles? Despite the fact that they seldom work well in our climate or light, we persist in planting copies of English perennial borders—even in the deserts of southern California! So far, at least, American garden design (does the phrase evoke *anything?*) has achieved little of the distinctiveness found in American writing, music, art, or even cooking. Garden design remains the one corner of our culture in which our dependence on England has never been completely broken. Those who care about the look of their gardens still hire English designers (or their imitators) and study English gardening books. Even at this late date, anglophilia continues to rule American gardening.

And yet from the English perspective, some of our most prized gardens scarcely deserve the label. I'm thinking here of Central Park, surely one of the most successful man-made landscapes in America. So how is it that Russell Page can offhandedly dismiss Olmsted's masterpiece as "a stunted travesty of an English eighteenth-century park"? The first time I read this, I bristled at the judgment. But now I think I understand what he means. Even by the relatively informal standards of the English landscape garden on which it is modeled, Central Park is woefully literal and underdesigned (Page faults it for a "total lack of direction"). Yet this radical informality and utter lack of artifice is probably what we like best about it. Central Park pretends not to have been designed. It is less a garden than a counterfeit natural landscape, and New Yorkers seek in it the satisfactions of nature rather than art.

A society that produces "gardens" (or "antigardens") like Central Park is one that assumes nature and culture are fundamentally and irreconcilably opposed. And it seems to me that in order to design true gardens of distinction one must have a vision of how the two can be harmonized. It may be this that we lack. Americans have historically tended to regard nature as a cure for culture, or vice versa. Faced with the question of what to do with the land, we always seem to come up with the same crude alternatives: to virtuously subdue it in the name of "progress," or to place it strictly off-limits in "wilderness areas," hallowed places we go seeking an antidote to city life.

A people who believe that nature is somehow sacred—God's second book, according to the Puritans; the symbol of Spirit, according to the transcendentalists—will probably never feel easy bending it to their will, and certainly not for aesthetic reasons. Indeed, at least since the time of Thoreau, Americans have seemed more interested in the idea of bending *themselves* to nature's will, which might explain why this country has produced so many more great naturalists than great gardeners. We evidently feel more comfortable taking moral instruction in bean fields and at the feet of trees than arranging plants into pleasing compositions.

We even seem to approach our gardens as naturalists. Consider the typical American gardening book, which is organized like a field guide, plant by plant. It is much less often that you find rock gardens, herbaceous borders, or annual beds considered whole, as you do in English garden books. Instead, each cultivar is given its due, considered as an individual, its habits, character, and flaws appraised. "Flowers one can like or even love for themselves," wrote Katherine White, for many years the *New Yorker*'s garden columnist, "but gardens inevitably relate to man." Alas. It is as if making gardens were somehow unfair to the plants in them, a denial of their individuality and freedom. How long can it be before Americans rally behind the banner of plants' rights?

But back to compost. Eventually I did find the buried treasure. I was digging around the barn one day last fall when suddenly my spade slipped through a patch of particularly airy soil. I turned over a chunk of sod and there it was: the blackest earth I'd ever seen. I was elated, but only momentarily. Because by then I had read enough about compost to know that finding it didn't really count. Yes, it would be a boon to my vegetables and perennials. But this was a one-time windfall, the moral equivalent of finding a deposit of fossil fuel. I didn't even mention the strike to any of my serious gardening friends. For I now understood that if I wanted to perfect my gardening faith I would have to begin my own compost pile.

Which I promptly did. I built a slotted box out of some scrap lumber, found a shady spot for it (so the compost wouldn't dry out in the sun), and after the first frost had finished off the warm-weather plants, I piled the box high with blackened bean vines, squash leaves, zinnias, sunflower stalks, corncobs, and half a dozen club-sized zucchinis that had eluded timely harvest. I topped off the pile with a shovelful of the compost I'd found (in order to introduce the necessary microorganisms, it's best to begin a compost pile with a bit of compost, on the same principle as sourdough bread making). I mixed it all up, hosed it down, and forgot about it.

By the time I returned to the compost pile in April, I had read enough about American gardening to know that composting was a pretty silly fetish. It would never produce a beautiful perennial border, just a mor-

ally correct one, and wasn't that a little absurd? Well, I guess it is, but
when I lifted off the undecayed layer of leaves on top and ran my hand
through the crumbly, black, unexpectedly warm and sweet-smelling
compost below, I felt like I'd accomplished something great. If fertility
has a perfume, this surely was it. Mixed in were incompletely composted bits and pieces—vague brown shards that I could still make out
as former corncobs and sunflower seed heads. They looked like the
shadows of last year's harvest. I have to admit, I was starting to see
tropes. This heap of rotting vegetable matter looked more lovely to me
than the tallest spike of the bluest delphinium. Right then I realized
that, like it or not, I was an American gardener, likely to cultivate in the
garden more virtue than beauty.

*

From *Second Nature: A Gardener's Education.* Michael Pollan (1955–). New
York: Atlantic Monthly Press, 1991. Over the last decade Pollan has become one of the most influential voices in the often intertwined commentary on nature, food, and animals and the rituals they inspire in American
society. Whether his subject is the inner workings of the organic food or
meat industries, genetically altered seeds, or the dangerous health and environmental problems caused by the overproduction of corn in this country,
the editor of the Modern Library Garden Classics series and frequent con-
tributor to the *New York Times Magazine,* combines a measured, ethical approach and the skills of an investigative reporter.

What is refreshing in Pollan's writings is the wit and intelligence he uses
to dissect cherished cultural attitudes (old and new), such as Romantic notions of the "Otherness" of nature separate from humankind and its arts,
the Anglophilia of American garden design, suburban obsession with
lawns, the biocentric view that bestows "rights" on trees, and even the
uppityness of the better class of garden catalogue. Anyone who writes—as
he does in his contemporary classic, *Second Nature*—of the "metaphysics of
compost" is sure to be an adventurous thinker. Pollan is that very species,
in the essay printed here tackling the piety and self-improvement cult that
attends the perennial American quest for healthy soil which is now, according to a recent *Wall Street Journal* article, an $800-million-a-year industry.
Mind you, Pollan is second to none in enjoying the feel of warm compost

spilling through his fingers. But, his real intention is to constantly renegotiate the relationship of nature and culture, emphasizing aesthetics over moralism. His recent book, *The Botany of Desire*, considers beauty and co-evolution in the theatre of plants.

Pollan is a hands-on kind of guy, writing from his own experience of place, cataloguing the habits of flowers and vegetables. He wonders what makes a tree a tree—is it a word or a concept? He lets the reader into his garden and into his thoughts, seeding his own canny observations with the words of poets, novelists, and ancient philosophers. "Writing and gardening, these two ways of rendering the world in rows, have a great deal in common," he observes.

DEER

DIANE ACKERMAN

ONE DAY, WHEN THE LAST SNOWS HAVE melted, the air tastes tinny and sweet for the first time in many months. That subtle tincture of new buds, sap, and loam I've learned to recognize as the first whiff of springtime. Suddenly a brown shape moves in the woods, then blasts into sight as it clears the fence at the bottom of the yard. A beautiful doe with russet flanks and nimble legs, she looks straight at me as I watch from the living room window, then she drops her gaze.

Like fireworks, five more deer make equally spectacular leaps, and land squarely on the lifeless grass. But once they touch earth all their buoyancy seems to vanish, and they lumber around the yard, droopy, gaunt, exhausted. A big doe lifts a hind foot to scratch her shaggy cheek. I think that's the doe I named Triangle last year because of the geometrical pattern in her coat. But at the moment, the deer are in molt, which must feel itchy, and since they don't shed evenly, their usually sleek coats look crisscrossed by small weather systems. Mainly the deer seem frantic with hunger. They start eating the dried-up lavender leaves, whose pungent smell usually keeps them at bay. They've lost their winter fat, but there's nothing in bloom. Their living larder won't be full for weeks. Desperate, they devour the bittersweet and pull bark from aspens and other trees they don't prefer. In summer's banquet, they can afford to be sloppy and eat whatever they fancy. Now, searching for the highest-protein foods, they hunt carefully among the garden's leftovers.

I love watching the deer, which always arrive like magic or miracle or the answer to an unasked question. Can there be a benediction of deer on a chilly spring morning? I think so. Their otherworldliness stops the day in its tracks, focuses it on the hypnotic beauty of nature, and then starts the day again with a rush of wonder. There is a way of sitting quietly and beholding nature which is a form of meditation or prayer, and like those healing acts it calms the spirit.

Come summer, of course, the deer will ransack my herb garden, plunder my roses, destroy the raised beds, leaving their footprints as calling cards among the decapitated flowers. They are terrorists in the garden. That's why I've planted most of my roses in a special fenced-in garden with a solid gate. It feels a little odd, being in competition with deer, but that's what comes of cultivating so much land. If we replace their vegetation with buildings and crops, we leave the deer no choice but to raid our gardens. And humans have been known to raid deer, even cultivate them as a crop. For millennia, Chinese herbals have included deer parts, favoring antler velvet, bone marrow, spinal cord, penis, undigested milk, fetus, brains, thyroid gland, and much more as remedies. If human beings were not sitting smugly atop the food chain, what curios of our bodies would others use as medicines? A thought explored in gory detail by many science fiction books and movies. These deer are beautiful and whole, not a sum of their parts, and I'm happy to share everything but prize flowers with them. But how to protect those flowers? Friends have recommended such deer deterrents as bags of hair from a barbershop, used tampons, cougar pee, mothballs, salsa, bars of smelly soap, and barking dogs. I find that an oily soap called Hinder works reasonably well, and won't harm child or animal, but you have to spray it after every rainfall. This year I finally hit on a solution: pinwheels. I planted one beside each treasured bush or flower. Spinning randomly and sparkling in the sun, they seem alive and so the deer avoid them. I also like how festive the pinwheels look, decorating the garden with color and motion and the soft whir of their blades.

But I leave all the apples from both trees just for the deer, I let them eat their fill from the raspberry vines, and I feed them in hard weather. Sometimes in colder months I leave apples beneath the twin apple trees where deer would expect to find them. For a decade, the apple trees have helped the deer survive winter. What with the changing current of El Niño and several volcanoes hurling dust high into the atmosphere, the apple trees were sparse this year and the deer found few apples beneath the snow. Despite thick, burro-like coats, they looked thin. I suppose I am "conflicted" about the deer, as psychological folk like to say. But mainly I am grateful to have these emissaries of the wild so close at hand, and when they visit all I can manage is praise.

We've worked hard to exile ourselves from nature, yet we end up longing for what we've lost: a sense of connectedness. For many home-owners, suburbanites, and travelers, backyard animals such as deer, squirrels, birds, and raccoons become an entryway to the bustling world of nature. Studying animals is easy when they're close at hand, and there's nothing like the thrill of recognizing individual animals with unique looks and personalities: the doe with the white half-circle beneath one eye, who stands up on her rear legs to pick apples off the trees; the young buck who always does a small war dance before he leaps a fence. When that happens, we lose our "us against them" attitude and start to feel part of a kingdom of neighbors. Deep in our instincts and cells we remember living wild in nature, fitting into the seamless circle of the seasons, reading the weather and landscape, facing frights and challenges. In a real sense we are out of our element now, and it's small wonder that we relish rare visits to nature—picnics, jogs, and bike rides; journeys to parks, camp grounds, and zoos.

We may feel cozy and safe in our homes, protected from both blast and predator, but we pay the price with slack muscles, weak hearts, and glum spirits. Deprived of fresh daylight, we sink low during winter months. And yet when we search for remedies to those distresses, only the artificial springs to mind: gyms, pills, lightboxes. By retreating farther and farther from nature, we lose our sense of belonging, suffer a terrible loneliness we can't name, and end up depriving ourselves of what we need to feel healthy and whole. Children know this instinctively, and quickly learn the joys of nature. When a tree stump or marsh beckons, they dive in, wide-eyed, all hands.

I suppose what we fear is loss of control, of ourselves and of our planet; and there's no doubt, nature is chaotic, random, violent, uncontainable, no matter how hard we try to outwit it. But it's also dazzling, soothing, all-embracing, and restorative. Wonder is a bulky emotion;

when it fills the heart and mind there's little room for anything else. We need the intimate truths of daylight and deer.

Deer panic so easily that the only way to be among them without frightening them is to hunker down low and positively not look. Eye contact, even glancing, may distress them. Most often, wild animals make eye contact only when they wish to fight, eat, or mate. If you seem to be ignoring them, you pose little threat. And so I steal out, bent low, carrying a sliced-up peach I place on the grass near the apple trees, then, still without making eye contact, I creep back indoors. Soon two deer sniff their way to the treasure, so unfamiliar yet so sweet, and stand eating peach slices with juice dripping from their mouths. I've noticed that squirrels seem comforted by the sound of my voice when I'm among them, but deer require silence.

One noon last summer, I saw two fawns sitting on the grass in the shade of a large tree in my front yard. Quietly I crept out with con-cealed purpose—I walked easily across the years, as if on an errand unrelated to the deer. Because I seemed preoccupied by human things, they watched me, ever alert, but didn't bother to stir as I sat down in the grass near them, averting my eyes, picking a blade of grass or two, only now and then studying them with long, thick glances. A passing car startled them and they half-stood, then settled down again. Deer don't fold their legs like dogs, but slide down over the tops of their knees like camels. As I continued my mock grazing, they curled up and snoozed.

Where was their mother, and wasn't she afraid to leave them alone among humans? Typically, a doe will have one or two fawns and hide them in a secluded spot while she forages, returning only to nurse them. During the first few weeks of life, fawns don't give off much scent. Small, quiet, camouflaged, and nearly odorless, they're not easily dis-covered, so the mother may drift off without much concern. On the other hand, I might well have been in her sights, and dismissed as an-other creature out grazing in the sun. Humans are familiar to suburban deer.

By midsummer the fawns were eating a vegetarian diet which in-cluded hundreds of species of buds and leaves, and they were roaming a wide area. They left scent clouds in the forest. Late in the day, I would often seem them wander into open areas to nibble broad-leafed plants, watch them position themselves downwind, slowly roaming upwind, always alert for the smell of predators. Deer tend to twitch their tails just before lifting their heads, so whenever I see the tail-twitch, I stand still and drop my eyes. If I scare them, they'll pronk away in an awkward, tail-flashing pantomime that says, "I know you see me, but I'm too fast for you! Too strong for you! It's no use chasing me!" To my mind, prey calling attention to itself as a bluff seems dicey, but apparently gazelles do the same thing.

Now, nearly a year later, the fawns are grown, their speckles have disappeared and their bellies look gaunt. The lovely reddish-brown coats they wore as gawky juveniles have been replaced by the somber gray-brown of adulthood. These coats are more loosely woven, but each hair is hollow so that trapped air will heat up like a comforter on chilly nights. I cannot tell if they're male or female—not from a distance, anyway. Their mother is young, so most likely the fawns are female; deer tend to produce females early in their breeding life. Later on, as a doe ages, it's advantageous to have males and fuss over them, suckling them longer, making sure they're strong so that her genes will flourish as her offspring grow to best their rivals and dominate harems. Many animals are instinctively able to choose the sex of their offspring. Do humans make such unconscious choices? I wonder.

Remembering what I was saving for the squirrel and bird feeders, I grab a jacket and hurry into the garage, returning soon with six ears of corn. Then slipping slowly out back, I toss the corn across the yard. The deer stare squarely at it from a distance, tentatively approach the corn, realize what it is, and eagerly gnaw one cob apiece. What about the utility apples I was saving for a pie? Filling my pockets and hands with apples, I creep outside once more. As I toss apples to her, the largest female regards me solidly, eye to eye. An apple lands about three feet in front of her, and still she watches me carefully, then walks toward the apple, slices it with one bite, and eats with a mixture of surprise and relish. Apples in April! She looks back at me, allows me to settle low on my haunches and watch her and her family. I try not to move.

In time, she wanders toward the others, also happily eating apples and corn. The deer will survive at least one more day because of this food, maybe a few days, maybe long enough to get to the next decent meal. Knowing that, my heart lightens. It is a moment sealed in a glass paperweight, a scene to be reflected in a gazing ball, a time of peaceful communion with nature. And there I sit on the grass until evening drops a gray screen over the air and daylight drains away. At last the deer become startled by something real or imaginary and trot back toward the woods, with the largest doe leading the way along the fence. When she finds a place she feels comfortable with, she lines up squarely and hurdles it. The others pace nervously. One stands before the fence, lifts a foot as if to jump, thinks about it again, backs up, paces, then once more aborts the attempt and finally risks it: a five-foot jump straight up. Her hooves graze the top rail as she clears it. Soon the others follow, launching themselves from the tidy world of humans back into their familiar pandemonium of green.

*

From *Cultivating Delight: A Natural History of My Garden,* Diane Ackerman (1948–). New York: HarperCollins, 2001. Whether she is watching the courting rituals of rabbits, bicycling to the rhythm of birdsong, or standing with her nose to fragrant oak beams, Ackerman finds poetry and wonder wherever she goes. "I don't mind Japanese beetles having sex on the roses, I just wish they wouldn't eat at the same time," laments the author of the popular title *A Natural History of the Senses.* Her literary flair is enhanced by the empirical skills of a scientist to make her commentary on the natural world entertaining and wise. Forget triumphing over nature, she admonishes the gardener—cultivate delight instead. For a woman who captures backyard squirrels, offering them enchanting necklaces and several kinds of nuts, in an effort to charm while she observes their behavior, it seems perfectly reasonable that she has learned to appreciate the deer in her yard. "Can there be a benediction of deer on a chilly spring morning?," she muses. Observing nature is a form of meditation or prayer for Ackerman, who reminds her readers that gardeners spend a great deal of time on their knees.

My Garden (Book)

Jamaica Kincaid

My attachment in adult life to the garden begins in this way: shortly after I became a mother for the first time, my husband gave me a hoe, a rake, a spade, a fork, some flower seeds to mark the occasion of that thing known as Mother's Day. It was my second Mother's Day; for the first one he had given me a pair of earrings and I put them on a table in the kitchen and they were never seen again, by me, nor anyone else, not the lady who cleaned the house, not the women who helped me take care of my child, not my husband, not my child—no one admitted to ever seeing them again. I can't remember if the seeds and tools were wrapped up, but I can remember that immediately on having them I went outside and dug up a large part of the small yard, a patch that had never been cultivated, and put all the seeds in the packets in the ground. And that was that, for nothing grew, the ground was improperly prepared, it was in the shade of a big oak tree and a big maple tree (those two trees really did grow in the same vicinity and I did not appreciate them then; so annoying, their leaves falling down in the autumn and dirtying up the yard, I thought then).

A man named Chet lived in the house right next to me and he could breathe properly only while attached to canisters filled with oxygen; then every once in a while he would come outside and smoke a cigarette, and while smoking a cigarette he would tend to these enormous tomatoes that he grew right up against the side of his house. The tomatoes were exposed fully to the sun in that position and he did not worry about poisonous toxins leaching out of the materials from which his house was built into the soil in which his tomatoes were grown. His tomatoes prospered near his house and they tasted most delicious; my plot of back yard upturned by me, which had made my hands blistered and unpleasant-looking, looked as if an animal of any kind had mistakenly thought something was buried there and had sought in vain to find it; no one looking at the mess I had made would think that a treasure of any kind, long lost, had finally been unearthed there.

I moved into another house not too far away and with a larger yard. Chet died and I am still ashamed I never saw him again after I left my old house, and also I never attended his funeral, even though I knew of it, and when I now see his wife, Millie, she avoids me (though I am sure I avoid her, too, but I would rather think that it is she who is avoiding me). I moved to a house which had been the house of someone named Mrs. McGovern and she had just died, too, but I never knew her or even heard of her and so moving into her house carried no real feeling of her for me, until one day, my first spring spent in that new house and so in that new property, this happened: the autumn before, we had paid someone a large amount of money to regrade the lawn out back and it looked perfect enough, but that following spring lots of patches of maroon-colored leaf sprouts began to emerge from the newly reconstituted lawn out back. How annoyed I was, and just on the verge of calling up the lawn person to complain bitterly, when my new neighbor, Beth Winter, came over to see me and to talk to me about how enjoyable she found it to live with her family of a husband and three children in the very same house in which she grew up; on hearing of my complaints about the lawn person and seeing the maroon-colored leaf sprouts I had pointed out to her, she said, "But you know, Mrs. McGovern had a peony garden." And that was how I learned what the new shoots of peonies look like and that was how I came to recognize a maple, but not that its Latin name is *Acer;* Latin names came later, with resistance.

That first spring in old Mrs. McGovern's house (but she was long dead) I discovered her large old patch of daylilies (*Hemerocallis fulva*) growing just outside the southwest kitchen window and Rob (Woolmington) came with his modest rototiller and made a largish square with it for my vegetable garden and then followed me around the outside perimeter of the house with the same modest rototiller as I directed him to turn up the soil, making beds in strange shapes, so that the house would eventually seem to be protected by a moat made not of water but the result of an enthusiastic beginning familiarity with horticulture.

This is how my garden began; then again, it would not be at all false to say that just at that moment I was reading a book and that book (written by the historian William Prescott) happened to be about the conquest of Mexico, or New Spain, as it was then called, and I came upon the flower called marigold and the flower called dahlia and the flower called zinnia, and after that the garden was to me more than the garden as I used to think of it. After that the garden was also something else.

By the time I was firmly living in Mrs. McGovern's house (or the Yellow House, which is what the children came to call it, for it was painted yellow), I had begun to dig up, or to have dug up for me, parts of the lawn in the back of the house and parts of the lawn in the front of the house, into the most peculiar ungardenlike shapes. These beds—for I was attempting to make such a thing as flower beds—were odd in shape, odd in relation to the way flower beds usually look in a garden; I could see that they were odd and I could see that they did not look like the flower beds in gardens I had admired, the gardens of my friends, the gardens portrayed in my books on gardening, but I couldn't help that; I wanted a garden that looked like something I had in my mind's eye, but exactly what that might be I did not know and even now do not know. And this must be why: the garden for me is so bound up with words about the garden, with words themselves, that any set idea of the garden, any set picture, is a provocation to me.

It was not until I was living in Dr. Woodworth's house (the Brown Shingled House with Red Shutters) some years later that I came to understand the shape of the beds. In Dr. Woodworth's house, I had much more space, I had a lawn, and then beyond the lawn I had some acres. The lawn of Dr. Woodworth's house was bigger than the lawn at old Mrs. McGovern's house, and so my beds were bigger, their shapes more strange, more not the usual shape of beds in a proper garden, and they became so much more difficult to explain to other gardeners who had more experience with a garden than I and more of an established aesthetic of a garden than I. "What is this?" I have been asked. "What are you trying to do here?" I have been asked. Sometimes I would reply by saying, "I don't really know," or sometimes I would reply ". . ." (with absolute silence). When it dawned on me that the garden I was making (and an still making and will always be making) resembled a map of the Caribbean and the sea that surrounds it, I did not tell this to the gardeners who had asked me to explain the thing I was doing, or to explain what I was trying to do; I only marveled at the way the garden is for me an exercise in memory, a way of remembering my own imme-diate past, a way of getting to a past that is my own (the Caribbean Sea) and the past as it is indirectly related to me (the conquest of Mexico and its surroundings).

*

From *My Garden (Book)*, Jamaica Kincaid (1949–). New York: Farrar, Straus and Giroux, 1999. As a novelist, essayist, and editor of *My Favorite Plant: Writers and Gardeners on the Plants They Love*, the Antiguan-born author in-fuses the usual topics of plants and planting, garden visits, weather, and seed catalogues, with a unique postcolonial perspective. A garden is a world—her own in Vermont admittedly resembles a map of the Caribbean and the surrounding sea—which cannot exclude race and politics. An es-sential theme of her garden writing is the conquest of European empires and their repossesion of plants uprooted from native soil. Thus, "cocoxo-chitl" is renamed "dahlia, after a Swedish botanist," in its European hybrid. In one of her articles, which appear regularly in the *New Yorker*, she re-minded her readers that Thomas Jefferson's Monticello and the celebrated plantation at Middleton Place in Charleston were the work of slaves. Kin-caid brings the novelist's keen intellect and the memorist's transparency to understanding who she is: the garden is a narrative field which generates new histories of plants, cultures, and continents that shape her sense of rootedness in the world.

MR. JACK TOMATO

WILLIAM WOYS WEAVER

BOTANICAL NAME: *Lycopersicon lycopersicum*

FAMILY: *Solanaceae*

PEOPLE OFTEN ASK ME HOW VEGETABLES get their names and my pat response is that there is no set rule. Some names are purely convenient and descriptive, like the Green Grape tomato. Others bow to a touch of poetry like Queen of the Earlies. Since I breed plants, now and then I am presented with the opportunity to name one of my creations. In the case of my Mr. Jack tomato, I would like to think its robust flavor matches the personality of its namesake.

Mr. Jack is Jack McDavid, whose dedication to saving farms and bringing the best of America's regional produce to the table is well known in Philadelphia. He owns a couple restaurants in Philadelphia and he cooks in bib overalls. Because he likes good food and knows a good tomato from a mediocre one, and because he has been such a good friend to the garden community, it occurred to me that someone ought to name something after him. He makes a lot of ketchup and hot sauces, so a tomato seemed like a natural choice. To honor him, I chose a tomato that chefs would understand. It has the right shape, it has the right flavor, and it came into being quite by accident.

One of my small, red pear-shaped tomatoes crossed naturally with a Mexican tomato from Oaxaca called sometimes Zapotee Pleated and other times *tomate enrrollado rojo.* This is a very old tomato, rosy red in color, heavily pleated, and usually hollow like a pepper. It is a type of tomato that was grown in Mexico before the Spanish conquest, and what it lacks in slick appearance it compensates in flavor.

One summer day several years ago, I happened to notice among my Zapotecs one vine that was completely off—this is where patient observation sometimes pays off in the garden. The fruit was pear-shaped, plump, juicy, bright red, and hugely flavorful. I consulted my field notes: yes, the previous year (1990) I had worried that the Zapotecs had been planted a little too close to the red pear tomatoes. Things happen, especially around pear tomatoes. I am now positive that a bumblebee sealed the kiss that previous summer—open pollination at its accidental best.

All the characteristics were right, even to the shift in foliage color (the Zapotec tomato has gray-green foliage; the pear tomato does not). I began to grow the new tomato in isolation. In 1998 a pink one emerged. This is now called Mrs. Jack in honor of McDavid's Pennsylvania Dutch wife, a capable companion to the red. Both are just the sort of tomatoes a farm-loving chef would appreciate: they continue to ripen after they are picked, they have good flavor and lots of meat to make sauces thick and tasty. And they keep for almost a month without rotting, a plus for people with very busy schedules. It took about ten years to get Mr. Jack under control, but now I think I've finally got this tomato where I want it and its best characteristics are fixed. The recipe development I leave to Jack the chef.

*

From *100 Vegetables and Where They Came From,* William Woys Weaver (1947–). Chapel Hill: Algonquin Books, 2000. Weaver is a plant breeder and food historian whose passionate interest in where plants come from, how they got there, and how to cook them has led him to cultivate his own heirloom garden of close to 3,000 vegetables, flowers and herbs at Roughwood in Devon, Pennsylvania. His garden supplies seeds and plants to Monticello, the New York Botanical Garden, and Seed Savers Exchange. Weaver inherited his love of plants and a vast knowledge of them, including some heirloom seeds themselves, from Mennonite and Quaker family members who were involved in plant cultivation and homeopathy since the nineteenth century. One of his ancestors, Joshua Pierce, had a local arboretum that became the heart of Pennsylvania's famous Longwood Gardens.

Weaver is the author of numerous books, including *Heirloom Vegetable Gardening, Pennsylvania Dutch Country Cooking,* and *Sauerkraut Yankees,* which serve to demonstrate the increased affinity in the last decade between garden writing and food writing. In fact, he recently became Professor of Culinary Arts and Food Studies at Drexel University's Center for the Study of Food and Wine. Ever attentive to the local and the historical, he views the heirloom vegetable as "material culture," promoting garden history to a branch of American Studies. This acknowledgment is long overdue. In preserving the heritage of nineteenth-century plants from Pennsylvania gardens, and bringing to life his own new offerings, such as the "Mr. Jack" and "Roughwood Golden Plum" tomatoes, Weaver credits Pennsylvania's Quaker and Amish background as an underpinning of his own deeply felt spiritual connection to the lives of plants.

THE PARABLE OF THE POPPY AND THE BEE

GARY PAUL NABHAN

I want to find our cousin
somewhere in the dawn, sporting
the pungent gleam of dew and sun,
our secret cousin Glimmer of honey,
our crazy cousin Wild bee's delight.
Some call the wild bees gone, their hymns
extinct. Some call the glade still and cold.
Yet I call her and call her back.
I call our cousin's many names,
who sang the psalms that saved us.
KIM STAFFORD, *Oregon Reunion of the Rare*

*

WE WANDERED FOR SEVERAL HOURS IN THE DESERT heat, up and down faint trails on gypsum-laced bluffs, before we saw it. At times, I sensed we might not see it at all. The landscape looked barren, torn up by years of off-road vehicle racing and overgrazing by livestock. Few flowers, insects, or even lizards were active during the dry spell of early summer. I was easily convinced that "it" was indeed rare in this valley near the Nevada-Utah border.

The "it" that brought me to the Virgin River basin was not the Joshua tree, not the crimson canyon, not the casinos, the health spas, or the white-water raft trips. I was after a rare wildflower, a small poppy called the dwarf bearclaw poppy, which was federally listed as an endangered species in 1979. Although legally protected, it had suffered from a five-year drought, during which nearly every elderly bearclaw had died off, and only a few new seedlings had sprouted to replace them. But drought had not merely affected the bearclaw poppies; it affected the other native organisms interacting with them as well.

I walked the trails and gazed out over the desert shimmering in the heat. Steve Buchmann, my bee-minded counterpart, was seeing more than midday mirages. Apparently spotting the first poppy, he whistled for me to come over to the bluff where he knelt a few hundred yards away. I did just that.

"I haven't found any yet," he said, sighing and gazing down at a patch of feathery, blue-gray poppy plants.

"Yes, you have," I replied. "That's *Arctomecon humilis* right at your feet." They looked like little cabbages set against the chalky soils of the gypsum outcrops. Seeing just one of the plant's velvety white blossoms, I was sure it was a poppy. I wondered if the heat had gotten to Steve, who ordinarily would have known a poppy when he saw one.

"The bees, I mean—I haven't yet seen any native bees. I've seen several open flowers, but none of the new species of bee, *Perdita meconis*, that Vince and Terry have been working with here in the Virgin."

Steve seemed to notice every open white flower in sight. While I had come to this place to see a rare plant, Steve had come to see an even rarer bee. Each of us had our biases, mine botanical, his more entomological. Both of us had come to see "it," but "it" had a blossom in my mind, while Steve's "it" had wings. We were witnessing an endangered ecological interaction of considerable antiquity. Few of us fathom how vital this pollination process may be to the reproduction and survival of rare plants, let alone to our own survival.

The poppy-loving bee had been described by scientists only in recent years, even though the poppy it loved had been known by botanists for more than a century. Fortunately, the bee had finally received the attention it deserved from Steve's colleagues in Logan, Utah, entomologists

Terry Griswold and Vince Tepedino. When Terry identified *Perdita meconis* as a new species, specimens had been collected only from the area in which we stood and from the Kelso Dunes, 200 miles to the west. Vince and his students had carefully determined that in each of these localities, this bee pollinates only one kind of plant: a prickly poppy in the Kelso Dunes and the endangered bearclaw poppy here in the Virgin.

Meanwhile, I was thrilled at this glimpse of the poppy so thoroughly studied by one of my botanical heroes, Kim Harper. Dr. Harper and his Brigham Young University students had organized counts of all known bearclaw poppies year in and year out. They had determined that the small patches of poppies were already quite genetically uniform, per-haps because inbreeding had been going on for generations. At last I could see such patches of poppies "in the flesh."

Steve, I soon realized, was less than satisfied with the mere sighting of the poppy. After several hours of searching, he was frustrated that he would have little news to pass on to Terry and Vince, for the poppies bore no bees on this particular day in June.

Or at least they bore no native bees this late in the flowering season. Steve pointed out to me a feral (nonnative) honey bee that approached a dwarf bearclaw poppy, then zoomed away to a flowering buckwheat nearby. This type of bee may casually visit the poppies, but it did not do so this day. A single far-ranging bee can serve as an effective pollina-tor for the poppies earlier in the season, but we were too late for that. Even though these poppy plants are not exclusively dependent on *Per-dita meconis* for producing their fruits and seeds, we noticed that the number of full black seeds within each fruit among the hundred some poppies was still low. Despite the presence of honey bees—as well as earlier visitations by poppy-loving and other solitary bees—the poppies were not filling all of their fruits with seed.

Scientists once believed that the only plants that could be threatened by low pollination rates were ones dependent on a single insect partner to spread their pollen around—the yucca with its yucca moth, for in-stance, or the fig with its fig wasp. We now know that the majority of flowering plant species can suffer low seed set when pollinators are scarce—even if they have a wide variety of pollinators under ideal con-ditions. In less than ideal conditions, most of these animals will make fewer and fewer visits to a rare plant population when it becomes too small to provide them with sufficient rewards.

In the case of the bearclaw poppy, its habitat is protected but its most dedicated pollinator is not. When I called on Vince Tepedino in Logan to ask him about the vulnerability of the poppy-loving bee, his answer was immediate: "This bee should perhaps be listed as an endangered species just as the poppy is, since it is known from so few places"— fewer localities, in fact, than the poppy itself.

It is unlikely that Dr. Tepedino's concerns for protecting the bee will be heeded in the near future. When he spoke with me, there was a moratorium on listing *any* more species as federally endangered. Given the current antienvironmentalist climate in some states, the mere thought of championing "some spineless little critter" like a bee would give some politicians a headache. The flower-loving fly of the Delhi Dunes of California, which is federally listed as an endangered species, is an example of a pollinator that has already suffered the ridicule of the "Wise Use Movement" and the sarcasm of commentators on the six o'clock news. And yet, fewer than 500 of these flies persist anywhere in the world, and they need only a few football fields of sand to survive.

Rare invertebrate species have become fall guys for the antienvironmental movement, which has argued that the government should only concern itself with bona fide "wildlife"—in other words, game animals—and leave the fates of plants or bugs to chance. During the summer 1995 debates about the reauthorization of the Endangered Species Act, lobbyists kept quoting a segment of a book called *Noah's Choice*, which pitted a little-known beetle against a highway project that would have provided rural dwellers with better access to a hospital. The take-home message was that the survival of beetles and other creepy-crawlies in their habitats could not possibly contribute to the well-being of humans. Bugs only get in the way of our economic endeavors.

If you are a bee, fly, or a beetle, this has not been your best time: more rollbacks of environmental legislation have been proposed during the past decade than ever before in U.S. history. Is it any wonder that the few spineless critters I've watched in the past few months were all ducking underground, frantically trying to get out of the way of the antienvironmental bulldozer? That bulldozer pretends that all bees and beetles are replaceable by others and that none of them has special habitat needs.

As Buchmann and I drove back from the Virgin basin toward Saint George, Utah, I naively asked him a question that many pollination ecologists have been asked by resource managers: "If an endangered plant can be pollinated by introduced honey bees just as well as by native bees, why not move a few hives into each rare-plant habitat and solve the problem that way?"

"Gary," he groaned, feigning shock, "you should know better than to fall for quick fixes! A mobile beehive for every rare plant might have been a reliable stopgap solution a few years ago, but today, honey bees are dropping like flies. Over the long haul, it's never wise to put all your eggs—or pollen grains—in one basket. By investing exclusively in honey bee pollination, you're making things risky both for the rare plants and for the native bees that have coevolved with them."

With two decades of research under his belt at the USDA Carl Hayden Bee Research Laboratory, Steve could recite on a moment's notice the grim statistics regarding honey bee declines. Since 1990, nearly half of the managed honey bee colonies in the United States have been lost to diseases, parasites, pesticide poisonings, or infestations by fierce Africanized bees. In one part of the Southwest, 85 percent of all feral bee colonies in rock shelters, caves, and tree trunks have succumbed to mites over the past five years. Other states are reporting a near-total loss of their feral honey bees.

There are now fewer honey bees in North America than at any time since before World War II. More than two-thirds of the remaining hives are infested with pests and diseases that are not easily controlled; in fact, some of the mites are developing resistance to formerly lethal miticides. And Africanized bees, which first arrived in the United States in 1990, have now spread to more than a hundred counties. Because so many people now fear these so-called killer bees, bee-keepers in heavily-populated areas are having to abandon their businesses under the threat of lawsuits from neighbors.

These trends are a painful reminder that without sufficient honey bees to provide the pollination services essential to U.S. crop production, we will have to rely increasingly on wild pollinators or face food shortages. Already, dozens of native bees pollinate as many flowers of alfalfa, cranberries, blueberries, and sunflowers as does the European-introduced honeybee. Should honeybees continue to disappear from the southern half of the United States, wild pollinators will have to take up the slack in pollinating other crops. It is estimated that within a few years, pollinators other than managed honey bees will need to provide four to six billion dollars of annual crop pollination services to American farmers.

Yet many of the native bees that pollinate our food crops are also vulnerable to a variety of threats. Like the poppy-loving bee, they are finicky about which flowers they visit and where they nest. Almost all pollinators have nesting requirements that scientists have not yet learned to simulate or artificially duplicate. Their habitats must also be kept pesticide-free, for most native bees are smaller and more sensitive to chemical poisoning than honey bees are.

While nearly 200 kinds of bird and mammal pollinators of plants are known to be globally at risk, no one knows how many insect pollinators are vulnerable to extinction. The recent *Global Biodiversity Assessment* lists fewer than 3,000 insects as endangered, but that number is low due to lack of data. The world's more than 100,000 invertebrate pollinator species are as affected by deforestation, contamination, and habitat fragmentation as any organisms can be, but definitive listings of threatened species have been published only for European butterflies. Hardly any reliable information exists with regard to the numbers of bees, wasps, flies, or moths that may be on the brink of extinction.

Yet paying exclusive attention to the extinction of species may divert us from recognizing other kinds of losses—the extirpation of pollinator populations, the disruption of the "traplines" they follow from one flowering plant to the next, the depletion of nest-building materials, the compaction of nest holes by trampling or plowing, and the fragmentation of migratory corridors. In autumn of 1996, I encouraged the Arizona-Sonora Desert Museum to convene a task force of eighteen conservation scientists and resource managers to consider what to do about the extinction of plant-pollinator interactions. Authorities from four countries, from the Xerces Society for invertebrate conservatism, Bat Conservation International, government agencies, and numerous universities drafted an international policy proposal for protecting pollinators. They suggested that such extinctions will be averted only by setting aside sizable tracts of pesticide-free habitat and by restoring the "nectar corridors" of flowering plants required by migratory pollinators.

Such pollinator conservation measures will not merely help bearclaw poppies in Utah; they will also aid Hawaiian silverswords, the evening primrose of California's Antioch dunes, the night-blooming cacti of the Arizona-Mexico border, and a primrose now languishing without seed set in the suburbs of Tokyo, Japan. The parable of the bearclaw poppy and the poppy-loving bee can remind us that plants may be vulnerable without coevolved pollinators, and vice versa.

Native pollinators have consistently provided our croplands and wildlands with the kind of support that has kept our country fruitful. Let us remember them every time we smell a poppy or take a bite into a delicious, succulent fruit, honoring our collective debt to them. Hopi maidens mark the autumn with the Butterfly Dance; the Yaqui Deer Dancers spin and rattle their way through their ceremonial cycle wearing silk-moth cocoons around their calves; and the Hindi of peninsular Malaysia devote hundreds of hours each year to rituals that placate, charm, and sing poetry to the giant Asian bee, *Apis dorsata.* We should emulate the wisdom of these native peoples and celebrate, respect, and support our native pollinators. In doing so, we will clearly be expanding our sense of community, acknowledging at last the presence of other members who have been in service to us all along.

*

From *Cultures of Habitat: On Nature, Culture, and Story,* Gary Paul Nabhan (1952–). Washington, D.C.: Counterpoint, 1997. Nabhan's "parable" underscores his characteristic use of narrative, myth, and folklore to bring a larger context to his writing, especially in the politically charged issue of endangered species. In books as varied as *The Desert Smells like Rain, Endangered Seeds,* and *Coming Home to Eat,* he interweaves the ordinary, the social, and the sacred whether focusing on farming, plant hunting, scientific experiments, ethnography, or foodways. Everywhere in his work, Nabhan celebrates the local with an eye on the significance of human acts, making a major contribution to our understanding of Native American agricultural practices in the Southwest from his base at Northern Arizona University, Flagstaff, as Director of the Center for Sustainable Environments. His writings are a blueprint for safeguarding both plant diversity and cultural diversity within a broad ethical perspective of "ecological restoration." In Nabhan's imaginative view of the nature/culture theme, which he explores in *Cultures of Habitat,* to restore a place means to "re-story it, to make it the lesson of our legends, festivals, and seasonal rites. Story is the way we encode deep-seated values within our culture."

Eating My Yard

Joan Dye Gussow

Let her dyet proceede more from the provision of her owne yarde,
than the furniture of the markets; and let it be rather esteemed
for the familiar acquaintance shee hath with it, than for the strangenesse
and raritie it bringeth from other Countries.

—Gervase Markham, *The English Hus-wife,* 1615

I STRUGGLE TO KEEP OTHER SPECIES FROM grazing my yard so I can do the harvesting. But even when Nature and her creatures cooperate fully, I don't come close to feeding myself; Alan and I never did. I do try to live as much as possible on what I grow. But the extent to which I'm not self-sufficient reminds me constantly that I depend, as we all do, on neighbors—increasingly remote neighbors—to carry on for us the demanding work of food production. Because farmers keep planting and harvesting, tending trees and vines, and caring for animals and birds, none of us is required to survive on our own production capacity.

Consequently, the invisibility of these people as the *source* of our food never ceases to alarm me; witness a commentary by Dave Hage recently published in *The Nation* asking why taxpayers should be rescuing farmers who are once again in financial trouble. The first answer, the author says, is because Congress always responds to the farm lobby. "A second answer is that a government should cushion its people against the cruelties of the market." I'm waiting here for him to mention the fact that farmers grow our food and we'd starve without them, but he says, "Finally, farmers give the nation a certain economic and social diversity. They provide a counterweight to the grain and meat-packing giants that control our food production, and they undergird a rural culture that millions of families still find preferable to suburbanized America." I'm certain that this writer knows that we need farms to produce food, but he seems to feel no necessity to point out that these providers of economic and social diversity, these undergirders of rural culture, feed us.

I don't at the moment grow grains or any animal products (flesh, eggs, milk), and I eat—among other things—bread and muffins, homemade granola, eggs, milk, lots of cheese, and a little meat. I also eat more fruit than I have yet been able to grow, though I'm trying. And I don't grow all my own fertility. According to calculations by intensive-grower John Jeavons, who has thought more about saving our planetary soils than anyone, I would need to plant at least half of my garden beds with compost crops to produce on site all the nutrients I need to keep the other half growing vegetables. So I bring in manure and wood chips as I've reported, add chopped-up newspapers to my compost pile, and supplement with purchased blood meal, bone meal, ashes, and mineral powders.

Some small-farm families grow almost everything they eat, but most farmers don't. The great majority of U.S. farmers have been convinced that growing their own food is a waste of land—which could better be planted with crops they can sell—as well as a waste of time, because everything can be bought fast and cheap and even ready to eat. The bargain chicken the farmer eats, however, may have grown up on feed she sold off her farm. That sort of logic has led to lots of farmers going broke and others depending on food stamps, since low prices for the "raw materials" that are turned into processed foods translate into even lower prices on the farm. Cheap chickens mean even cheaper corn.

There is an article much quoted among people concerned with creating a food system that the planet can support indefinitely. In it, a University of Maine economist named Stewart Smith points out that the farmer's share of the food dollar has declined so steadily since 1910 that if the trend simply continued, there would be no more "farming" in agriculture by the year 2020. His graphs show that by then our food dollars would go entirely to pay for the inputs (fertilizer, seed, pesti-cides, herbicides, machinery, interest on debts, etc.) and for the cost of getting the food from the farm through the processing plant and the supermarket to our table (transportation, processing, advertising, retail-ing). These pre-farm and post-farm sectors are where more and more of the money flows. Smith called his paper "Is there Farming in Agri-culture's Future?" This trend makes it hard to understand the govern-ment's reluctance to help keep farmers solvent. Someone, of course, will need to produce food, but maybe our leaders have decided that losing our farms is just one more instance of "progress" that can't be stopped. Perhaps they have concluded that we'll get our food from poor coun-tries south or east of us where farm workers are paid so little that food cheap enough for us rich folks can still be produced profitably.

Because my "farm" is only 1,000 square feet of growing space twenty minutes north of New York City, I couldn't really feed myself if I wanted to. But I do grow all my own vegetables, and I therefore eat differently than most people—better, I think. In deciding what to eat, I bind myself to the seasons, augmented by what a small upright freezer will hold. And—what impresses me most—I'm almost always able to plan meals for myself and for frequent guests based on what's fresh in the garden or what's stored in the cold cellar or the guest bedroom closet. I eat fresh tomatoes between July and December or January when the last one harvested green has turned red (dried tomatoes or frozen sauces take me through winter and spring). Sometimes on a cold morning I have a roasted sweet potato for breakfast. I eat no lettuce when no lettuce is in the garden or cold frame, and in its place (in tacos, for example), I use chopped kale. And for salad? I'll get to that.

What do I grow? Always potatoes (six or seven kinds) plus sweet potatoes, tomatoes (several kinds), a variety of hot and sweet peppers, eggplant (short and long), zucchini, green beans, dry beans (pinto, scar-let runner, and black), storage onions (red and yellow), leeks, garlic, carrots, parsnips, kale, spinach, lettuce, mesclun, edible-pod peas, green soybeans, broccoli, parsley, basil, and other herbs. Sometimes cabbage, beets, turnips, collards, leaf celery, ruby chard, and butternut squash. Depending on which of these things is available, I plan my meals, aug-mented mostly by cheese, eggs, milk, bread, and grains. The mix is obviously nutritious since I am, at seventy-plus, absurdly healthy. And, hearing no complaints from guests, I assume that they find my seasonal local meals as delicious as I do.

As to how this works out in practice, there I was on July 3, having just come home from the supermarket with tortilla chips (I'm not perfect!), eggs, apricot and grapefruit juice, English muffins, and . . . Coca-Cola (I'm *really* not perfect—and I had someone coming who would ask for it). I also had to get bottles of seltzer, because the man who brings me a wooden case of ancient heavy-glass spritzer bottles when I need them seems unaccountably to have disappeared. That was my Fourth of July shopping. I was at the market early, when other people were loading up with bags and bags full of meat and buns and snacks and the like. And I was a little anxious, because I was trying, as usual, to make things from my garden the center of a meal for seven or more.

Watching those other shoppers line up with two or three cartloads of groceries, I realized how odd I was. And, feeling a momentary twinge of self-pity, I understood that it was hard to do what I was trying to do, to count mostly on what I had grown, and thereby symbolically to use only what belonged, at any particular time of year, in the place where I lived. Then I walked over to get my tortilla chips, and realized what *hard* really was. Because I don't watch television or read women's magazines, I don't see food advertisements. This means that I don't know how to decide which of the dozens of different kinds of tortilla chips—bite-sized, restaurant-style, white corn, yellow corn, chili-lime, avocado-sour cream, and so on, filling half the length of a supermarket aisle—I need to buy. Why would I want circles instead of triangles? What does it matter if the chips were made with all-white corn? Why would I buy chili-lime-flavored chips if I'm going to serve salsa with them?

Then I realized that the store had twenty aisles of such time- and energy-sinks, centers of artificial diversity that raised silly questions and induced you to occupy your mind making non-essential distinctions—non-essential, but necessary if you were going to escape the store without simply fleeing. I don't have to do much of that kind of choosing—and I won't starve if I simply flee. Many of my choices are made for me by the seasons, and by my once-a-year planning for what I will grow. And stressful as it might be to wonder if I can put together a meal for seven at the beginning of July, before the tomatoes and peppers and eggplant have fully begun to fruit, it is, on a profound level, easier than the alternative.

We're going to start our Fourth of July meal with those tortilla chips (not local, I'm afraid), and a "fresh" salsa made from some tomatoes I froze whole last year, and some roasted hot peppers and salsa cubes both left in the freezer—stuff I need to get rid of before the new crops of tomatoes and peppers come in. We'll also have a really seasonal offering that will be the most popular appetizer, the last of my sugar snap peas, briefly steamed whole and dressed with my home-dried tomatoes softened in balsamic vinegar. For the main event, we'll have Grilled Andouille Sausage and Sweet Potato Salad (lots of last year's sweet potatoes still occupy the guest room closet), some kind of bean salad (I have lots of pintos, some black beans, and a handful of white beans that I'm taking the trouble to cook separately so the dish will be more interesting to look at). We're also going to have a frittata made with various garden greens (beet, collard, kale, lettuce that's bolting from the heat), scallions, and herbs, with some lime juice from my home-grown limes (the tree comes inside for the winter). If I can find enough un-bolted lettuce that my fellow community gardeners don't intend to pick, I will also have a salad, but it's not the best time of year for that. Lettuce and spinach don't like 90-degree days any better than I do.

As it turned out, I burned the white beans getting distracted by all the different things I was trying to do. But when I looked in the freezer, I discovered that I had some snap beans left over (with the fresh ones already coming from the garden), so we had a salad of black and brown and green beans. And I never made the lettuce salad because the peas were such a hit that everyone was almost full before the main dishes were served.

I recognize that it's a faily quixotic enterprise on which I have set out. Trying to grow as much as possible of what we eat began as a way to prove to myself and others that eating locally year-round did not imply a season of cabbage and old potatoes, even if you lived in New England. I demonstrate that every time I serve a splendid meal in the dead of winter. But the impulse to make such a demonstration grew out of my conviction that we all had to relearn our dependence on the land, getting to know and count on people who worked the land around us, farmers who were not-too-distant neighbors.

So my ultimate goal is to keep local farmers in business by increasing

their customer base. Obviously, I would do this more directly by buying their food than by growing my own. So I'm much less troubled by
the fact that I can't grow everything I eat than by the fact that I mostly
can't support local farmers by what I buy; it's usually easier to grow it
myself than to find food that is locally grown.

One day last summer, I went to the nearest giant supermarket to pick
up a couple of things and realized that I wanted apples.

AUGUST 6—I found myself feeling profoundly misplaced as I walked
through, chilled from the open freezer cases, in a kind of trance since the
store was largely empty, wondering who bought all these things. The
number of choices is simply overwhelming. . . . I started peering into
other people's carts and wondering how they decided which of the sizes
and flavors and shapes of things they chose. I got Brita filters and oat bran
muffins (there must be 14 flavors—I get mine because I can't get whole
wheat), but gave up at the frozen food section, which was even more
overwhelming—and cold (all those chilled aisles using up electricity
whose production helped warm the planet!).

And then I got some apples even though they were utterly placeless. I
went to someone in the produce section and asked whether there were
any apples from New York state. He looked at me absolutely blankly and
said "WHAAT?" I said, "Are any of your apples local, from this state? I
like to support local farmers." "I have no idea," he said with obvious
disinterest. "It might be on the box they come in." And I realized suddenly that I didn't have the energy to ask to see the manager and make
the fight. I'm a single "old lady"; the manager could have looked in my
cart and seen that I don't buy enough to be a "valued" customer. In that
brightly lit twenty aisles of stuff that I mostly don't buy, I felt too alien
and isolated to make a useful fuss.

So I bought Macintosh apples, and for all I could tell, the ones I bought
might well have been shipped across the country from Washington State,
although Macintosh is a New York State standard. But I wanted to make
Apple Pan Dowdy with my homegrown blackberries the next day, and,
after an hour of driving around New Jersey vainly looking for a simple
bamboo blind (ah, yes, the suburbs!), it seemed wasteful and irrational to
drive five miles north to Davies' Orchards to get local apples. The energy
cost—fossil and human—would have been absurd.

How difficult and time-consuming it is to try to live simply in this
culture of frenzied consumption. ShopRite was a kind of epiphany. I felt
as if I simply didn't know how to shop there, how to make choices, how
to find things. It made me feel helpless and alien. And how in hell do
people make rational choices from among all those bewildering and complex items?

And when I came home, the four hay bales I had ordered for the community garden were sitting at the end of my driveway, so I put away the groceries and then went outside to clean up the shed before the bales were moved in. I did that, reordered it, swept it out, and felt great about how it looked. I weeded some in the driveway, then I went to tie up the tomatoes that were not in cases. . . . I found myself so peaceful and happy and open-hearted at that task. I realized that ShopRite had really made me crazy. It was all so artificial and had nothing to do with food. I am overwhelmed with the realization that for most people, ShopRite is their experience with what passes for food: dead, uniform, odorless, and sanitized. How do we make people raised in such environments remember what food is? And how do we help them remember that it takes farmers to produce it?

The simplest and best idea I ever heard for beginning to support local is to spend at least $10 a week on local food, and for a few months in the summer I can do that by going to the farmers' market that a friend started in a neighboring community. There I can buy locally baked bread, farm-raised trout, locally produced tofu, local cheese, local corn (which is too space-consuming to raise in my little garden), and fruit. I can also buy local cheese and butter at the small marking in my community. And I've found a nearby place to buy local tortillas, which come fresh, three dozen for $1, produced for the large Latino population in the area. (I could have *made* local tortilla chips for Independence Day!)

But fruit remains a dilemma, especially in the winter. I paid $2.90 for a box of clementines at my nearby oriental market in January—well aware that they had been shipped in from Spain. As I stood peeling one this morning, I found myself thinking about the unsweetened grapefruit juice I regularly hunt for in the juice section of the supermarket, and my mind flipped to the issue of making responsible choices. The juice section is, of course, just one aisle of the product playland most markets have become, thirty running feet or more, loaded from floor level to its topmost shelf with canned and boxed mixes of fruit concentrates, sugar and water whose often fanciful names give only the slightest indication of their actual contents.

Even my grapefruit juice is not simply grapefruit-squeezings, but "filtered water and grapefruit juice concentrate." Here at least, the name on the package tells me fairly well what I am getting— "Unsweetened Grapefruit Juice"—and in smaller letters underneath, "from concentrate." But the juice is distributed from Chicago and carries no indication of where the grapefruit was squeezed, so I have to take all this on faith, and on signals from my own taste buds, which remain attuned to actual foods. Are most breakfast drinkers, their taste-buds blunted by "juice cocktails," prepared to detect fraud?

What was on the label of the "orange juice" made with "watery or-ange byproducts," sugar, and unapproved preservatives, which was dis-covered quite by accident several years ago to have been distributed in twenty-five states? It was manufactured in Michigan from concentrate supplied by a Chicago corporation from juice presumably extracted in Florida, California, and some other orange-growing region whence it made its way to Chicago. One can only hope that this well-travelled mixture was not marketed as "fresh." Are enough consumers left who have drunk "real" orange juice to notice?

The adulterated juice news story reported that the Food and Drug Administration was "committed to pursuing adulteration cases," but knowing what I know about understaffing at the FDA, the moral I drew from this depressing story was that if you ate from the standard U.S. food supply, you couldn't hope to employ enough policemen to make your food trustworthy. In a global marketplace, your eating and drink-ing really can't be protected from economic fraud or worse, however hard the regulatory agencies try.

When I peeled my clementine this morning, however, I wasn't wor-ried about safety or integrity. I simply wished I knew something about how many miles that fruit had traveled to get to me; I wished that something in the store could let me know its unit cost in environmental terms. I can't be self-sufficient, nor do I think I need to be. But I want to be ecologically responsible, and I would like to know which of my choices—from that juice rack, for example, or from those bins of fresh fruit—would have imposed the least burden on the environment. What did it really cost to get that pear juice to my grocer's shelf? the peach nectar? the cranberry juice (from concentrate)? Water *is* heavy to ship. Making concentrate from fruit where it grows and adding water locally would make travel sense. But adding water in Chicago and sending it east seemed not to—and where was the concentrate made?

On the face of it, apple juice would seem the winter beverage of choice in the apple-growing state I live in. But I am wary of that since the time I bought a small carton of "100% pure apple juice" from a Manhattan mini-mart and discovered on the label that it was made of concentrate from West Germany, Austria, Italy, Hungary, and Argentina. Now, I only recently learned, China has set out to be the world's leading producer of cheap apple juice. If we want to be responsible to ourselves and the planet, then the best most of us can do most of the time is to shorten the chain from the farm to our table, get as close to the producer as possible whenever we can, and for the rest, until the food system unwinds, take the chance on regulatory agencies we really don't trust.

I'm okay for vegetables year-round, pretty well off for fruits in the summer, resigned to using "imported" grains and their products (although I try not to buy pasta sent from Italy). I buy unbranded bread baked either in this country or at least in the region, but I don't know where the ingredients come from. I make my own granola from organic rolled oats, New York State–produced honey, organic cold-pressed unrefined corn or peanut oil, and a variety of nuts and seeds whose provenance I don't know (though my organic sunflower seeds come from farmer friends in North Dakota). And I buy sardines from Port Clyde, Maine, if I can find them, because that's the port from which the mailboat to the Maine island I know best leaves, and it's as local as I can get. Since New York is a dairy state, I ought to use mostly local dairy products. But except for New York State cheddar, goat cheese, and butter, until recently I had been opting for convenience over conscience.

When our children were young and we were very poor, I started making milk from skim-milk powder, and kept doing it long after it was a budgetary issue. I was troubled by the fact that the cows whose milk was dried surely weren't local and the system has never paid a decent price for their product. But I drink almost a quart of milk a day and often run out just when I want to make myself a cup of warm milk before bed. The store within walking distance is closed then, and I've told myself that driving farther afield just for milk is environmentally irresponsible. Fortunately, someone heard me say this and asked the obvious question: "Why don't you buy local organic milk for most of the time, and keep powdered milk around for emergencies?" Amazingly simple. Now I can help my state's dairy farmers—who are going broke even as I write—and still have my bedtime toddy.

And then there's the critical issue of salads. Mention local eating in the Northeast, and one of the first things most listeners want to know is what they would do for salad, by which most people mean, of course, something like the standard American salad of iceberg lettuce and tomato. If people are surveyed about how important it is for them to have certain fruits and vegetables fresh year-round, they rank lettuce and tomatoes among the most important.

It's certainly not nutrition that's driving this need. When I learned many years ago that per capita consumption of iceberg lettuce was twenty-five pounds a year, I looked up its total nutritional value. A year's supply of iceberg lettuce contains pitifully few nutrients; three to four days worth of iron, for example, and enough vitamin C for a week and a half. Yet many people seem convinced that they cannot satisfy their daily nutrient requirements without an iceberg lettuce fix.

I was so intrigued by the question of how a watery crunch of lettuce and a sectioned orange golf ball had come to represent salad that I did some research and found out that the word *salad* derives from the Latin for *salt*, and according to Maguelonne Toussaint-Samat's *A History of Food*, was first applied to a dish "popular on festive tables in fifteenth century Milan." It was a very liquid, very salty ragoût, "flavored with preserves, mustard and lemon, and decorated with marzipan." That sounds really awful, and it sure ain't lettuce.

Looking further, I came to the conclusion that the word *salad* had arrived later than the idea of eating dressed raw greens, which goes back to antiquity. Indeed, Waverley Root and Richard de Rochemont begin their history *Eating in America* with an observation that when Columbus discovered America, the Indians "were given to greens . . . which they ate raw, as salads, or popped into whatever happened to be cooking." Obviously, the "Indians" were not eating iceberg lettuce, but local greens, in season.

What salad evolved into when the home economists got hold of it toward the end of the nineteenth century comes close to a return to ragoût with marzipan. By 1920, Fannie Farmer's *Boston Cooking School Cookbook*, then in its tenth edition, contained ninety-seven salad recipes and fifteen dressings. Here is one of the recipes just as presented:

BERSHIRE SALAD IN BOXES

Marinate one cup cold boiled fowl cut into dice and one cup cooked French chestnuts broken in pieces with French Dressing. Add one grated red pepper from which seeds have been removed, one cup celery cut into small pieces, and Mayonnaise to moisten. Trim crackers (four inches long by one inch wide, slightly salted) at ends, using a sharp knife; arrange on plate in form of box, keep in place with red ribbon one-half inch wide, and fasten at one corner by tying ribbon in a bow. Garnish opposite corner with a sprig of holly berries. Line box with lettuce leaves, put in a spoonful of salad and mask with Mayonnaise. Any colored ribbon may be used and flowers substituted for berries.

I found my stomach clenching with pity at the thought of a struggling homemaker trying to tie those crackers into a box with a red (or some other color) ribbon with a bow at the center.

The salad entries in the 1934 edition of Mrs. Simon Kander's *The Settlement Cook Book* are equally appalling and require a level of obsession and skill that would daunt Martha Stewart. If "salad" in the "New World" had come to this by the early twentieth century, iceberg lettuce and tomato was surely a victory for women's liberation and nutrition.

But we have choices, even in the cold Northeast, that are neither well-travelled iceberg lettuce or Bershire Salad in Boxes. My salad research led me to Meta Given, whose *Modern Encyclopedia of Cooking* had sold 500,000 copies by the time of its sixteenth printing in February 1954. She tells us that

> people have been enjoying the foods that go into salads for four or five thousand years. . . . Raw vegetables were included in the menu for a number of reasons: their crispiness was a pleasant contrast to the soft foods in the meal; their fresh flavor seemed to highlight the whole meal; they were usually slightly tart and peppery and perked up the appetite for the foods that were eaten with them, and they were beautiful in color and form and pleased the sight as well as the appetite.

So winter salads need to be beautiful in color and form, slightly tart and peppery, and crisp—boiled or roasted beets marinated with raw onions, root vegetable slaws of infinite variety, cold dressed grains and lentils brightened with sundried tomatoes softened in vinegar, seasoned puréed dry beans with nuts for crunch—all of them more delicious and usually more nutritious than iceberg lettuce. These are some of the alternatives to winter greens in the Northeast winter.

But there is another responsible solution to the salad problem. On the Maine coast, Eliot Coleman grows "candy carrots," tiny little spears of sweetness, and a variety of cold-tolerant greens in an unheated greenhouse, with the vegetables inside covered with a light-admitting spun fabric for extra cold protection. At my house, twenty minutes north of

Manhattan, I don't even have to work that hard. I have a cold frame covered with an old 3-by-6-foot storm window that I don't manage very carefully. Mostly I just leave one edge propped open to keep the plants from overheating on sunny days when the inside temperature can go up into the nineties.

> January 14—I went out and picked a salad today. The Lollo Rosa lettuce and frisée in there is just perfect, and beautiful. Untouched by the 10° nights! A woman called about coming down to see my cold frame—saying I was the only person she had found in the Hudson Valley who had anything growing!

And out in the garden, not in the cold frame, but under a light cover of that same spun fabric (called Remay), I have a bed full of mâche, a small compact rosette of leaves that seems entirely undaunted by the cold. If I can produce these greens, farmers can grow them for all of us, but only if we're willing to pay them a reasonable amount to do so.

*

From *This Organic Life: Confessions of a Surburban Homesteader*, Joan Dye Gussow (1928–). White River Junction, Vt.: Chelsea Green Publishing Company, 2001. Gussow combines the experience of four decades of gardening in the lower Hudson Valley and a passion for healthy eating to articulate an ethics of the responsible consumer. A former Chair of the Nutrition Education Program at Columbia University Teachers College and author of *The Feeding Web*, she decries the current food politics that has generated a system in which food is grown so far from where it is consumed and trucked across the country, when more fresh foods can be grown closer to home. In her view, it wastes energy resources and impacts land use and water rights, besides allowing commercial companies to patent seeds which should be freely dispersed. Her solutions to current problems seem highly practical, starting with the encouragement of local farms to raise more crops and animals, and the revival of processing plants for food products. On a personal level, for Gussow it has meant growing as much of her own food as possible, supporting community gardens, co-ops and local farmers (even if it means paying more than at supermarkets), and searching for ways to enhance the sustainability of the food system. She is part of a growing community of activist gardeners and environmentalists calling for changes in the way America produces, distributes, and consumes its food supply.

The Sentient Garden

Jim Nollman

I HAVE BEEN SPOTTED, ON ONE OR TWO OCCA-sions, sitting in the sawdust of my own sentient garden, whispering sweet nothings to the cabbages. I'm not sure why I do this, although I recognize it as a manifestation of the co-creative point of view. It seems the natural thing to do.

This activity commenced after I discovered for myself what has been a truism for plant breeders for millennia: that every cabbage plant sprouted from the same seed packet is not identical. They may all display a common rosette pattern of nine leaves spiraling up from the center, but each one is also as unique as each human baby is unique, as unpredictable in its growth pattern as the weather that nurtures it. Two cabbage seeds planted just eighteen inches apart will grow in two different ways. One sprints to a broad four inches and then remains that way for two weeks or more. Meanwhile, the other one grows spindly. It falls prey to earwigs and slugs while its cousin has nary a mark upon it.

I pay a visit to the garden one June morning and am very surprised to notice that the two cabbage heads are about the same size. I suddenly start humming into the nonexistent ears of the two cabbages as my way of expressing an aesthetic encouragement to their growth. I sing a Tibetan mantra over and over again in the same opportunistic manner that the walrus was found to recite sweet poetry to the oysters in *Alice in Wonderland.* The act is spontaneous. There isn't meant to be much logic to it.

I stop singing and notice that the cabbage that was chewed up as a sprout has grown strong just to protect itself from further predation. This one grows quickly over the next several weeks. We harvest it at six pounds on the 1st day of July. Most of the tough outer leaves are noticeably beaten up, but the heart is as perfect as one might expect from a vigorous, healthy, organically grown cabbage.

Meanwhile, the other one is taking its sweet time to mature. The second cabbage is harvested ten days later than the first, also at six pounds. My wife shreds it into cole slaw. We sit down to dinner; my two daughters recite "blessings on the meal," and the four of us set to the task of devouring it. It tastes superb. Life is perfect. A few weeks later, at a well-attended neighborhood barbecue, I tell the story of the two cabbages to the general throng. Someone mentions the auspicious timing of the two cabbages.

"The auspicious timing? What's that supposed to mean?"

"Well, my family doesn't like to eat cabbage more than once every ten days. Does yours?"

"Well, yes, I suppose you're right."

"And ten days is what you got, isn't it? Sounds like there may be something to it."

It is at this juncture that this admitted nonexpert recently seen discussing cabbages at a friendly barbecue is now seen hurling himself boldly off the twentieth-century rationalist cliff. I land not in cool water where I am brought to my senses, but rather on the warm August soil of a 1930s cartoon world where anthropomorphic plum trees dance the cakewalk while a bounding purple cabbage points out the words of a Tibetan chant. Om Mani padme huuuuummmmmm! Some people spend their entire lives unsuccessfully trying to communicate to their spouse or their kids. Other people firmly believe that the government should invest more of the so-called defense dividend into communicating with dolphins because that species holds the key to planetary bliss. This crazy gardener wants you to believe that cabbages do it just as often. And just as well.

I am standing in the center of the sentient garden. This time it's February. I have wandered down the deer path to my sentient plum tree and wish I knew a way to ask it if its actions really do affect the deer's actions. And vice versa. Or it's September. I wear a foolish grin as I start singing an old Beatles tune—"Will you still need me, will you still feed me, when I'm sixty-four?"—to a row of broccoli. Or it's June. I stand before a flower bed and offer congratulations to the gallica rose Belle de Crecy, for honoring me with such an incredible display of color, shape, and fragrance. The arrangement of petals seems perfect, and yet the flowers are so much smaller than I ever imagined a perfect rose could be. Or it's October, and I find myself verbally apologizing to one of those same broccolis before harvesting the head.

But it's too easy to turn metaphysically effusive. Let us turn skeptical instead. What other stretches of elasticized logic might just as easily explain the case of the synchronized cabbages? There are many other explanations. For instance, let no one underestimate the power of circumstance. It could just as easily have been a coincidence. For that matter, if I orchestrated the ripening moment of the two cabbages, I must have also modified the eating habits of several insect predators. Do I believe my little mantras have altered the culinary druthers of local slugs and cabbage moth larvae? And how do I explain the fact that a nearby willow casts a slight shadow over the more northerly cabbage? Did I test the chemical variations in the soil? And why am I so unwilling to acknowledge that genetics played some part in this drama?

In other words, a simple scientific query easily evinces any number of other factors affecting the ripening times of cabbages. Evidence also suggests that I may be suffering from a common malady known as after-the-fact wishful thinking. I stand guilty of applying cause-and-effect sentience to my own desires. All may be true. Yet I still insist upon talking and listening to the plants. I sometimes wonder if I can affect four cabbages over thirty days next summer as I did two over ten days this summer.

There is something more at stake here than simply trying to justify why a gardener might wish to talk to plants. Traditional peoples around the world have always asserted that the process of food gathering is an act of gift giving from prey to person. It is said that the spirit of the gift increases even as the body of the gift is consumed. The predator who expresses gratitude for the gift receives more gifts. The predator who forgets to acknowledge the gift suffers dire consequences. Lest this relationship be misunderstood out of context, let it be known that in the above story, I am a predator of cabbages. Cabbage is my prey.

Why is this important? Many aboriginal critics of contemporary culture believe that the environmental crisis is exacerbated by our own culture's neglect to honor the profound gift given *from* prey *to* predator. But how can we be expected to honor something we do not recognize? In fact, there can be no honoring until we first learn to acknowledge the consciousness of other creatures. This is the reason that Inuit people in the High Arctic express real fear over the consequences of a dominant civilization bent on denying the value of common aboriginal beliefs about animal and plant consciousness. They believe that unless modern people are able to revitalize and redefine these same aboriginal perceptions about ecosystems existing as neigbborhoods—and on a global scale—none of us has much hope of surviving. To the traditional person, the very idea of animal and plant consciousness promotes an atmosphere of mutual esteem across species. It instills humility wherever the relationship is honored. No matter if this relationship is sung, danced, touched, carved, planted, worn, hugged, dug, or eaten, it is always honored.

Paradoxically, the positive effect this ancient spiritual repertoire *could* excert on our society (such as treating food as a conscious gift from plants and animals) may be more important to the welfare of the planet in this late twentieth century than our society's unswerving desire to debunk it wherever it rears its nonlinear head. One might rightly wonder about our own skewed sense of "progress" that replaces traditional values with cold hard data—no matter how much wisdom the original belief granted to its believers, their families, and their communities. But let it also be understood that honoring the gift between predator and prey, recognizing the sentience of all life, is not the same thing as glorifying the primitive. To regard them as a paraphrase of each other only trivializes what is a genuine modern longing to reconnect with the natural world. Reconnecting is what biocentrism is all about. And biocentrism is rising fast as the reality for our children's generation.

In that sense, I like to believe my cabbage anecdote offers a kind of ecological *myth* (like the well-known case of the one-hundredth monkey) whose value—as with most myths—sometimes offers more to a person than its debunking ever could. I *wish* to believe in this idea of negotiated relations between human and nature because it enhances my

life. Thus I continually find myself promoting its expression, even if
my logical education constantly reminds me I may have my head
screwed on backward. No matter, this belief makes more sense to me
than the predominant depiction of nature as a vat full of names, catego-
ries, and resources.

Nor am I unaware of the fact that those of us who exalt cabbages
may be guilty of grabbing at the same proverbial straws as William
Kirby, who exalted the lowly louse in a parallel attempt to explain his
own new worldview to denizens of the old. Yet the more we face up to
these very personal biases, the more we discover that the relationship
between ourselves and such as cabbages and plum trees and deer is just
as much about truth as it is about ethics, simple faith, or even about the
postmodern philosophy that depicts every view of reality as a personal
preference. In such a manner, it becomes our working reality.

There is an old saying: If you look too hard, paradise disappears. If
this is true, there is a risk to scrutinizing the sentient garden too inten-
sively. Yet there are still important questions waiting to be answered.
For instance, if not circumstance, if not weather, if not soil chemistry,
if not genetics, then how *do* I explain the cabbages ripening at such a
perfect ten-day interval?

Unfortunately, it is here that my reasoning turns most recondite. I
have no clear answer, although, inscrutably, that is not quite the same
thing as admitting I do not know. What I did was visualize an unspoken
(and mostly subconscious) wish to have the harvest turn out well.
Sounds innocuous enough. Regard it as a simple gardener's prayer
mumbled directly to the sentient garden. But this is no hocus-pocus; I
offer no burnt offerings to the god of this garden, don no feathers, bend
no elbows to the four directions. Nor do I possess any hidden agenda
of promoting myself as the next generation of consciousness athlete. Or
perhaps I make too much of an event that occurred only once. The
scientific method would beg me to repeat the experiment next year, and
then again the year after that. Not a bad idea.

Which halfheartedly leads to a final series of questions. Cooperating
cabbages is one thing, but claiming a unified conscience for the entire
garden seems quite another. If what I contend is true, at what point in
the process of constructing a garden from scratch does this bold leap to
consciousness presumably occur? Is it sudden? Gradual? And to what
extent is the mind of the gardener tangled up in the process? Is it just

gardens that are loved intensely, sweated over profusely, or admired roundly that gain consciousness?

In fact, all such questions remind me of Victor Frankenstein sewing body parts together, giving them a jolt of electricity, and then forever agonizing how to regain control over a creation who had started making real demands on his peace of mind. This entire line of thought leads nowhere because it presupposes that we sentient gardeners promote a robotic (herbotic?) garden—some kind of naive pop mysticism for the horticultural set. This is not a case of listening to birds sing and hearing cabbages. Permit me to swap the word *garden* for *art*, below, and thus paraphrase author Ken Wilber as he paraphrases Schopenhauer to express the same idea this way:

> Bad gardens copy, good gardens create, great gardens transcend. What all great gardens have in common are their ability to pull the sensitive viewer out of him or herself and into the garden, so completely that the separate self-sense disappears entirely, and at least for a brief moment one is ushered into a nondual and timeless awareness. A great garden, in other words, is mystical no matter what its actual content.
>
> *(Grace and Grit)*

Or regard another image taken from Keith Thomas's *Man and the Natural World*, which earlier gave us sweet-smelling horse manure and instructive lice:

> One of the most treasured memories of an old lady friend of mine, recently deceased, was of her visits, some sixty years or more ago, to a great countryhouse . . . and of her host, who was then old, the head of an ancient and distinguished family, and of his reverential feeling for his old trees. His greatest pleasure was to sit out of doors of an evening in sight of the grand old trees in his park, and before going in he walked round to visit them, one by one, and resting his hand on the bark he would whisper good night. He was convinced, he confided to his young guest, who often accompanied him in these evening walks, that they had intelligent souls and knew and encouraged his devotion.
>
> (W. H. Hudson, *Far Away and Long Ago*)

An old man wanders around his garden a hundred years ago, chats up the trees, and charms his young friend, who herself has recently died of old age. The image demonstrates that a sentient garden transcends purely ethical inclinations to do good work or good foraging or even attain a reintegration of activities. Here is an image of the sentient garden as a *charmed* garden where all the myriad parts—including the human part—interpenetrate to create a sense of place. The gardener who acquires such a sense connects more closely to the divine mystery of life.

*

From *Why We Garden: Cultivating a Sense of Place*, Jim Nollman (1947–). New York: Henry Holt and Company, 1994. Any gardener who sings the Beatles' song, "Will you still need me, will you still feed me, when I'm sixty-four?," to a row of broccoli surely has a special relationship with his plants. Nollman, in fact, seeks out their "personalities," preferring individual growing characteristics to the objectivity of scientific names. He wonders why garden literature is mostly silent about the intuitive relationships of gardeners to their gardens. Questioning the lack of acknowledgment of "place" in the Judeo-Christian heritage, he looks to Native American and Asian teachings that consider heaven and Earth as equally sacred and nature a living rather than inert mass under human control. In a style that blurs the distinction between nature writing and garden writing, Nollman's spiritual perspective is rooted in the politics of the local—his own garden on an island in Washington's Puget Sound—at the same time that it addresses global environmental issues.

Purslane and Immortality

Sara B. Stein

To rip a weed from the earth is satisfying. There is a pale, crackling sound heard in the head and felt in the hand as the tenderest root fibers break from their holdfasts; then a bright, cheery crunch as the clump itself gives way. I like the weightiness of the clump; I like the way the weight lightens as the soil, shaken out, beaten out, spatters its sustenance back to ground. There is a fine sensation of murder.

But is an uprooted weed dead? A person is dead when vital organs fail, when heartbeats cease and brain waves flatten. Plants have no comparable organs. They have structures—roots, leaves, stems—that are like organs in that they are organized. But these structures are, at least in the short run, not vital to life. A person in pieces is certainly not alive, but a daisy cut from its roots and stripped of its leaves lives on in a glass of water. I have seen bees pollinate a vase of wild roses, and kept tabs on these rootless remnants as their petals fell, their ovaries swelled into young fruits. A banana plucked green continues to convert its acids and starches to sugars unaware that it is off its tree. It is still alive when ripe, and eaten. Presumably, it lives for a while in the stomach. Why not?

The test for death in a plant is breathing: as long as a weed respires, it lives, and it respires as long as it has the chemicals to do so. The chemical most likely to run out first is water. On a hot day, out in the strong sun, pulled-up weeds die of desiccation.

The gardener, however, may only think he has uprooted a weed, or may too carelessly assume he has exposed it to dying. Many weeds, and grasses especially, can get enough moisture from a single root left in the ground to support the plant until new roots can be sent to soil. A weed uprooted entirely, but left root side down in a moist or shady spot, may well have time to do the same. Or it may rain. I'm sure a creeping grass, even if left with its roots in the air, simply turns them down and digs back in during a drizzle.

Purslane, whose stems and leaves are plumped with juice and waxed against dessication, can husband water long enough to ripen seeds. By the time this succulent weed shrivels in the sun, its mission is completed, its seeds are sown. Purslane multiplies faster than it dies.

Purslane is an annual, like crabgrass and ragweed. Annuals live for one year, no more, and frequently much less. Biennials have a two-year life span. Their first summer is spent as a bouquet, a nosegay, the furry rosette of a young mullein, or the bunchy cluster of leaves that is a first-season burdock. The bouquet arrangement, in which each leaf radiating from the crown is nicely spread to the sun, maximizes the amount of light the weed receives and minimizes the amount of energy that would otherwise have to be distributed along avenues of stems and branches. The weed concentrates growth underground, that first year, in fleshy storage roots, taproots like edible biennial beets, turnips, and carrots. The second summer mullein and burdock throw their hoarded energy into tall flowering stems, go to seed, and die exhausted. Queen Anne's lace, the wild carrot, is seldom noticed until its blossoms bloom the second year. Domesticated carrots would bloom like that the summer after planting if the gardener didn't rob their pantry for himself. Parsley, a close carrot relative, is grown for its first-year nosegay of crenellated leaves.

Annuals and biennials are considered to have a predetermined life span, a built-in schedule for their youth, their flowering into maturity, their senescence, and their death. So do humans, who, no matter what the circumstances of their lives, must be children for thirteen years or so, come to sexual maturity on schedule, and get stiff in the joints before they die a natural death. But many biennials can become annual when it suits them, and vice versa. Shepherd's purse that germinates too late in the season to bloom before winter snugs in for the cold season as a rosette, then blooms and dies the following summer, like a biennial. The same seed germinating in spring rushes into bloom and does its stuff in a single season, like an annual. Two common species of plantain, narrow-leaved and broad-leaved, are described respectively as an annual that becomes perennial, and a perennial that is sometimes annual. A plantain that lives, blooms, and seeds all in a single summer in North Dakota may not bother to grow up during its first year in California, and needn't die so young. This flexible life plan is comparable to deciding as a child that life is risky, and one had best start a family as a schoolchild to assure one's lineage or, alternatively, that circumstances are so good as to warrant waiting.

A friend of mine from Trinidad was disappointed at the behavior of pole beans in the North. Back home in the Caribbean bean vines grow for years, climbing high into trees, where, as a boy, he used to climb to pick them. Tomatoes, eggplants, and peppers, all annuals here, are perennials in their warmer native lands. Their life span depends on the weather.

The potential life span of a species, the length of time it can live under the best of circumstances, is genetically determined. Because genes can change, life spans can evolve. Unlike that of other mammals, the life span of humans extends beyond their reproductive years, presumably because grandparents, spoilers of grandchildren, contribute something to the ultimate success of their youngest descendants, who in turn carry forward whatever it was that made their helpful grandparents live so long. Mice have evolved an opposite strategy. A female house mouse is sexually mature at the age of one month, might give birth three weeks later, usually gets pregnant again on the day the first litter is born, and gives birth for a second time on the day the firstborn are weaned. Mice, a basic food of almost every predator there is, behave as though there is no tomorrow because for most of them there isn't. Their sexual precocity evolved under the pressure of certain and swift mortality. The Ice Age had the same effect on certain plants.

Back before the Ice Age, when climate was reliably warm year round and alligators basked in Nebraska, grains that grew around the Mediterranean were perennial grasses. They matured at a leisurely rate and lived for years. As climate deteriorated, those individuals that matured quickest, that got off their seed before the cold got them, became more numerous. Ultimately some such species were made up exclusively of sexually precocious plants, mousy annuals. Mortality is thus an accommodation to circumstances.

Not all populations chanced upon that fatalistic strategy. Garden centers sell seed of annual ryegrass that one can plant assured of its transcience; of winter ryegrass that behaves like Shepherd's purse and is used as a manure crop, sown in fall, plowed into the ground in spring; and of perennial ryegrass that grows into a permanent lawn. The genes that control such things as speed of maturation and the ability to survive dormant through cold or drought can be passed around among varieties and even among related species to alter the behavior of the hybrid offspring. Annual wheat could be bred back to perennial wheat if we wanted to wait longer for our bread.

The genetic instructions of some plants apparently lack any information at all about how to get old and die. The American Museum of Natural History has on exhibit a slice of giant sequoia trunk labeled with the dates of growth rings at hundred-year intervals. It germinated from a seed weighing less than one three-thousandth of an ounce in the year 550. The tree was a stripling when the last wave of barbarians overwhelmed Roman civilization. Its trunk was five feet in diameter when the Normans invaded England, ten feet when Columbus discovered America, and sixteen feet when it met an untimely death at the hands of lumbermen in 1891. During its 1,342-year life, it had grown to sixty-five billion times its original weight, or nine tons. The giant did not give up its life easily. It took two men thirteen days to fell it with axes. There are bristlecone pines still living that germinated four thousand years ago, back in the Bronze Age. The oldest of these living trees show no sign of senility, no hint that they are slipping toward their end. Murder aside, the fact that they ever die is apparently an accident—a disease, an avalanche, a bolt of lightning.

A gripping garden tale is Mea Allan's account in *The Englishwoman's Garden* of restoring a neglected garden in Suffolk, England, and researching its history. An olive tree proved almost undoubtedly to have come from the John Tradescants, elder and younger, who were gardeners to Charles I in the seventeenth century, and famous plant collectors. The olive species was inventoried among the plants propagated in their London nursery garden in 1634. Miss Allan's specimen, apparently a gift from the Tradescants to Suffolk kinsmen, was judged by botanists to be at least three centuries old. The Tradescants' plant lists noted a yellow jasmine collected from Russia in 1618. That, too, grew in Miss Allan's garden, and so did "Tradescant's great rose daffodil," identified from an old botanical print.

Mea Allan pointed out that this many-petaled daffodil cannot reproduce by seed. It hands on its genes by cloning bulblets around the original bulb. Presuming that plants arising from these bulblets were identical to the original one, Miss Allan was satisfied that the daffodils that bloom in her ancient garden are in effect those planted in the 1600s, even though the central bulbs from which they grew no longer exist. No one keeps records on wild garlic. Who knows how old my bulblets are?

No clone feels its age. Whatever clock times the normal life span of a garlic plant is rewound in every bulblet. The same is true of other clones, of sprouting snips of stem and root, pieces of purslane. Each turns the clock back to infancy, rejuvenated by amputation.

My son in agricultural school told me that our apple trees, densely planted to form the bosque my husband had envisioned as the second axis in his grand scheme, were rejuvenations of eldery clones. I called Jim Lawson, purveyor of old-time apples, to check this out. He told me about an elderly woman—he figured she was in her eighties—who came to him with a problem about her granddaddy's tree. It was what she called a Tenderrind apple, and it was getting pretty old. Mr. Lawson grafted bits of the old tree to new rootstock. When the youngsters fruited some years later, he sent the apples to a meeting of the North American Fruit Explorers in Geneva, New York. They identified them as Tenderskin apples brought over by the early settlers, and thought to be extinct. The oldest clone Mr. Lawson could recollect offhand dates from the sixteenth century. Its name is Rambo.

In 1937 researchers in France began an experiment in the potential immortality of plants. They obtained cells from the interior of a carrot and induced them to live and divide in a nutrient medium, where each cell formed a mass of embryonic carrot callus. Forty years later, the tissue is still alive and growing, although the carrot from which it was taken would have lived no longer than two years. Cells from the callus remember everything they knew four decades ago. They can be induced to shift from their shapeless sort of growth to organized growth:

each cell can grow into a complete carrot plant. But mortality is a part of the new carrot's total recall. At the age of two, it dies.

Unless its recollection has been foiled by removal of its flower buds. Without a substance produced by its own flowers, the plant never learns that it is supposed to senesce. Ignorant of its age, it lives on, perennially.

Thinking about this brings on a giddiness of the mind, a sensation akin to the once-upon-a-time elation of spinning in a swivel chair. The immortal carrot dies when some substance or substances, which it can make but is not necessarily obliged to make, inhibits it from living. Death is not a passive acquiescence to the passage of years, but an active halting, performed by the individual, a suicide.

One night I stayed up late with my night-owl oldest son talking about death. Why, if senescence requires some chemical complexity to bring it about, should mortality have evolved? What is the point of dying? He developed a theory. The longer an individual lives, the greater the chance that genes in both cloning cells and sexually-reproducing ones will be damaged. The offspring of immortals would be monsters. Individuals that evolved a mechanism for dying in effect protected their genes, handed them on whole to wholesome descendants. The idea put dying in a new light. To die is altruistic. Yet it is also, on the contrary, the ultimately selfish act, because it best preserves integrity.

There is another way of looking at mortality, and it strikes to the heart of a troubling issue: When does a life begin? I was startled years ago to hear a physicist grumble at the naïveté of students who ask, "What was there before the universe began?" To a physicist, such a question is not askable. Time began when the universe began; there is no "before." To a biologist, the question of when a life begins is similarly naïve. Nothing living has ever been dead. Every life can trace its livingness in an unbroken line to the very first living organisms, and perhaps even further to organisms that, because they lived so differently from those today, we might fail to recognize as alive. No seed, or egg and sperm, from which a new life grows was ever dead, not in four billion years. There is no gap to life, even though life that first fermented in bacteria now respires in oak trees.

Not that individuals haven't died without reproducing offspring to reproduce in turn, and therefore have failed to hand on their lives, but nobody is descended from those bodies that failed. Any life alive today is here because countless ancestors, one after another after another, handed life on to the next generation. That's what weeds, cloning and seeding, are trying to do, and I'm sure many are succeeding. Who am I anyway to chop them from their destiny? What if someone had come along and slain the dragons from which my kind is descended? I have seen pictures of those reptiles, therapsids whose sweat glands were beginning to make milk, whose cold bodies were heating up under scales becoming fur when the world was deep in dinosaurs, and I might easily have made a dreadful mistake if I had been around then and seen a hairy therapsid galumphing toward me and had had a shotgun handy to wipe out him or her, and any possibility of me. Who knows what future lurks in the genes of weeds?

Judging by how much energy is left in our star, our sun, this planet has about as long a future as it has had a past, and I'm not about to judge purslane's potential over that period of time. So some stems clone, some seeds escape. So what.

*

From *My Weeds: A Gardener's Botany*, Sara B. Stein (1935–). New York: Harper & Row, Publishers, 1988. One January, Stein was envisioning her new azalea garden, led on by the seductive pages of a catalogue that exuded fresh aromas along with its images. When spring arrived, reality offered a harsh reinterpretation of her dreams. The young azaleas were overwhelmed by so many towering weeds. She did what any curious writer-gardener, who had already written on evolution, biology, physical fitness, and aging, would do. She decided to write a book about weeds, being of the opinion that "gardens grow weeds, but plans omit them, books don't mention them, photographs don't show them, and gardeners don't know much about them, although they spend as much time killing weeds as growing food and flowers." She set about studying, researching, planting, until she developed an intimacy with her garden through struggling with it, unsentimentally. She asked questions like, "Where does weed wisdom reside?" "Who knows what future lurks in the genes of weeds?" Stein found some answers in thinking about sex and garlic. Purslane was the starting point for ruminating on the question of time and the life span of plant and human species.

INDEX

This index is primarily a listing of notable people, books and essays, gardens, organizations. Books by authors of the individual selections follow in each biographical note, and only those mentioned by other authors are included here.

Abby Aldrich Rockefeller Garden, 274
Adams, John, 244
Addison, John, 249
Agricultural Society, The (South Carolina), 182
Allen, Gay and Asselineau, Roger, *St. John de Crèvecoeur: The Life of an American Farmer*, 19
American Horticulturist magazine, 284
American Philosophical Society, 169, 182
American Seed Trade Association (ASTA), 147
American Society of Landscape Architects, 274, 316
Augustine, St., 319; *Confessions*, 298
Antoinette, Marie, 312
Arnold Arboretum (Cambridge), 204, 209, 223, 274
Asgrow Seed Co., 148
Ashbridge, 250
Austen, Jane, 315

Bacon, Francis, "Of Gardens," 8, 32, 248, 276; "Naturall Historie," 33
Bailey Hortorium, 132
Bailey, Liberty Hyde, 124-33, 226; *Hortus*, 78, 81, 133; *Manual of Cultivated Plants*, 41
Banister, John, 111-2
Banks, Sir Joseph, 313
Bardswell, Mrs. Frances Anne, *The Herb Garden*, 39
Barton, Benjamin Smith, 212-3; *Elements of Botany*, 188
Bartram, John, 13-19, 41, 112, 161-70, 179, 211
Bartram, William, 112, 169, 171-80, 188, 211; *Travels Through North and South Carolina, Georgia, East and West Florida*, 211
Battersea Park (London), 113, 115-6
Beaufort, Duchess of, 312
Beauvais, Abbott of, 316
Beecher, Henry Ward, 50-4

Belfield Farm, 244
Belle Isle Park, 270
Berry, Wendell, 67-70
Betts, Edwin Morris, 243
Bierstadt, Albert, 271
Bigelow, Jacob, 231-3
Biltmore Estate, 270
Blackwell, Elizabeth, 315
Blenheim, 250
Boorstin, Daniel, 244
Botanic gardens: Cambridge, 189; Denver, 278; Memphis, 278
Boyceau, 312
Brainard, DeWitt Clinton, 105
Breintnall, Joseph, 162
Bridgeman, Thomas, 55-9
Brimmer, George W., 231-3
Bromeliad Society, The, 198
Bromfield, Louis, 318-20
Brooklyn Botanical Garden, The, 42
Broughton, Lady, 312
Brown, Capability, xix, 264
Browning, Elizabeth Barrett, 122, 263
Bryant, Edwin, 194
Bryant, William Cullen, 271
Buist, Robert, 116
Burnett, Frances Hodgson, 225
Burpee, W. Atlee, Co., 148

California Institute of Technology, 274
Calvino, Italo, *The Baron in the Trees*, xviii
Candolle, Alphonse de, *Origin of Cultivated Plants*, 41
Capitol Grounds, 253, 270
Carrel, Alexis, *Man the Unknown*, 62
Carver, George Washington, 279
Catesby, Mark, 112, 164, 169; *The Natural*

History of Carolina, Florida, and the Bahama Islands, 169
Cato, Carl, 282
Cato, Marcus Porcius, 295
Central Park, 235-6, 253, 265-71
Charles III, King of Spain, 35
Charlotte, Queen, 313
Chatsworth, 250
Clayton, John, 166, 169
Colden, Cadwallader, 164-6, 169
Colden, Jane, 170, 313
Cole, Thomas, 252
Coleridge, Samuel Taylor, 180
Colette, 153, 157
Collinson, Peter, 161-5, 169
Conard-Pyle Co., 157
Correvon, Henry, *Le Jardin de l'Herboriste*, 41
Country-Life Commission, 133
Crèvecoeur, Michel-Guillaume St. John de, 13-9, 37, 182
Culpeper, Nicholas, 41; *Complete Herbal and English Physician*, 81
Curtis's Botanical Magazine, 216
Cushing, Frank Hamilton, 44-9

Dalibard, Thomas, 167-9
Dana, Frances T., 138-9
Dana, Richard Henry, 123; *Two Years Before the Mast*, 189
Darlington, William, 168
Darwin, Charles, 132, 322
David, Abbé Armand, 209; *Abbé David's Diary*, 43
DeKalb Hybrid Wheat, 148
Democritus, 308
Desert Seed Co., 148
Dillenius, Johan Jacob, 166, 169
Dorman, Caroline, *Flowers Native to the Deep South*, 81
Douglas, David, 199-202, 217
Downing, Andrew Jackson, 125, 131, 233-6, 245-53, 258, 264, 271
Drake, Sir Francis, 87
Dumbarton Oaks (Washington, D.C.), 272-5, 316

Earle, Alice Morse, 5-12, 259; *Old Time Gardens*, 317
Eckbo, Garrett, 276-8
El Paso International Airport, 278
Elgin Botanic Garden, 215, 217
Ellwanger and Barry Nursery, 220
Emerson, Ralph Waldo, 123, 189
Enslen, Aloysius, 214
Evelyn, Charles, *Lady's Recreation*, 310
Evelyn, John, 292
Ewing, Juliana Horatia, 314

Fabre, J. Henri, 327
Fairchild Tropical Garden (Miami), 226
Fairchild, David, 218-226
Farrand, Beatrix, 272-5, 316; *Beatrix Farrand's American Landscapes*, 274
Fernie, William, *Herbal Simples*, 41
Field, Henry, Seed and Nursery, 148
Food and Agriculture Organization (FAO), 146
Fothergill, John, 179, 211
Fox, Helen Morgenthau, 39-43
Francis, St. (of Assisi), 319
Franklin, Benjamin, 165-9, 179; *Poor Richard*

Improved, 169
Fresno Mall, 278
Friend, Hilderic, *Flowers and Flower Lore*, 78
Funk's Seed, 148

Garden Club of America, 66
Garden Club of Virginia, 281-2
George III, King of England, 15, 169
Gerard, John, *Grete Herball*, 30, 41, 85
Girardin, Louis-Rene, *De la Composition des Paysages*, 250
Graines des Plantes Officinales, 40
Gray, Asa, 132, 271
Greeley, Horace, 271
Greene, J.L., *Time's Unfading Garden*, 284
Greenwood, 234, 236
Gregory, St. (the Great), 316
Grieve, Mrs. Maude, 41
Gronovius, Joannes Fredericus, 165, 167; *Flora Virginica*, 169
Gurney's Seed and Nursery, 148

Hall, Captain, 229-30, 233
Hamilton, William, 212, 237-9, 244
Hampton, F.A., *The Scent of Flowers and Leaves*, 41; *The Toilet of Flora*, 41
Harris, Joseph, Company, 148, 155
Hassam, Childe, 123
Hawthorne, Nathaniel, 123
Hazlitt, William, 19
Hedrick, U.P., 54; *The History of Horticulture in America to 1860*, 94
Henderson, Peter, 113-7; *Manual of Floriculture*, 256-7
Henry Doubleday Research Association (HDRA), 146
Hillside Garden Club (Lynchburg), 281-2
Hoffmann, Georg Franz, *Flora Germanica*, 215
Holland, Lady, 312
Horticulture magazine, 137
Horticulturist, The magazine, 233, 253
Hosack, David, 215-7
Howard, Sir Albert, *An Agricultural Testament*, 60-1, 63
Hudson's Bay Company, 194, 202
Hunnewell, H.H., 115-6

Indiana Farmer and Gardener magazine, 54
Indiana Horticultural Society, 54
International Union for the Protection of New Varieties of Plants (UPOV), 145-47
Irving, Washington, 271; *Astoria*, 189

Jackson & Perkins, 156-7
James, Henry, 264
Janiculum Hill, 272
Jardin du Roi, 37
Jefferson, Thomas, 95, 182, 237-44
Jekyll, Gertrude, 7, 274, 314, 316
Jewett, Sarah Orne, 123; *Country Byways*, 5; *A Mournful Villager*, 10
Johnson, Thomas, 85
Josephine, Empress, 312
Josselyn, John, 85-90; *New-Englands Rarities Discovered*, 85-6, 89-90

Kalm, Peter, 41, 166-7
Kent, William, 249

Kew Gardens, 313
King, Louisa Yeomans, 65-6
Krutch, Joseph Wood, 321-8; *The Gardener's World*, xx

La Quintinie, Jean Baptiste de, 307
Lacy, Allen, 82, 297-301
Lafayette, Marquis de, 35, 37
Lamb, Charles, 19
Laurel Hill, 234
Lawrence, D.H., 19
Lawrence, Elizabeth, 75-82
Lawrence, John, *New System... A Complete Body of Husbandry and Gardening*, 311
Lawson, John, 107-12
Lawson, William, *Countrie Housewife*, 310
Le Conte, John, 216
Le Nôtre, André, 43, 247, 315
Leighton, Ann, 229-236; *American Gardens in the Eighteenth Century*, 112
Lévi-Strauss, Claude, 49
Lewis and Clark Expedition, 95, 182, 188, 213, 217, 244
Lewis, Meriwether, 213-4, 241-2
Library Company, The (Philadelphia), 161
Lille, Abbé de, "Les Jardins," 250
Linnaeus, Carolus, 18-9, 165-7, 169, 313
Lodi Park (Delhi), 278
Logan, Martha, *Gardener's Kalendar*, 315
Loudon, John C., 248, 252, 312
Louis XIV, King of France, 246, 307
Lowell, James Russell, 123, 254
Lutyens, Edwin, 316
Luxembourg Gardens, 312
Lyon, John, 212, 215

M'Mahon, 91-5, 125-7, 129, 188, 214, 242, 244, 251-2; *The American Gardener's Calendar*, 94, 125, 251
Malabar Farm, 320
Malmaison, 312
Markham, Gervase, 6
Marshall, Humphry, *Treatise on the Forest-trees of North America*, 211
Mason, George, *Essay on Design in Gardening*, 249
Mason, W., "The English Garden," 249
Massachusetts Horticultural Society, The, 40, 231-3
Mather, Cotton, 229
Medici, Marie de, 312
Merck's Index of Fine Chemicals and Drugs, 41
Michaux, André, 179, 181-3, 217; *Flora Boreali-Americana*, 188, 212, 215
Michaux, François André, 179, 181-4, 188-9; *North American Sylva*, 184, 188-9
Middleton Place (South Carolina), 183
Miller, Philip, *The Gardener's Dictionary*, 161, 166, 169
Milton, John, *Paradise Lost*, 248
Missions: La Purisima Concepcion, 192; San Buenaventura, 192-3; San Diego de Alcala, 192, 196; San Fernando, 192, 194, 196; San Gabriel Archangel, 192, 194, 196; San Juan Capistrano, 192, 196; San Luis Rey de Francia, 192, 196; San Xavier, 190-1; Santa Barbara, 192-4, 196; Santa Ines, 192; Soledad, 193
Mitchell, Henry, 71-4
Monardes, Nicholas, 87
Montagu, Lady Mary Wortley, 309

Montaigne, Michel, 31
Monticello (Virginia), 237-44, 284
Morrison, Benjamin Yoe, 42
Mount Auburn, 232-35
Mount Lebanon, 105-6
Mount Royal Park, 270
Mount Vernon (Virginia), 34-7, 284
Mount, The, 264, 274
Mühlenberg, Rev. Dr., 211
Murray, Lady Charlotte, *The British Garden*, 315

National Register of Historic Places, 280
National Seed Storage Laboratory (NSSL), 147, 151
New Farm, The, magazine, 64
New York Botanical Garden, The, 42-3
New York State College of Agriculture, 132
Niagara Falls, 271
Northrup King Co., 148
Nuttall, Thomas, 95, 184-9, 200, 214, 217

Oberlin College, 274
Office of Seed and Plant Introduction, 220, 225
Olmsted, Frederick Law, 265-71
Organic Gardening magazine, 64

Padilla, Victoria, 190-8
Panama Pacific Exposition, 207
Park, George W. Seed Company, 155; *Park's Flower Book*, 155
Park, Bertram, *Guide to Roses*, 156
Parkinson, John, 79, 85, 138, 311; *Herbal*, 41; *Paradisi in Sole*, 41, 311
Parkinson Society, 314
Parkyns, George I., 238
Parmentier, André, 252
Parrish, Maxfield, 264
Pavillion Colombe, 264
Peale, Charles Willson, 243-4
Pennsylvania Horticultural Society, The, 95
Pepys, Samuel, 302
Perényi, Eleanor, 296, 306-17
Peter Henderson & Company, 116
Petre, Lord, 166
Pettingill, Amos, 20-8
Pfeiffer, Ehrenfried, *Bio-Dynamic, Farming and Gardening*, 61
Picturesque Pocket Companion, 233
Piesse, George, *The Art of Perfumery*, 41
Pilat, Ignaz A., 265-71
Plant Variety Protection Act of 1970, 147
Pliny the Elder, 7, 30, 138; *Natural History*, 41
Pliny the Younger, 309
Pompadour, Mme. de, 312
Pope, Alexander, "On Verdant Sculpture," 249
Poplar Forest, 243
Poucher, William, *Perfumes, Cosmetics and Soaps*, 41
Poughkeepsie Garden Club, 41
Powell, John Wesley, 49
Prevention magazine, 64
Price, Uvedale, 252; *Essays on the Picturesque*, 249
Princeton University, 274
Pursh, Frederick, 210-17

Raleigh, Sir Walter, 87
Redouté, Pierre Joseph, 183
Rehder, Alfred, *Manual of Cultivated Trees and Shrubs*, 41

Reid, Hugo, 195
Repton, Humphry, 252, 264; *Observations on the Theory and Practice of Landscape Gardening*, 250
Riley, Charles V., 323, 326
Robinson, William, 274; *The English Flower Garden*, 117
Rodale Research Center, 64
Rodale, J.l., 60-4
Rohde, Eleanor Sinclair, *A Garden of Herbs*, 41; *Old English Gardening Books*, 30; *The Story of the Garden*, 311
Roosevelt, Theodore, 133, 264
Rousseau, Jean Jacques, 19, 315, 319
Rowntree, Lester, 140-44
Royal Botanic Garden (Dresden), 217
Royal Botanic Gardens (Edinburgh), 42
Royal Horticultural Society (London), 202
Ruskin, John, 252

Sakamoto, Motozo, 206, 208
Salvidea, Padre, 195
Santa Barbara Botanic Garden, 275
Sargent, Charles S., 209, 223, 274
Sargent, H.W., 115
Savage, Henry, Jr. and Elizabeth J., *André and François André Michaux*, 183
Schling, Max, Inc., 24
Scott, Frank, 254-9
Seed Savers Exchange, 145-52
Serra, Padre Junipero, 191, 197
Sévigné, Mme. de, 315
Shakers, 96-106
Shipman, Ellen Biddle, 316
Shoals Marine Laboratory, 123
Sissinghurst, 72
Smithsonian Institution, 253
Solymosy, Sigmond, 78, 80
Spencer, Anne, 279-84
Steiner, Rudolf, 64
Stewart, Charles D., 327
Stout, A.B., 43
Stowe, Harriet Beecher, 123
Sturtevant, Edward L., *Notes on Edible Plants*, 41
Suzuki, H., 204, 218
Swain, Roger B., 134-7, 152

Taft, Mrs. William Howard, 220-2
Temple, William, 249; *Garden of Epicurus*, 311
Thaxter, Celia, 118-23
Theophrastus, 41; *Inquiry into Plants*, 33
Thorburn, George, 116
Thoreau, Henry David, 123, 287-96, 320
Tracy, W.W., Jr., *American Varieties of Vegetables*, 151
Tradescants, John I and John II, 314
Tresco Abbey, 71-72
Trollope, Mrs. Frances, 230
Tusser, Thomas, 313
Twickenham, 242

Ulrica, Queen of Sweden, 17
U.S.: Bureau of Entomology, 221; Bureau of Ethnology, 49; Department of Agriculture, 42, 147, 151, 222, 225; Department of Parks, 219; Office of Public Buildings and Parks, 220
Ugarte, Padre Juan de, 191
Unamuno, Miguel de, 301
University of Chicago, 274
University of New Mexico, 274

Vallejo, Guadalupe, 195
Vancouver, George, 193
Varro, Marcus Terentius, 295; *De re rustica*, xvii
Vaughn's Seed Co., 155
Vaux, Calvert, 270
Veitch, Joseph, 209
Versailles, 246, 312
Vick, James, *Flower and Vegetable Garden*, 78
Villa Borghese, 263
Villa Lante, 263
Vilmorin-Andrieux, *The Vegetable Garden*, 41
Virgil, *Georgics*, 232
Voltaire, 319

Walden Pond, 296
Walpole, Horace, 249-50; *History of Modern Gardening*, 250
Warwick Castle, 250
Washington, George, 19, 34-8, 95
Welty, Eudora, 80, 82
Wharton, Edith, 260-4, 274
Whately, Thomas, *Observations on Modern Gardening*, 244, 249
Whealy, Kent, 145-52; *The Garden Seed Inventory*, 150, 152
White Flower Farm, 20-8
White House, The, 253, 275
White, Jane Baber, 279-84
White, Katharine S., 82, 139, 153-7; *Onward and Upward in the Garden*, 28
White, Stanford, 264
Wilder, Louise Beebe, 29-33, 154; *The Fragrant Path*, 33, 154
Will Tillotson's Roses, 157
Williamsburg, 284
Wilson, Edmund, 49
Wilson, Ernest H., 203-9, 225-6
Woburn Abbey, 250, 306
Women's National Farm and Garden Assoc., 66
Wood, Alphonso, *Flora Atlantica*, 78
Woodlands, The, 212, 238, 244
Wordsworth, William, 180
World's Fair (Chicago), 270
Wright, Richardson, 302-5

Yale University, 274
Yokohama Nursery Company, 218, 220
Yosemite Valley, 271
Young, Arthur, 34-7

Zuñi Indians, 44-9